BECOMING GEORGE

www.penguin.co.uk

Also by Fiona Sampson

Poetry:
The School on the Coast Road
Come Down
The Catch
Coleshill
Night Fugue
Rough Music
Common Prayer
The Distance Between Us
Travel Diary
Folding the Real
Picasso's Men

Non-fiction:
Collaborative Poetry Translation (with W. N. Herbert and Francis Jones)
Starlight Wood
Two-Way Mirror: The Life of Elizabeth Barrett Browning
In Search of Mary Shelley
Limestone Country
Lyric Cousins
Beyond the Lyric
Percy Bysshe Shelley
Music Lessons
A Century of Poetry Review
Poetry Writing
On Listening
Writing: Self and Reflexivity (with Celia Hunt)
Creative Writing in Health and Social Care
The Healing Word
The Self on the Page (with Celia Hunt)

Translator:
Evening Brings Everything Back by Jaan Kaplinski
Selected Poems by Jaan Kaplinski (co-translator)
Day by Amir Or

Becoming George

The Invention of George Sand

FIONA SAMPSON

doubleday

TRANSWORLD PUBLISHERS

UK | USA | Canada | Ireland | Australia
India | New Zealand | South Africa

Transworld is part of the Penguin Random House group of companies whose addresses can be found at global.penguinrandomhouse.com.

Penguin Random House UK, One Embassy Gardens,
8 Viaduct Gardens, London SW11 7BW

penguin.co.uk

First published in Great Britain in 2026 by Doubleday
an imprint of Transworld Publishers

001

Copyright © Fiona Sampson 2026

The moral right of the author has been asserted.

Every effort has been made to obtain the necessary permissions with reference to copyright material, both illustrative and quoted. We apologize for any omissions in this respect and will be pleased to make the appropriate acknowledgements in any future edition.

Penguin Random House values and supports copyright. Copyright fuels creativity, encourages diverse voices, promotes freedom of expression and supports a vibrant culture. Thank you for purchasing an authorized edition of this book and for respecting intellectual property laws by not reproducing, scanning or distributing any part of it by any means without permission. You are supporting authors and enabling Penguin Random House to continue to publish books for everyone. No part of this book may be used or reproduced in any manner for the purpose of training artificial intelligence technologies or systems. In accordance with Article 4(3) of the DSM Directive 2019/790, Penguin Random House expressly reserves this work from the text and data mining exception.

Typeset in 12/15.5pt Minion Pro by Six Red Marbles UK, Thetford, Norfolk
Printed and bound in Great Britain by Clays Ltd, Elcograf S.p.A.

The authorized representative in the EEA is Penguin Random House Ireland, Morrison Chambers, 32 Nassau Street, Dublin D02 YH68.

A CIP catalogue record for this book is available from the British Library.

ISBN: 9781529924336

Penguin Random House is committed to a sustainable future for our business, our readers and our planet. This book is made from Forest Stewardship Council® certified paper.

For Peter

> I don't aspire to the dignity of man. It seems to me too laughable to be much preferable to the servility of woman. [. . .] So take me for a man or a woman as you wish.
>
> GEORGE SAND TO ADOLPHE GUÉROULT, 6 MAY 1835

> I am truly *myself*, in a word, which doesn't stop pleasing me.
>
> GEORGE SAND, HISTOIRE DE MA VIE

> . . . the essence peculiar to *François le Champi*. Under its so ordinary events, such normal things in such everyday words, I felt a kind of tone, a strange emphasis.
>
> MARCEL PROUST, DU CÔTÉ DE CHEZ SWANN

Contents

Introduction	1
Chapter One: Dawn	7
First impression *In the garden*	38
Chapter Two: The very rich hours	43
Second impression *Criss-cross*	74
Chapter Three: Reveries of a solitary walker	79
Third impression *Complicity*	110
Chapter Four: Entering on tiptoe	113
Fourth impression *Costume drama*	146
Chapter Five: Becoming a writer	151
Fifth impression *Chinoiserie*	176
Chapter Six: The years of rebellion	181
Sixth impression *The soloist*	224
Chapter Seven: Duet	229
Seventh impression *Fame in a black lace mantilla*	272
Chapter Eight: Dear master	277
Final impression *Of mastery*	322
On language and sources	*329*
Acknowledgements	*333*
Picture credits	*335*
Notes	*337*
Index	*371*

Introduction

Nobody makes a revolution by themselves, and there are some, above all in the arts, which humanity accomplishes without really knowing how, because everybody has taken charge of them.

– *La Mare au diable* (*The Devil's Pool*, 1846)

WHEN I STARTED TO WRITE about George Sand, I imagined myself following a trail of the writer's connections. I pictured untangling webs of mutual influence, parsing address books, calculating the result of a particular friendship, or critical reaction. All writing, I thought, is a form of dialogue. It talks to the writing that's gone before it, to what's going on in the surrounding culture and, on a more practical and immediate level, to the author's editors and critics and – most of all – her readers. What's written for publication can't help but speak to the world of fellow protagonists, past and present and (perhaps) future. As readers, we too take part in this great, multivocal conversation with what we're reading, and everything that what we're reading is in conversation with, and on – in a ceaselessly ramifying net of connections.

I first came across George Sand during my life as a musician: this writer who was Fryderyk Chopin's lover and whose name seemed a signifier of mysterious authority, a way of doing things which was left unspecified but felt musky with sophistication.

Compared to 'Sand', 'Chopin' meant something altogether more familiar, a contained and lucid music. Since then, I've come to think of Sand as an exceptionally vivid example of how intrinsically collaborative literature-making is. A highly connected writer with a peculiarly public life, she was influentially innovative in her writing and had a large body of devoted readers. She was also a famously voluminous correspondent. Here, I thought, was a life deeply and visibly concerned with connection; lived, despite the Romantic norms of her era, against the grain of ideas about the solitary nature of 'genius'.

Nothing I've learnt while thinking and writing about Sand has changed my mind on any of this. But another story has increasingly emerged within and through my first idea, like the palimpsest of an overpainted canvas. In this other story, too, Sand is an unusually well-drawn example of something that surely must be true of all writers, to a greater or lesser extent. But perhaps also of everybody alive. The emphasis in this version is less literary, more biographical. For what's been painted over turns out to be a human face, and this second, hidden story is about someone who had to struggle to become herself.

In this version, the woman who was born Amantine-Lucile-Aurore Dupin de Francueil in Paris in 1804 reveals something about the nature of all lives as self-invention. And, since self-invention is precisely resistance to given circumstances, in doing so she slips the limits of country or language. Her story ceases to be a kind of costume drama and emerges as timeless. To become George Sand required will, imagination, chutzpah. In an era when both revolutionary and traditional forces were pulling at the social fabric within which she lived, she managed to emerge as one of the boldest precursors of that perhaps final hope modernity holds out: that we might choose what we become.

As one of the great novelists of the nineteenth century, George

Sand knew everyone, *le tout monde* of the famous from poets to emperors. And a much larger, international everyone, 'the public', knew her. She was one of the most famous writers in the world, at a time when books had something of the glamour that would later surround, say, Hollywood movies; and in a century when their reach was increasing exponentially.

Some of her fame was also more personal. By the age of twenty-three she was a cross-dressing, cigar-smoking, highly successful novelist, living a racily metropolitan existence in Parisian bohemia. She had famous, or possibly infamous, love affairs with a series of famous and not-so-famous men, and at least one celebrated woman, and was the composer-pianist Fryderyk Chopin's partner for nearly a decade. All this made it easy for contemporaries, particularly those men of the literary and journalist establishment – critics, editors, rivals – who were bothered by the idea of a woman writer, to caricature her as a figure of immoderate productivity and vast appetite.

This image of her as larger than life, a 'female Don Juan' cutting a figure straight out of Jonathan Swift or François Rabelais, persists. As with other great women writers of the nineteenth century (I think about Mary Shelley and Elizabeth Barrett Browning), her personal life has been used to occlude her work, and so obscure her place in the literary canon. *Vita longa, ars brevis*. While cultural literacy in twenty-first-century Europe still broadly includes *La Comédie humaine* (*The Human Comedy*) by her contemporary Honoré de Balzac, it may not stretch to awareness of the seventy novels that make up what George Sand might have called her *Female Comedy*. Her groundbreaking debut *Indiana* is every bit as moving as Emily Brontë's later *Wuthering Heights*, a novel influenced by its author's admiration of Sand; yet it's spawned no pop-rock classic. *Lélia*'s hugely influential feminist critique of marriage is seen as no longer relevant; yet Victor Hugo's

Notre-Dame de Paris (*The Hunchback of Notre-Dame*), published two years earlier and equally embedded in the particular social injustices of that time, tells a story which remains in popular consciousness today. Sand's pioneering novels of rural life, such as *La Mare au diable* and *François le Champi* (*François of the Fields*) began to appear in the 1840s, predating Thomas Hardy's Wessex fiction by decades. But for much of the twentieth century they were relegated to staples of the French school curriculum. Only relatively recently has their early role in the development of ecological thinking begun to be recognised.

And so on. George Sand deserves to be re-embraced as a writer: our own sense of literature will inevitably be shifted by our doing so. It will become that bit richer and more complex, its chronology of innovation rearranged. The paradox of her posthumous reputation – all personality, little art – is not only that in death Sand was described by Gustave Flaubert (whose *Madame Bovary* remains essential reading) as someone whose 'name will live in unique glory as one of the great figures of France'. It's also that in life she was deeply immersed within the to and fro that is the fertile humus of literary activity. That world of rivalrous coteries, of literary 'little magazines', of gossip and tendentious reviewing in bars and clubs as much as on the page, produces a continual buzz as of conversation, and it is as profoundly connected as it is riven by competing ideas and egos.

George Sand plunged into this world just at the moment when publishing in the global North becomes recognisable to us today: with the advent of mass literacy came the mass production of books and new periodicals. Editorial offices (and city bars) were replacing the closed world of artistic salons directed by aristocrats. Sand was no *salonnière*, unlike earlier writing women including Mme de Staël – or indeed her own great-grandmother, Maria Aurora von Königsmarck – but the very model of the writer as freelancer, calling in at the newspaper bureau to chat to her editor, or mailing in copy. This working, professional life, with its ceaseless, perfectionist standards exercised over details hardly apparent to the reader, is also a meeting of minds obsessed by literary writing: which Sand navigated as if born to it. As she wrote to a friend in 1831, 'It's a big thing to make yourself useful and necessary in a literary office. It gets you everywhere, even without *camaraderie*, and without one's *personhood* appearing in the slightest.'[1]

So much, so sexless. But of course George Sand was handicapped by perceptions of her gender. Small wonder she so often dressed to pass – though she could not in fact disguise herself successfully – as a man. Instead, by suiting up as a *garçon* she was, criss-cross, acknowledging that to be a writing woman is a little off-centre: is queer. That to do everything she did – riding astride, going out and about to Paris theatres and bars, taking her desk in the intellectual mosh pit of *Le Figaro*'s office – as a woman was to violate the canon of acceptable behaviour.

Playing the *garçon* required a certain robustness, even from this woman who was barely five foot tall. In a writing profession that was shifting its historical association with private income the stakes were rising too: meagre publishers' advances or poor reviews could mean literal penury. At the same time, in the early decades of the nineteenth century there were fewer professional writers than in the twenty-first, and fewer genres available to those there were, so that the intellectual community of even a great literary city like Paris or London really did resemble a turbulent, rivalrous village. This was a man's world of networking in smoke-filled rooms, and George Sand was almost the first woman to join in with its long, continuing argument. (George Eliot, for example, would only emerge in London a couple of decades later.)

Sand didn't enter these rooms by being somebody's muse, some Alma Mahler of her particular time and place. Nor was she helped along by a powerful older partner (as George Eliot, say, would be). On the contrary, after the failure of her marriage she consistently chose romantic liaisons with men who were younger, and generally less distinguished, than herself. The male arm on which she entered Parisian literary life, for example, belonged to one such lover, the student Jules Sandeau, with whom, as 'J. Sand', she co-authored her first published fiction. Soon, however, he was proving unable to keep up the literary pace, and she was taking on the whole of their joint commissions. So that, though writing under (almost) his name was what allowed her to start taking part in the writing world, he was far indeed from any kind of mentor. Indeed, what he most resembles is a sort of literary beard.

All biography includes an element of recuperation. It's a kind of rereading of the facts of a life that – like translation, like editing – is necessarily interpretive. It also has everything to do with reputation. And this puzzle of reputation-making turns out to be at the heart of George Sand's story. It has helped and hindered the reading of her work; it also shaped her life. Within and also beyond the ways that she wrestled with gender, what she was *seen* to be determined who she *got* to be to an extraordinary extent.

In the second quarter of the twenty-first century, personal identity gets rehearsed but also performed. Fake it till you make it; or at least make yourself appear however you want (selfies all round). A century and a half earlier, George Sand was the pioneer of the convincing impression. We respond to each of her performances, just as her contemporaries did. From this distance, we can see how she responded to their responses – how she created herself within their attention. It's a collaborative, corresponding relationship. Now, rereading the author and her works, we help recreate her once again. For reading is the most inclusive form of literary dialogue and, as Sand wrote, change happens 'above all in the arts' when 'everybody has taken charge'.

ONE

Dawn

WHERE ELSE TO START BUT with dawn, and the girl whose name that was? Dawn – Aurore – was born Amantine-Aurore-Lucile Dupin de Francueil on 1 July 1804.[1] Or rather, on 12 Messidor Year XII, according to the French Republican calendar then in use. She had been conceived in the French Republic; by the time she was born the First French Empire was two and a half months old. Her parents' secret marriage on 16 Prairial, a month before her arrival, had gained her legitimacy and the patronym Dupin de Francueil; and her father named her Aurore after his own aristocratic mother, Marie-Aurore de Saxe. But Aurore's mother was a working-class Parisienne, and her birth was a moment of slippage: in history, in class, in identities.[2] In geography, too. By the time she was four, Aurore would be living not on the impoverished city block where she was born but in her grandmother's historic manor at the heart of rural France. This great house would become one of the most stabilising influences and longest loves of her life.

Light, dark: spider, cloud. If childhood is a plunge into vividness, country childhood is a plunge into what was until recently a shared world of vivid experience. Before industrialisation almost every child growing up in Europe, whether their father was the village baker or led a battalion in the French Army, understood the crunch of trampled leaves, the way ice fractures in a puddle. Ordinary children played outdoors. As, albeit in other, more often organised ways, did those living lives of privilege; who took riding lessons, or botany walks with tutors. And so, in different ways in their differing neighbourhoods, did city children, for, *rus in urbe*, eighteenth-century countryside still interpenetrated all but the densest European metropolis. Livestock and wild creatures in bizarre variety – baskets of thrushes, yoked buffalo – were trampled through town to market. Rats and mice, birds and bats were co-inhabitants of town houses, shops, city shanties. In the absence of industrial pesticides, spaces indoors and out were sewn with insects. Wasps at the meat safe; daddy-long-legs behind shutters.

At the turn of the nineteenth century most French children, whether they were growing up in a slum or a chateau, knew that horseflies are iridescent, or how to catch the leaves falling from plane trees. Aurore's childhood was in this respect absolutely typical. Villages like the one she would be raised in were inseparable from the surrounding fields and forests on which they depended. Many would remain that way for the rest of the century even as, elsewhere, industrialisation gathered pace. In the famously enduring glimpse Marcel Proust gives of his childhood at Combray, in the Normandy department of Calvados, blackthorn still flowers along *Le Côté de Guermantes* (*The Guermantes Way*) in the 1870s. Even in the twenty-first century, at first glance nothing much seems to have changed in those regions by now relegated to a kind of minority status as *la France profonde*.

The 1870s would be the final decade of Aurore's life in her own country home, further south than Combray and close to the very centre point of France. Today, that home is one of a pair of settlements double-barrelled as Nohant-Vic, in what's now the central

French department of Indre. Nohant itself is spared the D943 road which spatchcocks its slightly larger neighbour Vic. Tawny-stuccoed and limestone houses still stand quietly around the modest square linking its church and manor house, those twin pivots of traditional power. Yet, for all the attractive immediacy of the raked sand and neat poplars, the pretty shuttered dormers, the church of Sainte-Anne with its homely narthex – wooden pillars and a catslide roof – Nohant is no longer typical of contemporary French life. It's become a museum piece, emptied of the quotidian.

In the second quarter of the twenty-first century, less than one-fifth of the French population still lives in the countryside, a loss that prettification by *Les Plus Beaux Villages* schemes can do nothing to disguise. And Nohant's little *manoir* is literally a museum. In 1961 the Maison de George Sand opened in what the novelist herself described as a 'modest manor from the time of Louis XIV [...] part of the hamlet, forming, with no more pomp than any house in the village, one side of the rustic square'. This description in her 1854–5 autobiography *Histoire de ma vie* (*Story of My Life*) pulls back to describe its 'humble, calm and quiet surroundings', where 'there are some twenty [dwellings] clustering about the manor like neighbours, so to speak,' and sharing a view of 'the rich brown furrows, the great walnut trees with their full crowns, the shaded lanes, the tousled bushes, the overgrown churchyard, the little tiled belfry, the ancient portico, the tall, half-ruined elms'.[3]

Pull back a little further and, under a mile north of Nohant, contemporary life returns, albeit sleepily, in neighbouring Vic. A busy road separates the Romanesque church of Saint-Martin from what remains of the rest of a village square. This leg of the departmental road rules a diagonal across the level countryside between Châteauroux and La Châtre, in (Sand again) 'the

Noire valley, a [...] central location in the most level part of the country, in a large belt of grain land [with] a wide blue horizon'. It's deep France indeed: just thirty miles from the country's geographical centre, a fact that's still marked by a monument raised in 1799 in another of the region's unassuming villages, Bruère-Allichamps.

This celebration of the Romantic era's emergent discipline of scientific geophysical measurement was peculiarly apt to the First Republic, then seven years old, and its revolutionary redistributions of property and opportunity. Henceforth terrain might be a question of geophysical fact, not mere hereditary ownership. This new, literally earthy territoriality was of a piece with the calendrical revolution which had taken place six years earlier. In October 1793, the French Constitution abolished the Gregorian calendar, with its ramifying religious and pagan cultural history: including the Catholic feast days whose regular pleasures cemented the hold of the Church on the population. The new, secular Republican year started with the spring equinox. Its twelve months, slightly out of step with traditional divisions, were called after their country season: germination, blossom, harvest. Every day of the year was renamed for flora or fauna or after the tools of practical crafts and rural tasks.

Thermidor, fructidor, écluse and *escourgeon*. Today it's hard to hear in this clutter of nomenclature a hitherto disenfranchised population reclaiming the world around them. Instead, it's as if surviving elites had raided their education in that genre spanning the classical centuries – from Hesiod's *Works and Days* of c.700 BCE to Virgil's first-century *Georgics* – with results not in the end so different from the rustic kitsch of their late Queen Marie Antoinette's Hameau de la Reine at Versailles.[4] The anglophone ear snags on pastoral curio. To much of the post-communist world, on the other hand, the Republican calendar seems to foreshadow back-to-the-land anti-intellectualism, or the heroically mindless labour celebrated by social realism.

In the event, after just over a dozen years the whole unwieldy system was abolished by Napoléon on 1 January 1806. But reading backwards is inevitably anachronistic. The idea Gilbert Romme had advocated in 1793 was intended to draw on the shared experience of the farming – which is to say the gustatory – year as a framework of social complicity. Ironically, given the Republican separation of Church from State, the religious iconography it was attempting to replace had long banked on this same humbling sense that 'we're all the same in the end'. In the stone flora swarming the Cluniac Romanesque churches of the Camino de Santiago in south-west France, or the Gothic cathedrals of the north, medieval masons celebrated the familiar world surrounding them. Lavish nature was quotidian, and universally available.[5]

In the early nineteenth century of Aurore Dupin's childhood, Nohant and its countryside were still of a piece with such rural, medieval landscapes. One could have recognised them, for example, in the pages of *Les Très Riches Heures du Duc de Berry* (*The Very Rich Hours of the Duc de Berry*). That famously extravagant illuminated manuscript in the International Gothic style had been commissioned four centuries earlier, around 1412, by the great patron (and astute statesman) Jean de France. His duchy encompassed the whole of twenty-first-century Indre and Cher, including Nohant, where the chateau's late-thirteenth-century turrets and crenellations, a more modest version of those pictured in the *Heures*, would survive as the ruined bastion Aurore came to know. (That the *Heures* was probably produced in Paris by artists from the Low Countries who never visited the Duchy of Berry only underlines the continuity and ubiquity of the rural experience it portrays.)

Its now-familiar images portray the calendar of Christian

prayer, bookmarking that annual cycle with rural seasonal tasks and phenomena – snowfall, ploughing and, oddly to our eyes, astrology – just like the Republican calendar. And these illustrations are somehow childlike in their gem-like vividness. They have the unmediated brightness of things noticed for the first time. Lucid colours and attention to detail, like the close-up, childish concentration of the kind that Aurore would remember as an adult:

> Between me and the fire was an old screen on feet, decorated with green taffeta. I could see a bit of the fire through the worn taffeta, and it produced little stars whose brightness I increased by squinting. So little by little I lost the sense of the phrases my mother was reading [to me]. Her voice threw me into a sort of drowsiness of spirit, where it was impossible to follow an idea.[6]

In the *Heures*, the ploughman doesn't trouble us with his inner life, he just ploughs. The meadow is entirely and always meadow. It's a vision of things that can be relied upon. In the fifteenth century, as in the nineteenth, continuity is central to rural life. Farming, predicated on predictably recurring conditions, works months in advance: country dwellers are surrounded by sights and sounds older than themselves. The 'great walnut trees with their full crowns' Aurore would remember from her childhood arrived in France with the Romans; the 'tall, half-ruined elms' were indigenous. This childhood immersion in the rich natural and cultural layers of the Berrichon landscape would prove so influential that it eventually led a future George Sand to produce some of the first ecological literature, and pioneering fictions of rural life.

If an ecclesiastical calendar gives almost metaphysical status to continuity and predictability, childhood takes these on faith.

For the child, what was here already has been here forever. To four-year-old Aurore, a line of poplar trees in Nohant, a wall crumbling under its stone coving, the gardener and his dog, will be as old as the world, and part of what defines it. There's a reason why Marcel Proust's great multi-volume exploration of time and memory, *À la récherche du temps perdu* (*In Search of Lost Time*), starts with the once-upon-a-time magic conjured by that single word, *longtemps*, which means both *long ago* and *for a long time*.

Perhaps it's no coincidence that Proust was influenced by his grandmother reading to him from the novels, many of them set in the Berrichon countryside, that little Aurore would grow up to write. Continuity: discontinuity. Growing up in Nohant's manor house as a descendant of aristocrats, Aurore would simultaneously have understood herself, a child born under the Republican calendar, to be a *citoyenne* of the new department. She would have been aware that she lived both in Indre and in what had been the Duchy of Berry. The old names for the French regions, changed only in 1790, would have remained in the living memory of the adults around her. A parenthetical vocabulary – half-occluded regional identities, the ghostly rhythm of an old calendar – was still stored in the collective understanding. It offered an early lesson in the distance between a name for something and its identity; in how things can get shaken loose from their starting points.

After all, there never was a child called George Sand at Nohant. There was, though, Aurore Dupin. She would grow up to write, under her famous nom de plume, around seventy novels and, among her non-fiction, the engaging, autobiographical *Histoire de ma vie*, from which we learn much about how that childhood appeared to her. *The Story of My Life*: French uses the same word, *histoire*, for both *history* and *story*. English is keen to separate what happened – *history* – from the telling of it, or *story*: a linguistic divorce bearing the weight of Anglo-Saxon empiricism, which believes that facts are wholly free-standing and exist regardless of who relays them. French suggests this distinction is spurious: that there *are* no facts independent from our account of them, since unless they're witnessed, whether by scientists or policemen, scholars or bystanders, they simply can't be in our human ken. But *histoire* as a tale can become the tale as a lie; we *could* hear Sand's title as *The Lie of My Life*.

There is something particularly inhabited about George Sand's writing, and *Histoire* is no exception. Part of its gregarious charm lies in its occasional, meandering repetitions; it travels, so to speak, the country mile. It lingers especially on the early years, as memory does: and as we – analysts, biographers, admirers – do when we try to retrace how a self is formed. This is memoir as reconstruction, a reworking by a master storyteller of her most important story: the one about herself. Sand, who compiled large parts from earlier letters, started work on the book in 1847, but its five volumes weren't published until 1854–5.

Even the story of her birth, for example, becomes an anecdote. One day, friends and family gathered at her parents' apartment to celebrate the marriage of her mother's sister to her father's friend:

> They had formed some quadrilles, my mother had a pretty pink dress that day and my father was improvising a contradance on his trusty Cremonese violin (I still have this old instrument to whose sound I was born). My mother, a little unwell, left the dance and went into her room. As her expression hadn't altered, and she had gone out very quietly, the turn-taking continued. On the final eight bars, my aunt Lucie went into my mother's bedroom and immediately called out, Come, come, Maurice, you have a daughter.[7]

Sand tells us that her aunt, noting the colour of the new mother's dress, prophesied good luck for this baby born 'to music and in the pink': a creaky pun on *la vie en rose*. But the detail I like best about that passage is its mention of the Cremonese violin. As her contemporaries would have been aware, Cremona is where all the best stringed instruments were made in the seventeenth and eighteenth centuries; most famously by the Stradivari and Guarneri families. It's one of the glitter points with which the writer highlights her father's standing as an officer and a gentleman.

Maurice Dupin de Francueil was a serving officer in the Napoleonic Army. Until a couple of months before his daughter's birth in July 1804, he had been based at the large encampment at Boulogne. (Two months later this would be raided by the British Navy.) But his new wife was a Parisienne, and seems to have wanted to get home before the baby came. Sure enough, Aurore was born in the capital at 15 rue Meslée (now number 46 rue Meslay).[8] This modest thoroughfare ran parallel to the boulevard Saint-Martin in what, since the Republic created the Parisian arrondissements in October 1795, had become *le troisième*. It squeezed alongside the unfashionable Marais, a district of formerly fine mansions from which the Revolution had chased out the gentry, before debouching beyond the porte Saint-Martin at the stuttering end of rue de Bondy. Seven years later that unprepossessing space would be landscaped with a huge fountain and named first place du Château d'Eau – and eventually place de la République.

But not yet. One of Auguste Bruno Braquehais's astonishing series of photographs documenting the 1870–71 Siege of Paris and the Commune shows a burnt-out block at the corner of rue de Bondy and boulevard Saint-Martin. In the left of the picture, back from the ruined facades where balconies still hang intact, huddles the little Café de Bondy, proprietor – so its fascia announces – a M. Lesage. All hipped roof and picture-book second-floor gables, it's a piece of small-town vernacular that has survived Haussmann's elegant remastering of the capital city. And it suggests the lively subculture of seventy years earlier in which a young army officer, who has just made an honest woman of the *demi-mondaine* he fell in love with, might celebrate with friends when a brother officer decides to marry his sister-in-law, Aurore's aunt Lucie.

Subculture, and also to some extent counterculture. The rue Meslée had a tradition of civil disobedience. During the riots of August 1788 it suffered so many deaths that the bodies from this street alone became an early feature of the Paris catacombs. A decade before Aurore's birth it was a politically bohemian, sexually relaxed neighbourhood. In 1791 the Haitian Julien Raimond lived at number 33 during his successful campaign for civil rights of 'free-citizens of colour, from the islands and colonies of France'.[9] Philosopher and feminist Mary Wollstonecraft stayed at what was then number 22 from December 1792 to summer 1793, the period during which she met and fell in love with the American blockade-runner Gilbert Imlay, and while she was contributing to the new Republic's education policy.[10] In 1797–8 a clandestine publisher of fiction was operating out of the street.

But by the time of Aurore's birth, the distinguished cabinet-makers Jacob Frères, settled in rue Meslée for three decades, had just changed their name to Jacob Desmalter & Co. and were creating extraordinary Empire furniture for Emperor Napoléon himself. The atelier of Louis-Léopold Boilly, portraitist and commercial artist, was at number 12. Five years on from the chaotic decade of the French Revolution, radical passions had given way to the quieter counterculture of artistic bohemia: not that the term *bohémien* would come into fashionable use for such alternative lifestyles for almost half a century.[11] Still, this was a place where love 'across the barricades' of social divide was part of a recognisable pattern. One such relationship was the match between Aurore's parents: Maurice Dupin de Francueil, aristocratic army officer and heir to the manor at Nohant, and working girl Sophie Delaborde.

For Antoinette-Sophie-Victoire Delaborde was, for all her splendidly numerous names, properly urban, and no better than she ought to be. Translated to London, we might imagine her full of cockney cheek and with the proverbial heart of gold. Her father, Antoine, 'was a "master fowler" and "master birdcatcher", in other words he sold canaries and finches on the quai des Oiseaux; having kept a small café with billiards in I don't know what corner of Paris, where, anyway, he did no business', although her stepfather 'had an illustrious name in the world of birds: he was called Barra, and the name is still legible in the boulevard du Temple above a huge stack of cages of every size'.[12]

When it came to her own name, the woman her daughter would come to know as Sophie-Victoire embraced the pragmatic doublethink of her era. At first, as shown on her marriage certificate, she was Antoinette. George Sand tells us that her mother was called this as a child. The Revolution made the name unfashionable, especially after October 1793 when Marie Antoinette was guillotined. By the time she met Maurice Dupin in 1800, therefore, she was embracing Revolutionary struggle as Victoire. After their marriage four years later Dupin summoned up hopes of domestic wisdom and called her Sophie.[13]

He may have had reason to do so. For all the sociability of their shared life, with its music and dancing, the Victoire he had fallen in love with was a member of that 'world of ambiguous morals', as the Académie Française still defines '*demi-monde*', 'made up of frivolous women, often venal or kept, on the fringes of good society, but frequented by its men'.[14] Nor had she ended up there through escapist middle-class whim. M. Barra may have excelled commercially, but he was clearly no protector of his stepchildren.

According to Sand's *Histoire*, he abandoned Victoire when she was fourteen. Though three years younger, her sister Marie-Lucie (to give her full name) was presumably cut adrift at the same moment. As Victoire's daughter would point out, at the end of the eighteenth century what this meant for girls was 'the venality of rich men who wait until hunger strikes and then blight innocent girls; and the pitiless rigour of social opinion, which permits neither return nor expiation'.[15]

Despite the enormous upheavals of Revolutionary French society, the liberty and equality both sexes had joined in the struggle to attain remained an overwhelmingly masculine privilege. Actually, when her father, Antoine Delaborde, died on 2 December 1781, Sophie-Victoire was only eight and her sister Marie-Lucie five, and we have no conclusive proof that they were able to remain at home even for the next six years. Their mother, who survived until the elder girl was seventeen, seems not to have intervened to support them. Perhaps she felt powerless too. She remains in the shadows of Aurore's story, one in a succession of problematic mothers.

At whatever age the double catastrophe of abandonment and sexual exploitation befell Sophie-Victoire, we know that child prostitution, then as now, was fuelled by powerlessness and desperation. Sand calls it 'This storm where [the sisters] were carried away like two poor little leaves that spin without knowing where they are, in this confusion of troubles, terrors, and incomprehensible emotions.'[16]

By 'fifteen or sixteen', Victoire was a chorus girl, a *compars* in 'a small theatre'. By the time another decade had passed she was indubitably no longer innocent. In 1799 she gave birth to an illegitimate daughter, Angélique-Caroline.[17] Despite the social cost, she didn't abandon this baby to a foundling institution but chose to keep her. It was just the following year that she met Maurice

Dupin, sometime during the two months to September 1800, while he was stationed at Milan.

For Dupin, Milan was a brief interlude of compulsory idleness, in which his military ambitions were forced to take a backseat to pleasure. As he wrote to his mother:

> We pass our time here in carriage rides and dinners. [. . .] In the evening, we go to races and shows, which are magnificent. There is a female singer and a tenor who are admirable. The ballets are very badly danced, but the decorations superb. In sum, forced *by order* to have fun, I decide to all intents and purposes to *have* fun.[18]

One of these execrable dancers may have been Victoire, who, as her daughter would write,

> belonged to the vile and vagabond race of the gypsies [*bohémiens*] of this world. She was a dancer or, rather, something lower than a dancer, in one of the most disreputable of the Paris theatres, until the love of a rich man rescued her from this abject condition, only to impose upon her one more abject still. When my father first took up with her she was thirty, and living in a whirl of wild indiscipline.[19]

Yet capable of strategy, all the same. When, three months after his stay in Milan, Victoire turned up in Asola during the very December weeks that Maurice's regiment was stationed there, it was more than simple coincidence. She was taking the gamble of surrendering her current 'older protector' for a relationship with a coming man; and a good-looking one at that. An anonymous portrait painted sometime around 1800 shows the dark-eyed youth, collar swathed in a cravat, near-black curls combed dashingly forward from a side parting. He doesn't meet our eyes but gazes past us towards something more important: dreams of military glory, perhaps.

At Asola, the twenty-two-year-old Maurice had just been made aide-de-camp to Lieutenant-Général Dupont. As he wrote proudly to his mother, along with the commission came 'a yellow plume, and a fine red sash with a gold fringe'.[20] In practice, ribbons don't put food on the table, and his commissions would prove a financial burden as much as a professional reward. In 1807, promoted to aide-de-camp for Napoléon's brother-in-law, Général Joachim Murat, who had himself been made *Prince français* and Grand Duc of Berg, he would find that glamorous proximity to power so costly that, as he turned thirty, 'his expenses [. . .] exceeded his means [. . .] he had debts for uniforms, horses and tackle'.[21]

But back in 1800, when Victoire tracked Maurice Dupin's regiment seventy-five miles down the Po Valley from Milan, she was evidently mounting a campaign of her own. This required some patience. In Milan, the young officer who had fallen for her had become increasingly confused about what was going on. 'Sometimes I believed myself loved, and then I saw, or believed I saw, that I was not,' as he would tell his mother in a letter dated 29 Frimaire Year IX (20 December 1800). In the end he left the city to get over the affair, travelling via Bologna, Florence and Rome.

This havering was not simple coquetry on Victoire's part. It's complicated at the best of times, and in most cultures, for a woman to signal to a man how much she might be interested in him – to have him understand the nuance – without, for example, cramping his style. If she's a woman society regards as immoral and promiscuous, it's harder still: like driving with the brakes on, as Maurice's account makes clear. At first, at Asola:

We spoke to each other little; we scarcely looked at each other. I seemed spiteful, [. . .] she showed pride, despite having a tender and emotional heart. This morning, [sent to investigate a military alarm] at the moment of mounting my horse I turned to see behind me this dear woman, flushed, confused and casting upon me a long look expressing fear, interest, love [. . .] I returned bringing news to the General. *She* was still there. Ah! How I was welcomed! How full that dinner was of laughter and affection! What delicate attentions she paid me![22]

Yet that same evening, despite throwing herself weeping into his arms when 'by unhoped for chance' he found himself alone with her, Victoire refused to sleep with him. As she had to, if this were not to become just another sexual liaison. She had learnt by heart, as it were, what happened to an impoverished woman at the start of the nineteenth century if sex preceded declarations of fidelity.

All the same, it was a turning point. That night, since he was unable to sleep with this 'dear woman', Maurice instead wrote to tell his mother about her. And Victoire, having taken the plunge of emotional declaration, did not hold out for long. She seems from then on to have stuck close to her lover. The following May, when he went to see his mother at Nohant, Victoire followed, staying five miles from the manor in the little market town of La Châtre. Sand – who was of course by definition not there – can't resist painting a picture of a returning youth newly toughened up by his military career: 'He was bigger, thinner, stronger, paler; he had grown an inch since his enrolment, quite unusual at the age of twenty-one but probably brought about by extraordinary marches into which he had been forced by the Austrians.'[23]

War hero or no, in a town of fewer than 3,500 people Maurice's assignations with Victoire at the local Black Head Inn soon caused a scandal.[24] News got back to his mother, Marie-Aurore de Saxe. Every inch the aristocrat, she was distraught. From the next two years, and until after Aurore's birth, Maurice would be torn between the two women: each paradigmatic of her own class, each as fiercely single-pointed as a diva, and each experiencing any attention he paid to the other as abandonment. 'He would have to choose between his mother and his mistress, to deceive or cast into despair one or the other [. . .] This was more than a battle between two loves; it was the battle of two duties.'[25]

There was, though, a particular hypocrisy to this parental resistance. Victoire's history was indeed chequered. But, as his mother well knew, Maurice had also already had a child out of wedlock; the asymmetric social consequences of these two births would run like a fault through Aurore's childhood. Maurice had fathered his son Hippolyte in 1799, when he was twenty-one. The mother, Catherine Chatiron, a carpenter's daughter from (as her name suggests) La Châtre, was dismissed, and her baby taken away to be raised instead by a peasant family living conveniently alongside Nohant's manorial stables.

This sounds like an almost rational mid-course between snobbish abandonment and acknowledged paternity. The Dupin estate believed it had paid Catherine off fairly and, in an era when mere survival was closely aligned with prosperity, Maurice's son could grow up protected by, even educated at, the manor.[26] But of course it ignores human feeling, a problem which would recur in Aurore's upbringing. Why couldn't Hippolyte's own mother raise him under his grandmother's sponsorship? The boy was even renamed, as if to scrub clean his identity: can the name chosen, Pierre Laverdure – *laver dure: wash hard* – really be a coincidence? Or do we read it instead as *la verdure, the greenery* of rustication? Family code for Hippolyte was '*la petite maison*', a usual way to say 'cottage' in French, yet carrying here the comparative sense of the 'great house' of Nohant manor. The aristocratic de Saxe family is the House of Saxony, and the illegitimate son a kind of 'outhouse'.

Whatever his emotional backstory, Hippolyte was toddling around at the manor by the time Victoire arrived in La Châtre in May 1801.[27] And so it fell to a key figure in the inner circle at Nohant to scare off this latest figure of scandal. Maurice's mother retained a former abbot as her estate manager, source of practical expertise and all-round masculine authority figure. Jean-François Deschartres had been Maurice's tutor – and would in time tutor his children too. An educated man, who left the Church in 1789 to avoid anticlerical Revolutionary violence, this family protector seems altogether to have lacked sexual motivation around women.

Sand, in whose childhood he was to figure large, would later portray Deschartres as more assiduous than wise:

> Under the Restoration, he would have gladly resumed his title of abbot [. . .] but he had never taken orders [. . .]. He had been a pretty youth, he still was when my grandmother took him on: clean, well shaven, bright eyes, and a prominent calf. Finally, he had a very good governor's manner. But I am sure that no one, with the best will in the world, had ever been able to look at him without laughing, so clearly was the word *pedant* [*cuistre*] written in every line of his face and every movement of his body.[28]

Cuistre is one of those conceptual bundles hard to decipher in translation, since it means both pedant and bumpkin. That is, until one understands its original meaning: the lay helper charged with petty procedure within a church, where he has not been ordained, or university, where he has not been educated.[29] A *cuistre* fusses over form without understanding content, aping a distinction he doesn't possess: Deschartres was a *cuistre* in literal fact as well as style.

Yet there's a sense, too, of something baulked, of aspiration beyond possible achievement, in the torsion of that *cuist—*. It opens up space for compassion and understanding – and that's how Sand continues:

> He should have been ignorant, greedy and cowardly. But far from that, he was highly learned, very sober and madly brave. He had all the great qualities of soul combined with an unbearable character and delirious self-satisfaction. He had the most absolute ideas, the crudest manners, the most arrogant language. But what devotion, what zeal, what a generous and sensitive soul![30]

Two truths coexist here; as they seem to have done in that provincial inn during the early summer of 1801, when Mme Dupin de Francueil's family manager tried to run her son's lover out of town – and failed. For Victoire sent Deschartres packing: 'More prompt than cautious in response, gifted with a liveliness of speech [. . .] sharp and biting like a true child of Paris,' as Sand would portray her.[31] Very possibly a sense of being wronged helped Victoire stand her ground. It's likely she saw herself as – or hoped to be – not so much a mistress as a partner. Wives follow armies. Why should she not accompany her husband on a visit home, if not actually to his mother's house?

Sand's naturally sympathetic account draws a veil over the fact that Victoire was five years older than Maurice, and at a delicate stage in her sexual marketability. When the couple met she was twenty-seven – not young for someone whose life expectancy when she was born in 1773 had been less than thirty – and any suggestion of ageing is particularly alarming to a woman reliant on sexual charm for her survival.[32] So it would be no surprise if this single mother in her late twenties pushed to cement mere feelings – however genuine – with the institution of marriage.

Eventually, against his mother's opposition, Maurice set up household with Sophie. He married her in the nick of time in summer 1804, a month before Aurore, their first child, was born.[33] But it's hard to paint him as ensnared. Their home seems to have been happy, Maurice playful and charismatic even in a domestic setting. From the rue de Meslée the family moved to 22 (now number 13) rue de la Grange Batelière, a twenty-minute stroll east in the direction of the boulevard Haussmann. Their daughter would recall a father who played with her and showed her off:

> I vaguely remember quiet dinners in the light, and a dish of sweets that was certainly very modest, because it consisted of vermicelli cooked in milk and sugared; my father pretended to eat the whole thing just to amuse himself with my greedy disappointment. I also remember that, with his serviette knotted and rolled in various ways, he made the figures of a monk, a rabbit and a puppet, which made me laugh a lot. He must have spoilt me horribly, because my mother was forced to intervene so he wouldn't encourage all my whims instead of repressing them [...]. I've been told that [...] he played with me for entire days, and that even in full uniform he wasn't ashamed to carry me in his arms in the middle of the street and on the boulevards.[34]

But the young officer was often away from home on military campaigns. That Victoire (now consecrated as Sophie) continued on occasion to follow him suggests perhaps that theirs remained a kind of love match. And in April 1808, either because the three-year-old Aurore was now judged old enough to travel or because the trip promised to be a long one, Sophie-Victoire took her along too.

Their destination was Madrid; they were following the French army of occupation into the city it had taken days earlier, on 23 March. Sophie-Victoire secured a lift for herself and her younger daughter in the light, soft-top *calèche* of another army wife she knew, a Mme Fontanier, who didn't want to travel to Spain with only a twelve-year-old groom for protection. Yet Caroline, no more than nine years old, was left behind in Paris. Leaving a girl child in a wartime city – even if she's properly lodged where your sister can keep an eye on her – seems risky as well as heartless. This odd decision is never explained. Aurore would remember:

> I don't believe I was upset at being separated from my sister, who stayed on in the accommodation, and from my cousin Clothilde. As I didn't see them every day, I could not imagine a longer or shorter duration of the separation that I witnessed start again every week.[35]

In a clever retrieval of childhood's curious logic, the adult writer describes how instead she was heartbroken at having to leave her doll – more real than her sister – 'in this deserted apartment where she must have been so very bored'.[36]

Aurore was about to be transported into what must have seemed at her age like a fairy tale: high-lit and dark, fantastical and grotesque.[37] In *Histoire*, her account of this early passage through world history is framed by the portrait of a childish psyche still engaged with what Bruno Bettelheim would call 'the uses of enchantment', or as Sand puts it, the way 'children [dwell] between the real and the impossible'. It's a strategy that, whether or not intentionally, makes the whole episode feel like a nightmarish dream sequence, a kind of fugue state. Sure enough, as the two women, the child and the youth travelled through the battle-scarred north of Spain, 'the more we advanced on our route, the more terrible the spectacle of war became'.[38]

Something of that spectacle can be glimpsed in Francisco Goya's horrifying contemporary series of intaglio prints *Los desastres de la guerra* (*The Disasters of War*), which the Spanish court painter made in secret in the decade from 1810: especially the first suite of forty-seven, protesting against this very occupation of the city in which he lived by Napoleonic forces, as well as against the wider Peninsular War which would continue until 1814. In scenes unrelieved by any suggestion of meaning or higher cause, Goya shows human bodies becoming, over and over, the playthings of grotesquely imaginative evil.

Before this trip, Aurore 'had killed a lot of people in my [fantasies and] military games. I knew the word [death] and not the thing.' *Histoire* details the deadly war games which now surrounded her from the miniaturising perspective of a child. They include a puzzling echo on the balcony of a requisitioned palace, and the scabies, caught from infantrymen fresh off the battlefields, with which she would return home to France. Of a piece with this childish scale, Aurore learns what death really means by way of a pet pigeon. 'I had never had such a beautiful toy, and a loving toy, what a treasure! But he soon proved to me that a living being is an inconvenient plaything, because he always wanted to run away.' Petulantly, the little girl wants the bird killed. But, taken to the kitchen to see pigeons being slaughtered for supper, in a moment of comprehension she 'saw the movement of the bird which died violently and the final convulsion,'[39] burst into tears and would not touch the meal, even though the adults around her had in fact saved her own pet.

Another dreamlike sequence. In the yard of a rural coaching inn a serving girl hoisted her up to glimpse, through the windows of 'the carriage of the queen', the Infanta María Luísa, travelling in the opposite direction on her way into exile.[40] The infanta was obeying Napoléon Bonaparte's summons to join the rest of the Spanish royal family in Bayonne; her departure from Madrid, a few days earlier on 2 May, had triggered the doomed Dos de Mayo Uprising by the Spanish populace against the French occupiers. Public affairs: intimate encounter. Where and when might this lamplit glimpse have occurred? The adult Sand could recall only that the inn was either near Burgos or seventy miles further north, near Vittoira – today Vitoria-Gasteiz – in the Basque region, just south across the Pyrenees from Bayonne.[41]

Aurore and her mother could scarcely have been reunited with Maurice in Madrid before 8 May. But once there, they found themselves right at the heart of things. The family would spend two months living in the gilded splendour of a second-floor apartment in the palace of the deposed Spanish First Secretary of State, Manuel de Godoy. Though this sounds like a storyteller's fantasy, it goes with the practical territory of realpolitik. Godoy was a symbol: not just Spain's equivalent to a prime minister, but the Achilles heel of the outgoing regime. His Francophile sabre-rattling against Britain had led to the Spanish rout at Trafalgar; yet even after this costly naval defeat he had retained disproportionate influence as a royal favourite. Defeat is always economically and socially costly for ordinary people. Eventually, desperation produced a popular uprising and soldiers' mutiny, the Tumult of Aranjuez, which on 17 March 1808 had intercepted the royal household just outside Madrid. The party were attempting to flee south from Napoleonic occupation of the north of the country. Instead, Godoy was now taken prisoner, and King Charles was forced first to sack him and then to abdicate in favour of his son.

This was the crisis that had given Napoléon the opportunity to send in his army of occupation, including Aurore's father, to the Spanish capital – while claiming they were only there to stabilise the situation. (He had occupied the north of the country in just the same way, after pretending that he merely wanted access to Portugal.) Général Joachim Murat, commander of the French forces in Spain, entered Madrid on 23 March 1808. It was both practical and symbolic that he should occupy the *piano nobile* of Godoy's splendid, centrally located baroque palace, which had been built for a previous First Secretary, the Marquis de Grimaldi, right next to the Royal Palace.[42] Natural too that, as his aide-de-camp, Maurice Dupin should be housed to hand within the same building, albeit in more modest quarters. The Dupin family would remain at the Palacio de Godoy until Murat departed for Italy, to be crowned King Joachim Napoléon of Naples on 15 July.[43]

Even in wartime this was a glamorous setting. What little girl wouldn't enjoy the princess fantasy of living in a palace – and perhaps learn a lesson of exceptionalism? The date of their arrival would have allowed Aurore and her mother to miss some of the conflict's gruesome underbelly, including the immediate aftermath of the failed Dos de Mayo Uprising of at least six days earlier. The occupying forces – in which of course Maurice himself had a leading role – massacred the city's civilians, turning even the lack of available weapons against the Madrileños and choosing to take any tool they possessed, from a lathe to a needle, as proof of their participation.

This militaristic revenge too is captured by Goya in his

nightmarish chiaroscuro *El Tres de Mayo* (*The Third of May*). The Spanish peasant kneeling before the French firing squad throws up his arms in a gesture that is both the universal language of surrender and a crucifixion. The scene takes place at night outside the city walls, on the hill of Príncipe Pío: a Spanish Golgotha.[44] The victim's white shirt is like a shout among dun tones of night, earth and drying blood. His face is astonished, brown – that is, explicitly southern as opposed to French – and painted with a kind of cartoonish modernity, unlike the slightly mannered precision with which bystanders are rendered. His whole being is exclamation. In contrast with the other condemned civilians who mill behind this target, the faceless firing squad are all death. Immaculately equipped and uniformed, each adopting an identical stance to form a phalanx, they are a professional killing machine.

But tragedy can also be intimate in scale. On 12 June Aurore acquired a baby brother, a major life event for a child of not yet four. Maurice announced to his mother 'a big boy who whistles like a parrot'.[45] But Auguste Dupin would survive for less than three months, and Sophie-Victoire always believed that the Spanish surgeon who attended her deliberately harmed him because of ill will against the French occupiers: 'She imagined she had seen [. . .] this surgeon press his two thumbs on the new-born's two eyes and that he had said between his teeth, "This one will not see the Spanish sun."'[46]

Sand's own recollection of her little brother's blank stare suggests more than simple blindness: something closer to congenital illness or developmental difficulties. Perhaps the baby was oxygen-starved at birth, or maybe Sophie-Victoire – travelling under difficult conditions, then camping out in a deserted palace in the middle of a war zone – had picked up one of the many infections that can harm a foetus.

Whatever the reason for Auguste's impairment, the whole family left Madrid in the first half of July, as soon as the surgeon pronounced Sophie-Victoire strong enough to make the trip. Together they passed through battle lines and shared transport with war-weary infantrymen:

> It was no longer the Madrid palace, the golden beds, the oriental carpets and silk curtains. It was filthy carts, burnt out villages, bombarded towns, roads covered with the dead; ditches where we searched for a drop of water to quench our burning thirst and where one suddenly saw clots of blood floating. Above all it was horrible hunger and a scarcity that became more and more menacing.[47]

Both children caught scabies, and this infection would prove fatal for little Auguste.[48]

But it's possible he was not the first baby the couple had lost. Sand seems to have believed there was a previous son, born in 1806, who also failed to survive. She transcribes a letter Maurice apparently sent Sophie-Victoire in May 1807, in which he writes that 'our three children will soon need the resources and attention of their father'. One of the three was Aurore herself, and a second her half-sister Caroline; she assumes that the third was a child lost in infancy, though it may of course have been her half-brother Hippolyte.[49] If a child was indeed lost when Aurore was a toddler, it's true that she would scarcely have understood or registered what was going on.

To lose a baby sibling just as you turn four, on the other hand, is unavoidably traumatic; the whole family, plunged into grief, may be unable to provide a little girl with much in the way of reassurance. Besides, at four Aurore was of an age to grapple with clumsily emergent maternal feelings:

I don't remember ever believing that my doll was an animated being: yet I felt a real maternal affection for some of those that I owned. It was not exactly idolatry [but] something analogous, relatively, to what fervent Catholics feel when faced with certain devotional images. They know that the image is not the object of their adoration itself. [Children] need to care for or scold, caress or break this child or animal fetish that is given to them as a toy [. . .]. By breaking it they protest against lies. For a moment, they thought they had found life in this mute being who soon showed them her brass wire muscles, her misshapen limbs, her empty brain, her entrails of bran or straw. [. . .] I loved breaking dolls [and] began to fall into the state of doubt that children have about the reality of these kinds of beings. A truly singular state where nascent reason on the one hand, and the need for illusion on the other, fight each other in their hearts.[50]

The child's dolls are transitional objects just like the novelist's characters. But is this only a portrait of the artist as a child with dolls? It follows straight after a passage in which Sand recounts her mother's curious decision to take one daughter, and not the other, with her to Spain. The puzzle remains of what could so trump a mother's care for little Caroline. Perhaps Sophie-Victorie wanted to play house with Maurice once more, appealing to him with (just) his own child? Underlining the oddness of her decision, she was heavily pregnant – 'seven or eight months' gone according to *Histoire* – when she undertook the arduous journey to join him in Madrid. For the birth of Aurore she had managed to persuade Maurice to follow her from Boulogne to the relative safety of Paris; this was exactly the reverse. It's hard not to agree with Sand when she speculates that there may have been 'a pinch of jealousy' in the decision.

There's a trace of something else, too: the faintest sense that as a child Aurore was a sort of doll for her mother. In the French for doll, *poupée*, we hear the English *puppet* and all that implies of mimicry and manipulation. 'She wanted to bring me, and I was still a rather inconvenient personage,' Sand drily observes. 'It wasn't a very prudent undertaking on my mother's part.'⁵¹ It's as though the adult is the childish one in this relationship:

> She spoke purely, as birds sing without having learnt to sing. She had a sweet voice and distinguished pronunciation; her least words charmed and swayed me [but she] was truly crippled in relation to memory, and had never been able to link together two facts in her mind.⁵²

It's not inconceivable that Sophie-Victoire could have followed Maurice to Madrid on a similar childish impulse before Aurore was born, in 1802–3; although it's not clear what the couple might have been doing there. Spain was still at peace, and there's no record of a regimental posting. Yet, according to *Histoire*:

> Several people [. . .] pretending to have seen me born, informed me that, for family reasons easy to divine in a secret marriage, I had not been legally given my true age. According to this version, I was born in Madrid, in 1802 or 1803, and the birth which carried my name had been, in fact, that of another child born since, who died a short time later.⁵³

As Sand points out, there might indeed be room for doubt. In 1804, the French state didn't yet keep rigorous records of births, marriages and deaths; by the time she was writing her memoirs, there was no one left to ask about her origins.⁵⁴

It's perfectly possible that such rumours have a truth the wrong way round. That there was indeed a 'forgotten' baby who died soon after birth, but who came before, not after, the future George Sand (and so can't be the third living child Maurice referred to in 1807). Rates of perinatal mortality were eye-wateringly high at the turn of the nineteenth century, at 41.2 per cent for those born in 1800, and it wasn't unusual to name a subsequent child after one lost in infancy.[55] (In fact, four decades later Aurore's own daughter would do just that.) An earlier baby might indeed have been called Aurore, and the child born in 1804 named after that lost older sister – taking on what is, after all, a careful naming of Maurice's first daughter after his mother. This seems somewhat more likely. It would have required a strong nerve in the emotional days immediately after a death for Maurice and Sophie to register the birth of their second-born but not her death, in order to fake legitimacy for their first. It would also have put Aurore's childhood development wildly out of step – and amid all the detail she records there is no hint of any exceptional precocity.

Perhaps this all feels like calendrical detail. But for Sand it was lived experience. Children conceived after the loss of a sibling are on record as feeling haunted by the original offspring whose 'replacement' they are. As if they're living as a dependent clause, whose identity is not in and for themselves, but somehow in relation to the vanished child. They love and need their parents in ordinary childish ways, but what role do they perform for those parents? Are they simply themselves, or are they some sort of consolation, substitute or distraction?

These kinds of anxieties about the self are deep-seated. Who we think we are sits at the core of who we are in practice, and of what we let ourselves become. To put it another way, identity lies at the heart of identity. Sand says, strikingly, that she 'suffered this doubt for a dozen years', until shortly before starting to write her autobiography: 'It's no more than two or three years that I've known positively who I am.' She claims that it was only in deciding to explore the question for *Histoire* that she found 'in some old unexplored drawers' – as if at the denouement of a gothic novel – the mysterious confirmation that

> I was indeed born in Paris 5 [*sic*] July 1804; I am truly *myself* in a word, which doesn't stop pleasing me, for there's something troubling about doubting one's name, one's age and one's country. [. . .] I could have died without knowing whether I had lived – in person – or in someone else's place.

Apparently, the proof of her own birthdate lies in letters exchanged between her father and grandmother. But – most unusually, in a memoir that quotes extensively from letters – she never shares these with the reader.

In these passages of *Histoire*, the adult Sand seems to review her childhood as if in the kind of double exposure which suddenly reveals the ghostly print of another self here beside her. If she did spend a dozen years fearing she was 'not herself', and was living not 'in person' but by proxy, she must have experienced a profound internal displacement. Her vagueness about her actual 1804 birthdate – she oscillates between 1 July and 4/5 July – comes into focus as a symptom of this distress. The separation of self and identity, of identity and name, quickly slips from fun with names to an existential insecurity.

Sand started writing *Histoire de ma vie* in 1847. So we might calculate that she could have continued to worry that she was 'not herself' right up until, say, 1848, and that those dozen years of uncertainty may have begun sometime after she turned thirty, in 1834. Not early enough, therefore, to account for the vertiginous trajectory of her twenties, but coinciding with the period from thirty to the mid-forties that is for most artists and writers when they 'come into their own'. This being so, her period of doubt overlaps with some of her years of Romantic rebellion, her relationship with Fryderyk Chopin, and up until around the publication of her first pastoral novel, *La Mare au diable,* in 1846. It's a definitional stretch of her life.

Almost the only touchstone certainty in those years of doubt was Nohant. The manor would offer a symbol of continuity to both young Aurore and the adult George Sand who would inherit it. Yet for all its apparent solidity, even it seems to oscillate between fiction and fact. Rebuilt only in 1770, albeit on the site of a fortified medieval castle, whatever looks ancient here is at least partly made up. Nor had the property been in her family for generations. Her grandmother bought it, for 230,000 livres, on 23 August 1793.

Marie-Aurore de Saxe herself believed she had been ruined by her 'descent' to this estate with its twelve-acre park, its extensive common lands and home farm, and the round towers left from the old fortifications.[56] But the modesty she saw in it must have afforded her a degree of protective disguise, especially during the first years of ownership, since her ancestral royal connections would have been both burden and risk in those Revolutionary times. The property's vendor, squire (*écuyer*) of Serennes and former governor of Vierzon, Pierre-Phillippe Péarron de Serennes, had himself chosen the alternative of selling up and leaving France rather than risking the guillotine.[57]

Aurore's grandmother would prove quite unable to resist continuing his highly visible work of seignorial reinvention. According to the writer and journalist Edmond Plauchut, who would frequent Nohant in future decades when it had passed to her granddaughter:

> A great lady in her tastes and her actions because she had been raised by the Dauphine Marie-Josèphe, Madame Dupin

created a park, orchard, greenhouses and a garden; she laid out carefully sanded paths and bowers; she planted a profusion of limes, poplars, chestnut trees and elms, whose high and massive crowns today give Nohant the character of a seigniorial residence that it never had during the time of feudalism.[58]

First impression: *In the garden*

THE FAMOUS AUTHOR SITS IN her garden, raising a parasol against unusually strong spring sunshine. The manor house behind her is all bright stonework and open shutters. On its raised ground floor, salon windows and a French door have been opened wide. Foliage obscures the true height of the building and makes it appear – at least by the standards of a French country manor – domestic, even cosy.

It's an impression confirmed by other photographs Placide Verdot has taken on this late-April visit to Nohant. Here's the ivy-clad medieval tower in the park wall, here a shabby fence, here ivy creeping over the crumbling banks of a pond. Verdot notices these things because 'Views of the Monuments and archaeological curiosities of Indre' are his speciality. As his calling card announces, he's even received an award for this work from the French Archaeological Society. Which might explain why in this photo the figures on the lawn are no closer than the middle distance, and are so frustratingly out of focus.

Placide Verdot's studio at 54 rue Grande, Châteauroux, in the medieval high street of the department capital, is less than twenty miles away. He's a local photographer. But this doesn't make him a provincial also-ran. In 1875 photography is still an unusual combination of innovative technology and something which may or may not be art – the era's jury is out on this. New and rare enough, at least, for its practitioners to have the status of experts. The decisions which he's making here about how to capture a place and its way of life may or may not reflect an interest in Nohant's famous owner: portraits will come later. But they undoubtedly contribute to the emerging understanding of how to use photographic plates *en plein air*.

George Sand sits for him with her granddaughters – who've brought their dolls out to pose, too. She has just over a year left to live, but the scene appears timeless. And perhaps in a way it is. These little girls will remain so in love with the way of life the Bonne Dame Nohant has created that they will do their utmost to preserve it here over the *longue durée* – and that *durée is* long. Incredibly, nine-year-old Aurore, kneeling here in the sun, will live on until 1961.

The girls' parents face them, on chairs brought out to the garden's raked gravel for this photograph. Hands on knees – strawhatted, be-smocked – Sand's artist son Maurice looks thoroughly relaxed. Her beloved daughter-in-law Lina, back to the camera, is perhaps slightly less so. The cedars beneath which they sit were planted to commemorate Maurice's birth, and that of his sister Solange: an oddly literal version of a family tree. Seizing their share of immortality in the background beyond the dark branches are a housemaid and the top-hatted bystander – perhaps a groom? – who will manage to appear in most of the views Verdot takes today.

It is among other things a portrait of an idyllic country afternoon, which captures a completely inhabitable moment and transports it across a century and a half. Nothing's yet in full leaf. Dazzle and shade shift through branches, insects scritch, spring pollen floats on the still air. Perhaps there are voices coming from the lane beyond the manor wall, or from deep in the house's stone interior.

But what looks at first glance like a pattern of drowsy leisure is actually a powerhouse of creativity. Excellent things, this picture says (whether it means to or not), can be made in quiet, provincial spots, under trees, within earshot of sheep and cows. As in fact they always have been; perhaps Verdot still finds this familiar and unremarkable. Only now, as he takes this picture three-quarters of the way through the nineteenth century, have politics and art slipped away from the countryside to concentrate in metropolitan centres. In the eighteenth century, J. S. Bach or J. W. von Goethe, Jean-Jacques Rousseau or Voltaire, could shift the culture of a continent while living and working outside their respective capital cities. (Not, admittedly, for the best of reasons, since power and money were regionally dispersed by resting in the hands of the old aristocracy.) George Sand is, remarkably, a kind of bridge figure in this process. Herself of aristocratic descent, her life has spanned the decades of industrialisation and flight to the city. She herself embarked on Parisian literary life only after years trapped by domestic ties in the muddy 'desert of France', but, once in the capital, she changed things at the heart of national and European culture.

More than that, in her success she's come back to settle in rural Indre. It's a double transition that makes her a patron saint of the 'nowhere nobody'. Here in Nohant she has turned her attention to ecology, the environment, rural ways of life. She's published a number of masterpieces about the countryside that will remain required reading a century and a half from now. She's turned her home into a centre of excellence, a place where great literature and (in the hands of her guests Franz Liszt and Fryderyk Chopin) music gets written. She's established two theatres in the house: an incubator stage, and her son's pioneering marionette theatre. She's welcomed distinguished visitors – writers, artists, musicians, politicians and thinkers – from all over Europe to this Berrichon hamlet. And, although by now she has joined the national artistic establishment, she remains that radical figure, a highly productive, always exploratory artist.

All of which makes the trees in the picture, its foreground irises, icons of something radical. One way radicalism and novelty are muted is by being distanced from the social mainstream: difference gets put out like the cat at night. But being away from the centre of things may not always be disempowering. Right now Sand's close friend and closest literary confidant Gustave Flaubert is transforming the French novel from his mother's riverbank home outside Rouen.

Like Aristotle's lever, long enough to move the earth, distance might be the very thing that can effect change. Perhaps it's easier to innovate away from the groupthink of fashion. As Rebecca Solnit, that bold writer working a century and a half from now, will say in *Recollections of My Non-Existence*, new ideas come into being at the periphery; the movement of change is from the periphery to the centre. George Sand reminds us that change may be centripetal.

TWO

The very rich hours

AT FOUR YEARS OLD, Aurore Dupin de Francueil was held in a cat's cradle of family relationships; if some of its strings were a little tangled, perhaps that served to tighten them the more. This was life *en famille*. Though in many respects she would be raised as an only child, Aurore was surrounded by strong characters. None of the adults around her seems to have made any particular attempt to downplay their personalities, or the differences between them, on her account. One gets the impression of a continually strobing shadow play, its huge and exaggerated figures a sort of Guignol pantomime.

The central tension of the little girl's upbringing would prove to be a struggle between the maternal and paternal sides of her family, with their widely different ways of showing love – and of choosing to live. For years to come, a class war – politesse versus street savvy, education versus instinct – would be fought over her small person. But four is an age of sitting under tables watching the feet of adults, of the dreamy uncertainty that surrounds emerging childish certainties: the cupboard opens like this, I dress my dolly like that. While Aurore could only just peer over a tabletop, such adult campaigns might pass literally over her head.

So when she, her baby brother Auguste and her parents

arrived at her grandmother's country home for the first time at the end of August 1808, she may have been too young to notice adult tensions. But this was also a rare moment of family unanimity. After all, the quartet were returning from the Spanish battlefields; they arrived at Nohant to be celebrated as survivors by the manor's chatelaine, the great Marie-Aurore de Saxe. The drama of having escaped with their lives trumped even maternal questions about the suitability of Maurice's marriage.

Not that his family were in good shape. Feverish, off her food, unable to shake the scabies which she had caught on the terrible return journey from Madrid, with its 'suffering, thirst, heat and fever', little Aurore only 'came to [her] senses on entering the courtyard of Nohant', which seemed to her childish eyes every bit as imposing as the Godoy Palace had been in Madrid.[1] It was love at first sight; and the child fell not only for the beautiful limestone manor with its tree-shaded facade, but for a whole way of life:

> It was not the first time I had seen my grandmother, but I have no memories from before that day. She also seemed very big to me, although she was only five foot, and her pale and pink figure, her imposing air, her unvarying costume composed of an extra-long brown silk dress with flat sleeves, which she had not wished to modify in accordance with the requirements of Empire style, her blond wig with a forehead curl, her little round bonnet with a lace cockade in the middle, made her for me a being apart.[2]

This glimpse of an aristocracy that was already anachronistic and more than a little eccentric is suffused with affection – and gratitude. Though she was filthy from the journey, and covered with boils, Aurore found herself scooped up by her grandmother and put to bed in this 'so delicate, so refined' lady's own room, a 'fresh and airy [. . .] paradise'.

Is there a slight, novelistic exaggeration in the way the adult George Sand juxtaposes the state her child self was in with the delights of her grandmother's house? Chiaroscuro tones of grime and illness used to throw life at Nohant into high relief? Perhaps. But then, this is a formative moment. After the hell of Spanish battlefields, and a purgatorial voyage home through the Bay of Biscay, a small girl arrives in what will prove to be her personal paradise. Small wonder if the memory of this arrival is full of images of light and air.

The spacious stone house that now entered Aurore's life was a concrete symbol of family as something not invented on the fly but instead robust, undeniable, even hard to escape. From its first chapter *Histoire de ma vie* makes explicit how, for the future writer, home would be the stage of real human drama: 'the idolatrous cult of the family is false and dangerous, but respect and solidarity within family are necessary'. 'Idolatrous', a characteristically emotive term, sends the writer plunging on. Even France's violent political history, she points out, can be viewed through the prism of family:

> In antiquity, the family played a major role. Since this role exaggerated its importance, nobility transmitted itself like a privilege. [. . .] The eighteenth-century philosophers shook the cult of nobility, the revolution overturned it; but the religious ideal of the family was dragged into this destruction [. . .] and the people who had suffered from hereditary oppression [. . .] became used to believing solely in their own resources. [Yet] each family has its nobility, its glory, its claims: work, courage, virtue or intelligence.[3]

The language may be high-flown, but the insight's accurate. Heredity, conflating degrees of privilege with genetic belonging, had indeed defined pre-Revolutionary French society, and so the 1789 Revolution itself. Aurore was a daughter of this Revolution, which though officially ended by Napoléon Bonaparte in 1799 was continuing to reverberate even beyond the borders of France: her parents had married across its battle lines. The rackety, quasi-bohemian life they had cobbled together as a result, in Paris lodgings and following army postings, was all the four-year-old had known. Now at Nohant she was confronted with another kind of family: the 'great lady in her tastes and her actions' for whom she had been named.

It wasn't just what Marie-Aurore de Saxe and the rest of Aurore's paternal ancestry represented, but also what they passed down to her, that would shape the future writer. Her grandmother's educated anecdotes, the patrician style and exacting manners, could confirm her sense of self-worth – but at the same time open a rift in her sense of family. 'We'll call her Aurore,' Maurice had said when his daughter arrived, 'after my poor mother, who is not here to bless her – but who shall bless her one day.'[4] But Marie-Aurore de Saxe, who was fifty-five when her granddaughter was born in Paris – as she herself had been – was very far from being either frail or pious. Proudly the illegitimate daughter of the eighteenth-century French military hero Maréchal Maurice de Saxe – himself the illegitimate son of Augustus II, King of Poland and Elector of Saxony, by aristocratic court favourite Maria Aurora von Königsmarck – she had named her own son Maurice after the marshal, and carried her grandmother's name just as her grubby four-year-old granddaughter carried hers.

Calling an accidental child after the father's mother blanket-stitches her continuing presence – and hence that of the father himself – into that child's life.[5] As in a fairy tale, little Amantine-Aurore-Lucile now found herself to be the great-great-granddaughter of a king and to have, in her great-great-grandmother, a conspicuously talented and adventurous forebear. Maria Aurora von Königsmarck, a member of both German and Swedish nobility, became the first official mistress of the future King Augustus II in the 1690s.[6] But when Voltaire called Maria Aurora 'the most famous woman of two centuries', it was because of her literary and stage work.[7] Poems and plays have come down to us, as have the scores of two opera-ballets for which she supplied libretti and in which she performed as dancer. The racy-sounding *Fastnachts-Lust* (*Carnival Desire*) survives from 1696, the year she gave birth to the future marshal.[8] During the 1680s she played a central role in the Swedish intellectual feminist circle around Sophia Elisabet Brenner, a female scholar of international standing then known as the 'second Sappho', who was the first to publish poetry in Swedish. The poem that established her posthumous reputation as a proto-feminist pioneer, 'The justified defence of the female sex' (1693), is thought to result from the two women's friendship.[9]

It was just before he turned fifty-two that Maria Aurore's equally distinguished son, Maréchal Maurice de Saxe, had the affair with an eighteen-year-old actress, Marie-Genevieve Rinteau, that resulted in the last of his several illegitimate children.[10] The girl born in September 1748 was named Marie-Aurore for the marshal's mother, but received neither financial support nor the de Saxe patronymic from him. The first decades of her life were a struggle for a tenuous respectability. In 1755, the year she turned seven, her mother's subsequent lover and protector abruptly died. The dauphine, who was Marie-Aurore's first cousin, was petitioned for help.[11] Perhaps knowing the marshal's behaviour as well as the way society worked, she responded. But her generosity was high-intervention. Marie-Aurore was separated from her mother and sent to boarding school, first in an Ursuline convent in Saint-Cloud and then at the Maison Royale de Saint-Louis, founded by Mme de Maintenon, both outside and to the west of Paris. When she reached seventeen, the dauphine arranged her marriage to a Comte de Hom – who was killed in a duel eight months later. Three weeks before their wedding, on 15 May 1766, parliament had been persuaded to grant Marie-Aurore the de Saxe patronym in order to legitimate this match. But it availed her little in her widowhood the following year, when the dauphine herself also died.

Marie-Aurore was forced to step back across the chasm between respectability and the demi-monde to live with her actress mother. When she was twenty-seven this compromising figure died, and she moved to a Paris convent. It was at the Dames Augustines Anglaises in rue des Fossés-Saint-Victor – which was to feature large in her granddaughter's life – that she was visited and courted by an older widower. She may have seen Louis-Claude Dupin de Francueil as a family friend or even an uncle, since he was a former lover of her mother's actress sister Geneviève. He would be sixty-two when she married him at twenty-nine – in the nick of time for her own marriageability.[12] It was an excellent match. Her new husband took the name de Francueil from a village within the estate of the great chateau of Chenonceau, of which his father had been chatelain. Nevertheless, when this second marriage produced a son, he agreed to name the boy Maurice, criss-cross, for his maternal grandfather.

Be careful what you wish for, perhaps. Just like his grandfather, Maurice had grown up to be an outstanding army officer, and to fall in love with another *demi-mondaine*, Sophie-Victoire Delaborde. And so although his little daughter Aurore had royal ancestry, a sequence of illegitimacies (and her own conception outside marriage) ran through that lineage like a zipper, always ready to be pulled apart. And the grandmother for whom the four-year-old had been named, and who now placed this soiled and sickly near-stranger tenderly in her own bed, understood the contingency of family fortune.

Perhaps she stressed what was aristocratic in her lineage in order to try to outreach what was rackety: the recurring family themes of extramarital liaison, the stage and soldiery. The way she chose to 'rescue' her illegitimate grandson Hippolyte from his impoverished mother no longer seems surprising or gratuitous once we realise it's the same model the dauphine had used to 'rescue' her own seven-year-old self. This in turn changes how we understand her future attempts to do much the same with Hippolyte's half-sister, the granddaughter who, for now, she put protectively to bed.

The sustained effort of will it required was crystallised by her manorial life at Nohant. When Maurice and Sophie-Victoire arrived with their children that August, gardens and parkland beckoned the family outdoors. And Aurore, reaching the transformative moment when the prolonged reverie of infancy tips into childhood, was just old enough to explore them.[13] On her very first afternoon she woke after napping for a couple of hours to find her half-brother Hippolyte presenting her with an 'enormous bunch of flowers'. At nine, he was still young enough to be delighted by the arrival of a playmate, however small. And, eager to play herself, 'I felt so good that I ran into the garden with Hippolyte. I remember that he held me by the hand with extreme care, believing that I was going to fall at each step.'

But 'I was a little humiliated that he believed me to be such a little girl, and I soon showed him that I was a very resolute boy.' There's learning a place, and also learning to play. In the ensuing sibling push and pull,

Temperamental and bossy, because I was thoroughly spoilt by my father, I could neither think ahead nor pretend. Hippolyte soon saw my weakness, and to punish me for my whims and tantrums, he set about teasing me cruelly. He undressed my dolls and buried them in the garden, then put a little cross there and made me disinter them [. . .] I swore very often that I hated him. But I was incapable of bearing a grudge, and when he came looking for me to play, I didn't know how to resist him.[14]

Quand il venait me chercher pour jouer, je ne savais lui resister: it could be the motto of her adult relationships with men.

Despite this blush of childish excitement, Nohant couldn't make everything right. Aurore's baby brother had been called Auguste, in true de Saxe style, after their great-great-grandfather, King Augustus II of Poland. But the month he was named for would prove cheerless. By the time the family arrived in Indre, Aurore was over the worst of the scabies both children had caught en route. But 'fever was consuming [him]. He was livid and his poor dulled eyes had an expression of indescribable sadness.' This infant vulnerability trumped Aurore's nascent sibling rivalry. 'I began to love him when I saw him suffering.'[15] Daily, Sophie-Victoire brought Auguste outside to soak up the healthy country air, sitting in the shade with him on her knees. She tried to improve her own health through good food and exercise – even starting to garden a small plot beneath an old pear tree – in order to strengthen the quality of her milk, which she believed must be failing the little boy. But to no avail. He died in her lap on 8 September.

The baby was buried next day in the village graveyard. But he was not to rest there. Sophie-Victoire was so upset that, when darkness fell, Maurice Dupin went to the plot, dug up his son's body and brought it home. His wife kept the little corpse in her room all day, hoping with the irrationality of grief that there had somehow been a mistake; that the baby had simply seized or fallen unconscious. Only on the second night could Maurice prevail on her to accept the brute facts. One of the parents wrote their infant's name on a piece of paper, laid it between two pieces of glass and wired them together. Someone filled the little coffin with flowers. And then, under cover of darkness, they sneaked their boy into the garden plot his mother had been cultivating.

Over the next 'five or six days', according to *Histoire*, the young parents appeared to flout mourning convention with their bouts of eager gardening. They built up a grassy knoll with a spiral path and flower beds full of the Michaelmas daisies that were just coming into season. Soon Aurore and Hippolyte joined in – though without realising they were helping to raise a monument. All they knew was that 'as if by magic' the family had together created 'a real children's garden'. Sand would remember these days as a rare pause of great domestic tenderness; but even the children must have felt the lengthening shadows of the adults' sadness, and remembered that baby Auguste was dead.[16] Small wonder that Hippolyte could make Aurore cry by pretending to bury her dolls.

But these play-funerals would turn out to be practice for still greater calamity. Just over a week after her baby brother's death, Aurore's adored father was dead too. Again, she witnessed the extremities of adult grief. It was around six in the morning on 17 September and in the pre-dawn gloaming the small child, somehow already dressed, was watching her mother get up. Sophie-Victoire had put on a white skirt and a white short-sleeved blouse. She was just combing out her dark hair when François Deschartres, whom she had first met seven years before in those scenes at the Black Head Inn, burst into the bedroom without knocking – itself a sign that something was wrong. The steward's pallor and agitation gave the game away even before he managed to blurt out his news. 'He said to her in accents I will never forget for the rest of my life, "He is dead!" Then he gave a kind of convulsive laugh, sat down, and burst into tears.'

The previous evening, against Sophie-Victoire's protestations, Maurice had ridden over to little, local La Châtre to dine with friends. It's easy to understand the tension this provoked, and which *Histoire* records. For him to escape the house of mourning after a few days for an evening of drinking in the company of friends is so much the classic masculine strategy for dealing with emotion that in the twenty-first-century it's become a cliché. The pitch of jealousy and anxiety his young wife had worked herself up to in imploring him not to go – without any logical reason for her to worry about his safety on this unexceptional, early autumn evening – is just as recognisable. She's every woman who feels her man isn't supporting her in the extremity of grief; for whom the little death of abandonment feels like the final abandonment that is death itself. Now, in the darkened bedroom, as Sophie-Victoire's grim fantasy turned out to have come horrifyingly true, little Aurore covered her mother's bare arms with kisses that had no effect. 'I heard her wrenching cries. She was deaf to mine and didn't feel my caresses.'[17] Pity Sophie-Victoire. But pity more the four-year-old who was learning, in the very moment that she lost her father, that she was not the apple of her mother's eye; that she was simply not as important to her mother as her mother was to her.

Maurice came first; something that can have been no surprise to an adult observer, since Sophie-Victoire had already showed herself capable of leaving a daughter behind in order to follow her man to the battlefields of Spain. Perhaps he was the love of her life; perhaps he seemed to be her very life itself. He was, after all, so much more than she could reasonably have hoped for.

The fun-loving young soldier had become a distinguished officer and, just a fortnight ago, she had arrived at Nohant with the son and heir in her arms and been accepted at last into her aristocratic mother-in-law's house. Now all of this was ripped away.

As if immediately underlining this, it was her mother-in-law who rushed in the pre-dawn dark to the house just outside La Châtre where the dying Maurice had been taken. The young cavalryman had been thrown by his horse: a tragedy that must have seemed at once likely and unlikely. However low his mood, there was no evidence that he was either drunk or unusually inattentive when at the end of the evening he'd set out for Nohant, followed by his friend Weber. Their way led downhill out of town, across the Indre and, about 100 yards beyond the bridge, round a bend in the road on to a tree-lined straight. Here, Weber would testify, Maurice had spurred his mount into a gallop that was probably customary: he knew the road home well. But, invisible in the darkness, a pile of rubble had been left near the avenue's unlucky thirteenth poplar. His horse stumbled, reared and threw him. He landed about ten yards away, still conscious – but with a broken neck.

The family put much of the blame on his mount. Handsome, even exceptional, Léopardo of Andalucia had been given to Maurice in Spain by Ferdinand VII in recognition of his actions during the Tumult of Aranjuez. But Léopardo was a big beast, and notoriously hard to handle. Sophie-Victoire had always maintained that it was a death wish disguised as a gift. Certainly, the stallion represented a degree of hubris. And it had killed Maurice just, as his daughter would observe four decades later, 'at the moment when his military career at last opened before him, dazzling and unobstructed'.[18]

Four-year-old Aurore understood death as absence, but not yet its permanence. Later she would recall asking, 'Is my daddy still dead today?' and 'When daddy has finished being dead, won't he come to see you?' This bracing innocence stands in contrast to a sort of gothic hysteria which seems to have enveloped manor and village. There were so many sightings of Maurice's ghost that 'some burglar profited or attempted to profit from the terror of our people, because a white ghost wandered in the courtyard several nights. Hippolyte saw it [...] Deschartres also saw it and threatened it with a gun: it didn't return.'[19]

That Hippolyte at nine years old had been carried away by the spooky drama of sudden death is entirely excusable. As Sand reminds us, he didn't yet know he was Maurice's son, and so didn't realise he'd lost his father.[20] All the same, the adult memoirist herself will attach an aura of superstition to this shockingly unexpected death. There is that thirteenth poplar. And then there is the family story that, a week before his own death, when Maurice went to retrieve baby Auguste's body from the family plot, he disturbed the wrong grave by mistake. The bier sprang up and knocked him into its open hole, where 'he experienced a moment of terror and inexpressible anguish at finding himself so close to death'.[21]

Or maybe none of this is true. Every story has its storyteller. The child Aurore had no idea that the body of her baby brother had even been moved from Nohant's little graveyard. Only fifteen years later, in the early months of her own marriage, would his grave be uncovered during remodelling of the manor gardens – prompting the head gardener to admit that he had first discovered it some years earlier, while planting fig trees. Caught between the twin terrors, superstitious and legal, of disturbing a grave and stumbling across what he perhaps took to be infanticide, he'd chosen to rebury the makeshift coffin and keep its secret. To find out how it got there, the young wife – and posterity – would have to rely on that unreliable narrator, Sophie-Victoire.[22]

But if family stories grow hyperbolically, families themselves can shrink with alarming speed. As the only surviving legitimate child of her father, at the moment of Maurice's death little Aurore became her grandmother's heir (de facto legitimacy, however tenuously achieved, trumping Hippolyte's claim even though he was older and a boy). She would come to write her account of her father's death in the very rooms in which she had first heard the news as a child.

Becoming Marie-Aurore de Saxe's posterity would, however, not always be easy. At the outset her grandmother doted on her: 'because of my striking resemblance to my father. My voice, my features, my mannerisms, my tastes, everything in me reminded her of her son as a child [. . .] she often called me Maurice, and said "my son" in speaking of me.'[23] This isn't quite the first time we've glimpsed the child Aurore as a 'very resolute boy', but it's still a surprise to find such a recollection buried among others of a grandmother who was to try unusually hard to train her into ladylike behaviour.

Perhaps it was to correct her own tendency to turn Aurore into her lost son that Mme Dupin de Francueil decided to find the child a less boisterous playmate than Hippolyte was turning out to be. Ursule, the niece of her personal maid Mlle Julie, was half a year older than Aurore, and seems to have been considered, like the children of the Dupin family, a kind of blank who could be moulded in any way the adults chose. Sure enough, the girls were soon playing as equals, eating at the same table and sleeping together in the 'big bed' at the manor. They even, as little girls will, did each other's hair in matching styles. After a few months, when Deschartres resumed the role of family tutor he had first undertaken for Aurore's father, both joined in with Hippolyte's lessons. So firm a friendship did it become that the pair would still be writing to each other more than four decades later.

When she recalls what the girls quickly came to call 'the golden age' of their shared childhood, Sand insists that her child self was spoilt.[24] Hippolyte, who might have been expected to curb a little girl's whims, had instead – like her father – played along with them. It was different with 'Ursulette', the 'little bear', whose real name was Geneviève. 'Very intelligent and very brave', she resisted Aurore's attempts to dominate their friendship through coming from the more monied family.[25] There were physical scraps. Perhaps most potently, Ursule announced that, since the deaths of Aurore's father and brother, she no longer envied but pitied her wealthier friend.[26]

The aristocratic oligarchy of the Ancien Régime was over, and a future social radical was learning that privilege isn't absolute. Perhaps this friendship, with the lessons Aurore absorbed from it, was only possible because revolution had already shaken up the social narrative in France. But comparisons between privilege and disadvantage would be repeated through her childhood, as she struggled between what she came to call her 'two mothers': the aristocratic grandmother she called Maman and the former chorus girl she called Mama.[27] Even as a powerless child she would find herself faced, like her father, with the practical and emotional impossibility of choosing between these two intensely possessive women.

Already in the first months of life at Nohant, she was experiencing these conflicting loyalties as a moral responsibility. Sophie-Victoire wasn't a conventionally affectionate mother, but Aurore was 'passionately' attached to her. Perhaps, human psyches working as they do, her feelings were all the more intense because she sensed they might be unrequited. That tableau when Deschartres announced Maurice's death – the imploring child and the mother to whom, at this moment, she seems to mean nothing – crystallises a certain dynamic.

At the same time, every day at Nohant there was its chatelaine, Marie-Aurore de Saxe, that calm, predictable and encouraging presence. Aurore loved her too:

> These were really the two extreme types of our sex: the one white, blonde, serious, calm and dignified in manner, a true Saxon of noble blood, with great airs full of ease and protective kindness, the other brunette, pale, ardent, awkward and timid in front of society people, but always ready to explode when the storm rumbled too strongly within, with a jealous Spanish nature, angry and weak, wicked and good at the same time. [. . .] My mother was a great artist, lost for lack of training [. . .] She knew nothing; she had learnt nothing [. . .] she did it by instinct.[28]

'Two extreme types of our sex': these were, in particular, *female* role models. In adulthood, Sand would become notorious for trying out controversial ways to be a woman. She would also, perhaps, integrate her double familial inheritance in a writing life composed equally from creative disobedience and intense self-discipline. But not just yet. For now, she was a child whose mother dismissed precisely the ladylike manners her grandmother was trying to inculcate, allowing her to play freely outdoors, to 'roll on the ground, laugh noisily, speak [the local dialect] *Berrichon*'.[29]

Fairly soon, Aurore seems to have become anxiously aware that her grandmother had the wealth which protected the household; only for her mother to pose her the tendentious, manipulative question, 'But do wealth and talents create happiness?'[30] In the middle of this emotive polarisation one of Aurore's paternal uncles, the Abbé de Beaumont, came to stay at Nohant. He pitched in for Maurice's side of the family, urging Sophie-Victoire to hand over her child's care to the grandmother who could afford her the best of upbringings. Unfortunately the little girl herself, overhearing this, developed 'a sort of unformed terror of the wealth by which I was threatened', and, worse, a belief that she was being sold to her grandmother.

Which, in a way, she was. On 29 January 1809, her mother signed over charge of Aurore's education to Marie-Aurore de Saxe. On 3 February, in return for an annual allowance of 1,500 francs, she signed over the little girl's guardianship too.[31] She was at last financially and emotionally free to return to Paris and retrieve her elder daughter Caroline, whom she'd boarded out for the previous ten months. A fortnight later, Aurore and her grandmother followed Sophie-Victoire to the capital. The plan was that, for the next few months, the child would visit her mother but live with her grandmother, and so gradually get used to both a socially smarter way of doing things, and to life without 'Mama'.

This transition was never going to be seamless. Respectability, both a conceptual and practical puzzle, was crystallised in the person of Aurore's elder sister Caroline. Marie-Aurore de Saxe – herself famously the illegitimate daughter of an illegitimate son – had been flexible enough to accommodate Maurice's illegitimate son Hippolyte. Yet she refused absolutely to countenance Aurore's illegitimate half-sibling on her mother's side. Indeed, her refusal even to let Caroline visit Sophie-Victoire in Nohant had helped force her daughter-in-law's hand over Aurore.

At four and nine years old respectively, the girls themselves felt things differently. Aurore had parted readily enough from Caroline when setting out for Spain. At three, she had been too young to understand what was going on. But Caroline, five years older, must have understood perfectly well what it meant to be left behind when her mother set out to carry her younger child – and her pregnancy – into the foreign country with which France was at war. Even little Aurore sublimated a longing for some missing maternal intimacy in the imaginary games, dolls and invented stories which *Histoire* recalls. Caroline didn't grow up to become a famous writer, so we have no record of how she managed her longings. But she clearly attached family feeling to her younger sister. Once Aurore and her grandmother had arrived in Paris and Sophie-Victoire had established a routine of visits, she wanted to be involved.

And so one day she simply turned up at Marie-Aurore de Saxe's fashionable Paris home on the rue Neuve des Mathurins. This took courage: picture the smart address, with views of 'the huge gardens on the other side of the road', on a route out to the Parisian countryside which would in the future become the uptown address of Haussmann's opera house, Palais Garnier. Nine-year-old Caroline was admitted as far as the vestibule of the luxurious apartment by a maid called Rose who was, apparently, new and didn't quite understand the house rules. The child got no further, though she begged in a series of frantic whispers to see her sister. The aristocratic mistress of the household had her sent away, 'dismayed, broken, humiliated, wounded in her self-respect and in her naive love'.[32]

But Aurore was distraught too. She was there in her grandmother's drawing room while this was going on; she overheard her sister's 'stifled but heart-breaking sob, a cry from the bottom of the soul, which penetrated to the bottom of mine and awakened the voice of blood'. Even the bribe of a much-pestered-for doll failed to calm her, and her grandmother was forced for once to concede. The sisters could see each other, but only at their mother's apartment. Like most compromises, it was a bad idea. The intention was to prevent the younger daughter spending much time in Sophie-Victoire's world: in practice, the arrangement immersed her in it.

There was a chasm of income but also of taste, and it became immediately apparent to Aurore. Mme Dupin de Francueil's apartment was furnished in pre-Revolutionary style, with carpets everywhere, and her own room was lined with 'sky-blue damask'. The child could not now avoid noticing the painful contrast with the 'poor wood and tiled bedroom' of the maternal home, a little under a mile away in rue de la Grange-Batelière and, as a result, 'I did not at all enjoy these comforts of life to which my grandmother would have liked to see me more sensitive.'

Maman, all 'enlightened discernment' and 'naturally very elevated' taste, wanted to cultivate something similar in her granddaughter:

> She would say to me, 'There's a badly drawn figure, a colour match that shocks the eye, a composition, or language, or piece of music, or dress in bad taste.' [But] my mother [was] less complicated and more naive. Almost all the products of art or industry pleased her, so long as they had cheerful images and bright colours.[33]

Things came to a literal head with Aurore's hair. Her mother, who thought her grandmother dressed her frumpily, insisted on doing the child's hair 'in the Chinese style':

> It was the most horrible hairstyle that could be imagined, and was certainly invented for faces with no forehead. Your hair was brushed back by combing it against the grain until it had assumed a perpendicular attitude, and then the ponytail was twisted right in the middle of the skull, so as to make the head an elongated ball surmounted by a small ball of hair. One looked like a brioche bun or a pilgrim's gourd. Add to this ugliness the torture of having hair pulled like this against the direction of

growth [till] the skin of the forehead was pulled tight and the corners of the eyes lifted like figures on a Chinese fan.³⁴

But all sorts of things could prove painful in this battle of maternal wills. Though just a child, Aurore was taught to live inside the formal *vous*, and to address her grandmother in the third person:

Respect was necessary, and seemed to me icy. [My mother's anger] was just a painful moment to get through. [Though my grandmother] embraced me solemnly and as a reward for my good behaviour; she didn't treat me sufficiently like a child. [. . .] It was necessary to carry oneself correctly, to carry gloves, to be silent [. . .] To every spirit in my nature was opposed a little oppression, very gentle, but assiduous.³⁵

Small wonder that Sophie-Victoire's expressive immediacy continued to seduce Aurore to her core. So much so that, when the child sickened after a few months in Paris and was brought back to the fresh air of Nohant to recover, it was deemed necessary for her mother to follow – boarding Caroline out again in order to do so.

This oscillation was painful for everyone. Yet it continued for years, and must have made it abundantly clear to Caroline whose needs came last. Finally, Sophie-Victoire explained to her younger daughter that she had to abide by the custody agreement she'd signed in 1809, because she was financially dependent upon it. With childish logic, Aurore's response was that in this case they should simply earn their living together as seamstresses. Caroline should come too. It was a kid's fantasy of running away – but with, instead of from, her mother. *Histoire* has her going so far as to hide a letter full of plans for how to do so behind one of the portraits hanging at Nohant. This may be an embroidery: the surviving note contains nothing more than a farewell. Perhaps what the future writer would remember most clearly is most clearly true: that on this occasion of particular closure she was not allowed to see off her mother, who left in the middle of the night: 'How much I regret not being able to wish you goodbye in person,' her note reads. And in the morning she found no answering letter in the hiding place 'behind old Dupin's portrait'.[36]

Sophie-Victoire would always be an intermittent letter-writer. (Easy to guess that she probably disliked writing, having had little education.) But in this era there was no other way to stay in touch. A word Sand doesn't use, for the obvious reason that she lived before Sigmund Freud, is narcissism. Yet her reminiscences give us numerous suggestions of how narcissistic her mother, that determined, streetwise and yet childish survivor, could be. Maybe this had been key to her extraordinary upward social trajectory. But now, widowed at thirty-five, those years of self-invention were over. In Paris she was slipping back down the social and economic ladder to respectable penury. This later Sophie-Victoire is the one whose narrow, anxious face peers out from the frame of her bonnet in the pencil portrait George Sand would execute around 1833.[37] She looks, as she was, like a sufferer from the migraines her daughter would inherit. Her lips are thinned as if compressed by anxiety – or because she's lost her teeth. Though her eyes are as large and dark as her famous daughter's, there are dark circles beneath them. You can see what a pretty woman she's been, but also how completely she has surrendered that cardinal virtue of the ingenue: vivacity.

Imagination and invention were among Sophie-Victoire's gift to her second daughter, but they may have come to Aurore from

Maurice too. Fired by fairy stories and tales of heroism, the future writer invented a figure called Corambé, a gender-neutral deity who was part *genius loci* and part Green Man – or anyway, Green Person. So far so creative, though she seems to have daydreamed with almost neuro-atypical intensity. The Corambé myth would remain so important to her that she would return to it in her adult creative life. The little girl also enjoyed being read to while she sat at her mother's feet watching the lit hearth through a fire screen:

> Her voice put me under a kind of drowsiness, where it was impossible for me to follow an idea. Images drew themselves in front of me, and came to fix themselves on the green screen. These were woods, rivers, towns of a bizarre and gigantic architecture such as I still see often in dreams [. . .] One day these apparitions became so complete that I was almost frightened, and asked my mother whether she didn't see them [. . .] and she rocked me on her knees while singing to me to bring me back to myself.[38]

Which might be a sort of literary embellishment by the adult Sand – the fantasies themselves seem only mildly remarkable – until we read this passage alongside another in *Histoire*. After her father's death, Aurore's grandmother noticed how the orphan would sit 'saying nothing, my arms hanging, my eyes fixed, my mouth half open, and that I seemed stupid at times'. Sophie-Victoire reassured her mother-in-law that the child had always done this and was just daydreaming. ' "Probably so," replied my grandmother; "but it is not good [. . .] I also saw her poor father, as a child, fall into a kind of ecstasy, and after that he had a languid illness." '[39]

There couldn't be a more precise description of absence

seizures, which are most common in girls between the ages of four and fourteen, a quarter of whom will have a relative who also has seizures. Seizures of this kind, which used to be called *petit mal*, usually last around ten to fifteen seconds – as in that 'seemed stupid at times' – and are often mistaken for daydreaming. The medical literature makes a connection between 'delusions, illusions and hallucinations' and 'partial epilepsy'.[40] Most children – apparently including Aurore and her father, if they were indeed sufferers – grow out of absence seizures, although a minority go on to develop full-blown epilepsy. (Is there any point in speculating as to whether Maurice developed *grand mal*; whether he tumbled from Léopardo in a seizure? But it would be impossible to prove.)[41]

Whatever the truth of this, reverie is one of the great trump cards of childhood. As Sand reminds us, 'It seems that children like the mystery of their daydreams.'[42] The word she uses, *rêveries*, recurs throughout her *Histoire*, and the French means both dream and daydream, as well as that kind of noodling reflection which the English 'reverie' denotes. It implies pausing, observing, feeling, rather than trying to 'master' the world of experience. Late in life, writing for *Le Temps* in 1871, she will return to this kind of knowing-without-naming:

> There are hours where I escape from myself, where I live in a plant, or feel myself to be grass, bird, treetop, cloud, running water, horizon, colour, shape and sensations that are changing, mobile, undefined [. . .] where I live, finally, in everything that's developing into itself as if it were an expansion [a dilation] of my being.[43]

It's as if those childish absences have been transmuted, not into a flight from the self but into the dissolution of its boundaries.

A year after that piece, Sand will go further still:

All the earth and the sky act upon us all the time and, all the time, we act in return upon all the earth and all the sky without noticing. [...] I am in everything, and everything is in me.
And I don't have the freedom to separate myself from what makes up my life.[44]

And, a month after that:

the appetites of man have become imperious needs which nothing can tie up, and [...] if these needs don't, within a given time, impose some limit upon themselves, human demands and the productivity of the planet will no longer be in proportion. [...] Let's look after our forests, respect our great trees [...] but all of us, let us also protest, in the name of our own rights and fortified by our own courage, against idiotic and insane measures. [...] When the earth is devastated and mutilated, our productions and our ideas will line up among poor and ugly things striking our eyes all the time. [...] Man needs Eden as a horizon. I know that many say, 'After us, the end of the world!' It's the most hideous and the most disastrous blasphemy that man could proffer. It's the formula of his resignation as a man, because it's the rupture of the thread that unites the generations and gives them solidarity with each other.[45]

The explicitly ecological essays from which these passages come will be published between August 1871 and November 1872, when Sand is in her late sixties. They are part of a celebration, in her maturity, of a principle which will inform her entire writing life. For her, idealism is no cheap trick of taste but an essential part of purposeful writing – of literature's moral obligation. 'Childish, innocent principles that have stayed with me through everything,' as she will describe them to her friend Gustave Flaubert in October 1871.[46]

But this is more than half a century in the future. For now, writerly idealism took the form of *rêveries*. Besides, the cusp of adolescence was to produce a rupture with the Indre countryside. Marie-Aurore de Saxe was an older 'parent' than the woman who had dealt with Maurice's youthful high spirits. By the time her granddaughter turned thirteen, she was in her late sixties. In an era before modern medicine, this meant old age. Perhaps Maman could no longer meet the demands of bringing up a second teenager full of the family character. Whatever the reason, she seems suddenly to have lost patience in a game-changing way one day in 1817, when Aurore cheeked her too hard. After three days of being sent to Coventry by the entire household, the crestfallen thirteen-year-old was summoned to the grand seclusion of her grandmother's bedroom. Here Marie-Aurore de Saxe pre-empted any apology, announcing the great secret that Sophie-Victoire was a 'fallen woman'.

In the early nineteenth century this was perhaps the most wrenching blow it was possible to deal a young girl's self-image. Looking back across two centuries, it's hard to understand exactly what that shame must have been like: though perhaps nobody enjoys being told that their mother is a sex worker. Aurore surely felt simultaneously implicated and isolated. In the formal salons and chambers of her grandmother's home she was uniquely identified with Sophie-Victoire – to whom no one else there was related. Small wonder if, in this context, any adolescent lapse of behaviour made her appear to be 'her mother's daughter'. A secondary shame must have been the sense that everybody already knew this about her mother, and so about herself. A third, that she was coming into her own adult sexuality, with its confusing first desires and fears.

Such an announcement could only have intensified the stirrings of adolescent self-consciousness. Shame longs for privacy. But rather than hide her granddaughter away in the countryside, Marie-Aurore de Saxe now recognised that she needed an education. She decided to enrol Aurore in a convent in Paris, exactly as she herself had been enrolled. Or not quite exactly. The convent she chose wasn't where she had been educated – neither of those institutions had survived the Revolution – but the Dames Augustines Anglaises, where she lived during the happy months of courtship by her second husband.

Astonishingly, it was also the institution in which she had been immured during the Revolution. Though it was indeed anglophone, by the time of the Revolution the convent had been a Parisian institution for more than 150 years; ever since a group of British Roman Catholic nuns, fleeing Oliver Cromwell, settled here in the oldest part of Paris. Nevertheless, in 1793 the sisters, under double suspicion both as a religious order and as Englishwomen, had been placed under house arrest. Their foundation was turned into a de facto prison for foreign or aristocratic women, including the widowed Mme Dupin de Francueil, by then the mother of five-year-old Maurice. Incarcerations which were the real thing: eight of the women held there were eventually guillotined.[47]

But by the second decade of the nineteenth century normal life for the order had resumed, and the convent was again a place of refuge. The rue des Boulangers meets what was then the rue des Fossés-Saint-Victor (it's now the rue du Cardinal-Lemoine) at its highest point, a corner site in a bumpy Left Bank terrain of historic ruins and Roman remains. Starting with four old houses on this corner, the sisters had been cultivating an enclosed foundation since 1638. The site was both rambling and homely;

it included cloisters, a church and the nuns' 'immense kitchen garden [. . .] full of flowers, vegetables and magnificent fruit'.

A drawing made in 1858, some four decades after Aurore's arrival, shows the convent entrance with its three steps and classical Gibbs surround of dressed stone capped by an image niche. The old masonry looks inviting; softened and broken in by centuries of living. Above a garden wall more than two storeys high spread the canopies of mature trees, which Sand tells us are chestnuts.[48] *Histoire* describes the place that would be her home for nearly two and a half years as

> a collection of buildings, yards and gardens, which formed a sort of village rather than a house [. . .] this heterogenous ensemble had its own character, something mysterious and complicated like a labyrinth, a certain poetic charm which those who are cloistered know how to insert into the most banal things.[49]

Perhaps the memory of this homely beauty trumped other recollections when Mme Dupin de Francueil was deciding where to place Aurore. If so, that sense of remembered enchantment would eventually be shared. Her granddaughter would record how 'In every corner, vines and jasmine hid the dilapidated walls. The cocks sang at midnight as if in deep country, the bell had a pretty silvery sound like a woman's voice; in every corridor, a niche cut gracefully into the wall opened to show you a plump Madonna in seventeenth-century style.'[50] Perhaps, more simply, since the 1790 dissolution of religious orders who had traditionally carried out much of French education, there were substantially fewer institutions for Marie-Aurore de Saxe to choose between.[51] Or might there have been some other, personal tie? When she was arrested in November 1793, it was for concealing valuables from Revolutionary appropriation. Released from the convent nine months later, she went on to buy Nohant, having evidently avoided financial ruin: some economic resources, at least, must have been successfully transferred or concealed.[52] Could the convent have been involved in any way?

There's a further odd coincidence by which the adult Sand seems strangely unfazed. Sophie-Victoire had been imprisoned in the same convent at the same time as her future mother-in-law. Actors were subject to arrest by Revolutionaries: the entire company of the Théâtre-Français, for example, had been arrested because of its royal foundation. The Delaborde sisters – twenty-year-old Victoire (as she was then) and Lucie – 'on the stage' in altogether less exalted roles were, ironically, imprisoned for possessing sheet music of religious songs. This must have been uncharacteristic to say the least, and indeed their ultimately successful plea was that the material was not theirs but had been given to them by an 'abbot'.

Perhaps we shouldn't be surprised if Victoire Delaborde, in the midst of making a tenuous living as a chorus girl, should at the time have failed to bond with the patrician Marie-Aurore de Saxe. But it seems odd that she apparently raised no objection when her thirteen-year-old daughter was returned to the very institution from which she herself must have been glad to escape. Did she feel powerless to intervene – like her own mother? Or had she, like her mother-in-law, simply lost patience with Aurore? In *Histoire*, Sand puts into Maman's mouth a speech that perfectly articulates the lament of parents and caregivers when lovable little kids turn into recalcitrant teenagers:

> You had spirit, and you do everything in your power to become or to appear stupid. You could be nice, and you make yourself ugly at whim. [. . .] Your brain has become as deformed and

lanky as your person. Sometimes you scarcely respond and seem like a strong character who disdains everything. Sometimes you talk on and on like a magpie who babbles for the sake of babbling. You were a charming little girl, you must not turn into an absurd young person.[53]

Once a disappointing teenager, always a disappointment. When it came to saying goodbye as she entered the convent, on a chilly day in January 1818, Aurore put a brave face on the panic and upset she was feeling – only for her grandmother to misinterpret that as cold-heartedness.[54] In fact, the teenager was homesick. Staying away from home is tough at any age, and she was still in many ways a sheltered child; enough of one at any rate that in her first moments in the convent she was drawn into a childish game of tag (*barres*). Besides, there was much more than just her new purple serge uniform to master at rue des Fossés-Saint-Victor, where she would pass the next two and a quarter years without spending a single night in the outside world.

Change of this kind is vertiginous. Later, Sand would call the version of Aurore who arrived at the convent a 'peasant from Berry'. She noticed straightaway that her fellow pupils had excellent manners, unlike her own, and that there was a preponderance of aristocratic names among the students. More dizzying still, she found herself thrown into an entirely British world, where only English was spoken for much of the time, and the nuns (and their favourites) drank tea three times a day. And this new language was everywhere within earshot: even beyond its high walls, the convent was flanked by Scottish and Irish, not francophone, foundations. It was almost as if she had left the country.

At least being cloistered meant Aurore would no longer be passed to and fro between her mother and grandmother, an 'apple of discord between two beings I cherished'. Eventually, as the school year wore on, she would acquire an English nickname, *Some Bread* (from Dupin, *du pain*). But at first, despite being ahead of her age in philosophy, history and literature, she lived under the absolute handicap of knowing not a word of the language of the institution.[55] Yet she seems to have thrown herself into the life around her. First, she plunged into sociability and fun with her fellow students. Later, she became drawn to the mystical devotion of the sisters:

> The first year, I was more than ever the enfant terrible I had begun to be, because a sort of despair or at least hopelessness in my affections propelled me to stun and desensitise myself with my own mischief-making. The second year I moved quite suddenly to a burning and agitated devotion. The third year I maintained a state of calm, firm and joyful devotion.[56]

This sounds like someone growing up after trying out various personae: a typical teenager, in other words. But Aurore's full-on adaptability also sometimes reminds one of the excessive flexibility of children who grow up without a loving, consistent caregiver. Trained by her grandmother to believe that even family love was conditional, Aurore had learnt to adapt herself to whatever terms were required to win it. Kids looking for love become gifted at finding ways to express and elicit love; they can be almost preternaturally attuned to codes of approval, as every adult lurking to groom them knows.

But such adeptness need not end in abuse. *Cherchez la femme*, goes the cliché, but *cherchez le coeur* rings more comprehensively true. The adult Sand would claim that the intensely devotional period of her adolescence was sparked by witnessing the serenity of the convent chapel at dusk. But there was also a special presence at rue des Fossés-Saint-Victor. 'Mother' Mary Alicia Spiring was a 'pearl' who 'shone' in the modest, shadowy convent. She was not yet thirty, and was beautiful, 'even if she had too much nose and too little mouth'.[57] A Frenchwoman with an English father, she fluently managed both the English institution and its French setting in her roles as convent treasurer, and as a kind of personal assistant to the Mother Superior.

Perhaps it was this role in the institution's leadership that earned her the honorific 'Mother', which Sand always uses for her in place of 'Sister', even though there can be only one Mother Superior in a convent. Perhaps she also offered something of the maternal care Aurore was seeking. In the closed world of rue des Fossés-Saint-Victor, resident adults took favourites under their wing: a relationship Sand would characterise, despite her somewhat romantic description of Mother Spiring, as 'filial'. It was a way for both parties – homesick, sometimes orphaned girls and childless women – to manage the loneliness of institutional life.

Mary Alicia Spiring was intensely – that *intensely* is doing a lot of work here – admired by the student body. When her previous favourite grew up and left the convent, no one dared ask to take the girl's place, until Aurore developed the 'filial passion' that emboldened her to step up. The *Histoire*'s account of the interview that followed reads like the kind of instructive religious dialogue between archetypes of Good and Evil that the convent pupils were taught. Mother Spiring protests that Aurore is the worst-behaved girl in the convent, and no replacement for her 'sweet and wise' lost favourite. Sand has her teenaged self respond that this is exactly why she needs the very best help. She's not quite a devil tempting the holy woman by flattering her. But she is clearly drawing on a redemption tradition of which no convent girl can be unaware. In the Parable of the Lost Sheep in Luke 15:1–7, 'there is more rejoicing in Heaven over one sinner who repents, than over ninety-nine good people who did not need to repent'.

The Prodigal Son becomes the prodigal daughter, whom Mother Spiring must welcome all the more because of the distance she's travelled from past bad behaviour.

It was not to be the only occasion on which this dialectic would make itself heard in Aurore's life. Her time at the convent seems to open a dialogue between two aspects of her emerging personality; one that would continue for the rest of her life. On the one hand she was the engaged, sociable and sometimes rebellious 'Devil', convent shorthand for a headstrong pupil. On the other, she was the idealist with an exceptionally fertile imagination, prone to raptures, assiduous daydreams about forms of moral virtue, and those 'Childish, innocent principles that have stayed with me through everything'. If the first would emerge repeatedly in her private life, the second is everywhere in her work.

Second impression: *Criss-cross*

THIS IS A FASCINATING ENCOUNTER with the adolescent Aurore Dupin. She already has the signature fulness of face, the long cheek and rounded chin that August Charpentier's glamorous 1838 oil of the famous George Sand will capture. It's a remarkable continuity of resemblance. Distributed as prints made by the engraver Luigi Calamatta, Charpentier's portrait will also have its subject's distinctive mane of dark hair worn down, as here; though in the later portrait it's trained into ringlets and dressed with flowers. This younger version is wearing boy's clothes, as Aurore so often would to ride around the Indre countryside during the curious limbo of her later teens, after convent school and before her grandmother's death. At fifteen, sixteen or seventeen, she already has the sultry, heavy-lidded gaze familiar from later portraits: neither frank nor fearless but undeniably come-hither.

Except that – criss-cross – this portrait is not by Luigi Calamatta but his wife Joséphine, and its subject isn't Aurore Dupin but her son, Maurice. Just like his mother at the same age, he's living at Nohant; but he does so only in the summer months. And the house he knows isn't the sepulchral manor where his adolescent mother nursed her dying grandmother, but a family home that's if anything overcrowded by the presence of her current partner, Fryderyk Chopin. Who, practising and composing at the piano, can hardly be a silent member of the household.

When Maurice leaves his mother's house at eighteen to study painting in Paris, he won't go to work with either of the Calamattas, but in the atelier of another of his mother's friends, Eugène Delacroix. Yet by the time he marries, the bearer of this extraordinary family resemblance will be on the cusp of forty, and living full-time at Nohant with his mother. And his bride, a fellow artist half his age, will be the Calamattas' daughter Lina (Marcellina). He will bring her to live at the manor; their children will be born and raised here; and George Sand will tutor them just as she was tutoring Maurice at the time of this portrait.

Might all this not feel a touch claustrophobic to a young bride? Though she appears pleasantly characterful and intelligent in photographs, Lina may be used to finding the course of her life somewhat overdetermined. As the daughter of not one but two distinguished artists, a life in art may have felt inevitable: after all, even the choice of Jean-Auguste-Dominique Ingres as her godfather tied her into the family profession. She wasn't yet born when her mother painted this portrait of the teenaged Maurice; and their families have been friends for decades. Lina's Freudian joke will be that she marries Maurice because she can't marry his mother.

Like all such jokes, it may let slip more than she means it to. Isn't parapraxis its own kind of queer? If Maurice's creative, accomplished but not quite canonical work as an artist echoes his mother's accomplishment at one remove, Lina's marriage to Maurice, in which her own artistry is sublimated, is surely twice removed from the famous writer's life, even though they're living affectionately together under the same roof. This pleasant, artistic couple make the sort of mirror that close families hold up to an exceptional artist. Being so nearly – and yet entirely not – the one who becomes famous, they reveal another possible version of the famous life. They show how easy it would be for the great work never to have been made, the achievement never to be, in Elizabeth Barrett Browning's phrase, 'dared and done'.

THREE

Reveries of a solitary walker

ANY INSTITUTION CAN BECOME ITS own small cosmos, but to be cloistered is surely to be recused entirely from the wider world. In the second decade of the nineteenth century, pupils at the Paris convent of the Dames Augustines Anglaises are shut out, as much as they are sheltered, from all the messy experiments of adolescence; excluded equally from choice and responsibility. Though they're allowed to visit family twice a month they are not permitted, as later school boarders will be, just to saunter out into the Left Bank. Instead, crammed up against the convent's high walls, the medieval blocks of the lively working and residential neighbourhood in which they live are reduced to echoes: shouts, hooves and metal carriage wheels, a rattle of shutters and the rumbling of barrels over bumpy *pavés*. The outside world encroaches only through letters, or visits conducted at the grille of a dedicated parlour just inside the convent entrance.

Post-Revolutionary France is a country in which social order has not yet fully stabilised. But the lives of the girls and women on rue des Fossés-Saint-Victor are ordered by a medieval timetable of religious observances that is the foundation's original *raison d'être*. Teenaged girlhood can overlap awkwardly with innocence, and part of that innocence is a childish inability to believe the present might be contingent, the past and future real. So the cohort of pupils Aurore Dupin has joined must sometimes feel that any break with the resonant atmosphere in which they're immersed is almost inconceivable. As if the dramatic events of just a generation ago had never interrupted its routines, their life is both peaceful, and literally immured.

Exact timetables hold lives in place. This may have been both difficult and reassuring for the thirteen-year-old who entered the Dames Augustines Anglaises on 12 January 1818.[1] Small wonder if at first she rebelled. For the Aurore who arrived at the convent wasn't just socially gauche. For better or for worse, she had been formed by instability. When she was tiny her adored father, coming and going at the behest of his military career, had spoilt her erratically. After his death not only did the family's fortunes change, but so did even what – and who – counted *as* family. Since then her double life has see-sawed between the competing realities of her 'two mothers', 'Mama' and 'Maman', each with their own inconsistencies. The convent has offered her not changeable adult whim or emotion to navigate, but the predictability of a way of life informed by unchanging principles. What's more, for the first time she has guides to help her find her path: a mentor in 'Mother' Spiring and a confessor, the Abbé Prémord, for her spiritual life.

Monastic order opens a doorway into a world in which persons, and beliefs, exist in and for themselves, rather than to trigger reactions. In the two and a quarter years she spends within it, Aurore comes to love the cloister. But her departure from rue des Fossés-Saint-Victor will be as abrupt as her arrival. In the spring of 1820, her grandmother gives her one month's notice that she must leave this 'more perfect happiness than I had ever before tasted [. . .] my paradise on earth [where] I was neither a boarder nor a nun but something in-between, with complete freedom in an environment that I loved'.²

Though she hasn't seen it coming, several circumstances have conspired to end her convent life. Among them is, ironically, how very well she has adapted to it. Encouraged by Mary Alicia Spiring's mentorship to make the shift from 'devil' to 'devout', and by her confessor to row back from the extremes of mystical devotion by which she's briefly tempted, she's become a paradigm of successful formation. Too able for the perhaps not very demanding lessons the sisters offer, she's been allowed free rein to write and stage plays for the convent community, and to mentor younger pupils. She's become that elusive, powerful thing, the popular girl: perhaps herself therefore, in this heightened emotional atmosphere, the object of schoolgirl crushes.

Rooted and thriving, of course she wants to stay where she is. Perhaps not surprisingly, therefore, she now discovers a vocation to become a nun herself. Her grandmother is horrified. Though culturally Catholic, Marie-Aurore de Saxe is a thoroughly secularised, intellectual woman: an admirer of Voltaire, whose Enlightenment mixture of philosophy with anticlerical scepticism may well have released her into atheism as well as strengthening her pragmaticism about the ways of the world. She placed Aurore in the convent for her *social* formation – as Aurore experiences it, to discipline her – and the last thing she may have been expecting is the creation of a little saint. Privately, aware that this is her only legitimate grandchild, she may also be eager to see marriage and maternity preserve the family lineage of which she is so proudly aware.

But other things are also playing on her mind. At seventy-one, she's becoming increasingly unwell. Intimations of mortality concentrate her mind. If she dies now, what will become of her fifteen-year-old granddaughter? If Aurore stays where she is, there's a real risk she might take holy orders. But if she leaves the convent and her grandmother dies, she will be alone in a predatory world. Both sides of the girl's family offer object lessons in the risks unmarried women run in a society where only men can earn their living with a degree of respectability.

Perhaps a third way would be to secure her granddaughter's future through an advantageous marriage. Though Aurore will experience this suggestion as emotional blackmail, it's in fact another of Maman's – perhaps clumsy – attempts to rescue her granddaughter:

> My daughter, I need to marry you off quickly, because I'm on my way out. You are indeed young, I know, but however little you wish to enter the world, you must make an effort to accept the idea. Remember that I would end my days in terror and despair if I left you without a guide and support in life.[3]

'I would end my days in terror and despair.' Mme Dupin de Francueil's mind is further concentrated by the threat of renewed political upheaval with which, in the city beyond the convent walls, 1820 has opened. On 13 February, the Duc de Berry was stabbed outside the Paris Opéra at the Salle de la rue de Richelieu, just ten minutes' walk from her own Paris apartment on rue Neuve des Mathurins. He died a day later. This is no random attack but the assassination of a leading aristocrat; the unluckily named Charles Ferdinand was the nephew of the king, Louis XVIII. His assassin, an anti-monarchist saddle-maker, may have hoped to trigger renewed political and social turmoil; and might easily have done so. In the event, he fails by a hair's breadth; partly because the prolific duke left, among no less than four posthumously born children, a legitimate heir.[4] Perhaps, after the decades-long attrition of revolution and Napoleonic warmongering, the national appetite for bloodshed has finally shrunk. But the king is sufficiently shaken to demand the demolition and replacement of the Salle. Marie-Aurore de Saxe was herself formed by proximity to the monarchy, and her middle years were dominated by revolution. So her anxiety now is both real and realistic. The Paris of the assassination is the same city where her granddaughter is at school and therefore, a few days later, she arrives on what will prove to be her last trip to the capital for a stay in rue Neuve des Mathurins. Within two months she has withdrawn Aurore from the convent.

Aurore leaves the cluster of old houses on its gentle rise in the fifth arrondissement on 12 April. She has been not so much sprung as hatched. The happy minutiae of life on the rue des Fossés-Saint-Victor are suddenly replaced by real-world responsibilities. Her return to Nohant is preceded by a few days in the capital, but they offer little to soften this transition. Sophie-Victoire takes the opportunity to establish that she won't accompany her younger daughter to the Berry countryside, nor visit her there, until her mother-in-law is dead. Aurore has been accustomed to receive and pay visits with her mother and half-sister during her time at the convent: now these relationships are to be interrupted. Bitterly hurt, even decades later she will overlook the kernel of truth in her mother's excuse that Caroline, now too old to be boarded out, can't safely stay alone in the city.

Even worse is losing the convent community and all it contains: friends, mentors, a spiritual life – and the sense of a writing self. For at rue des Fossés-Saint-Victor, 'I become an author and director of shows – Unheard of success [. . .] before the community.'[5] All writers write themselves into being writers, and that's what Aurore has done in her last months at the convent. In creating plays which genuinely entertain and unite a community, she has discovered writing not as blind self-confession but as something framed by its audience. She's understood that this is a practice to which it's possible to make a public commitment. Most important of all, in learning how to elide people-pleasing 'good' behaviour, spiritual idealism and the committed effort, she's discovered how to give herself licence to write. The sisters have taught Aurore that writing is a socially useful, morally good and disciplined practice. (Perhaps Mother Spiring is her ideal reader?)

In the spring of 1820, though, the fifteen-year-old is still more intensely aware of being forbidden to follow what she believes is her religious vocation. Her grandmother's fiat requires spiritual as well as emotional navigation: how do you weigh obedience, that primary moral duty of the nineteenth-century young woman, against faith? But she must navigate it alone. The philosophically – if not politically – progressive, secular household to which she's returned has little time for the devotional literature in which she's recently been immersed, and in whose study she has excelled. And her supportive network has vanished, apart from occasional visits from school friends.[6]

Back in Nohant, the alarming prospect of an arranged marriage continues to mix with an overarching discouragement. It seems nothing more stimulating awaits the fifteen-year-old than ad hoc tuition from Deschartres, and the occasional English lesson. In place of popularity and attention: silence, mud. The manor abuts the village square, but little transpires on this modest patch of grass and sandy gravel between the manorial gates, the church of Sainte-Anne and a couple of cottages. Soon, depression sets in. Alone in her country bedroom, Aurore composes lines of longing and emotion in place of the entertainments she produced in Paris, her adolescent energy seizing on the diction of Romantic *Sturm und Drang*. This new intensity echoes her formerly passionate religiosity: meaning is shifting its ground.

The social silence is something else. Mme Dupin de Francueil's formerly commanding presence is being reduced by the encroachments of age. Before Aurore was sent away to school, her grandmother was still very much in the swing of things. As well as supporting a full cast of servants, Nohant was often busy with visitors; and, of course, Hippolyte was in situ. Over the years the half-siblings had shared games, and lessons with Deschartres; and Hippolyte played the trickster, for all the world like the medieval German folk figure of Till Eulenspiegel, his persistent naughtiness drawing out her own.[7] Now he's away at cadet training, and one reason Aurore has been returned to Nohant is to keep her grandmother company in the otherwise unpeopled great house.

Their relationship continues to be quasi-filial. For all Aurore's genuine gratitude and affection – for all that she is apparently of marriageable age – it remains a matter of duty and respectful obedience. Surely neither intended what started so well to ossify in this way. But perhaps it's as impossible for the grandmother to shake off the constraints of a cultural formation by the Ancien Régime as it is for the granddaughter to escape the too-feelingful Romanticism of her own era; perhaps the former can no more forget her personal experience of social peril than the latter can fully renounce her dangerously *déclassée* mother.

But the two Aurores try. They establish a routine in which the adolescent reads aloud to her grandmother. In the twenty-first century this will sound improving, even restfully monastic, but in the nineteenth it's a form of shared narrative entertainment that is the closest equivalent to crowding on to the sofa to watch appointment TV together. The two chat; they exchange views. Perhaps, as they sit in one of the manor's classically proportioned reception rooms, all clean tiled floors, long windows and judiciously disposed furniture, their surroundings contextualise the formality with which they interact and make it a little more understandable. Here, what surrounds the young Aurore is a wordless argument for perfection through elegance. The gleam of silverware, the high gloss on parquet floors, make an argument for beauty through restraint.

She still has one private, malleable resource: her writing. Letters offer her a continuation of humanly connected life, and so she begins to write to convent friends; to live through, if not by, the pen. We've no way to estimate the volume of her correspondence over the next couple of years – how urgently she pushes back against her new isolation – because we only know the letters that survive. But we do know that a lifetime of prolific correspondence starts here. Over 17,000 letters by the future novelist will make it through the white noise of intervening events; the authoritative edition prepared between 1964 and 1991 by Georges Lubin for Garnier Classics will run to twenty-five volumes and roughly 24,000 pages.

This is a stupendous quantity of writing. Its sheer volume towers over *Histoire de ma vie* and other published works, including *Lettres d'un voyageur* (*Letters from a Traveller*) and *Un hiver à Majorque* (*A Winter in Mallorca*), in which George Sand also seems to address us directly 'from life'. Which doesn't, of course, mean it creates an accurate self-portrait. Letters aren't necessarily more spontaneous or authentic than literary writing. We all invent ourselves in correspondence – if that weren't so, social media wouldn't claim so much of our attention – while on the other hand, books are signed just as letters are, and can only be composed from their author's viewpoint. Besides, letters are as multivarious as their occasions: Aurore's will include romance, familial and practical necessity, engagement with officialdom, travel news, literary advice-giving and friendship. Selfhood, too, is multifaceted. 'I am large, I contain multitudes,' in Walt

Whitman's so-modern insight from 'Song of Myself', which will be published in the same year as Sand's *Histoire de ma vie*.

For the moment, though, Aurore may feel less resourceful than simply like someone with very different outer and inner lives. The returnee is making her bedroom at the manor house into a retreat where she studies, writes and reads far into the night. She turns sixteen as the summer evenings are at their longest. Open windows, lamps, the country stillness with only an occasional owl or dog to break it. July evenings at Nohant can be more fresh than oppressive. This is not the Midi: the River Indre, less than a half a mile away, is too modest to fill the night air with mosquitoes.

But, at least at first, letter-writing lacks the spontaneity of chatter in a school corridor. Jane Bazouin, for example, takes more than one exchange to warm up from a formal *vous* to the intimate *tu* in her responses, even though she's a close friend. And when she does, she neglects to reveal that she's about to leave the convent and return to home life in Paris – from where she next regrets that she cannot see herself ever coming to visit Nohant.[8] Undeterred, Aurore, who seems to be writing and living in a completely different register, almost as if she were talking to herself and not to Jane, responds that she 'often weeps and suffers' – presumably from loneliness and frustration.[9]

How much is this authentic confessional, and how much an adolescent's worked-up, Romantic sensibility? For there's also a glorious, peacocking Aurore who stands on her hands – performs cartwheels – in these letters. She initiates correspondence with another convent friend, Marie-Émilie de Wismes, in a rhetorical *coup de theâtre*: 'Who could be writing to me? What is this stamp? this handwriting? this person in fact whom I don't know at all? Behold Émilie most intrigued. Come, my dear, recognise a convent companion . . .'[10] That 'behold' – a flourishing '*voilà*' – is the writer as conjurer, an abracadabra reveal of fresh talent. It's also a 'Once upon a time', variants of which have opened stories since years immemorial, and which turns this 'cold call' into the upper hand of showing off. The gamble is on, proving irresistible. Look, says Aurore's letter, I know you found it too boring to write to our mutual friend Louisa, but how can you possibly resist *me*? And as if fearing that the reader's attention will flag, it breaks out in underlining and macaronic English and Italian: 'I saw *Louisa there is some time ago*: the poor *Ragazza* told me sadly that no letter from de Wismes had soothed her worries for a long time, and the last she'd written remained without a reply.'[11]

Jumping around between languages as if they were registers is both playful and a great way to sound effusive, as if French by itself weren't enough to contain the writer's energies. This sensation of breathless enthusiasm – of thoughts speeding on to the page unrestrained by formality – is only helped by how clumsy Aurore's raids actually are on English – that non-existent construction is a literal translation of the French idiom *il y a quelques temps* – and Italian, which doesn't capitalise nouns as she does here. (Possibly Maman is correct when she mocks the level of education the convent has provided.)

Aurore may not know it, but she's setting the direction of future travel. The correspondent who will become George Sand is developing her notion of the ideal reader. For writing is really always transitive: it's addressed *to* someone, even if that someone is unknown, or generalised; or indeed, as in a diary, a future self. As readers, we notice how some writers declaim, others pray, confide, hector or ponder. Then there are those whose writing is truly a form of correspondence, in the double sense of addressing and matching up with some other reading self. Theirs is what we might call the Scheherazade principle: seeking primarily to engage this reader and take them along too with such engaging stories, such seductive prosody, that they can't resist.

Which is the bet the young Aurore's correspondence makes. Her next letter to Émilie is thick with Romantic tropes:

> My god! How lucky you are and how I envy your trip on the Loire, I who am so responsive to [*si sensible aux*] the beauties of nature! [. . .] And then to travel on a river, by moonlight! How I'd have liked to be in ecstasies with you over the beauty of night, the freshness of the countryside! What *flowery ideas*, what *imagination*, what *spirit* in fact, since one must say the word, we would have had together!¹²

Is this really as gushing as the exclamation marks and onrushing emphases suggest? Or is it just a little arch? The writing's certainly aware enough of itself to emphasise the word *spirit*, so full of religious overtones for these recent convent schoolgirls. But then the next sentence veers off, like concentration that can't contain itself: 'I also loved the mischief of your letter.' (Émilie recounts having to descend a steep ladder in the tower of Nantes Cathedral, directly over the head of a colonel who had gallantly not looked up.) 'It's to die laughing for.' Some more schoolgirl humour about having to practise the harp, and then back into Romantic vein: 'my dragging health gives me a *lazyness* of spirit, a kind of disgust for everything [. . .] then I'm the worst and most stupid person who exists'. From 'sensibility' to '*une espèce de dégoût pour tout*': it's the gamut of Romantic attitudes.

Now the letter pivots again. Hippolyte is home. He's arrived in a glamorous flurry of regimental leave and is spending a substantial portion of his holiday teaching his half-sister to ride – and on difficult horses at that. She's not mounted side-saddle like a girl, but astride, *à l'anglais*:

> We still get up to a bit of mischief, that's to say breaking, shattering everything, maddening the dogs, throwing them in the water, etc. We often go horse riding: he has shown me how to ride in the English style and though I'm not very skilled, because I am very brave we have delightful trips.

But her illegitimate half-brother remains a tricky figure. Even to Émilie, Aurore doesn't admit a sibling relationship. Instead she calls him 'this young pupil of the military school at Saumur with whom I was raised' and 'from whom I showed you several letters at the convent'. Showing a boy's letters around while not admitting he's a relative sounds a little like the history of a crush. 'He's like a brother to me' is not at all the same, when it comes to young girls boasting, as actually being siblings.

About a month after her letter to Émilie, the sixteen-year-old writes to another convent friend, Apollonie, enjoining her to secrecy and breaking into English, perhaps in an attempt to conceal a confidence: 'I have been very happy for three months. Hippolyte, about whom I spoke to you secretly in the convent, has been here on quarterly leave. Don't speak about that, he is gone to Nancy now.'[13] In her next letter she both thanks this confidante – 'You console me for a very strong and very strongly-felt [*sensible*] sorrow' – and yet in a postscript seems to cover the tracks of that confidence: 'What then don't you understand in my letter? And this h . . . .? I no longer understand anything about it myself.'[14]

Is this 'h . . . .' Hippolyte? We're quickly back with Émilie, and the hand-standing and grandstanding: 'It's really true to say that *the extremes touch*. Seeing two beings whose tastes, character, situation are so different in all respects, one would be astonished to know that we like each other.'¹⁵ Ostensibly, Aurore is talking about their own friendship as their lives diverge. Winter gives way to the spring of 1821, and her letters increasingly evoke a contrast between what she pictures as Émilie's social whirl and her own dull life. But it's hard not to notice how apt 'the extremes touch' is to that surprising rapport with Hippolyte. They too seem to be opposites who attract. The bold, cheerful and chaotic youth has embarked on a military career; despite a similarly scrappy education, his half-sister is a future member of the intelligentsia.

Whatever holds them together, she continues to disguise their sibling relationship even to close friends. When Émilie asks about Hippolyte's name, Aurore responds with 'Hippolyte de Chatiron', ennobling the actual 'Chatiron' with that fictional 'de'. Later, when she bemoans not having danced with him before the end of his leave, she sounds like any teenager with a crush:

> Hippolyte has gone, so we are absolutely alone. I shorten the day by getting up late, I breakfast, I chat with my grandmother for an hour or two sometimes, I go up again to my room, where I busy myself, I play harp, guitar, I read, I warm myself, [. . .] I go over memories in my head, I write in the ash with the tongs, I go down for dinner, and [. . .] go up again to my room and scribble some ideas in a kind of green notebook, which is now full up.¹⁶

This sounds less like Romantic posturing than adolescent uncertainty and boredom. She may be doing little more than 'scribble . . . ideas', but where else is the beginning writer to start, with neither audience nor deadline as her frame? So bored is Aurore that perhaps even marriage starts to appear less restrictive than life as a lady's companion with Maman. This same letter now turns, as if by an association of ideas, from Hippolyte to 'Mr de Colbert', Louis-Pierre-Alphonse, Comte de Colbert and Lieutenant-Général and Commander of the 13th Division at Rennes. No, she protests to Émilie, 'you exaggerate [*prodigue*] in suggesting he pleases me. I assure you it's only to a certain point [. . .]. What I liked about him was his generosity to children, because I was really still a child [when I knew him] and I've always remembered his friendliness.'

Aurore was indeed 'still a child' of no more than eleven when she encountered Colbert back in the summer of 1815. Then a mere general, he was billeted with fellow officers at Nohant manor for a fortnight.[17] But for just a moment, as we follow her through the rather obscured trail of surviving evidence, it seems as if that younger self has come back to haunt her. For early in 1821 it transpires that her grandmother is still interested in securing for her the relative safety of an establishment marriage. This latest plan involves a general who is 'immensely rich, but fifty years old and with a big sabre cut across his face'.[18] Whoever the mysterious officer is, however – whether or not he even exists – we know for sure that he's not the child-friendly Comte de Colbert, who even six years ago was already a married father of daughters – and who has not subsequently been widowed.[19]

In any case, towards the end of February, Maman promises Aurore that she won't force her to marry the unnamed general.[20] But it's hard to know how truly she means this. For later on the night she makes this promise, Marie-Aurore de Saxe has a major stroke. She's discovered early the next morning, lying on the floor of her room. Although she survives, she will be partly paralysed for the rest of her life. And, while she regains the ability to recognise Aurore with affection, she will never again be able to keep her granddaughter intellectual company, plan her future or even guide her present. Her memory is gone, and with it most of her capacity. The years-long habit of protecting her granddaughter is reduced to asking after her health.[21]

The routines of Aurore's childhood are over. Life in the stuccoed manor with its tall, shuttered windows can no longer sustain any sense of itself as an extension of the chatelaine's pre-Revolutionary aristocratic life. Like her, it has 'undergone a great weakening'. Truthfully, it lapses into the provincial. As spring goes on, Aurore will describe herself to Apollonie, the confidante with whom she seems most to relax into sincerity, as 'A real countrywoman, going out in boots, bareheaded whatever the weather, on foot, on horseback, in our Berry *sludges* [*boues*] which are frightful; I come and go but without pleasure [...] I live like a creature of habit.'[22]

As for the potentially life-changing decision which was upstaged by her grandmother's stroke, this collapse casts that whole conversation in a different light. Gradually, we understand that a warning mini-stroke came first. During the evening, Mme de Saxe is suddenly unable to concentrate on what Aurore is reading to her. She hallucinates: 'What you're reading to me is so strange that I'm afraid of being ill and understanding something other than what I hear. Why are you talking to me of the dead, of shrouds, of bells, of tombs?'[23] Aurore is shocked: she's just finished reading a 'fresh and amusing page' about the savannah. After a few rounds of cribbage her grandmother, with the air of marshalling her concentration, tells her, 'This marriage won't suit you at all, and I'm happy to have broken it up.'[24]

'What marriage?' Sand will recall herself responding: she knows nothing about the idea. In retrospect, Mme Dupin de Francueil's sudden announcement feels like one of those abrupt changes of emotional climate that often accompany stroke. Or again, the entire story of the scar-faced general could be an hallucination of the kind characteristic of a mini-stroke. Except that Maman offers her granddaughter proof of the existence of this suitor, in the form of a letter in which René, François Vallet, Comte de Villeneuve, regrets the decision to abandon this marriage plan. Twenty-seven years older than the teenager who is his step-cousin at two removes, de Villeneuve has the authority that comes from his social and family standing. After his mother's death when he was three, he was effectively adopted by Aurore's grandfather's stepmother, who was his aunt: he joined that part of the family, in other words, who still own the astonishing Renaissance chateau of Chenonceau, seventy-five miles from Nohant on the border of Indre-et-Loire.

Built like a bridge across the River Cher, Chenonceau's arcade of silvery arches will become iconic to the point of cliché with the advent of twentieth-century mass tourism. But for Mme Dupin de Francueil, if not perhaps in quite the same way for her granddaughter, the famous image reflected in the waters of this Loire tributary may have something of the elusive quality of mirage. It must at least represent a tantalising near-miss, since it belonged to her husband's stepmother, who left it not to him but to her grandson René Vallet de Villeneuve. Establishment to his fingertips, de Villeneuve now urges his aunt at Nohant to marry Aurore off to the successful older man, since 'one can find lots of young people [to marry], but one cannot be sure of their character, and the future with them is indeed uncertain. In place of which: high position, fortune, respect.'

Like the storyteller she is, three decades from now George Sand will claim to have his letter before her as she writes up 'this sad evening' in her *Histoire*. But it's hard not to suspect this is too good to be true. On the one hand, she will by then be living once again at Nohant, where old correspondence, accumulating as is its wont in drawers and attics, may conveniently not have been thrown out. On the other, the famous novelist who publishes her memoirs will have become confident in the malleability of fiction. There's flex in *Histoire*'s veracity. If we accept its reported conversations, which we know can't have been recalled verbatim, perhaps we should accept this 'letter' in the same spirit. For example, of this fateful evening she writes:

'And so, Maman,' I cried in terror, 'are we going to Paris?'
'Yes my child, we're going in eight days. But, be reassured, I don't want to hear talk of this marriage.'

Yet this is a complete fiction. We know from the sixteen-year-old's letters that she was aware of the planned trip to Paris at least a month before her grandmother fell ill.[25]

In the ten months left to Maman after her stroke, Aurore's life sinks into formlessness. Nursing her grandmother is exhausting. She often has to sit up all night, particularly when the invalid is suffering night terrors. The sickroom is stuffy; to stay awake, she resorts to her grandmother's snuffbox, to black coffee without sugar, sometimes to brandy. Ingesting all this – especially on top of sleeplessness – leads to upset stomachs and 'unspeakable nervous anguish' of her own.[26] She's on the verge, if not actually of a nervous breakdown, then certainly of wrecking her health.

Freshly respectful of her as the manor's acting chatelaine and his new boss, Deschartres is all concern as he observes her losing weight, becoming lethargic and aimless. With urgent pragmatism he presents her with a filly, Colette, and urges her to go out riding, taking only a local lad called André as her escort. It works. Soon she's developed the habit of leaving the manor every day at first light and galloping 'twelve leagues in four hours', in a silence broken only when she and the boy stop to rest.[27] The pace is gruelling, but it doesn't prevent her absorbing the beauty of the Berrichon countryside. The observations which are laid down now may lie dormant for almost two decades, but they will emerge to blossom in the pastoral novels of her forties.

At the same time, this extreme exercise has a note of self-punishment; an edge of catharsis. Aurore is effectively carrying her worries alone. Confiding to Apollonie how lost she's feeling, she adds bravely, but not entirely truthfully, 'My grandmother is going on much better; she is convalescing. I thank you dearly for the interest you take in her health. I had mortal worries in that regard.'[28] 'Dearly', *tendrement*, is a conventional intensifier, but sums up the tone of the letter. This is the quality that's missing from her life – and has been for perhaps longer than she realises.

So she seems to be feeling very raw when, on 18 November, she writes a long letter of protest to her mother. Sophie-Victoire, who is enjoying the sociable Paris her daughter longs for, has taken it upon herself to admonish the seventeen-year-old for not being a good enough carer to her grandmother. Which is deeply hypocritical, of course; not least because her own refusal to visit Nohant until the old lady has died means she's relying on second-hand gossip. For Aurore this criticism, coming when she's sinking under the weight of doing the right thing, is clearly a kind of last straw.

Her response is both furious and frosty. For the first time in her relationship with the mother she's tried so hard to woo she uses the formal *vous*. Perhaps she does so in order to underline that – as her grandmother's granddaughter – she knows how to behave correctly. The result is to displace Sophie-Victoire from family intimate to correctly addressed older relative:

My grandmother being so ill, you say, I leave her to go racing through the fields
   [. . .]. I don't know who the person is who has told you I neglect to fulfil my dear and sacred duties to the one who

brought me up with such generosity and tenderness. I don't believe I have this monstrous wrong to reproach me, and on the contrary I have the consolation of receiving every day from my excellent grandmother testimonies of love and affection that prove to me that she's in no way displeased with me. [...] You also reproach me, mother, for having neither shyness, nor modesty, nor gentleness [...] neither decency nor style: to so judge me you would have to know me. [...] You say that [my tutor] has given me lessons in my room; where would you like me to receive people who come and see me? It seems to me that my grandmother, suffering or asleep, would be very inconvenienced by a visit. [...]

It's a folly, you say, dear mother, to learn Latin. [...] Why must a woman be ignorant? Can't she be educated without exploiting it and without being pedantic? Suppose I should one day have sons [and they need help with their lessons]? But for that to happen one has to be married. I will only find, you say, a monster or a coward [*poltrone*].[29]

In arguing one by one against the elements of what seems to have been a perfect critical storm, she reconstructs all the unkindnesses of her mother's assumptions. And though she ends on a conciliatory note, she also reminds Sophie-Victoire that, at seventeen, 'I know how to walk.' Accustomed by now to running the household at Nohant, she will no longer accept being admonished like a naughty child.

All the same, no seventeen-year-old wants to be told that only 'a monster or a coward' could want her. It's another of those direct hits to the heart of Aurore's emerging femininity that the women of her family are so good at scoring. Why on earth, apart from pure heedlessness, should Sophie-Victoire write such a letter? She knows her younger daughter is triply unhappy: at leaving the convent, at being alone in the country looking after her grandmother, and about her grandmother's failing health. She knows how she herself has refused to visit Nohant and has offered her daughter no support in these isolating duties, 'despite [her] beseeching'.[30] Perhaps she envies her younger daughter, even now. For she can't have forgotten that at seventeen she herself had been turned out of the family home by her stepfather and was surviving Paris as a chorus girl in a revue.

It might be that in the future Aurore will dress as a boy in part because she has come to lack confidence in her femininity; that she becomes promiscuous in her search for affirmation of her womanhood. But if for now she's able to deflect the most intimate part of Sophie's attack, knowing that she *is* attractive to an admirer, it seems possible that responsibility for this falls close to home. Hippolyte left Nohant when his leave expired, but he's very much still in his half-sister's life. This summer, adopting an air of extreme secrecy, she sent him a letter care of Émilie.[31] Now she embroiders a story, asking Émilie to post a letter to Hippolyte 'from his sister' (true enough as far as it goes) because she, Aurore, owes this invented alter ego a favour. 'It's a little trick she's playing on him,' she explains: this to one of her closest confidantes. Can what she's doing really be just sibling playfulness, or is it a trace of something more?

Eighteen twenty-one is a time of emotional impasse at Nohant, an interlude of 'sadnesses, walks and daydreams', as the Sand of *Histoire* will summarise it, in a chapter title worthy of Jean-Jacques Rousseau. We might indeed borrow from him and call these 'the reveries of the solitary walker'.[32] But one thing she has escaped is the threat of an arranged marriage, and so of 'passing immediately from my grandmother's domination to that of a husband'. She'll come to believe that, had that happened, she might 'never have become myself'. Instead, the muddy Indre countryside is a kind of vale of soul-making: 'it was decided by chance that [...] external influences would stop and I would belong entirely to myself for almost a year in order to become, for good or ill, what I had to be for pretty much the rest of my life'.

Again we encounter the sense of how important it will be to George Sand to become herself. As with her concern that she might not really be the child born on her own birthday, this seems to mean not simply some freedom to do whatever she wants – *agency* – but a particular contract with *authenticity*. Briefly, we glimpse through her eyes a kind of conceptual stammer: an astigmatic vision in which two overlapping versions of the self – one slightly displaced by circumstance, one somehow intrinsic – can't quite line up.

Without her role as convent favourite, Aurore is working hard to find a new identity. Over the next ten months nothing will be expected of her except that she be available to look after Nohant and its failing mistress. And with her grandmother in no fit state to offer 'moral or intellectual direction' she experiences, for the first time in her life, the autodidact's unsupervised freedom. She starts to read seriously at last, undergoes a spiritual crisis – and takes steps to resolve that crisis herself.

The adult Sand will label the self she was before she embarked on this process 'asleep', *endormie*. Once again we glimpse a sort of doubled self-image. She admits that 'it's rare that [a girl] finds herself abandoned so young to her own devices'. But on the other hand, as if impatient for that 'girl' somehow to catch up – with what? or whom? – she calls her teenaged self '*insensible*', unaware, of the intellectual challenges her grandmother has been trying to set her, and describes this period of her life as a 'hesitation between the development and the dumbing down [*abrutissement*, brutalisation] of the spirit'. In an echo of her grandmother's own position, this seems to imply that the contentment found in the religiosity so encouraged by the convent is a kind of dumb quiescence.

What, then, happens to her own idealism? Aptly for Aurore's times and temperament, the French word *l'esprit* captures the Romantic idea of mind as something animate. Like one of its many English derivatives, 'spirited', it supports a halo of meanings to do with nimbleness – wit, indeed – and doesn't separate the reasoning mind from the religious sense of spirit or soul. It's all the same thinking, responsive, morally responsible entity. Analogously, during these months of isolation in 1821, she comes to the conclusion that there is no category distinction between philosophical thought and prayer. They are both, as the religious might say, ways in which the spirit moves. But French does separate the lively mind from the brain and, later, when Sand sums up this period as 'great impotence of my brain, victory of my heart', she uses 'my brain' (*mon cerveau*) to specify the rational part of her mind.[33]

Nursing someone who is dying is inescapably thought-provoking. These months bring Aurore to the point of wanting to understand her own life, and this new desire shifts her idea of education from a chore to a need.[34] She turns, not to the anodyne devotional material that made up so much of her convent education, but to a translation of Thomas à Kempis's *The Imitation of Christ*.

Much of the reading that follows will be accompanied by the sounds of rain. Indre has an Atlantic climate, and 1821 is an exceptionally cold and rainy summer.[35] 'Racing through the fields' on horseback becomes less attractive; bad weather opens up the periods of uninterrupted time that concentrated study demands. À Kempis's *Imitation*, written in the Netherlands in the fifteenth century, is infused with the Devotio Moderna (Modern Devotion), a late-fourteenth- and fifteenth-century movement within Catholicism which flourished in the Low Countries and Germany. Founded by Jean Gerson, it called for less emphasis on outward observance and more on developing internal piety. The case it made against potentially corrupting observances – such as the selling of indulgences – meant it would be overtaken by the rise of Protestantism; but even in the twenty-first century the *Imitation* will remain highly influential among Catholics – such as Aurore.

Kempian piety, a kind of custody of the soul, is all about modesty and humility, the damping-down of unthinking, hedonistic impulse. For a young person already thoroughly damped down by duty and loneliness, it offers few consolations. So it's perhaps not surprising that Aurore's local confessor at La Châtre should recommend a fillip. He suggests François-René de Chateaubriand's *Le Génie du christianisme, ou Beautés de la religion chrétienne* (*The Genius of Christianity, or Beauties of the Christian Religion*), already hugely successful in the two decades since its 1802 publication. Chateaubriand composed the work in exile in Britain during the violently secularising French Revolution. Consequently it promotes Christian culture as a response to horrors carried out in the name of atheism.

Its celebration of the best of artistic production – such as Gothic cathedrals – is infectiously exuberant, and in these early decades of the nineteenth century the book is doing much to inspire young people in France to recommit to Christianity. Its conflation of beauty and meaning is proving influential even for French Romanticism. As the adult Sand will put it, 'Chateaubriand, the man of feeling and enthusiasm, became my priest and my initiator.' The text as confessor and intimate: the sexy, sinful resonances of that '*initiateur*' aren't coincidental. Sand will credit this book, and the overweening confidence it instils in her, with leading her into temptation: not to romp in the hay but to descend into 'the abyss of examination'. From a religious perspective, Chateaubriand introduces the 'poison' of intellectual arrogance; a belief that she can think it all – life, God – out for herself.

But what the seventeen-year-old does work out, sitting by candlelight with her grandmother or charging across the Indre countryside on Colette, is not that either reason or art trumps faith, but something altogether more morally sophisticated. She sees that the self-perfecting piety of Devotio Moderna is 'anti-evangelical and [so], taken literally, a doctrine of abominable selfishness': its adherents care only about their own spiritual salvation.[36] *Le Génie du christianisme*, on the other hand, suggests '*shared* religion' as a way to develop oneself. Returning to the shared external world of witnessed words and deeds – particularly artistic ones – *is* a way to practise faith. It's just like those lost convent performances, in which she could integrate faith, or anyway good faith, with what it was in her gift to do.

Of course, the girl reading alone in her room in the middle of the countryside doesn't see this all at once. For some time she agonises between Gerson and Chateaubriand, terrified that all her best motives – such as her loving care – have in fact been her worst. That, far from loving and caring for her grandmother, she's been doing everything for the most selfish of reasons: to secure a ticket to Heaven. She also worries deeply about what will happen if her grandmother dies having refused the last rites. In the end she seeks advice on this from a more trusted guide than local priests, her confessor back at the Dames Augustines Anglaises. He reassures her that it would be wrong for her to force her grandmother to take the sacraments, and the crisis passes.

Soon Aurore has moved on to Rousseau, that beacon of secular, Romantic ideas about the self and community – who is also a distant family connection. (Her grandfather had lost his lover, Louise d'Épinay, noble-born literary *saloniste* and divorcée and the mother of his two illegitimate children, to the philosopher, who was employed as a tutor at Chenonceau by his stepmother.) Disenchanted in her faith by the provincial clumsiness of local churches, Aurore devours Rousseau's *Du Contrat social* (*The Social Contract*) and the *Discourses*, the novel *Émile*, the 'Profession de foi d'un vicaire savoyard' ('Profession of Faith of the Savoyard Vicar') and *Lettres écrites de la montagne* (*Letters Written from the Mountain*):

> Jean-Jacques's language and the form of his arguments seized me like superb music lit by a great sun. I compared him to Mozart; I understood everything! What joy for a clumsy and stubborn pupil finally to manage to open her eyes completely and no longer find clouds before him [*sic*]![37]

It's a sudden insight into the seventeen-year-old's future. Great writing, she already believes, is gloriously clear at the level of both word and thought. No space here for pretension, or throat-clearing obfuscation. 'Language and the form of [. . .] arguments [. . .] like superb music lit by a great sun [. . .] compared [. . .] to Mozart': almost an *ars poetica*, this vision of art is well suited to a writer who will be unafraid of popularity: who won't see writing actually *to and for* her readers as any kind of literary failure.

Perhaps less intuitively, Aurore is also reading the mathematician and philosopher Gottfried Wilhelm Leibniz, who 'seemed the greatest of all but how hard he was to swallow!'[38] But then, recollecting all this in *Histoire*, Sand suddenly breaks off: 'If I wanted to take account of everything I read and its effects on me, I'd have to embark on a critical book which could run to many volumes [. . .] besides, I'd risk putting my present-day impressions into my account of the past.' She knows, in other words, that influence flows through time in both directions. What she's reading as a teenager is formative; it will still be shaping her thought decades later when she comes to write her life story. But memory's influence is retrospective, working backwards on experiences to transform them. This matters for a reason Sand as memoirist can scarcely bring herself to admit: it undermines the truth of memory as witness.

The fiction that will make George Sand famous isn't of course 'true' in the same way as experience itself. Her novels are made up. But there is always, in its raptness, a sense that it's true *to* something. Years after *Histoire* has been published she will identify this something, in her letters to Flaubert, as idealism. We might call it by another name: sincerity. Aurore isn't reading philosophy in order to solve ontological riddles about the nature of the world, but much more simply and sincerely as a guide to action:

> when I bent my understanding [to] abstractions [...] I found only emptiness or uncertainty flowing from them. My mind was and has always been too vulgar and too little inclined to scientific research [...] I was a being of feeling, and feeling alone decided questions for me.[39]

At seventeen, she's also encountering feelings as an increasingly practical problem. Inevitably, the question of admirers has arisen.[40] The young medical student Deschartres has hired to teach her anatomy is 'less fun than [the] skeleton' on which she's learning the science of the body. But the neighbourhood starts to gossip, and even her confessor at La Châtre doesn't believe her indignant denial that the two have become intimate. There is also her older married cousin, the patrician René Vallet de Villeneuve, who rides out alone with her, contrary to respectable convention.

In fact Aurore is 'too far removed from any flirtatious notion and very far from any idea of love' to care for any of this.[41] She remains wedded to the figure in the sickbed who, as winter comes on, is sinking fast. Maman no longer gets up, and speaks only rarely. 'All of December' is 'dismal'. On 22 December, Aurore is woken in the middle of the night. Her grandmother wants to give her a knife inlaid with mother-of-pearl. Whether it's a paperknife, a penknife or a fruit knife, it's easy to picture the attractive bibelot which may, perhaps, have been lying around in the sickroom: even invalids open letters and eat fruit. Sand will write that her grandmother is unable to explain its significance. All she can say is, 'You are losing your best friend.'[42]

In fact these words, which prove to be her last, explain the symbolism of the gift: long tradition has it that giving a knife represents severing the relationship of giver and receiver. With no outward sign of suffering, Maman slips into a coma, while Aurore and Deschartres continue to watch at the bedside. She dies at dawn three days later, on what Sand will, oddly, misremember as Christmas Day. Outside, across the square, the bell in the village church is chiming for Mass. In fact, it's 26 December, the feast day of Saint Stephen, the first Christian martyr.[43]

Birth and death: it seems as though, outside the shuttered windows of the ground-floor bedroom, the world continues to turn. Released from their vigil, neither Marie-Aurore de Saxe's steward nor her granddaughter have tears left to shed: they've done that as they waited at the bedside. But there are still rites to observe. The first, in the middle of a 'clear and cold' night, is unorthodox in the extreme.[44] Deschartres fetches Aurore at about one in the morning. The gravediggers have disturbed her father's coffin in making space alongside him for her grandmother. It has partly opened. Deschartres has been moved to kiss the skeletal forehead of his former young master, his first pupil. Now he offers Aurore the chance to do the same. This must be in secret, in the middle of the night, because of the risk of a scandal about, perhaps, necromancy. So Aurore, lightheaded with bereavement and after three nights without going to bed, and 'sufficiently moved and excited' not to think of challenging the idea, climbs into the grave and kisses the skull of her father 'religiously'. Maurice has been dead for fourteen years. It is also fourteen years since, in the last days of his own life, he climbed into an open grave in the middle of the night in this very churchyard.

But no curse gets perpetuated. His daughter will survive for over half a century. There is, though, to be a thickening of the husk of loneliness in which she has been living. A further rite is the reading of her grandmother's will to the assembled family. In an undoubted blow to Hippolyte, Aurore turns out to have inherited almost everything, and René Vallet de Villeneuve to have been appointed as her guardian. Cousin René invites her to share life in the Renaissance galleries of Chenonceau, offering her a kind of 'finishing' of her formation with ease, grace and aristocratic affluence.

It seems like the start of a new, happier chapter. But it's not to be. Instead – perhaps because she had expectations of something life-changing for herself – Sophie-Victoire now explodes, sabotaging Aurore's expectations. She makes such a scene at being left out of arrangements that – just as Marie-Aurore de Saxe must have feared, and as she had arranged her legacy specifically to prevent – the young woman is consigned to her mother's care. It's back to the mean parental apartment in central Paris, and continual surveillance by an increasingly petulant former chorus girl.

No surprise that, within four months, Aurore has found a man to marry. Nor, perhaps, that he should be older than her. Casimir Dudevant is nine years her senior, almost to the day. But not in fact old. 'Slim, quite elegant [and] with a cheerful face and military style', he is after all only twenty-six himself.[45]

Perhaps tellingly, Aurore has recognised in him the same kind of fun she had with Hippolyte. She tells her brother, 'I have here a companion [*un camarade*, she uses a term with military connotations] whom I like a lot, with whom I jump and laugh as I do with you.'[46]

Even their meeting is a kind of bagatelle, though Aurore notes to herself, 'C inerasable memory. Prophetic.'[47] On a spring evening, Aurore and her mother are among a group eating ices at Tortoni's, the café on the corner of rue Taitbout and the aptly named boulevard des Italiens that has been a Paris institution since 1798. It's in the smart ninth arrondissement, close to both the Bourse and the Opéra (which is now reopened, after the assassination of the Duc de Berry, on rue Le Peletier, five minutes' walk away). This, together with its late opening hours, has made it a magnet for beau monde and demi-monde alike. Tortoni's will enjoy a long posterity on the page, celebrated in fiction by almost every great nineteenth-century French novelist from Stendhal to Balzac, and later by Henry James and Marcel Proust. In life, meanwhile, it's noisy and crammed, its famous staircase and pavement terrace perfect for people-watching until the small hours.

Aurore's 'prophetic' encounter comes at around eleven on a Friday night. It's 19 April 1822, and the party have been to watch the Opéra-Comique at the Salle Feydeau, a five-minute stroll away. A young man approaches the table and greets their hosts, Angèle and Jacques Roëttiers du Plessis, who ask affectionately after his father. It seems he's a family friend. Then he notices Aurore, and asks Mme Roëttiers du Plessis who she is. When Mme du Plessis replies loudly and jokingly – summoning the group's attention – that Aurore is her own daughter, the young man seizes on the spirit of the moment to respond, 'Ah, so this is my wife? You know you promised me the hand of your eldest daughter.' This reference to an earlier gallantry (the Roëttiers' eldest, Winiphride, has just turned nine) may not constitute conversational brilliance. But it's enough to amuse a tableful of people who are out to have fun – and to stake a kind of claim.

It seems counter-intuitive that at seventeen the future George Sand should be thrilled by someone of no particular brilliance. This smiling youth is Dudevant, and he is a relatively undistinguished country landowner. But Aurore, of course, does not yet know that she will become George Sand, and consort with some of the most brilliant minds of her day. She's still 'far from any flirtatious notion and very far from any idea of love'.[48] After spending her adolescence first at the convent and then in country seclusion, she is inexperienced, innocent and ripe – as is perhaps the purpose of such upbringings – for marrying the first man who comes along.

Right now, one suspects, she's also looking for a fresh start with happiness. And perhaps, after the vertiginous changes of the last three years, all she can cope with is happiness in a familiar form. Like her, Casimir Dudevant is slightly provincial, military-at-one-remove, on the cusp between patrician respectability and illegitimacy. Like Hippolyte, he's the illegitimate son of a distinguished military officer and, in this case, the officer's housekeeper.[49] His father, Jean-François Dudevant – who has acknowledged him – is a former parliamentarian and, despite having served in the royal household, proved able to cross the barricades and join the winning side, being created a baron in 1811.[50]

Within a few weeks Aurore has accepted a real offer of marriage from 'C'. On 17 September 1822, five months after their first meeting – and nine after losing her grandmother – she's married on the very anniversary of her father's death; as if by this gesture she could mend that loss. The Napoleonic civil contract is ratified by a ceremony at the church of Saint-Louis-d'Antin, whose fashionable neoclassical style is in keeping with its ninth-arrondissement address on the rue de Caumartin; the stylish Roëttiers, by now firm friends of the new couple, host the wedding party. Sophie-Victoire does not attend.

Third impression: *Complicity*

THIS IS MORE LIKE IT. When I look at this portrait of the seventeen-year-old Aurore Dupin, I feel I understand what the fuss is about.

The young soon-to-be heiress is painted by an artist almost as young as herself, a twenty-year-old called Jean-Baptiste Bonjour who grew up in the countryside near Neuchâtel. Eighteen twenty-one is his first year as a professional artist; the turning point at which he's taken an untrained knack for capturing a likeness and resolved to make a career of it. What makes this extraordinary is that he doesn't come from the kind of bourgeois or privileged background that might have exposed him to lots of art. He's an agricultural labourer and vintner, a prodigious autodidact who has managed to solve centuries-old puzzles of realistic representation by himself – and latterly during studies in Paris with Claude-Marie Dubufe. Now, with his family's blessing, he is setting up as an itinerant portrait artist.[51]

The clarity and flatness of his picture of Aurore aren't exactly naive, but they remind us that he learnt to draw without studying artistic convention. (Another puzzle is how Jean-Baptiste has managed to master paint so completely. Line is one thing, colour and form are quite another. One theory is that before he left Switzerland he took watercolour lessons from Gabriel Lory.) Over time his portraits will become forensically detailed and yet more limpid, his sitters' skin ever more luminous and Dubufian. But this is an early work and, indeed, there is something ever so slightly American primitive about it: those perfectly regular eyelids, the dark outline of chin and eyes.

His subject is at a similar turning point in her own unconventional, soon-to-be artistic life. Bonjour is the first of the Jean-Baptistes for whom she will sit. In her famous future she will be painted by Jean-Baptiste Isabey, sometime around 1835, and Jean-Baptiste Bizard in 1847. But in 1821 she is waiting for life to start: nursing her grandmother, running Nohant, reading, thinking, and hoping to avert any marriage of social convenience.

Who chooses Jean-Baptiste Bonjour to paint her portrait? Does Aurore know his background, and does it speak to any kind of affinity in this seventeen-year-old, the bareback rider who so often disappears to race across great tranches of the rolling, apparently empty Berrichon countryside? Two worlds – two classes – meet in their sittings, but both these very young people may feel like outsiders. For all the heavy black with which Jean-Baptiste outlines Aurore's eyes – almost like kohl – there's complicity in her gaze. You think that, if only those spots of reflected light in her irises could be enlarged, you'd see the painter himself reflected in them.

Who is she looking at? That knowing tilt of the head, the certainty of Aurore's slight smile, suggest someone who knows how to be looked at, and how to take an intimate initiative. She may appear clear-skinned and untried, but she doesn't seem innocent. It is, to put it bluntly, a very dykey image, not least because this young woman has a boy's haircut and is wearing men's clothes: jacket, cravat and waistcoat. Yet the object of her seductive gaze is a man.

FOUR

Entering on tiptoe

SUDDENLY, A NEW VOICE MAKES itself heard. It's late in July 1823, and a young wife is writing from a fashionable Paris address to her husband, who is in Indre. He's gone down to check on the country property of which he is now chatelain through marriage, and his wife proudly addresses her letter 'Mr Casimir Dudevant, in his chateau of Nohant'.

Perhaps there's calculation in this as well as pride. Possibly the writer is willing her husband to fall in love with her country home. For, in sidling up the alphabet from Dupin to Dudevant, Aurore both has and has not changed more than her name. Installed on the fashionable rue Neuve des Mathurins, where both her fiancé and (among those walls lined with blue silk) her late grandmother once kept homes, she's now the married mistress of her own establishment. But also not: under the Napoleonic Code she enjoys no autonomy in property decisions.[1] And so Casimir is making his solo visit to the manor.

In the family's absence, Nohant is being run by François Deschartres. He's turned out to be as reliable – and, perhaps, as inflexible – as ever. Soon, he and Casimir will clash over modernisation. The new master of the house is a born country squire, for whom Nohant may be a novelty but the life of the rural gentry is not. Small wonder if he knows what he wants. But for the ageing steward the proposed changes spell tragedy. His position quickly becomes untenable; within a month he will have been forced out.[2] Unemployed at sixty-two, cut adrift from his home of decades and from the family of whom he had come to seem a part, he leaves for Paris, but will never manage properly to re-establish himself.

It's a brutal end to a long association. In the years since she ceased to be his pupil, Aurore has come to feel real affection for Deschartres. She recognises that the man she's in the habit of calling 'great' for his height rather than his social stature has been a genuinely caring elder, if not exactly a parental figure, in her life. But even if she does want to object, there's little she can do as a woman of just nineteen: she has another two years before she legally comes of age.

Married life at Nohant, where she and Casimir have by now spent their first winter, seems to be something of a fait accompli. The happy country lifestyle of their original matchmakers, Ange-Justine and Jacques Roëttiers du Plessis, appears to model their own future. The Roëttiers' Château du Plessis-Picard, some twenty-five miles south-west of Paris in the Seine-et-Marne village of Réau, has become interwoven with their own marriage. It's where they got engaged last summer, and then where they started their life together.[3] The Roëttiers' domestic idyll – they are raising five daughters in this elegantly pedimented, classically proportioned country mansion – must feel perfectly emulable to the Dudevants, as they start along a similar path roughly a decade later. Ange-Justine Roëttiers, known as Angèle, is just ten years older than Aurore, and got married at the same early age. To the nine years separating the Dudevant couple, Angèle offers the fourteen that separate her from her husband, who has, like Aurore's husband, a degree of social instability. (Though not illegitimate like Casimir, Jacques is the grandson and namesake of a gold- and silversmith whom fashionable success carried to a peerage. To contemporary eyes, it's new money that has bought and furnished the Château du Plessis-Picard.[4])

In a way, though, the Roëttiers are a little too golden to be a useful model. Their chateau is bigger and more modern than the revisionist, vernacular creation that Aurore has inherited. And Nohant is a great deal further than Réau from the bright lights of the capital; seven times as far, to be exact. Married life in Indre is already proving to be no happy continuation of the metropolitan partying from which the Roëttiers dip in and out, but a chilly hibernation remarkably similar to Aurore's time caring for her grandmother.

Nor are the Dudevants particularly well off. As an illegitimate son, under the Napoleonic Code Casimir is at risk of inheriting, if not virtually nothing like Hippolyte, still only part of his father's estate.[5] It was Sophie-Victoire, that battling survivor, who alerted the couple to this fact. Only after much productive meddling on her part was a marriage settlement from Baron Dudevant of a substantial 60,000 francs levered into place just three weeks before the wedding. Their marriage contract also stipulates that the young husband give Aurore an annual allowance of 3,000 francs, and that she retain her own inheritance of 500,000 francs, even though she's not allowed to manage it herself. This unusually complicated prenuptial paperwork will eventually achieve some of its originator's protective aims, but not at first. Casimir will burn through the settlement only to find, when his father dies in early 1826, that he has indeed inherited little else.[6]

All the same, marriage means more than a change of name. There are actually not one but two new voices making themselves heard in this letter, which Aurore starts to write in the changing light of a long summer evening in the capital. She's staying on the rue Neuve des Mathurins not at a family apartment but at the Hôtel de Florence, and the reason for her presence here is in her arms much of the time. Her little boy Maurice was born just a month ago, on 30 June, and the couple came to Paris to be near good doctors for the birth.

In fact Maurice's timing is impeccable, since he arrived exactly forty-one weeks after his parents' wedding, 'without difficulty' and so quickly, as his mother will later report, that she didn't even have time to get back to her room. He was born in the summerhouse at the bottom of the garden.[7] And, as if he were indeed proof of the couple's desire for each other – as perhaps he is – Aurore reports his excellent progress to his father: 'Your little angel Maurice has slept well this night, fed well this morning, done a good wee and poo [*pipi et caca*], etc.' Babies are irreducibly bodily. Even so, this frankness seems remarkable for the era, especially compared to the formality and artfulness of Aurore's first letters to old school friends. But then, although her husband has promised her 'friendship', this is not a letter to a friend. Discussion of infant body functions isn't the only kind of 'babytalk' it breaks into: 'Good night, my love, my dear little mimi, I'm going to lie down and cry all alone in my bed.' Indeed, from its first line to her 'poor little cat', the young wife seems to be writing in a kind of rapture of letting down her guard: 'It's so sad, my little good angel, my dear love, to write to you instead of speaking to you, to no longer know you're there beside me.'

This is the first surviving love letter written by someone who will become famous as a writer, and notorious for her love life. It's also the first time we hear Aurore sounding unconstrained by either social correctness or performance anxiety. In flowing, confident sentences, one phrase piling on another, she describes 'our little Maurice who's sympathetic, for he cries along with me. True, it's from hunger, but we both cry, and I love him more than ever, if that's possible, since I've had only him to console me.' A tender joke, since both parents know that, really, baby *is* just hungry.

Where does authenticity truly start and finish? Even if there is an element of play-acting the little wife here, something about having a physical lover, and becoming a mother, seems to have given Aurore new confidence. Physical intimacy can feel like intimate acceptance. It's important to remember this mood of relaxed, embodied – even carnal – happiness, because it is so often ignored in accounts of Aurore's marriage. Even though Casimir is only away in Nohant for a week she sends another letter, full of gossipy emotional intelligence, only a couple of days later.

Later biographers will make much of future occasions, after things stop going so well, when Casimir reproaches his wife for rejecting him sexually. They will also cite the advice Aurore gives Hippolyte, twenty years from now, when his daughter Léontine is about to be married. She warns her brother of the shock sex is for a girl brought up with no knowledge of it: 'Nothing is so awful as the terror, the suffering and the disgust of a poor child who knows nothing and sees itself raped by a brute. We raise them like saints [*saintes*], then hand them over like fillies [*pouliches*].'[8]

This arresting insight will become famous. But it has to be wrenched out of context if it's to imply its author doesn't enjoy sex for, on the contrary, her previous sentence enjoins, 'Tell [the bridegroom] to spare his pleasure a little and wait till his wife is gradually brought by him to understand it *and respond to it* [my italics].' Good sex therapist's advice indeed. But even so, not necessarily autobiographical. Despite her convent schooling, Aurore herself can never have been a 'saint' who 'knew nothing'. She had plenty of opportunities to witness creaturely life in her country childhood at Nohant, that region of farms, yards and byres full of animals, in a nineteenth-century countryside still teeming with wildlife.

Yet, however sexually knowing she was or was not on her

wedding night, it's true that the Dudevant alliance seems to be closer to a friendship with benefits than *amour fou*. The couple's courtship was a six-week whirlwind, but also just a game. At Plessis-Picard the pair played at calling each other 'husband' and 'wife' before Casimir proposed, couching his offer of marriage (with perhaps less than complete gallantry) in terms of 'eternal friendship', the domestic contentment of their hosts, and Aurore's own 'good and reasonable' air.[9] And at the age of only eighteen she accepted these terms. There must be deep peace in a marriage bed, to paraphrase Oscar Wilde, after the hurly-burly of life with Sophie-Victoire. Perhaps this first surviving love letter which Aurore writes one Tuesday in July 1823 and which repeats, '*Comme c'est* [. . .] *Comme il me semble*' 'How [. . .] How it seems' – an equivalent to that gushy, not always authentic, English intensifier 'so' – is after all simply practising the seductions of an apparent eagerness. But surely nothing is damaged by a little fanning of tender emotion.

Whatever its relationship with felt truth, this is the first surviving occurrence of a tone familiar from the published work. Some future critics will carp that this eager, outreaching 'voice on the page' is uncontrolled and labile. But here we see the future George Sand writing as someone who, in intimacy, is both communicative and emotionally present. All the same, it's paradoxical, even ironic, that the style which will make her famous is emerging at a moment of what we might call maximum gender essentialism, when she's a young wife and new mother. Aurore will always identify with *male* intellectual life.

Participation in that life, however, will not be easy for her. Even after Napoleonic educational reform and the establishment of fee-paying boys' *lycées*, roughly equivalent to grammar schools, intellectual literacy and high literary style remain associated with classical education, which Aurore as a girl lacks.[10] Whatever her convent education cost Maman, it seems to have been largely an exercise in piety and good manners. Years of training in Ancient Greek and Latin – language and rhetoric, ideas and style – still shape the sensibility of European men of the decision-making upper and emerging middle classes. But Aurore missed out on these subjects even when she was being tutored at home.

Still, her resistance to doing things like a girl dates from that 'golden age'. In girlhood, riding bareback and astride, she resembled another future writer growing up on a country estate on the other side of the Channel. Just two years her junior, the future Elizabeth Barrett Browning

> could run rapidly & leap high,—and [. . .] had very strong wrists. [. . .] She cd. climb too pretty well up trees—[. . .] And she liked fishing, though she did not often catch anything. And best of all, though she cared for bows & arrows, & squirts & popguns—best of all, did she like riding [. . .] galloping till the trees raced past her & the clouds were shot over her head.[11]

Resistance to the boredom of early-nineteenth-century girlhood – a primarily domestic existence – could be most easily expressed by acting the tomboy. In their teens, both girls chose autodidacticism, though only Elizabeth Barrett put herself through a gruelling formation in Ancient Greek prosody.[12] When both have become famous, and they finally meet, the poet will observe the difference in temperament that will come to define the novelist's reputation:

> she seemed to be in fact the man in that company, & the profound respect with which she was listened to, a good deal impressed me [. . .] scorn of pleasing, she evidently had—there never could have been a colour of coquetry in that woman.

[. . .] I liked her . . . I did not love her . . . but I felt the burning soul through all that quietness, & was not disappointed.[13]

But that's three decades in the future. On this summer evening in 1823 Aurore is just a country chatelaine waiting alone in the capital, which at the moment offers her no amusements; a young wife missing her husband and perhaps suffering a little from baby blues. She must be exhausted – and sleep-deprived. The couple have employed a nursery maid, Mme Aimable (whose name is so suggestive of a soft-porn au pair fantasy), but not a wet nurse. Unusually for a woman of her class, Aurore is nursing Maurice herself; just as her grandmother, influenced by Rousseau's ideas about natural childrearing, nursed the other Maurice for whom this new baby is named. So she wheedles:

> But above all tell me about yourself, tell me that you love me, and that you'll always love me the same. As for me [. . .] I've nothing new to say to you, I'll just repeat that I adore you, that I love you as much as it's possible to love on earth. Farewell . . . goodnight . . . My god this is sad!
> *Wednesday morning*
> There's one night gone, my angel [. . .] You've passed it very ill, poor little cat, in the midst of the chaos of the diligence. You've thought about your little wife, at least, haven't you? Your little [dog] Mascarille has already come 2 or 3 times to the foot of my bed to see if you're there.[14]

Attentive and almost submissive, this is a correspondent who doesn't lose sight of her intended reader, but builds her letter around him and what she can work out he is doing. It's hard to imagine any of the men who will become her literary peers writing with such a degree of deprecation and vulnerability, even to a lover. But this thin emotional skin will turn out to be a literary superpower. A majority of nineteenth-century readers of fiction are women. The contracted world of their experience – centred on interpersonal relationships, and so emotional intelligence – has become central novelistic territory. Aurore's powers of emotional perception have been honed by scrying the intentions of her widely differentiated cast of caregivers, and when she comes to write fiction will allow her to explore emotions and behaviour with forensic nuance.

But not yet. For now she's a young mother who needs all the confidence intimacy can provide. Luckily, her little son continues to be bonny. He's the first baby Aurore has been close to since her brother Auguste died when she was a child, and the contrast between the infants is marked. Three months after Casimir's trip to Nohant, she recounts to Émilie de Wismes how Maurice has recently been unwell, but 'Imagine my relief: he has a tooth and he's only four months [. . .] He laughs in peals, his father adores it. They spend whole hours together rolling on the ground on a rug. The little one is nearly always naked: he has such strength and energy, astonishing for his age.'[15]

This happy letter is in unignorable contrast to one she sent Émilie back in January – that grim season of the country year – when she was four months pregnant, and which seems to allow us to look over her shoulder into the backstage, as it were, of her marriage. Its postscript appears to offer the key to its sombre tone. Hippolyte is marrying a woman about whom this most prolix correspondent can bring herself to record only that she's so small the groom 'could put her in his pocket, or in his boot': shrinking the figure of the new sister-in-law almost to vanishing point in gloriously Freudian style. With a rare display of spite, Aurore's letter then segues to a twenty-eight-year-old mutual acquaintance, 'without fortune, without birth, without talents, and far from having an agreeable figure. [. . .] Apparently having a great taste for the young she has just married a man of 23.' A sneer which her own future preference for younger men will render ironic indeed.[16]

Still, as this new wife waits, tied down by provincial distances and by pregnancy, for the arrival of her brother 'and his *spouse*' (she underlines the word as if spitting it out), it's worth recalling not only her mystified, giggling exchanges with school friends, but also how much her husband reminds her of Hippolyte. He matters to Aurore. It would be novelistic to construct an unexpressed romantic jealousy from this, but *something* is going on: something more nuanced and complex than romance, probably, but at the very least a possessiveness that might be either sentimental or familial.

By a hop and skip of internal logic, in the same letter Aurore gives her old school friend advice on how to make her own imminent marriage work. (This too will appear ironic in retrospect.) Émilie has evidently been expressing anxieties both about married life itself and about the future pregnancies which are its almost inevitable corollary. Perhaps the strange intimacy of a letter, which 'speaks' to someone who's not right in front of you but is concealed, as if behind the grille of a confessional – or of a convent visiting parlour – encourages confidences. Whatever the reason, 'I agree that the annoyances which arise from the diversity of tastes and characters are all too real in most households,' writes Aurore:

> Also one must be persuaded that it is *absolutely impossible* to meet a person whose mood and tastes in everything are exactly the same as one's own. [. . . N]ature doesn't use the same mould for two people. So every time one spouse or the other wants to hold on to their ideas and concede nothing, they will find

themselves unhappy. I believe that one of the two, on marrying, must renounce themselves entirely, and abnegate not only their will but their opinion, decide to see with the eyes of the other, to love what they love, etc. What torture [...] when one unites with someone one hates. What sad uncertainty [...] when one marries a stranger [*un inconnu*]. But also what an inexhaustible source of happiness, when we obey what we love in this way. [For] since *on the side of the beard there is omnipotence*, and moreover men are not capable of such attachment, it is necessarily up to us to bend towards obedience. [...] Like you I used to have a sad opinion of marriage up to the moment when I attached myself to Casimir, and if I've changed that, it's only in my own regard.[17]

It's a passage straight from the *Men Are from Mars, Women Are from Venus* school of self-help, instructing the woman to make up for her man's shortcomings. But is it also, as some future biographers will diagnose, a cry of pain? I read it instead as a kind of boast. Aurore is offering her still-innocent friend reassurance: first that pregnancy isn't too difficult, and then that marriage itself isn't either. The difficulties of the former are physical, but those of the latter are psychological, and the author of this letter proudly believes she's overcome them.

Advocating the 'surrendered wife' is clearly not the proto-feminism we're tempted anachronistically to expect from this writer who will soon become a model for risk-taking women. But a belief that circumstance can be moulded *is*, and three things seem to be working together here. One is a kind of ecstatic passivity. Aurore has just passed through the tiring first trimester of her first pregnancy. Another is strategic pragmatism. At puberty, resistance exiled her to boarding school. Now she's six years older and wiser, the path of least resistance looks the altogether rosier option. Finally, there's a trace of idealism in this image of a successful partnership entailing absolute, unqualified understanding rather than give and take, the bodge and compromise of most good-enough domestic lives. In order to incorporate the differences between herself and her husband that are already apparent after six months of marriage, this nineteen-year-old *must* 'be persuaded that it is *absolutely impossible* to meet a person whose mood and tastes in everything are exactly the same as one's own'. If she were to meet someone who did offer this kind of 'exact' affinity, in other words, the whole grounds of her belief in her marriage would collapse.

She has married young, very quickly, and to pretty much the first person who's taken an interest in her. Given the tenor of her months with Sophie-Victoire after Maman's death, it's not hard to work out why. The age at which she married isn't by any means exceptional, as Émilie's approaching wedding confirms. But – perhaps by social design – both young women are too sheltered to have any clue at all about their own 'mood and tastes in everything'. There may be trouble ahead. The *tabula rasa* virgin makes for a malleable bride but, should she prove to have strong interests or personality, can prove the most mismatched of wives.

Aurore's own talent is going to burden her marriage until it capsizes. But all she knows for now is that the husband she imagined would truly understand her and whom she would deeply understand in turn is in fact '*un inconnu*', an unknown quantity. Before the wedding, Casimir's similarities to Hippolyte made him feel familiar. But marriage is not siblinghood. What makes it so definingly intimate is not just sex, but the thousand details of taste and ideas which create a way of life. The rough manners of a country gentleman, so enjoyable in Hippolyte or when Aurore and Casimir play-acted their future marriage at Château du Plessis-Picard, feel boorish close-up. Unlike Aurore herself, both the men in her life enjoy riding and hunting but struggle to read a book; both will become great drinkers. And it works both ways. Everything she finds difficult in Casimir must modify the way she understands her brother, even as she seems to be losing him to his own marriage.

Yet it's largely down to Hippolyte's emotional generosity that the half-siblings manage to remain friends for life. As he will point out, four years from now:

> If you had reflected more on the similarity of our origin, which your father's marriage made disappear in time for you [when Aurore, who was also illegitimately conceived, was 'saved' by her parents' marriage a month before her birth], if you thought how I was in my father's house five years before you, about the deep friendship this grandmother had for me, the effects of which only Deschartres's hatred prevented [you'd understand I am furious] but not with you, whom circumstances and the law has served as one would wish.[18]

No such tie of genuine affection holds Aurore's marriage together. Disenchantment starts with a modest acknowledgement in July 1823 that she feels isolated, 'if one can believe oneself alone when one is tête-à-tête with a husband one adores'.[19] Since this is unthinkable, wifely ennui gets blamed on Nohant. By spring 1824 she's telling Émilie:

> It's beautiful countryside, a charming home, but very sad because there is no Society. The people of Berry are unbearable creatures, even more boring than those of Limoges. We're looking to rent or buy a pretty country house near Melun or Montgeron and I imagine that we'll settle there soon. While we wait I'm enchanted to be in Paris, which I really love.[20]

After spending the summer once again at Réau, with the always-encouraging Roëttiers du Plessis, the Dudevants move to a new home. In the event this is not in either of the fashionable outlying communes Aurore hoped for but at Ormesson, forty miles further south-west from the capital. Forty miles less sociable, but also less expensive. Very soon, however, Casimir rows with the gardener of the estate they have rented, ostensibly over baby Maurice, who is by now toddling around, and presumably over, everything. After just ten weeks the couple give up the house and move to Paris. Here, after a brief stay with a paternal aunt of Aurore's, they find themselves renting yet another property, a furnished apartment on the rue de Faubourg-Saint-Honoré.

These changes are hectic and expensive, and even overwintering in Paris doesn't quite heal what's going adrift. So in the spring of 1825 Aurore contacts her old confessor, the Abbé Prémord, at the Dames Augustines Anglaises. A retreat at the convent ensues, though by special dispensation baby Maurice is brought in to his mother every day. This isn't a plunge into religion so much as a practical attempt to solve the depression which, a few years from now, she will describe so well in her first novel, *Indiana*: 'The Colonel's wife was nineteen [. . .] if you had seen her, slender, pale and sad, her elbow on her knee [. . .] you would have pitied the wife of Colonel Delmare, and perhaps the Colonel even more.'[21]

Seventy years before the development of psychoanalysis, in other words, what Aurore is really doing at the convent on the rue des Fossés-Saint-Victor is attempting to change the pattern of her life by changing herself. (In the twenty-first century she might have undertaken psychotherapy or gone on a yoga retreat. If this makes her sound like a yummy mummy, that's pretty much the mould she's trying to squeeze herself into.) In the first quarter of the nineteenth century, advice on life comes from one's spiritual guide. Not surprisingly, hers advises her to assume her burdens.

Even Mother Spiring pushes her back into the world, saying, 'You have a charming child [...] that is all that is necessary to your earthly happiness. Life is short.'²²

Soon the little Dudevant family are back in Nohant, no happier and 30,000 francs – a full half their marriage settlement – the poorer. Still, they persevere. Casimir spends yet more money on a piano for Aurore, and consolidates his own friendship with Hippolyte. But it's too late. Last summer, while they were staying with the Roëttiers at Château du Plessis-Picard, that special place which has meant so much to their relationship, he hit her in the face in full view of these closest – and smartest – of friends. The attack seems to have been a one-off, since in the future George Sand will recall being shocked as well as humiliated.²³ But once is of course enough for any woman to recognise in an instant both that the ultimate basis of her husband's power is in male violence, and that he must have, at least in his worst moments, little respect for her. That same night Aurore told Casimir that she would only continue to share a bed with him while they were staying with their friends.

So that by the summer of 1825 their marriage has settled into an impasse. Aurore has spent her young life trying to manage domestic insecurity: here it comes again. As she turns twenty-one she becomes run-down, suffering from a persistent cough and a racing heart. So the couple are easily persuaded to try yet another change of scene. They agree to follow two of their summer visitors, Aurore's school friends Aimée and Jane Bazouin, to the Pyrenean spa of Cauterets. Mourning the death of their elder sister, the Bazouins are in an equally bad way, and Cauterets, a little mountain resort in a high rocky valley close to the Spanish border, has long been renowned for its therapeutic hot springs. In the 1820s it's coming back to life after the war years. Private spa hotels offering thermal baths are springing up to dwarf the original settlement. These afford the three women the prospect of bathing and taking the waters, of wraps and rubs; while for Casimir there's plenty of hunting up on the hills.

The party set out, rather oddly, on Aurore's twenty-first birthday itself. Facing a journey south of more than 300 miles, and in something of a strange, premonitory mood, before departure that morning she notes in her journal, 'Adieu Nohant. I may never see you again.' This is ridiculously melodramatic, but in a way she's right. It's inconceivable that the present state of affairs will continue; and it does not. Once in the Pyrenees, Aurore will move restlessly out of the Bazouin sisters' orbit, as well as her husband's, to seize upon a new best friend.

Zoé Leroy is the vivid, twenty-eight-year-old daughter of a Bordeaux wine merchant. Like Aurore, she's eager to explore 'the most beautiful country in the world': the two share an affinity for Romantic sentiment. Once summer ends, it will be Aurore who pedals hard to keep that shared sensibility alive, writing from her father-in-law's house in the Gascon *paysage* that

> We go entire leagues without meeting a soul, without seeing the end of these long forests; we walk in sand up to our knees and have so much difficulty getting out that we lose the desire and the power to meditate. [...] But sweet reveries, *those* that *we* loved, my dear Zoé, are pleasant in cheerful meadows like your own...[24]

It's embarrassingly try-hard. But Zoé's friendship seems to offer the kind of intimate understanding Aurore has been pining for. And this first elective affinity has already opened the door to the second. Also in Zoé's circle down from Bordeaux are a young beauty, Laure le Hoult, and her fiancé, a rising young magistrate called Aurélien de Sèze. De Sèze is twenty-five, ambitious and intelligent, and destined for a life of public service: he has already been appointed Deputy Advocate General. He's also a long-nosed, dark-haired, handsome Gascon type. His father is Rector of Bordeaux Academy, and one of his uncles defended King Louis XVI: a connection that feels significant to Aurore, who hasn't forgotten her own distant royal descent, and who attended the interment of Louis XVIII in Saint-Denis only last October.

Despite his success, like many a smart young man before and since de Sèze is experiencing the lonely, disloyal thoughts that come from picking a partner for her beauty and not her brains. His fiancée is 'without ideas', he will tell Aurore, joining that eternal chorus of philandering men whose women 'don't understand them'. But Aurore, inexperienced and lonely herself in exactly this way, has no idea that it is a cliché.

The stage is almost inevitably set for an affair. A holiday mood, and the Romantic landscape of the area – mountains, bosky chasms, waterfalls – can only help. During their time in the Pyrenees, Aurore and Aurélien establish an understanding, in more or less unobserved moments snatched on group outings to beauty spots, which they pride themselves on keeping platonic. Of course, this is not really platonic at all: they've fallen in love, they kiss, they confide about how their partners don't understand them. But they manage not actually to have sex: which is one way to have your moral cake and eat it.

However, the liaison doesn't end with the holiday, when Casimir brings his wife home via Guillery, his father's country house near leafy, limestone Pompiey. Conveniently en route for Nohant, this house is pretty in itself. Even the flat, scrubby terrain of northern Gascony is not really the 'frightful desert, a desolate land' which Aurore describes to Zoé, with an outburst of pathetic fallacy, as 'Covered with cork trees [...] the saddest and drabbest tree, which [even] spring will not green up.'[25] It may not be a particularly happy household to visit, however, for Casimir has a wicked stepmother. The Baroness Dudevant has no children of her own, and her resentment of her husband's illegitimate only child – all too soon to be revealed by the paucity of his inheritance – is presumably only intensified by his arrival with not only a wife but her husband's only grandchild.[26]

In these strained surroundings Aurore's marriage has little chance to settle. Once again she's restless and unhappy; soon she manages to negotiate a couple of visits to her new friends in Bordeaux. The first takes place less than two months after Cauterets and, on the very first evening in their city hotel, Casimir surprises Aurore in a compromising embrace with Aurélien. Astonishingly, he not only forgives her, but grants her licence to act according to her own moral lights. Or perhaps it's not really so astonishing. Casimir must know Aurore is slipping through his fingers; after all, they no longer sleep together, and she has made no secret of her unhappiness. Although theirs is no May–December marriage, the age gap of nearly a decade probably appears enormous to the young wife. Certainly, both partners treat her as very much the younger spouse, almost childlike in her need to be looked after by her husband. At any rate, this is how she spins it.

'You who are so good to me, so tender, you who desire my happiness, who were ready to sacrifice yours, to take me to Bordeaux, to leave me free with Aurélien,' she writes to Casimir.[27] Is she really as manipulative as she seems here, running rings round a spouse who is, she's disappointingly realised, much stupider than herself? By the autumn of 1825 Casimir seems to have accepted and internalised her unhappiness, as so many married men and women must do in this era when divorce remains vanishingly rare. Possibly he's already come to realise that he could have a better time with other women himself. Why not, then, keep the peace by all possible means, so that the social and economic structure of the marriage into which he's sunk much of his inheritance can continue intact, even if emptied of romantic meaning? Either way, he seems to accept every sign of infidelity (however ardently denied), and in doing so lets the de Sèze affair play out.

Ten years from now Aurore will tell Zoé that 'Bordeaux was my crossing of the Berezina.'[28] The Battle of Berezina, a river crossing east of Minsk, famously sealed Napoléon's retreat from Moscow when Aurore was a child of eight. Her affair with Aurélien de Sèze, in other words, is a kind of surrender of her marriage. Or perhaps of the kind of person she had wanted to be. She floats through the rest of the autumn of 1825 at Guillery, unable to recommit to Casimir. In another piece of virtue signalling, she and Aurélien have agreed not to write to each other. But she starts a secret notebook of what will eventually total twenty-two 'letters' addressed to her lover.

She may not quite intend to send them: for the first time, she is writing to an ideal, rather than a literal, reader. But in fact they are first read by Casimir, who stumbles upon the notebook when she's completed sixteen of them. Who knows how he manages to find something supposedly so secret. And who knows whether, consciously or unconsciously, she was in fact laying out the real state of her heart and of their marriage for her husband. Either way, his response is again exemplary. He finds the journal on a day when he's leaving for Nohant to spend three weeks there managing their estate. In the following days, isolated at the manor in Indre, he sends his wife two long, self-flagellating letters of abnegation.[29] If hers confess longing and dissatisfaction, his are another kind of confession: a *mea culpa* that feels as if shamed out of him. 'I wanted to take my pleasure selfishly,' he writes, promising once again that there will be no more sex. 'I love you [. . .] with a calmness, a sweetness which desire does not permit. I love you like the most cherished of sisters.'

But Aurore isn't listening. Instead, she profits from Casimir's absence to pour out six more addresses to her lover in her journal, which she then posts off to Aurélien himself. She's been parrying her husband's importuning with conventional missives sending 'news of your little wife, your big Maurice' to 'my dear, my friend', 'my good friend'; their subdued formality throws into relief the trembling intensity of the 'letters' journal.[30] Now at last, on 15 November, she gives Casimir an answer: one that is over 8,000 words long and more essay than correspondence.[31] After reviewing their married life and what Aurélien represents to her, she outlines a set of 'Articles' she wishes Casimir to comply with.

In themselves, these Articles are surprisingly sensible. They include ways to stop arguing, an agreement that Aurore may continue to write to Zoé and Aurélien but never again in secret, and a promise from Casimir that he'll try to educate himself. What's shocking is that Aurore is prepared to use emotional blackmail to force them through. She frames the couple's happiness as entirely in Casimir's gift: 'I will await your decision with anxiety. If you accept [my plan] I can be perfectly happy.' But, she adds, 'If you [cannot] I'll keep silent but I will suffer and not recover. All these projects of trust, of intimacy, of the coming together of ideas, of matching feelings, [. . .] will no longer be able to exist between you and me.'[32]

The idealistic belief she expounded to Émilie de Wismes less than two years ago, 'that one of the two, on marrying, must renounce themselves entirely, and abnegate not only their will but their opinion, decide to see with the eyes of the other, to love what they love', has been turned completely around. No more 'omnipotence' from 'the side with the beard'. Now it's Aurore who has the power, and it's to her 'will' and 'opinion' that Casimir must acquiesce. Her trump card, that she *is* no longer 'persuaded that it is *absolutely impossible* to meet a person whose mood and tastes in everything are exactly the same as one's own', forces the hand of the husband who still wants their marriage to continue. This is graceless stuff; perhaps only excusable if we remember that the twenty-one-year-old believes she's fighting for her last chance of a tolerable life.

For a while it seems to work, and the marriage continues. When her father-in-law dies the following February, the true state of the Dudevant finances, sans further inheritance, are revealed. By April 1826, after yet more sorties to Bordeaux, she and Casimir are back at Nohant. At last there seems to be enough on the manor's doorstep to assuage Aurore's restlessness. As a wife, she no longer has to be chaperoned when she rides out on Fairy, the fine new mare Casimir has bought her. She resumes country routines she first developed while her grandmother was alive: gardening, and prescribing herbal remedies to local country people. And – perhaps to her surprise – she finds at La Châtre a community of young would-be intellectuals with whom she can make friends.

It's Hippolyte who, though no serious thinker himself, introduces her to this group, which includes François-Charles Delavau, with whom she takes up apothecary studies, and Alexis Pouradier-Duteil, a married lawyer who will end his career as Procurator General at Bourges. For now Pouradier-Duteil is throwing his unused brilliance into social exploits with other friends including 'the Madagascan', Jules Néraud, a married naturalist nicknamed for the East African island he visited some years ago.[33] Like clever young provincials everywhere, their circle bonds as much through a shared repudiation of local norms – dullness and mediocrity are equal crimes – as through the rapidly changing new philosophical and scientific ideas they're acquiring and exploring.

The combination of intellectual exploration with social resistance is a heady one, and Aurore is ripe for it. Making a gesture towards fitting in, when she joins the friends in the bars, cafés and homes where they meet to talk and argue she adopts her old riding costume of men's clothes. It's no disguise, of course; but nor is it intended as a fetish. On the contrary, it's a way to sidestep how conventional women's clothes would fetishise her gender. In 1826 necklines are demure, but high Empire waistlines still bracket breasts as if for presentation. Voluminous leg-o'-mutton – *gigot* – sleeves trammel the arm movements so essential to getting about on horseback. To say nothing of the nuisance of long skirts.[34] Besides, even with only the simplest of decorations – a pleat, a single ribbon – colourful dress fabric stands out against the brown study of the men's clothes, tobacco smoke, leather book bindings. And Aurore, an habitual chameleon, wants nothing more than to be inconspicuous.

There's an idealistic ardour about her engagement with this group, who may be affluent but each have something of the organic intellectual – the autodidact – about them. In nineteenth-century France, provincial transmission of ideas and culture is haphazard. Berry lies in the heart of the underdeveloped 'desert of France', far from the great universities of Europe. For as long as they remain in La Châtre, these young men are beyond the reach of cutting-edge thought, the kinds of public lectures by leading thinkers that are fashionable in London or Paris. They must pick up what they can from books that happen to come their way. Nothing about doing this is automatic; keeping up with contemporary ideas requires both commitment and discernment.

It's a shame that Aurore can't sustain quite this level of abstract engagement herself. Perhaps inevitably, she finds someone to represent it for her instead. Towards the end of summer an old friend, home from Paris for a period of rest and recuperation, joins the circle. Stéphane Ajasson de Grandsagne is the medical student Deschartres employed to teach Aurore anatomy during those long months of late adolescence when her life, as now, appeared to be on hold. It was their alleged intimacy that resulted in those accusations from Sophie-Victoire that she so passionately rebutted.[35] Five years older and no longer innocent, Aurore is now all too able to conceive of what was then inconceivable. By October she's writing to Zoé full of romantic 'spleen' and descriptions of this new-old 'friend who is all that a friend can be without inspiring love'.[36] He becomes a Romantic trope: 'a bit consumptive, a bit mad' with 'his hollow cheeks, his wandering eyes, his hunched figure'.

It's risky to write in these terms, and maybe Aurore is actually even more indiscreet, for the letter will survive only in fragmented form, as if it has been expurgated. Though what remains is plenty to make us squirm with embarrassment for her. She recollects herself in a postscript – 'When you write back, don't say anything about these stupid things I tell you. It's a great consolation for me that no one of mine suspects this or has reason to worry for me' – but doesn't seem to realise how inappropriate it is to confide in Zoé, close mutual friend of her *current* lover, about this. As for Aurélien himself, who has recently been complaining about her silence, 'Nothing seems to stop me writing and yet . . . ,' Aurore informs their go-between. 'Tell him that I'm going well, and that I'm not at all negligent, but sad.' Such a casual dismissal of the lover Zoé introduced her to would be bad enough. Worse, it's only in a penultimate paragraph, after eight pages of self-absorption, that Aurore proffers two brief sentences of condolence for Zoé's loss of an infant nephew 'in your arms'. 'I am united with you in your grief,' she notes. Well: perhaps.

So Zoé doesn't respond till the end of December.[37] Aurore's next surviving letter, dated 3 March 1827, continues in similar vein. She complains that she hasn't heard from her friend despite writing 'two months ago [...] I blame this cursed post.' It's an excuse we've all used when we owe a letter we can't face, but if Aurore did indeed respond to Zoé in January then her stay in Paris that month – which she rushes on to relate – is just when a letter from her friend, arriving at Nohant in her absence, could be expected to go astray. Casimir, staying behind at the manor with Maurice and Maurice's nursemaid Angel, might have felt perfectly entitled to open Bordeaux correspondence, in accord with Aurore's own Articles.

The tangle matters because of the light it sheds – or doesn't – on this somewhat mysterious visit to the capital at the start of 1827. Aurore tells Zoé she met up with a young cousin, old school friends and the sisters at the Dames Augustines Anglaises: 'Thank Heaven I was received with an outpouring of joy that I dared not hope for while wanting it like crazy.' She adds that these were surprise visits rather than planned ahead, and that during the trip she also 'experienced a deep grief [...] But there are things I no longer dare commit to paper.'[38] All of which, along with several rips in the letter which seem to excise a name, suggest something is the matter concerning a lover, presumably Aurélien.

Zoé's response appears to confirm this. 'You're surprised by Aurélien's silence,' she replies just five days later, before passing along excuses: his recently widowed sister has moved to Bordeaux, at work he is preparing to order executions. Neither circumstance would truly prevent a young man from mailing at least a scribbled line to a great love, particularly if she's in trouble – 'deep grief' – of some kind. But is that really what Aurore and Aurélien still are for each other? Even the letter to Zoé seems like a sort of act. If Aurore were really showing her correspondence to Casimir as promised, what could he possibly make of her confidence that there's something she can't confide, or of those later excised names? Or if mailing clandestinely, why not confide?

All the same, Aurore mentions 'very bitter tears the source of which I'd believed had dried up', which sounds genuinely like something coming to the surface: a child's experience of rejection, for example. If her relationship with Aurélien is in fact ending, she may find herself thrown back on the litany of her early losses: the deaths of Auguste and of her father, her mother's uncertain affection, her grandmother's often withheld approval and long dying; losses of the convent community, of close contact with Caroline and uninhibited friendship with Hippolyte, and of the marriage she hoped for with Casimir. But the young mistress of Nohant has a by now characteristic remedy for such feelings: finding affection elsewhere. During 1827, Stéphane de Grandsagne begins to occupy more of her attention. He returns to Paris – falls ill again – comes back to La Châtre to recuperate – and returns to the capital once more. And at the end of the year Aurore, chaperoned by his brother Jules, takes a trip to Paris herself.

This is not something spur-of-the-moment. Aurore must make sure she has care for her four-year-old son in place before she can leave home and, as she knows all too well, Paris is not next door to Nohant. She departs from the manor on 2 December but doesn't arrive in the capital till 5 December, when she checks into the same suite of rooms at the Hôtel de Florence in which she stayed for Maurice's birth. Jules de Grandsagne reserves more modest accommodation on the top floor. Aurore has told Casimir that she's feeling poorly again, and wants to consult Parisian doctors. Strangely, despite Stéphane de Grandsagne's medical background, these appointments seem hard to secure. When they do come, however, they are reassuring – as she reports home.

Perhaps she feels bonnier in the lively, smart city she loves. Hippolyte, who is fond of Stéphane and has kept in touch with him during the year, is around. She's fending off the ridiculous love letters which Jules 'the Madagascan' Néraud is sending her from La Châtre: little is more guaranteed to make one feel desirable than being desired, never mind by whom. Altogether, enough fun is being had for her to delay her departure from the rue Neuve des Mathurins. Her letters home start to thin, until on 15 December she writes to Casimir that she may need to have her tonsils removed. She will make a return trip to Paris if so, because she doesn't want to spend eight days convalescing before she can set out for Christmas at Nohant.[39]

It's unclear what's going on here. It would be reasonable to be alarmed at the prospect of such an operation without either anaesthetic or antibiotics. But it might be rather nice to have the excuse for another trip to Paris up her sleeve. Aurore could be creating an entirely fictitious alibi, or tonsils may be a euphemism, perhaps for something more gynaecological. In any case she sends home a sequence of announcements that she's about to leave, without actually doing so: on first 17, then 18, then 19 December. Finally, travelling with at least one of the de Grandsagne brothers, she arrives home on 21 December.[40] Almost nine months later, on 13 September 1828, she gives birth to a daughter. She names the baby Solange, after the shepherdess patron saint of Berry: a mysteriously un-aristocratic, rural peasant name.

In the future, this interval will be widely assumed to show that Solange was conceived in Paris, and that her father is Stéphane de Grandsagne. Aurore herself will insist the baby is premature – something future biographers, eager to smell a rat, will poohpooh. So what *is* really going on? Whoever is the little girl's father, unless she was conceived by 9 December (1828 is a leap year), she does indeed arrive early. The evidence doesn't suggest Aurore is in the throes of a sexual affair during her first week in the city, when she's writing long letters home every other day.[41]

But after 12 December there's a gap, and a shift in tone. If something happens, perhaps it's now, in the days when her return to Nohant keeps getting postponed. In this era before incubators, prematurity is likely only a matter of days. A baby conceived on 13 December, when Aurore's correspondence first slows, will be only four days premature if she arrives on Solange's birthday; if conceived in the hurly-burly of a Christmas homecoming, for example on 21 December, twelve days premature: still realistically possible. Casimir will so firmly believe the little girl is his that in the future he will try to force custody of her. Which would be unlikely if the Dudevants had absolutely no sex around the time of her conception.

When it comes to it, Aurore will allow Hippolyte to indulge in rumbustious celebrations of the birth of her second child as a triumph for her marriage. And after all, even exes do sometimes tumble into sex, and the Dudevants aren't yet separated, just a couple who don't share a bed, or who do so only rarely. Later, Aurore will claim that it's only during her second pregnancy that her 'secret antipathy [. . .] led to a complete separation of bodies'. Though of course, however problematic the marriage, she would say that, since she wants to offer Solange a narrative of legitimacy.[42] Perhaps Aurore rushed to sleep with Casimir on her return from Paris in order to cover her sexual tracks: knowing, for example, that she'd taken no contraceptive measures.[43]

But if she really was ready for fresh romantic adventure in Paris in December 1827, could Aurore have had a dalliance with anyone other than Stéphane de Grandsagne? We know little about her feelings for his brother Jules, but we do know he lodges in the same hotel as her, and that she doesn't want to travel home without him. And there is Hippolyte, the man in whose image she chose a husband. Of course this would be the most scandalous liaison of all; and in the absence of proof can never be more than futile speculation. Besides, there's something attractively tenacious and rather modern about their sibling alliance, which it would be a shame to lose to a fantasy of incest.[44]

But it's Hippolyte who supplies our one clue to what's been going on. In March 1828, when his half-sister is around three months pregnant, he writes her a curious note: 'My dear friend, so you are still pregnant? And it's for good [*pour de bon*] this time. I think like Doctor Charles that this child will take it all away.'[45] 'For good this time' seems to suggest a pregnancy scare or alternatively a miscarriage, especially as he writes just as she's leaving behind the miscarriage danger zone of the first trimester.[46] And what can pregnancy 'take away'? Infidelities, failures in a marriage? Depression: those 'very bitter tears' Aurore shed during her previous stay in Paris? If the latter, what might have caused those tears – a lovers' quarrel? In French, as in English, 'for good' means both 'without being cut short' and 'it's a good thing'; this too seems to suggest a lost pregnancy, whether accidental or aborted. In an era when the chief method of contraception is coitus interruptus, yet access to education means national birth rates are falling against the trend of the rest of Europe, abortion is a widely acknowledged resort in France. So widely acknowledged is it, indeed, that it has precipitated the rise of foundling institutions as an alternative to abortion for unwanted pregnancies. Aurore can't realistically have conceived Solange within a week of having an abortion, so it's unlikely that was the reason she came to Paris this December. But could she have had one last January? And if so what – or rather whom – would she have been tidying up after?

It's depressing to find oneself rummaging around like this in a great writer's reproductive system: would we do the same if she were a man, who could set aside considerations of pregnancy, childbirth and childcare? But the future George Sand's literary legacy will be framed repeatedly by speculation about her private life, and willy-nilly it's in these months in 1827 that she embarks on her notorious career as a sexual polymath. Aurore is not turning out to be who she thought she was: she is no longer Mother Spiring's morally conscientious protégée, the role model for younger convent schoolgirls. Her relationship with Aurélien had been, she believed, a love so profound that it trumped mere moral convention. (She even, disingenuously, made this argument for the affair to Casimir.) But now she's interested in Stéphane, and one can't have two loves who are both transcendent signifiers.[47]

Perhaps predictably, during her second pregnancy she's unhappy again. She finally realises what a bad friend she's been to Zoé and in February, full of hormonal feeling, writes an abject letter of apology.[48] Things with Aurélien are going even worse. He's losing faith in someone he has to prompt to write even when Zoé loses her father.[49] In February he advises, 'Resign yourself to living [. . .] write [to me] only a little.'[50] By May, he's refusing to be drawn by his lover's insomniac reflections on human nature.[51] Still, in the autumn he pays a visit to Nohant. Indeed, both he and Hippolyte are at the house when Solange is born, which really does suggest the baby girl has arrived earlier than her mother was expecting. Even in the most spacious of manor houses, one might not want a sometime lover around while giving birth to another man's child.

Eighteen twenty-nine grinds on, and with it the Dudevant marriage. Casimir has an affair with his daughter's Spanish nursemaid Pepita. In May Aurore accompanies him on a business trip to Bordeaux, where she spends nine weeks throwing herself at Aurélien until husband and lover join forces and persuade her to avoid scandal by returning to Nohant. More farcical episodes follow. Hippolyte, whose wife Émilie and six-year-old daughter Marie-Léontine are also staying at the manor, replaces Casimir as

Pepita's lover. Aurore goes again to Bordeaux and to Paris. Casimir is swindled into investing in a fictional merchant ship, the *Jeune Caroline*. Finally, in May 1830, Aurore makes a dash from Paris to Bordeaux only to find that Aurélien, mourning his father, is definitively no longer available to her.

This is not a passage which covers Aurore in glory. But through its frantic casting about she's coming closer to finding what she's looking for. And in her private dressing room at the manor she is beginning to write. First she tries to shape a travelogue from a trip she and Casimir made to the Auvergne in 1826. Next she works up some short stories, which she sends around to friends to read. But events overtake both these ventures. Life is becoming messy in the public as well as the private sphere, and a storm is about to break.

Eighteen thirty is an exceptionally hot summer; tempers, perhaps, are ready to fray. France's Bourbon monarchy, which was restored after 1814, has been drifting increasingly away from Revolutionary principles under the elderly and reactionary Charles X. Now, at the height of summer, he issues the Saint-Cloud Ordinances, which ban merchants and bankers, the newly emerging bourgeoisie that is becoming France's financial powerhouse, from joining the Chamber of Deputies: that is, the parliament. Their response is to shutter the Bourse, the nation's stock exchange, causing many factories to close overnight. Forced on to the streets, factory workers become a protest mob ready for action. To prevent reportage that might amplify the situation, officialdom compels newspapers to close. The inevitable rioting starts in Paris on the evening of 27 July anyway. By the afternoon of 29 July, the rioters have become revolutionaries and have occupied most buildings of national significance, including the Hôtel de Ville and the Tuileries Palace. These Three Glorious Days, *Les Trois Glorieuses*, lead to the abdication of Charles X on 2 August and the establishment of a constitutional monarchy. Copycat revolutions ripple across Europe, creating the Belgian state and founding a constitutional monarchy in Brunswick – though they fail in Italy and Poland.

Sequestered in Berry, though, it's hard to know exactly what's going on. Aurore's reaction – part anguish, part excitement – is captured in a letter she sends Maurice's tutor Jules Boucoiran. This newly significant figure in Dudevant family life is on a trip to Paris and gets caught up at the centre of events. But even deep in the countryside it's clear that seismic change of some kind has occurred. On 30 July, itching for news and talk, Aurore rides the twenty-five miles to Château du Coudray, summer home of Charles Duvernet, a progressive political thinker and writer from the La Châtre circle. Unsurprisingly, a group have already gathered at this tall, recently remodelled country house near the village of Verneuil-sur-Igneraie to talk over what they know about unfolding events. Among them is a fair-haired stranger, Jules Sandeau, who sits in the garden reading under a pear tree.

'The garden at Coudray is for us [. . .] the point of convergence, where our two planets aligned,' Aurore will later tell a mutual friend.[52] For unlike Aurélien, that doubly unavailable married man and leading citizen of Bordeaux, Léonard Sylvain Julien Sandeau is interested in a real relationship. Not that this nineteen-year-old law student, seven years Aurore's junior, is otherwise more suitable, or indeed better-looking, than his predecessor. His sandy hair will soon be lost to male-pattern baldness. He's comfortably round-faced, with the milky complexion of neighbouring Creuse, where he was raised in that tapestry-weaving capital, Aubusson. But what Sandeau shares with Aurore is discomfort with his current role – and the desire to become a writer.

She's just turned twenty-six, and the fourteen weeks of summer romance that follow this 'alignment of the planets' will lead her into a whole new way of life. So it can scarcely be inconvenient to 'discover' at this juncture that her husband does not after all respect her, as she had somehow assumed, but is out for furious revenge. In November, shortly after Sandeau has gone back to his studies in Paris, she stumbles upon Casimir's will and, she tells Jules Boucoiran:

> God alive! What a testament! Curses and everything! He had assembled there all his moods and anger against me, all his reflections on my *perversity* [...] Reading this at last ripped me from my dream. [...] My part has been done promptly and I dare to say *irrevocably* [...] without waiting another day. [...] *I want an allowance and I will go to Paris permanently, and my children will remain at Nohant.* [...] But in fact I expect to spend part of the year, six months at least, at Nohant near my children.[53]

As Maurice's tutor, Boucoiran is himself the safety net that will permit this leap. Ironically, although Aurore is in the habit of addressing him as 'my dear child', he's three years older than her lover, and evidently sensible enough to be trusted with practical as well as emotional matters.[54] His responsibilities now expand from simple teaching to the pastoral care of a beloved child. For, Aurore's letter goes on to explain, she doesn't feel that Maurice, at seven, is strong enough yet for the health risks of city life. This may be convenient for her personal freedom, but it's also realistic. Urban mortality is driven not only by poverty but by epidemics of cholera and typhoid, and infectious diseases from measles to tuberculosis, none of which respect class privilege in the capital's overcrowded, unhygienic streets.

So it is that 7 January 1831 sees Aurore writing to Maurice, 'My dear child, I have arrived in Paris. [...] work well with your father [. . .] and don't go outdoors without your boots.' She's mailing her young son not at Nohant itself but *poste restante* to La Châtre, because she worries that otherwise his father may not let her letters through to him.[55] The address she gives for herself is his uncle Hippolyte's apartment at 31 rue de Seine, where she will officially reside for the next three months.

Later in January, however, she sends a cheerful report to that inadvertent matchmaker, her La Châtre friend Charles Duvernet. It's written in the first-person plural, as if she speaks for all the members of their circle who have returned to the capital after the summer. But the real identity of 'we' soon becomes apparent:

> I've decided that I will associate [Sandeau] with my work, or myself with his [. . .] so much so that he lends me his name, because I don't want to appear, and that I lend him my help when he needs it. Keep the secret of this *literary association* for us. (Truly! I have a delicious turn of phrase.)[56]

The lovers are cohabiting: *literary association* is Aurore's 'delicious' euphemism for this. They have also, she goes on to tell their mutual friend, already placed a co-authored piece in the *Revue de Paris*, where, she can't resist gossiping, 'M. Véron, the editor in chief [. . .] hates women and does not want to hear about them. He has scrofula.' Aurore Dudevant has been in Paris less than a fortnight, but she's already immersed in the literary and sexual life that will be the making of her.

Fourth impression: *Costume drama*

You'd be hard put to call it a feminist image exactly. In this illustration for a gossip column printed sometime in 1831–2, Sand is on the protective, even chivalrous arm of a man, but she's also dressed in men's clothes. She carries them off well, with a swaggering cane, and shiny toes under trouser cuffs that fall just so (they must be tailored, not borrowed). The skirt of her frock coat flares cutely and she appears to have been buttoned into some sort of wasp-waist corset, even if the artist has exaggerated this line a little.

Actually Paul Gavarni, who executes this image, probably isn't exaggerating very much. He's certainly got the writer's sloping shoulders right. And the wasp waist will feature in all her future portraits until it suddenly vanishes, in photographs taken by Pierre Ambroise Richebourg, in 1852. Then all at once she'll turn into a little dumpling, the sort of woman who may not quite have got her figure back after having kids. And the voluminous frocks of her matronhood may conceal other discomforts: distension, flatulence. For in the last years of her life she will be troubled by terrible digestion and chronic bowel problems set off by a bout of grave illness, diagnosed as typhoid fever and gall-bladder disease, in the autumn of 1860.

A lifetime of excessively tight corsets can't be good for any of this. But here, near the start of her time in literary Paris, the new literary star is young and slim, and expects to stay that way forever. She carries herself with a confidence that perhaps makes her some sort of match for the artist: Gavarni is rakishly good-looking and just a few months older than his subject. He too has arrived from the French provinces to break into artistic, intellectual Paris at a slightly older age than usual; he too is just starting out. This engraving is among the first of his soon-to-be famous sketches of metropolitan mores.

If there is anything feminist to be found in the scene he's composed, it's the boldness with which Sand strolls through the dress circle of a theatre. She's the only woman here, and men turn to look at her. It doesn't do to imagine what they're thinking. But perhaps she knows anyway, thanks to years of living with Hippolyte and Casimir – neither of them models of politesse and restraint. When I look at this picture – in which, with her hair curling from under the brim of her top hat, she is clearly not pretending actually to *be* a man – I see again in her costume not the sexual fetishisation of her body that's usually assumed by those around her (and those who will come after), but her refusal of that fetishisation. *Count me out*, announce the smart tailoring, the neatly crossed black silk bandana. *I'm not playing your game.*

Which is not to say that this early incarnation of Sand is, as a future cartoon will have it, sexless:

> If this portrait of George Sand
> Leaves the mind a bit perplexed
> It's because genius is abstract and
> As we know has no sex.[57]

The rhyme comes from a caricature which Alcide-Joseph Lorentz will publish in 1842 (after he's benefited from an early commission to provide the frontispiece for one of his target's first books). He will title it 'Comedy Mirror', and it does indeed fail accurately to reflect George Sand, by then fully grown into her famous pseudonym. She does not lack a sex. The clothes she wears are just one of the ways in which a woman choosing to play by her own rules can appear.

Sand will already have said as much herself in May 1835, in a letter to the Saint-Simonist Adolphe Guéroult. As a representative of that movement in political economy which gainsays traditional social forms – instead seeing a world divided into parasitic 'idlers' and 'industrial' workers of all kinds, including writers – he has been fishing for closer collaboration with someone he understands as a fellow utopian and social revolutionary. At the same time (gender being as usual the protected exception) he's criticised her temerity in wearing men's clothes. But, she explains in her response, it's precisely men's privileges, not their identity, that she wishes to assume:

> If I were a boy, I would willingly make a stroke with a sword here or there, and letters the rest of the time. Not being a boy, I do without the sword and keep the pen [. . .] and my friends will respect me, I hope, just as much under my jacket as under my dress. [. . .] Be reassured, I don't aspire to the dignity of man. It seems to me too laughable to be much preferable to the servility of woman. But I claim to possess, today and forever, the superb and complete independence which you alone believe you have the right to enjoy. [. . .] So take me for a man or a woman as you wish.[58]

FIVE

Becoming a writer

MOST OF THE CEASELESSLY BRANCHING alternatives and decisions that make up a life evade reconstruction. Only occasionally does a wholly visible, undeniable step change occur. Aurore Dudevant's move to Paris in 1831 is one of these, even though it ushers in a period of alternating between the capital and Nohant. Her new life couldn't be more different from the role of country chatelaine she aspired to just a few years ago. In the future, she will call the period from 1831 to 1838 her 'Romantic Rebellion', and it would be easy to read her behaviour during these years simply as someone let off the leash. With its explosion of parties, outrage, sexual and creative energy it will fit her pretty much into the male fantasy of an ex-convent girl, and it is chaotic, risky stuff. She's going to have lots of sex in an era when both venereal disease and pregnancy can prove fatal.

But she's also going to embark on this and any number of other applecart-upsetting behaviours – such as gaining a divorce and winning a custody battle – while becoming a writer. In rebellion Aurore will, in no particular order, remain alive and healthy, create a stellar literary career, be fully accepted in male-dominated literary circles, gain the care of her kids – and even win back Nohant in her eventual divorce settlement. Only not all at once. There's a lot to live through first. For, whether or not she knows it at the start of 1831, the transition this country gentlewoman has chosen to make isn't a simple matter of just walking out of the marital home and into a bohemian love nest on the banks of the Seine. She may so far have seemed to those around her largely a creature of whim, but she's going to need stamina and willpower to make a success of her new life in Paris.

It starts with the Left Bank address where Aurore bases herself for an initial three months before her first planned visit home. This fourth-floor apartment at 31 rue de Seine belongs to Hippolyte, though he doesn't live there himself. The rue de Seine debouches into the waterside quai Malaquais, where Aurore will return to live a couple of years from now: presumably she enjoys this riverine district of the Rive Gauche, close to the Sorbonne.[1] But number 31 offers her more than its attractively bohemian neighbourhood, redolent with student life. So long as she stays here she is in a sense still living under the family roof; something that may also reassure Hippolyte, who is finding his sister's accelerating waywardness increasingly problematic.

It may also be reassuring for her family, and to Aurore herself, that she's committed to spending half of every year with the children in Nohant. This move to the capital is no impetuous flit, but an arrangement that has been carefully thought through. Ironically, she herself also has property inherited from her grandmother in Paris, but it's let out; the rent, together with income from the Nohant estate, provides much of what she and her estranged husband are living on. And she understands how badly they need this money, for she's on top of the finances too. With a pragmatism worthy of her Dupin forebears, she has contacted the family's Paris-based financial manager, Achille Salmon, in order to follow up for the first time the annual allowance which was in her marriage settlement, and which Casimir has never paid. Now she needs this money to live on – and to break the very financial dependency he has used to coerce her.

Aurore must thank the stars for her mother's success in procuring the unusually generous terms of the Dudevant pre-nuptial settlement. But she is following Sophie-Victoire's lead in another way, too. Despite her formative childhood experiences of abandonment, she's left her own children behind in the Indre countryside. The assumption is that, at just two and a quarter, Solange is too young to notice her mother's absence. In 1831, toddlers aren't generally believed to have much capacity even for feeling and, as is customary for children from a relatively wealthy background, the little girl has always been left for long periods in the care of nursemaids – including the alluring Pepita. This will prove to have been a terrible mistake. Solange will turn out to be no different from any twenty-first-century child in being damaged by such early separation from her mother, and for the rest of their lives this relationship will be strained.

But Maurice is another matter. Aged seven and a half, and like so many sons his mummy's boy, he becomes desperate at her departure. Aurore has had to bribe him with the promise of a complete miniature military uniform, and vow to come home soon: she will keep punctually to the agreed date of her return. All the same, two months into her stay in Paris she receives a letter from his uncle Hippolyte that is, she confides to his tutor Jules Boucoiran, 'sour to the point of bitterness' and that concludes: 'The thing you have done best is your son; he loves you more than anybody in the world. Be careful not to blunt that feeling.'[2] Which rather begs the question of Solange. Of course, she's at a double disadvantage as a girl, and the second child; but is Hippolyte, as he witnesses her parents' disintegrating marriage, also beginning to have suspicions about her paternity?

That 'the thing you have done best is your son', though, is the eternal reproof to women who try to do other things as well. Aurore was similarly reproved by Mother Spiring during her convent retreat in 1825, and she's shortly to be admonished in almost identical terms by the Parisian literary establishment. One can only hope it's pure coincidence that Hippolyte sends his letter within three days of her confiding to Boucoiran, who is of course at Nohant with Casimir, that 'I feel that my existence going forwards is fulfilled. I have a goal, a task, let's say the word, *a passion*. The métier of writing is one that is violent and almost indestructible, once it's seized some poor head, it can no longer be stopped.'[3] Whether or not the men of her former household do confer, Aurore has little option but to continue to trust Boucoiran, as Maurice's tutor, with the version of herself she wishes her young son to have. This letter, for example, opened: 'I only live for what concerns Maurice [. . .] so love him, my poor little one, don't spoil him and yet make him happy. You have what's needed to teach him without making him miserable, with firmness and with gentleness.'

Much is being stirred up by her move to the capital. For Hippolyte, separated from his own biological mother at birth, family separation must always be anxiety-producing, whether he realises it or not. (His foster status at the Big House casts a different, more anxious light on his earlier excessive amenability to his privileged half-sister.) Aurore's own heart had been broken by her father's death and her mother's absences by the time she was Maurice's age, so she understands very well what her little son is feeling. But the same personal history normalises parental absences; she may even rationalise that her own plan reliably to alternate three months in Paris with three in Indre will offer her children a comforting stability, unlike Sophie-Victoire's ad hoc visits to Nohant.

Aurore doesn't, in other words, see herself as someone who has abandoned her children. She does, though, know she has acquired a reputation as a 'female Don Juan', and is furious about it. To Boucoiran she denounces one of her accusers: 'Do you know that this woman adopts a half-joking half-serious tone to take me for a female *Don Juan*, formed in her own image, with a dose of boldness and more in the character?'[4] Which ignores the extent to which she is indeed 'formed in her [...] image', since 'this woman', now Mme Goüdain Saint-Agnan, is the same aunt Lucie who shared Sophie-Victoire's early life as a chorus girl. But the rumour, or something like it, reaches Hippolyte anyway and, evidently deciding he doesn't want to enable, or to be seen to enable, any sexual adventuring, he asks his sister to leave his property by the middle of March. Which effectively forces her to move in with her lover.

Jules Sandeau lives just 500 yards away, at 21 rue des Grands-Augustins.[5] Despite its proximity this is, in the way of cities, a whole different milieu; street and buildings alike are on a smaller scale than rue de Seine. But the district is not unrespectable. The future lexicographer Émile Littré, who will become revered as the author of the great *Dictionnaire de la langue française* (*Dictionary of the French Language*) known as *le Littré*, was born in this house in 1801. Four years ago, when his father, an ex-military tax inspector, died, Littré was forced to abandon medical studies. He's now working as a copywriter for the political daily *Le National*, under the charismatic Armand Carrel. Both Carrel and Littré, who will eventually succeed his mentor as editor, are intellectually gifted and fiercely democratic. Both fought on the populist Republican side in recent years. Littré and his widowed mother appear to be still living at number 21, perhaps as something in the nature of concierge or landlord, when Aurore moves in with Jules on the top floor.

A more bracing new context for her 'violent' 'métier' of writing is hard to imagine. The world of *Le National* couldn't be further from the ladylike noodling women of her class and era customarily settle for. In the first half of the nineteenth century writing a journal or reading poetry, like tapestry-work or sketching, enriches the existence of women who live in material comfort but lack freedom and outlet. But as Aurore sets out on her independent life in Paris, she reminds us that possibly the most difficult step in becoming a published writer isn't what you do with the blank page. It's what you do with the filled one. In 1831, to write professionally is to *participate* in political and civil society – and such participation is almost entirely a male preserve.

Five years from now, Armand Carrel will pay with his life for editing what will by then be the leading pro-democratic periodical of the day. His editorial line causes him to be insulted frequently in print, forcing him to fight a series of duels with the editors who publish these insults. His final duel will kill him at the age of just thirty-six. But in 1831, a twenty-six-year-old Aurore is still young enough to be excited by these high stakes for literature; as well as just old enough to have a sense of urgency about her own participation. A person's mid-twenties can be that tipping point when time passing begins to measure not progress but the stalling of some original trajectory. For young women in nineteenth-century France, confined almost entirely to gendered roles, fierce surveillance of their appearance can mean this is when even the small power which looks gave them starts to diminish. And Aurore is willy-nilly a woman. As, a month after her arrival in Paris, the elderly but influential gothic novelist M. Kératry will remind her, in terms which grimly echo Hippolyte's.

She's visiting the novelist, whose real name is Auguste-Hilarion and who is no mere Monsieur but the Comte de Kératry, at his home at eight in the morning. It's a time and place he's presumably set in order that she may witness the young woman lying naked in bed *in the same room* in which he receives her – as if thus holding up a mirror to her own young womanhood. It's a goatish display of sexuality, not far off exposing himself. But, two centuries on, women writers will remain familiar with such behaviour, and how often it's the context in which their literary inferiority is expounded. Something Kératry now proceeds to do, telling Aurore, 'Don't make books, make children.' So it's impossible to repress a cheer when *Histoire* records her riposte, 'My goodness, Sir [. . .] follow the precept yourself, if it seems good to you'; even if it is no more than *esprit de l'escalier*.[6]

Older men are the gatekeepers of the literary world, though not all of them are as old as sixty-one-year-old Kératry.[7] Nor, luckily, are they all as unhelpful. Aurore has arrived in Paris armed with more than just ambition and a handful of manuscripts. She has some literary contacts through friends in the La Châtre circle. In particular Charles Duvernet's mother, an accomplished harpist, understands first-hand how a woman's participation in the arts is every bit as dependent as a man's on actually being given the opportunity. She writes a letter of introduction to her nephew Henri de Latouche, the forty-five-year-old La Châtre-born editor of *Le Figaro*.

Aurore also has access to de Latouche through another Berrichon friend, Félix Pyat, who is on the team at the magazine.[8] One way or the other, she secures an appointment with this important editor within days of arriving in Paris, and – as she reports to Charles Duvernet in her letter of thanks – manages to mind her manners when she meets him: 'In front of him I'm charming, I curtsey, I take small pinches of tobacco, I throw as little as possible on his beautiful white carpet, I do not put my elbows on my knees, I don't lie on the chairs, in short I am genteel, you've never seen me like it.'[9] At de Latouche's request, Aurore reads aloud a sentimental story, titled 'Aimée', which she has brought with her in manuscript. 'It's charming, but lacks the common touch,' he tells her: 'To which I replied, "Fair comment." That it must all be redone. To which I replied, "That's possible." That I would do well to start over. To which I replied, "Enough."'[10]

In fact what Aurore starts over is not this early fiction, which she wisely abandons, but her writing itself. De Latouche has seen in her something more than just another genre novelist. Almost immediately he gives her a column in his paper, at seven francs a piece.[11] This isn't as great a leap as it sounds. *Le Figaro* is only five years old, and is still the weekly satirical and literary review it will remain for its first four decades: closer, in other words, to an independent 'little magazine' than to the broadsheet newspaper of record it will become. De Latouche has the paper, which he's owned for just a year, pretty much in his pocket.

But he's hiring her on the basis of writing she's done jointly with Julian Sandeau. Her letter to Duvernet goes on to reveal her disingenuous – and ambitious – side:

> I didn't talk to M. Delatouche [*sic*] about Sandeau: his protection isn't easy to achieve, I've been told, and without your mother's recommendation I could have chased after it for a long time without success. So I was afraid he wouldn't want to extend it to two people, and I told him that the name Sandeau belonged to one of my compatriots who had been kind enough to lend it to me.

This at a time when the couple are in fact writing well together. Their first, '*unbelievable* article' accepted by *Revue de Paris* (not the future English-language *Paris Review* established in 1953 by George Plimpton et al.), another newish literary periodical less than two years old, was submitted under the name Jules Sandeau. They chose to do this partly because Sandeau wrote 'three-quarters of it' while Aurore was ill with a fever. Partly also because, as Aurore has already learnt, the *Revue*'s editor in chief, Désirée Véron, 'hates women and does not want to hear about them'.

In fact, this article will be rejected a couple of weeks after Aurore announces its success to Duvernet. But within the month she, or rather 'Jules Sandeau', has successfully placed a story titled 'La Prima Donna' in the *Revue*, and at the end of February Véron becomes Director of the Paris Opéra, leaving the magazine in the altogether less misogynistic editorial hands of Charles Rabou. It's all part of Aurore's luck in arriving in literary Paris at a time of exceptional excitement and opportunity. There's energy in breakage and change. 'Literature is in the same chaos as politics. [. . .] One wants novelty and to achieve it, one creates something hideous,' she writes to Boucoiran.[12]

Actually she's learning to write with elegance and wit. For to be a columnist on *Le Figaro* means to be a staffer; and to be a staffer means working at your desk in the salon of de Latouche's villa in Montmartre. This early cross between the open-plan newsroom and a *salonist*'s paradise is where the editor holds court in an armchair, throwing out commissions to staffers and keeping the ball of political wit in the air, while also hosting visitors with conversation that's necessarily public. It all knocks the earnest talk of La Châtre's small group of intellectuals into a Napoleonic cocked hat – as de Latouche, having once been one of them himself, must be delightedly aware. Like many a provincial who's made it to the cultural centre, he believes profoundly in the power of contemporary culture-making; what later generations will call the zeitgeist. Also like many such figures he exercises the highest standards, as if to compensate for some early naivety. Far too ambitious and successful a literary figure to endanger 'his' *Figaro* by publishing slack writing, he remembers where he came from and how; so he can recognise the raw material of his younger self in an emerging writer. In Aurore Dudevant he evidently spots much more than their shared Berrichon memories: perhaps the itch of gift, a hunger to succeed.

Soon, she's not only getting copy in the paper, but parroting the *Figaro* line on cultural fashion. She goes to performances most evenings: theatre, opera and concerts. In March, Ludwig van Beethoven's Ninth Symphony, with the great 'Ode to Joy' which a future European Union will adopt as its anthem, has its Paris premiere. She hears, and very probably reviews, the violin virtuoso Niccolò Paganini. 'When one wants to write one must see everything, know everything, laugh at everything. Ah! Long live the artist's life! Our motto is *freedom [liberté]*,' she tells Boucoiran, in the course of a correspondence which has by now become her equivalent of writing home.[13]

Back in the office, she's one of the 'garçons', and *Le Figaro* is 'a postulate that journalism must pass through'. It's here that she recognises how 'It's a big thing to make yourself useful and necessary in a literary office. It gets you everywhere, even without *camaraderie*, and without one's *personhood* appearing in the slightest.'[14] Far from flirting her way on to the staff, in other words, the key to literary professionalism is to renounce her own 'person' and the distraction of gender roles. Perhaps it's no coincidence that she now pays a final visit to the convent on rue des Fossés-Saint-Victor; as if to assure herself which of two tough vocations – being a writer or taking holy orders – is really hers.

Nuns renounce personhood in part with the uniform habits they wear. Another kind of uniform allows Aurore to immerse herself in this 'artist's life'. For all the 'freedom' that's supposed to entail, she is 'following some advice you gave me', she tells Boucoiran, and dressing as a man. For men can go about the city without being sexually harassed. They gain entry to places, such as the cheap seats at the Opéra, from which women are barred.

What's more, in these wintry first months of the year, dressing as a man is both practical and cosy. It means metal-heeled boots, thick coats with raised collars, and the inevitable top hat. Best of all, the fashion *du jour* is a full-length, unbelted military-style coat called a *redingote guérite*. A kind of tepee of fabric originally designed for sentry duty, it's like a cloak of invisibility in which even a young woman can move freely through the city's streets and buildings.

In just three months she has got the hang of copywriting, of the city and of the buzz of contemporary culture. It's an extraordinarily accelerated learning curve. But in early April, just as she's hitting her stride, she keeps her promise and returns to Nohant. The Paris experiment has been a resounding success. Now, sprung from her desk at *Le Figaro*, she needs to see whether she can also transform herself into that more mobile, independent and best of all distinguished figure, the novelist. She may be back in the provinces for the spring but, armed with newly acquired technique, her task this quarter is to get past 'Aimée' and measure up to her fiction-writing contemporaries in the capital.

And they are non-trivial figures. Eighteen thirty-one is the year of Victor Hugo's first novel, *Notre-Dame de Paris*; his sexy, scandalous play *Marion de Lorme* premieres at the Théâtre de la Porte Sainte-Martin. Honoré de Balzac – whose novella *Sarrasine*, exploring hermaphroditism, appeared last year – publishes *La Peau de chagrin* (*The Magic Skin*) and 'Les Proscrits', both to be grouped among the *Études philosophiques* of *La Comédie humaine*; as well as another influential short story, 'Le Chef-d'œuvre inconnu' ('The Unknown Masterpiece'). These are novels of ideas, many of them socio-political. The membrane between literature and current affairs has been thinned by repeated revolutionary violence, creating the kind of ferment which gives the lie to the belief W. H. Auden will famously state a century from now, in his exequy 'In Memoriam W. B. Yeats', that 'poetry makes nothing happen'. In 1831, everything that's happening is unavoidably close at hand, even for poets; and literature plays a part in current affairs. During this period of chaos and novelty, it is one of the ways in which France talks to itself about what's going on.

Such volatility and excitement make it less unusual that an emerging writer as determined as Aurore should already have placed a second short story, again co-written with Jules Sandeau, before she went back to Nohant. *La Moue* (*The Pout*) is yet another new periodical, its name a reminder of how little magazines have had a predilection for funky titles since the dawn of time. The story it takes, 'La Fille d'Albano', is signed 'J. S.' but has a storyline that is pure Aurorean wish fulfilment. The heroine's brother talks her out of marrying a French country gentleman – say, a Casimir – in order to pursue her own 'poetry [. . .] soul [. . .] genius'. Which reads like shaking Hippolyte by the shoulders.

A certain pattern has been established. Before the end of this year a novel, *Rose et Blanche*, will appear under the name 'J Sand'. The ever-supportive Henri de Latouche, by now in on the secret of Aurore's collaboration with Jules Sandeau, has suggested the writing couple adopt this middle-ground nom de plume. The book's publication in the middle of December – for the Christmas market, as it were – will be a fillip to their relationship. But the themes that crowd its five volumes – abuse faced by women and girls, what happens to women of exceptional talent, a focus on feeling, parallels drawn between religious and artistic vocation, the puzzle of whom to rely on – suggest that Aurore is doing much of the running.[15]

But that's for the future. For now it's spring 1831, and she's at home in Nohant. After a delighted reunion with Maurice, and a shockingly less than generous assessment of Solange as 'enormous, monstrous and much given to bawling [*énorme*, *monstrueuse et très brailleuse*]', Aurore finds herself isolated once more.[16] She is, she confides to Émile Regnault, a medical student friend of Jules's, 'frightfully lonely here, where no one understands me'.[17] The Berrichon *paysage* once again feels like a trap: 'This countryside which I used to love so much, where I drugged myself with such sweet daydreams, where I walked away my foolish fifteen years-old and my dreamy and worried seventeen years-old, has now lost all its charms.'[18] It's as if adulthood never happened, and she's back reliving the slow, adolescent months of her grandmother's decline.

There's nothing for it but to write: and she does. Helped by the lack of distraction, in spring and early summer she plunges into her inner world: internal monologue, writerly imagination. A recent moneymaking scheme to decorate boxes and trinkets with paintings falls away. She reports somewhat unapologetically to friends who've commissioned her that she's too busy writing to paint. Still, since she's serious about making money, her decision is sensible. Writing for publication is a career: it can build momentum, unlike happenstance favours from friends. Yet she's not looking to take on hack work. She confides to a mutual friend that she and Jules Sandeau '*must*' love each other sincerely if the sacrifices she and her kids are making are to be worthwhile: and something similar applies to her writing. It 'must' be a real vocation, akin to a religious calling, to justify the enormous changes she's wrought in her own life and those of the people around her.

She'll feel less isolated in July, when she returns to Paris. Her relationships in the city continue to deepen. Perhaps inadvertently, Paul Gavarni captures the sense of this in his cartoon portraying her strolling on the arm of Henri de Latouche.[19] The image suggests something more than simple collegiality; a friendly complicity. It's also just camp enough to gesture towards homosexuality. Whether or not Aurore understands herself to be bisexual right now – convent pashes notwithstanding, she may well not – being a writing woman in 1830s Paris breaks some of the same rules as being a gay man.

Is that what de Latouche is? His 1829 masterpiece *Fragoletta*, subtitled *Naples et Paris en 1799*, is a gender-bending story which, in the best Shakespearean tradition, has a brother with a 'white and effeminate hand' stand in for the unavailable female love interest. In Balzac's admiring defence of this work, which would so strongly influence his own (in)famous *Sarrasine*, de Latouche's hermaphrodite protagonist is a 'frightening and graceful Adonis, [an] inexpressible being, who has no complete sex [*sexe*], and in whose heart the timidity of a woman and the energy of a man do battle, who loves the sister, is loved by the brother, and can offer nothing to either'.[20] De Latouche will die unmarried and, despite his relative youth, will retire from *Le Figaro* next year to *garder ses moutons* in the countryside of the Île de France, at hilly Val d'Aulnay. There he will spend two decades writing and enjoying the kind of ever so slightly camp good life often featured in twenty-first-century lifestyle magazines.[21]

In this, too, Aurore will eventually imitate her mentor. Meanwhile, great writers steal. Both *Rose et Blanche* and 'La Fille d'Albano' are set in the Italy that is his imaginative territory. And for now she's still 'kissing little Jules', as she deprecates it, and has once again turned to Émile Regnault, this time for help in finding a new city apartment. As she admits, anywhere she and Sandeau live together is going to need an emergency second exit, 'because my husband could fall, I won't say from the sky, but from the diligence, one fine day at 4 a.m. and, having no accommodation, do me the honour of disembarking at my home'.[22]

The attic apartment to which the couple move on her return to Paris this summer is once again on the fifth floor, in the mansard roof.[23] The set of three unfurnished chambers is just one room wide, but it enjoys a great location at 25 quai Saint-Michel. A small front balcony looks north across the pont Saint-Michel to the Île de la Cité. Nine years from now, in her novel *Horace*, George Sand will describe how 'We could see, in a single glance, the best part of the Seine; all along the Louvre, gold in the sun and crisp against the blue sky; all the bridges and embankments up to the Hôtel-Dieu. Opposite, Saint-Chapelle [. . .] on the right, the facade of Notre-Dame.'[24] This July, writing to Maurice, she summarises: 'Three lovely little rooms which look out over the river with a magnificent view and a balcony.'[25]

When they're apart, the only way she can express love and care to her son is through letters; the child seems at times to become the home she writes back to. But at just eight years old Maurice himself can scarcely be interested in his mother's life away from him. He simply wants her with him. And he really is *just* eight. His birthday falls on 30 June and, with a curious lack of emotional imagination – as if to observe the letter of her agreement and no more – she has chosen to leave Nohant for Paris and her lover the very next day.

'Away from the love object nothing is really beautiful,' she wrote to Regnault from Indre.[26] But who *is* the love object? Aurore is still dismissing the problem of separation from Solange while identifying with Maurice: 'I love her as much, but she's not yet old enough to feel my absence [. . .] it's the tears Maurice is going to shed that break my heart.'[27] As she shuttles between the quai Saint-Michel and Nohant, shifting from chatelaine of a country manor to mistress of a tiny apartment, Aurore is no longer the child whose mother keeps going away. Now she is the mother who goes away.

It's time for a bit of nest-building. The new attic apartment is unfurnished; she even needs to buy a lock for the door. This could be fun, but it's also stressful. Casimir is not, after all, paying her allowance, and real destitution looms. Only after threatening suicide in letters to both him and Hippolyte – who intervenes – does he reinstate it. So she seizes upon a commercial commission that de Latouche, knowing of their hardship, offers her and Jules. It's the chance to ghostwrite a posthumous novel under the name of bestselling author Alphonse Signol. Together the couple churn out five semi-plagiarised volumes of the aptly titled *Le Commissionnaire* in four weeks. It's their successful delivery of this marketable copy which persuades the publishers, B. Renault of 10 rue Notre-Dame-des-Victoires, to commission *Rose et Blanche*.

Rose et Blanche appears from a consortium of five publishers, which Renault leads. Its title page carries a sketchy, if deft, illustration which must be among the first professional commissions executed by the eighteen-year-old Alcide-Joseph Lorentz, who lives in the same street as Renault's business.[28] Rue Notre-Dame-des-Victoires lies in the quartier du Doyenné (Deanery), where the countercultural art scene of 1830s Paris is already beginning to coalesce. Young Lorentz is a member of what Théophile Gautier, just two years older, will come to call the 'Doyenné circle': a witticism, suggesting as it does the good behaviour of an ecclesiastical tea party. There really is an old Deanery building. And it's here that this group of writers and artists is settling in around, in particular, the poet Gérard de Nerval (Gérard Labrunie) and painters including Camille Rogier and Théodore Rousseau. Politically progressive and pro-democratic, they turn the necessity of house-sharing into something close to a commune. Two decades from now, Nerval will recall how:

> It was in our shared lodgings on rue du Doyenné that we recognized ourselves as brothers [...] The old Dean's salon [...] restored through the care of so many painters, our friends, who have since become celebrated, echoed to our gallant rhymes,

often crossed with happy laughter or nonsense songs [. . .] Rogier smiled in his beard from the top of a ladder, where he was painting a Neptune [. . .] a door opened with a crash: it was Théophile [. . .] he read his first verses – while [. . .] Lorry, or Victorine, swung nonchalantly in the hammock, extended across the immense salon, of Sarah the blonde.[29]

For this post-Revolutionary generation, creative excitement and possibility are in the air. Lorentz's childhood friend Théodore Rousseau is already taking the trips to the Midi to paint *en plein air* that will make him an influential precursor of the Barbizon school of landscape art. Gautier published his first story, *La Cafetière: conte fantastique* (*The Coffeemaker: A Fantastic Tale*) in May. It's a community of passionate, and still-developing, like minds that might resemble Aurore's old La Châtre circle, except that it's writ large by talent and by restless unconventionality.

Yet when Renault publishes *Rose et Blanche* at the end of 1831, Aurore's social life only tenuously overlaps with the Doyenné crowd. Jules's student peers differ from the artistic demi-monde, even if their relative poverty – and a taste for wine, women and song – seem pretty similar. This matters for his partner's social standing. Even – perhaps especially – when it comes to *la vie bohème*, the rules for women are different. Aurore is aware of her own mother's struggles to stay respectably ahead of disreputable milieux. She knows too that the address she herself is living at on the quai Saint-Michel, just round the corner from her brother's Parisian pied à terre, is by contrast respectable. And there are other problems with happy-go-lucky bohemian life. By spring 1832 Renault has gone bankrupt and so, although their novel has been fairly well received, she and Jules don't receive everything they're due for their hard work.[30]

In any case, it's the last time they will publish together.

Sometime during March 1832, cholera arrives in Paris. In the first week of April Aurore returns from a late-winter stay in Nohant to a disease-racked capital, from which the wealthy are fleeing in their thousands. Madness, panic, public lynchings, a mob refusing to believe in infection but convinced by rumours of sabotage . . . it sounds familiar to anyone who's lived through the twenty-first-century Covid pandemic. The German poet Heinrich Heine, who has settled in the city, files a dispatch to an Augsburg newspaper on 19 April. 'It is said that thus far more than 120,000 passports have been issued at the Hôtel de Ville,' he reports and, detailing the terror he's witnessed at Père Lachaise cemetery:

> I could see literally nothing but sky and coffins. I was among several hundred vehicles bearing the dead, which formed a queue or train before the narrow gate [for] several hours [. . .] it seemed to me as if the dead themselves were growing impatient and, tired of waiting, were in a hurry to get into their graves; and when, at the cemetery gate, one coachman tried to get before another, and there was disorder in the queue, the gendarmes came in with bared sabres; here and there were cries and curses, some vehicles were overturned, coffins rolling out burst open, and I seemed to see that most horrible of all *émeutes* – a riot of the dead.[31]

Catastrophe comes very close. For the first time, Aurore has brought the three-year-old Solange with her to Paris. It seems an unfathomable decision: did she not know how bad things are in the capital? News of the Three Glorious Days reached La Châtre promptly enough in July 1830. Has the Parisian epidemic been comparatively played down in the provincial press? Is she so desperate to get back to her literary life that she chose to ignore the risks? Or did she just want to be with her lover in this emergency?

She already believes in his frailty, worrying that he studies too hard and might even be consumptive.

Whatever the reasoning, Aurore, Jules, Solange and, perhaps, their close friend Regnault hunker in the apartment above the river while the epidemic rages around them. Eventually it comes close enough to kill even within the house itself. Ceaseless activity at the riverbank morgue opposite, meanwhile, is morbid evidence of the eye-watering fatality rates. In the next six months over 18,500 people, that is, almost 2 per cent of the capital's population, will die. Corpses arrive by night, sewn up in sheets because of the city-wide shortage of coffins, to be interred swiftly in quicklime for fear of contagion.[32]

Against this livid backdrop, the affair between Aurore and Jules begins to unravel. In bringing her child to their apartment Aurore has created an emotional and physical barrier to any kind of 'literary association'. 'In the morning [Solange] comes into my bed,' she tells Maurice. 'She couldn't be a better girl. Everyone [...] finds her beautiful and above all good. Only she doesn't like beards and doesn't want to kiss them.'[33] Whose beard might she be expected to kiss? Well: a portrait Aurore sketched of her younger lover a year ago shows a moustache and chinstrap beard.[34] Jules, who turned twenty-one just a couple of months ago, may be a little too immature to cope with the tensions that arise from sharing three small rooms – let alone his lover's bed – with a three-year-old. A seven-year age difference may feel more like a full generation when he has to listen to Solange's mother proudly recounting how, in the Jardin du Luxembourg, she

> saw the giraffe and pretended that she'd seen one in a field at Nohant. [...] She saw stuffed animals and didn't want to understand that they weren't alive. [...] She has a small cart and a small wooden shovel, she fills her cart with sand and

throws it into grilled openings which make rainwater run away. The municipal employees scold her and she calls them *stupid toads*.[35]

Émile Regnault is another kind of barrier. When she's away from her lover, in Nohant, Aurore confides her difficulties with 'poor Jules' to him. Perhaps she's not being truly manipulative; just going towards kindness wherever she finds it. And Regnault has been very kind indeed. Just before she returned to Paris this April she went beyond mere gushiness, making it sound as if she was returning to the capital just for him: 'Soon I will be in your arms. You'll give me the strength and life if you can. [. . .] Goodbye for the last time. Soon there will be no more question of goodbye. I embrace you with my whole soul.'[36]

You have to hope 'poor Jules' never read his friend's mail. But Aurore's quandary is genuine. It's hard to find an object of pity sexy, and Sandeau does seem to struggle on all fronts. A particular stumbling block is the way he failed to keep pace in delivering the instalments of *Rose et Blanche*. Fired by an urgent need for the publishers' advance, Aurore had her chapters finished two months early; Jules's delayed contributions forced her to cool her heels. Now, the distance between the couple as writers turns out to be not only quantitative but qualitative, for Aurore has brought back with her from Indre a manuscript that is entirely her own and that represents a step change in the calibre of her work. Her debut novel, *Indiana*, is published by Jean-Pierre Roret on her return to Paris. Appearing in May, it is the first book with 'G. Sand' on its title page. The revised *nom de guerre* is a lateral hop from the 'J. Sand' that denoted both someone who was and someone who wasn't Jules Sandeau. 'G.', which stands for 'Georges' and not yet 'George', denotes only Aurore.

The book itself opens a little stiffly. Its first pages, set in the drawing room of a 'small castle [*castel*] in Brie', give little sign that this breakthrough novel will be a tremendous, enduring success. As the characters are introduced they move awkwardly, like actors in need of a warm-up. There's Colonel Delmare, 'heavy and bald with a grey moustache and a fierce look, [who] made everyone tremble, wife, servants, dogs and horses' and who is casually brutal to his wife's dog; while the eponymous nineteen-year-old Indiana Delmare adopts a 'weary attitude, her long dark hair hanging down her emaciated cheeks, and dull rings under her dulled, inflamed eyes'.[37] A claustrophobic mode suggests depression, and resistance casts a gothic shadow around a figure lurking in the castle's twilit grounds. Soon the colonel has shot and injured this interloper, whom he assumes to be Indiana's lover, but who turns out instead to be a new neighbour, a nobleman called Raymon. His lover is not Mme Delmare but her maid, Noun. (Raymon is, oddly, the name Aurore first toyed with for Maurice.[38])

Now the writing begins to move – and is soon ranging widely. Raymon moves on from the maid to her mistress but – being Only After One Thing – refuses to accompany Indiana home to the colony known as Île de Bourbon (after the dynasty, not the drink), which will later become Réunion.[39] As the characters shift between France and this island in the ocean after which Indiana is named, the relationship between the territories becomes a metaphor for male–female relationships; gendered power as gender colonialism. But the distance between them also sweetly symbolises the effort true love demands.

Raymon renounces Indiana because he doesn't want to be merely her follower – echoes of Jules Sandeau? But then, avatar of sexuality that he is in the novel, he persuades her to make the arduous journey back to him, only to discover that – rather like Casimir at Nohant – he now occupies the house that used to be her home. Rescued by her English cousin Sir Ralph Brown, who like all the best heroes has been under her nose the whole time, Indiana returns to Île de Bourbon. There she and Sir Ralph live on together past the book's ending in a paradisal 'Indian Cottage': unmarried objects of society scandal, happily practising a countercultural model of the virtuous life in which, as Sir Ralph explains, 'The majority of our income is devoted to buying the freedom of poor, infirm, Black people. [. . .] If only we were rich enough to free all who live in slavery. Our staff are our friends; they share our joys, we tend their ills.'[40]

What stops this being patronising white messiah fantasy is that Indiana is Creole. That she and (white) Sir Ralph are equals across race and gender is demonstrated by their cousinship and like-minded coupledom. They choose further parity through friendship with their staff: the novel draws equals signs between everyone in this ideal community. There's more than a hint of the Edenic 'state of nature' advocated by Jean-Jacques Rousseau, and followers of his educational ideas like Aurore's grandmother, to this happy imaginary isle.

A similar fantasy of cottage life as a radical space was developed by another young woman writer, Mary Shelley, in her own triumphantly successful first novel fourteen years ago. In *Frankenstein*, first published in 1818, and in French translation in 1821, the invented creature acquires his intellectual and political formation by eavesdropping on a family of political radicals living in rural exile.[41] Books beget books. 'The best readings of art are art,' as George Steiner will write in *Real Presences*.[42]

This is perhaps especially true for women writers in the second quarter of the nineteenth century since, pseudonymous or not, they can't but stand out – and notice each other. The Brontë sisters will consume G. Sand's work. Is sexy Raymon, prowling outside Sand's imaginary castle, a kind of precursor to Heathcliff in *Wuthering Heights*, which Emily Brönte will publish as Ellis Bell in 1847?[43] That same year, the notorious 'madwoman in the attic' of Currer Bell or Charlotte Brönte's *Jane Eyre*, her inconvenient first Mrs Rochester, is designated a Creole. *Indiana* uses Creole identity as a stereotyped shorthand for more intense sensibility than that of European country gentry, too; but at least Sand's point is that her eponymous heroine is *correct* in feeling intensely.

In the late twentieth century, the *Oxford Companion to French Literature* will huff that 'This farrago of romantic passion punctuated by fainting-fits, typical of the early George Sand, is written with spontaneity and complete conviction.'[44] In fact, *Indiana* delivers an explicitly revolutionary message, about marriage and gender relations, for a supposedly revolutionary society. But what will make it last are the cross-currents of its characterisation and sharply realised nuance. Peopled by recognisable human individuals who flirt, gossip and confuse their own motives so frankly that we can end up accepting even the epic and symbolic elements of their story, it is that very modern thing, a character-driven book.

Which is the more remarkable because in 1832 psychological realism is not yet the literary norm, or even the way the world is customarily understood. Though the year will prove something of a literary turning point. The final instalments of Pushkin's verse novel *Eugene Onegin* are being published in Russia, although they won't appear in French till 1847. In the German Confederation, where Johann Wolfgang von Goethe died on 22 March, the second part of his *Faust* is being rushed into posthumous print; in Paris, the twenty-year-old Gérard de Nerval's translation of Part One of the tragedy appeared in 1828. In Britain, Sir Walter Scott, who will die in September, publishes his last two novels: his popularity in Paris perhaps reached its apogee during his 1826 visit for the avowed intent of writing a major study of Napoléon Bonaparte.[45]

Indiana powers through this distinguished and mature company. There's a new kid on the block. 'In Paris Mme Dudevant is dead. But,' Aurore writes home on 7 July to a La Châtre confidante, Laure Decerfz, 'Georges Sand is known as a vigorous youth [*un vigoureux gaillard*].'[46] The reviews are raves: in *Le Figaro* of course, thanks to de Latouche, but also in *L'Artiste* (this one admittedly by Aurore's friend Félix Pyat) and *Journal des débats*, which runs not one but two critiques. One of these, a piece by Jules Janin, calls *Indiana* 'the finest book of manners of our era': which infuriates Victor Hugo, who arrives at the Sand/Sandeau attic next day to inveigh against the snub to his *Notre-Dame de Paris*.[47]

Snubs notwithstanding, Aurore is launched. When her follow-up novel, *Valentine*, appears in November it will be equally well received. And now, as the epidemic continues to burn itself out, she is enjoying her first taste of celebrity. She was courageous in deciding not to wait around for Jules Sandeau, and in submitting her debut complete, rather than publishing in instalments. Now she must be courageous in a different way. She's suddenly a public figure, exposed to scrutiny. This season, when she walks out on Henri de Latouche's arm, she makes it to the gossip columns. At the summer reopening of Giacomo Meyerbeer's latest opera production, she's seated among the literary and artistic celebrities – Charles-Augustin Sainte-Beuve, Hector Berlioz – in the most conspicuous seats of the Salle Le Peletier.

Life will never be the same again. But some more intimate pleasures remain. Like any first-time author, 'G. Sand' sends out copies of her book to friends and colleagues, including Balzac. And she's delighted to welcome *le tout monde* of literary Paris to the attic on quai Saint-Michel. 'Literature is on my stairs like the angels on Jacob's ladder,' she tells Laure Decerfz. 'Nothing but novelists, journalists, spiritual handymen and dispensers of glory who come up and down.' What's more, she's beginning to have fun as her palimpsest self, a Mme Dudevant who is also M. Sand: 'Mr Georges Sand? – He's here. – May one speak to him? – He's at your service. – Where? – Before you. – What, Madame, you are Monsieur G. Sand? – With your permission. – I've come to thank you for having made *Indiana*.'[48]

Fifth impression: *Chinoiserie*

It's an era when talent seems prodigal. This elegant little portrait of George Sand is by the poet and dramatist Alfred de Musset. He executes it in 1833, as the two writers are becoming lovers. In the first months of this year George was seeing the actress Marie Dorval, a relationship with which she crossed the hetero/homosexual Rubicon. This summer, as she turns twenty-nine, she's been experiencing her first hostile press for the revolutionary novel *Lélia*. She's also the mother of two young children and a veteran of legal separation proceedings: certainly not untouched, in short, whether by heartbreak or metropolitan gossip.

Yet you wouldn't know any of this from the doll-like slim waist, deep curved back, or childish fulness of cheek and chin. Nor from the way she wears her hair, dressed but down. This is an idealised portrait by someone in love with his subject. In fact it's not so much a portrait (which surely tries to record a person) as straight idealisation. So it's all the more noteworthy that the image orientalises her. At first glance this is a straightforward piece of chinoiserie. George is outlined with black ink, although her fan breaks into colour. With her black brows and eyes, black hair and a wide, flawless face she could be a fantasy geisha.

In 1833, chinoiserie is no longer the cutting-edge luxury import it was in the seventeenth and eighteenth centuries. Design motifs which ape Chinese art are so conventional in France that 'chinoiserie' is becoming a derogatory term: put into circulation by two of George's own friends, indeed, to accuse those who exploit such designs of reductive racism. Charles Fourier uses it in 1823 to denote the commercial repetition of a style, emptied of meaning, 'which it ridicules': non-European culture understood not as art but as ethnographic trope. In 1836 it appears in *L'Interdiction* (*The Ban*), a novella by Balzac. A character remarks on 'these charming chinoiseries', and this sense of non-European art as purely decorative and without intrinsic merit forms part of his negative portrayal.[49]

Something George herself never refers to, but which recurs in ways she's described behind her back, is that in the France of her day her olive complexion, her dark eyes and hair, are unusual enough to attract comment. In 1866 Edmond and Jules de Goncourt will record in their great *Journal* of the literary epoch that she appears biracial: 'She is there beside me, with her lovely charming head and a mulatto complexion which has grown more pronounced with age.'[50] Three decades earlier Balzac, though a more affectionate witness, called her 'swarthy' in a letter to his lover Ewelina Hańska.[51]

In the twenty-first century we all understand how orientalism, like misogyny, protects social power by diminishing less powerful, or more or less dissimilar, people. We're no longer surprised that European male fantasies of the 'odalisque', which manage a double diminishment, should have taken hold in Paris by 1833. Alfred's drawing, which betrays a voluptuous kinship with such fantasies, dates from the early months of his relationship with George, before they know each other well. Before, for example, the reality of a feistily independent and equal self has landed.

Perhaps the picture makes it more evident that the Sand/de Musset affair will end badly. George will publish *Elle et lui* (*Her and Him*), an auto-fictional account of her relationship with Alfred, in 1859. That is: twenty-four years after the end of the affair, and two years after his death at the age of forty-six from heart failure and alcoholism. It's a long time to hold on to the story of a spoilt romance. Yet this won't purely be revenge literature. As she transposes her remembered relationship to a parallel world of painters and visual art, George exercises what her sometime publisher and agent Pierre-Jules Hetzel will call 'sublime clemency'. She reconstructs the messy patchwork that is human nature and motivation. Balzac, who after all knew both protagonists, declares that she portrays her de Musset figure, Laurent, 'in truth and in moderation'.

Still, she will have to rush composition, completing the book in just twenty-five days after a now-or-never when Paul de Musset threatens to take back his brother's letters.[52] Ironically, since he will protest the book on its appearance, it's this intervention which helps speed it into existence. When *Elle et lui* is a literary and a commercial success – and of course a successful literary scandal – it spawns not only *Lui et elle*, Paul's own hostile parody, but the copycat *Lui* by Louise Colet, *Eux (Them)* by Gaston Lavalley – all three published in 1859 – and, the following year, *Eux et elles* by Adolphe de Lescure.

In this blizzard of pronouns it would be easy, as is the way of blizzards, to lose sight of George Sand herself who, after Alfred de Musset's death, will be the only witness to what really went on at the intimate heart of their relationship. This drawing also survives, of course, as a mnemonic of how he saw her at its outset. In 1833 she still seems immaculately young, and with such a touchingly hopeful expression around the mouth.

SIX

The years of rebellion

WHEN THE ITALIAN VIOLIN PHENOMENON Niccolò Paganini takes Paris by storm in March 1831, *Le Figaro* joins in the rapturous critical reception. George almost certainly contributes one of the paper's raves. By this stage, the showman virtuoso can turn his fiddle upside down to play, ratchet up the excitement by tuning it a semitone higher (*scordatura*), and do any number of other crowd-pleasing tricks. He can also perform the prodigious tasks he sets himself in his own compositions – concerti and solo pieces of mind- and body-stretching difficulty – with a fluency which says: this instrument is not what you thought it was. It's no longer just the worthy, classical-era descendant of the viol family. This is a Romantic solo instrument, capable of extraordinary tonal effects and fistfuls of notes, and you can use it to express whatever you want.

Already, aspiring young violinists are working their way through the infamous studies composed by Rodolphe Kreutzer (1796), while pianists develop a technique fit for the era's complex and demanding new music through Muzio Clementi's *Gradus ad Parnassum*, 100 studies arranged in order of difficulty and published between 1817 and 1826 – just too late for Aurore Dupin.[1] She was thirteen by the time its first volume appeared, and managed throughout girlhood to dodge the chore of piano practice. So she may or may not be aware of the paradox that increasingly laborious technique underlies progressively more expansive musical expression.

It's not exactly the same with writing. After all, her own arrival on the Parisian scene will be something of a literary explosion, with not one but two triumphs – *Indiana* and *Valentine* – in a single year. But she does know all about hard work. Her front-and-centre fluency makes it all too easy to overlook what is the most important of the many qualities that will help her remain celebrated two centuries from now: a gritty stickability. She's stepping out on a professional life of continual graft.

She's also embarking on a stepwise private life. *Gradus ad Parnassum* indeed. Eventually, looking back on the years between now and 1838, she'll assume some responsibility for their difficulty, admitting they are her 'Romantic Rebellion'. But until the Polish pianist and composer Fryderyk Chopin becomes her partner and her private life settles around him for nine years, she will work through what cumulatively seem an almost unmanageable series of emotional and practical complexities. Eighteen thirty-two may be an *annus mirabilis* in publishing terms for the twenty-eight-year-old. But it's also the year in which – not least because of that literary triumph – she will have to accept that Jules Sandeau, effectively the man for whom she has left her husband, is not to be the *raison d'être* of her new life.

She hasn't, it transpires, found herself in a great, supportive meeting of minds where she can feel fully understood. She's once again been living with a stranger, another *inconnu* who turns out to be at some level incomprehensible to her. (He's an intelligent guy after all: why can't he keep up?) But breaking up with a partner, like Sandeau, is a great deal more stressful than breaking up with a lover, like de Sèze. The upheaval isn't just emotional, though that would be bad enough. It means changing a whole way of life, perhaps losing a friendship circle, having to make new living arrangements again. And there are to be many more break-ups in the crowded, lonely years to come. As she will tell a friend during one of the bumpy passages ahead:

> There are days when I want to stay and days when I want to go away. Make wishes that I'm able to stay, for whatever the storms and torments of youth, the isolation and regrets to which I'd dedicate my future would be sad consolation. We are old [...] and if we cure ourselves of loving, what will we do with the rest of our life?
> Pray for your old George, comrade.[2]

This first, game-changing break-up will take place in October 1832, when the newly crowned literary sensation fails to return to the quai Saint-Michel love nest from her summer in Nohant. Instead she will take an attic apartment a fifteen-minute stroll downriver at 19 quai Malaquais. Maurice, now nine, is to remain behind with his tutor in what is still – just – the family home. But Solange will again accompany her mother to Paris. The little girl is by now four, and needs space to run around and play, to break things and be childishly absorbed: having their own home will make this possible. The apartment on quai Malaquais is a godsend.

It's also a last big favour from the young writer's great mentor at *Le Figaro*. Henri de Latouche has retired from the paper to live in a cottage in the country, and is delighted to let his protégée use his Paris home. He's thrown in the carpets and the latest thing in heating, a combined fireplace-stove with metal flanges to direct the hot and cold air called a '*cheminée à la prussienne*'.[3] They strike the bargain on 6 September, when de Latouche sends her a hugely affectionate, protective letter: 'You shall have my apartment, and I love you with all my soul.'[4] In other words, some six weeks before her return to the capital Aurore already knows it is definitively over with Jules Sandeau, the man whose name she has 'taken' – though not like a wife.

So she must put together another new life. In an almost apologetic letter to Émile Regnault, her old confidant in matters Sandeau, she daydreams a communal future life. This could be nothing more than politesse – even an ironing-out of her earlier declarations – were it not remarkably close to how she will eventually live for more than a quarter of a century:

> Another year or two at most, we'll find a way to come back together under the same roof and have our garden, where we'll produce poems and vegetables, where we'll discuss science and cooking, literature and cauliflower, medicine and leeks. We'll be very kind and very gentle.[5]

The apartment Aurore Dudevant shared with Jules Sandeau overlooks the Île de la Cité. But number 19 faces directly across the Seine to the Louvre. Better still, this tall-ceilinged 'blue mansard' at the back of an enfilade of buildings includes a small salon whose elegant balconied window gives on to tree canopies. They fill the garden behind what for the last sixteen years has been the campus of the École Nationale Supérieure des Beaux-Arts, the now re-established national academy for art which was originally founded, in 1648, by Charles le Brun.[6] In the last couple of years, the enterprising architect Félix Duban has been turning this former convent and museum site in the heart of Saint-Germain-des-Prés into a hub for Parisian artists. Aurore's new home is cheek by jowl with this exciting development: art as simultaneously establishment and cutting-edge.

There must be a certain amount of bricks-and-mortar construction going on: the huge Palais des Études, for example, won't be completed till 1839. But even building work, in an era before power tools and radios, is evidently more peaceful than the clatter of the riverside quays. And reinvention is going on in the apartment up in the tree canopy, too. It's here that Aurore Dudevant's new name will flicker into life. Though flicker it does. By the time she moves into quai Malaquais she will be signing herself Georges on many, but not all, letters and still privately, as it were, be Aurore; she won't make the final shift into becoming George for another six months.[7]

Meanwhile, in this inspiring new context, the young writer chooses not to cruise on her first success, instead electing to work hard – and flex the muscles of her formal ambition. In December she will publish, of all things, a verse novel, *La Reine Mab*, two decades after Percy Bysshe Shelley's *Queen Mab: A Philosophical Poem, With Notes* appeared.[8] Perhaps more sensibly, her second novel is also issued late in 1832, again to widespread acclaim. *Valentine* is set in rural Indre, the author's home of the mind, where her eponymous heroine is unhappily engaged to a diplomat and falls in love across the class divide with a tenant farmer's son. Intelligent and exceptionally well read, Bénédict is as uncomfortable in his modest station as the artistically gifted Valentine is in her own huntin' and shootin' circles which, as the author describes them, noticeably resemble the life Casimir has built at Nohant. Such a liaison is forbidden by the mores of a provincial society which Sand captures with acuity. She's learnt to write about what she knows.

But what she knows is as much socio-political circumstance as it is emotional experience. *Valentine* segues from straightforward romantic fiction into the political argument that, even among the privileged classes, women's lives and gifts are largely wasted. This is not quite the point her new admirers among followers of the social theorist Henri de Saint-Simon had expected her to make. The group had lauded *Indiana*'s coruscating take on marriage, and the positive portrait of happy cohabitation in its place. But *Valentine* doesn't ultimately condemn the legal institution per se: only mismatched unions. Saint-Simonists, interested in a more just society built on greater financial equality, workers' and other rights, including women's suffrage, see marriage as an oppressive social institution ripe for abolition. They are less interested in what oppression *feels* like, and their disappointed reaction to this second book makes a conspicuous exception in a chorus of otherwise positive reaction.

Next year 'Georges Sand' will come closer to their position with her third novel, *Lélia*, a *j'accuse* which shows how structural inequalities overdetermine women's lives – and she will be penalised for doing so. *Valentine* tells a more traditional story, about people who find they are no match for society. It's the classic tragic configuration, where the exceptional individual – whether Oedipus or Tess of the d'Urbervilles – is trapped in an untenable situation. But because it focuses on the individual, not the structure by which she's trapped, tragedy can be flipped into a morality tale about punishment for individual transgression: you knew the rules and refused to follow them. Small wonder if progressive Saint-Simonists reject these tragic conventions as socially conservative. What they miss, of course, is Sand's greater radicalism in rethinking an entire world so that the individual woman might be allowed agency.

Georges is a revolutionary – but within limits. The enthusiasm with which she greeted the Three Glorious Days in 1830 belongs to a different life. To understand where she's got to by the time *Valentine* appears, we need to blanket-stitch back to the events of her summer. The Paris Uprising of 5 and 6 June, when a brief anti-monarchist insurrection was violently suppressed by troops, has disabused her of the glamour of interesting times. By 1832 Paris has become so desensitised to political violence that it will only be with the publication of Victor Hugo's *Les Miserables*, over three decades from now, that this uprising will be properly memorialised.[9] Yet the lived reality was grim. The bodies of many of those killed were dumped in the Seine where, barricaded behind mattresses in the attic on quai Saint-Michel, the writer and – worse – her small daughter were unable to avoid seeing them.

Solange was eventually persuaded that 'it was all a game like the battles she had seen chez Franconi [a circus] and in melodramas'. But folly isn't confined to little kids:

> They don't understand that they are all murderers and victims in turn. After all, it's a horrible thing to see blood running! to discover on the Seine below the morgue a red furrow [. . .] to hear the injured man it's forbidden to help moaning below the window [. . .] I needed all the horrible cold blood one has at such moments.

The Uprising was a salutary reset just when 'G. Sand' might have got carried away by literary success. A letter home to Laure Decerfz confesses: 'If I'd written to you before 6 June I'd have written to you with joy about the *success of Indiana* [. . .]. But *the 6 June has killed Indiana* for a month and has thrown me so brutally into real life, that it seems to me impossible at *present to dream in novels*.'[10] All the same, the human psyche is gloriously elastic. In the event *Indiana* is a continued success, and within a few weeks Georges had committed to her next novel.

Yet even here her relationship with Sandeau intervenes. She contracted with Ernest Dupuy for *Valentine* on 26 July 1832, two days before leaving for her late-summer stint at Nohant.[11] Her commitment is to deliver the novel print-ready sometime between the start of October and the end of November for a combined fee, payable on delivery, covering the first two or even three editions – the publisher gets to decide which. If this seems to more than play into Dupuy's hands, it may not have escaped her notice that his business address is literally on Currency Street, at 11 rue de la Monnaie. In any case, more than half the agreed fee is to be absorbed by four bills of payment endorsed by Dupuy and signed by Jules Sandeau. Dated at quarterly intervals starting in July, these are labelled 'For use in replacement insurance' (*Valeur en assurance de remplacement*).[12]

Their relationship may be fraying, but Aurore has bought Jules out of the draft. 'Replacement insurance' means paying a poorer man to undertake military service in his stead. It looks like a kind of blood money, yet the scheme is well established. There are even firms who specialise in it.[13] Aurore comes from a proudly military family, but her father and brother were career officers and she knows 'little Jules' would be unable to hold his own in their world. It's the first and possibly the most egregious example of what will become a pattern of rescuing her men, and doing so at cost to herself. But Sandeau is evidently up for being rescued. And Dupuy, contracting with 'Madame Dudevant' to publish under the name 'G. Sand, author of *Indiana*', must know he's on to a good thing, since it was he and his brother who issued that first success.

But the author herself remains desperate for money. In September, even as the sold-out *Indiana* goes into its third edition, she breaks off work on her next novel to deliver a short story, 'La Marquise', to the *Revue de Paris*. The magazine has already published her 'Melchior' in July. 'La Marquise' is another fine piece of writing, and when it appears in that prestigious periodical in

December her reputation will again be enhanced. These should be moments of literary pleasure. But her covering letter is preoccupied by payment.[14] She's forced to beg the *Revue*'s editor, Amédée Pichot, to cover a debt to Dupuy of 300 francs, due in a week's time.[15]

As the second tranche of Sandeau's conscription buy-out won't fall due till December, it's possible that this is an additional debt for living costs run up by the couple. At any rate, young Jules apparently has no intention of asking his family for help settling it.[16] Instead, in the way of young men who feel indebted, he's reacting to his lover's sacrifices with sullenness. He too is spending the summer of 1832 in the country, some 120 miles west of Nohant at the family home in Parthenay. His will be a very different *retrait* from Aurore's, marked not by increased domestic responsibilities but their complete absence. And Parthenay itself is a fistful of medieval landmarks built, in the gleaming limestone of western Aquitaine, on a crag above the River Thouet. Its slow pace of life must be something of a relief for the student, home from the metropolis after a year of epidemic, armed uprising, and the demands of keeping up with an older, wiser – and smarter – woman.

For Jules is at a crossroads. He can either grow up – or revert to a kind of prolonged adolescence. While his mistress works all hours to produce the novel which, by releasing him from conscription, may well save his actual life, he becomes increasingly lazy about even contacting her. He's more in touch with the couple's circle of friends, who are, of course, really all his. Gustave Papet, Émile Paultre and indeed Émile Regnault are young bachelors like Jules, like him just embarking on careers and still working out how to be adults. Over this summer the narrative arises between them – as so often when lazy, charming men are looked after by adoring partners (one thinks of the

Shelleys) – that it's not he but she who is the burden on their relationship.

So, as Aurore labours on at Nohant, she finds the agreeable new community she believed she'd built shrivelling away. Letters dry up; even Regnault becomes inattentive. It seems she's committing that worst of all female sins, being a drag. As she turns just twenty-eight she's being cast as a nagging old woman. As the warm, almost conspiratorial sense of a community of friends evaporates, it's painful to see this immensely gifted woman beg for reassurance: 'I know well that you love me, my good Émile. If I ask you, it's to make you say it again.'[17]

But in the end, she *is* more mature than this group of callow nobodies. 'When you know life better,' she tells Regnault, 'you will see clearly that I deserve not reproaches but pity [. . .] Where there is a mismatch of age and experience, one is blind [and] the other must come down from the pedestal where they've been placed.'[18] Self-respect and self-preservation demand that she break it off with Sandeau, even while she remains committed to paying his exemption insurance for almost another year. You have to hope this isn't the only reason why, back in Paris in the autumn, he pursues her for some months more. Luckily, she can ignore him because of de Latouche's gift of a home of her own. And perhaps it's to keep it this way that even now, astonishingly, she exerts herself to search out a new, smaller apartment in rue de l'Université and rent it for her ex.

For the first time there's a vacancy in her emotional life. But she's also living on her own terms as never before. Perhaps not coincidentally, 1833 becomes a year in which she doesn't return once to Nohant.[19] Instead, she uses her new-found freedom to continue working. *Lélia* will be published in July, just half a year after *Valentine*. Success means she's now of interest to major literary figures, who ask permission to call. Among them are two critics roughly her own age who, having started out earlier in the literary world, are already immensely influential. Charles-Augustin Saint-Beuve, six months younger than her, is the lead critic on *La Revue des deux mondes*. Gustave Planche, a cerebral anti-Romanticist whose tendency to swingeing critical judgements will earn him the nickname 'the Public Executioner', is nearly four years her junior.[20] A thoroughgoing Parisian, he too writes for the *Deux mondes*, among other periodicals, and he sends Aurore his admiring review of *Valentine*.

She's also being courted by publishers: Ernest Renduel and Charles Gosselin, known as the editors who can 'popularise a success' – in other words, turn a critical success into mass sales – as well as Balzac's publisher, Mame-Delaunay.[21] January sees François Buloz, with whom she has already signed an exclusive contributor's contract at the fortnightly *La Revue des deux mondes*, offering to pay a further 5,000 francs by March for her next novel in order to forestall her taking it to Gosselin. The magazine contract itself already gives her a guaranteed opportunity to earn between 250 francs and 350 francs per month, depending on the length of each contribution: comfortably matching her monthly allowance of 250 francs from Casimir.[22]

Buloz, one year her senior, is already proving his editorial brilliance at the magazine, which he has transformed. He took over just eighteen months ago, and is stuffing it with the best new writing. His contributors so far have ranged from Fenimore Cooper and Alexandre Dumas to Alfred de Vigny and Heinrich Heine. This is bracing, international company to keep; yet as a professional writer Georges is still astonishingly new. It's less than eighteen months, after all, since *Rose et Blanche* was commissioned. Despite the success of her first two novels, she's less experienced than she looks.

Now she makes the beginner's mistake of sending out work that isn't up to her usual standard, and the negotiations for the eagerly awaited new Sand novel are stymied by her own sample. The manuscript she circulates is a Celtic confection whose cod-Scottish title, 'Trenmor', is a character name lifted from the faked-up balladry of James Macpherson's reconstructed Ossian epics. (In fairness, the Ossian fakes have taken all Romantic Europe by storm.) Unlike *Indiana* and *Valentine*, the manuscript is a fiction without an engine of autobiographical anger, socio-political insight – or indeed narrative. Juxtaposing a one-dimensional saint and sinner to tediously symbolic purpose, it reeks of yardage. 'Trenmor' seems to be a dim descendant of those improving dialogues its author read at convent school. Dim descendant too of her own first professional work, since *Rose et Blanche* played at the same encounter between pious and worldly stereotypes, though it dismantled the convention.

In the event, therefore, Gosselin refuses her.[23] And Buloz, who is also her neighbour just around the corner at 6 rue des Beaux-Arts, havers too. Aurore's negotiations with him are being carried out by Gustave Planche, on whom she's come to depend so much – and so quickly – that some later observers will wonder whether the pair are lovers.[24] Though a negative can't be proven, this seems a suspicion too far. This is an Aurore, after all, who has never had to cope on her own before. A famous literary identity is coming into focus: it's a letter to Buloz dated 15 April that carries the writer's earliest surviving signature as George. But the woman herself is living alone (with little Solange) for the first time, and there must be times when that feels scary rather than exhilarating. It's a moment of remaking an identity, rather than of consolidating certainties. Why, after all, does she shift from the man's name 'Georges' to its near-homonym 'George', a name without currency in nineteenth-century France? What difference does cutting off that final 's' mark?

Planche himself – at least as caricatured by the brilliant young illustrator 'Benjamin', Benjamin Roubaud – looks to be a sexless creature, something of a bulgy-eyed haddock. He will die unmarried at forty-eight, after proving to be too much of an intellectual purist to accept the patronage of Napoléon III. He is waspishly brilliant, but his literary enthusiasms are uncompromising: he loves the work of Georges Sand and Alfred de Vigny, and detests that of Victor Hugo, with an almost nerdish singlemindedness. He's also too much of a literary geek to dissemble about 'Trenmor'. In a fit of pique, and despite being short of money, Aurore responds by undercutting his ongoing negotiation with Buloz, and returns to Dupuy for her usual advance of 2,000 francs – less than half, in other words, of what Buloz was offering. Sometimes youthful passion still shows through her epistolary manners.

Usually, though, she makes a good call. When Amédée Pichot of the *Revue de Paris* complains that she's signed to François Buzot's *La Revue de deux mondes*, her response is blunt. She points out that, though she did indeed publish first with Pichot, he didn't offer her the customary retainer and nor has he paid her at the same rate as his male contributors. Quite apart from any question of fairness, rights or literary *amour propre*, 'the survival of my little family depends upon me alone'.[25]

It all works out in the end, thanks mainly to several bursts of intensive rewriting. *Lélia* will come to be understood as one of the author's most important novels, in which she examines her own life and times. That she does so by exploring the inner life of a young woman trapped in a loveless marriage doesn't make its critique of post-Revolutionary French society less compelling or serious. The book takes it as read that women's rights are human rights; and it's an adjustment of the lens that many critics, at least at first, cannot accept. Unlike her friend Balzac, who embarked on the great fictional series of *La Comédie humaine* four years earlier, or Victor Hugo, whose *Notre-Dame de Paris* was published by Gosselin two years ago – or Charles Dickens, whose *Oliver Twist* will appear, albeit in English, before the decade is out – George Sand doesn't use a panoramic canvas for her social critique. Instead, she pays attention to the individual *experience* of social injustice.

The view from close up is vivid and detailed. To capture the nature of experiences, rather than simply observe them from the untouched distance of an omniscient narrator, *Lélia* borrows the Romantic *Bildungsroman* form, which tells the story of the awakening of an individual's reflexive self-awareness. The traditional protagonist is a young man: Sand makes hers a young woman almost a quarter-century before Elizabeth Barrett Browning's pioneering *Aurore Leigh* will do the same. Along with the form comes the seriousness with which that form is taken. The *Bildungsroman* was a way for Romanticism to think about how one becomes a particular person. From the first, this spoke to its era's cultural and intellectual concern with what personhood might be, considered in itself rather than in relation to God or any other synonym for an external 'Fate'. Goethe's *Die Leiden des jungen Werther* (*The Sorrows of Young Werther*), for example, which first appeared in 1774, isn't just the diary of a romantic crush. Its protagonist is a barometer of human range.

But unlike Goethe's lovelorn, eventually suicidal protagonist – or even Lord Byron's *Don Juan*, whose serial exploits have appeared between 1819 and 1824 – George Sand's *Lélia* receives a sentimental education that is almost entirely about limits. Her female protagonist must find a way to live *within* prohibitions on life experience, intellectual growth – and love. Which is as radical as it sounds. The novel quickly becomes regarded as scandalous for suggesting that marriage makes the same bargain as prostitution: a woman must pay for economic survival with sex.

Yet the force of this social critique is muted by a sometimes dreamy, often *in persona* narrative voice. Trenmor and his nemesis Sténio survive from George's manuscript sample, making it into the novel that appears in 1833 (and again, rewritten, in 1839) as very much the book's locutors. Much of the story is told *to*, if not *at*, Lélia, which makes for a claustrophobic read. The heroine often seems trapped behind the words. Trenmor's suicide note, for example, tells her: 'It would have been very easy for you to make me a happy man, a poet with fun ideas, with lively feelings; with a word a day, a smile every evening, you would have made me great, you would have kept me young.' Earlier in the same letter he propounds a more idealistic view:

> Love is not what you think; it is not that violent aspiration of all the faculties towards a created being; it is the holy aspiration of the most ethereal part of our soul towards the unknown. Limited beings, we incessantly seek [. . .] a goal for [this longing] around us and, poor prodigals that we are, we adorn our perishable idols with all the immaterial beauties glimpsed in our dreams.[26]

This sort of musing 'aloud' is as close as mid-nineteenth-century writing can get to literary modernism and its stream of consciousness. There's still more than half a century to wait before William James, brother of the by contrast profoundly conservative novelist, even names the notion in his *Principles of Psychology* (1890). But Sand's writing is radical in a different way. It makes the point that idealism *is* political. Democracy, models of economic equality, a world order governed by the rule of international law, are all principles based on ideals of human nature and behaviour; they are visions of human life and of social organisation. Idealism, frequently social or political, will mark all Sand's work, not least her later, great realist novels of rural life in Indre, moving like a vein of emotion through her writing. But because it's infused with feeling it would be easy to miss the fact that it is also a way of thinking: a set of ideas.

George Sand's canonical success will be created by readers and critics who do understand, one, that meaning and value are among the wellsprings of human life, and, two, that imagining a remedy goes a step further than just handwringing over suffering. It will become first fashionable and then traditional for critics, especially in the male tradition, to dismiss her emphasis on feeling and hope as a weakness. But her contemporary readers are under no such illusions: they spot the ideas Sand is propounding all too clearly. The hostile critical reception *Lélia* therefore receives in the summer of 1833 is not what either George Sand or Dupuy have become accustomed to; and it ends their working relationship.

Particularly intemperate is Jean-Gabriel Cappot de Feuillide, who has already satirised Sand in an article called '*Les bas-bleus*' ('The Bluestockings') in *L'Europe littéraire*. Now, in a 22 August issue of the same magazine, he compares *Lélia* with the works of de Sade, calling it 'Soiled, blackened, stinking of mud and prostitution [...] prostitution of the soul and body [containing] ignoble and shameless thoughts [and] corrosive pages.' Much similar vehemence will come Sand's way in the future, but it's worth pausing a moment to reflect on Feuillide's motives.[27] Both writers had their start on *Le Figaro*, Feuillide two years earlier than Sand, but his mentor there was not the editor de Latouche himself but Sosthènes de La Rochefoucauld, an ultra-royalist with conservative ideas about women. Feuillide may simply be suffering from competitive envy, exacerbated by being four years older than this new star in the literary firmament. Peers judge him to have 'a combative pen, a hot nature': next year he will injure Victor Bohain, the very editor who publishes his excoriating Sand review in *L'Europe littéraire*, in a duel.[28] But he may also be nursing that fiercest of all furies, detestation of a woman who steps in to excel in a man's world. La Rochefoucauld's own recent tenure as Director of Fine Arts and Theatres under Louis XVIII was noted for an obsession with decency: measuring the length of female dancers' skirts, applying plaster fig leaves to museum statues. A dubious ally, yet Sand remains under the impression he's a friend: at least until August, when she hears that he's badmouthing her. That month she even sent him a copy of *Lélia*, remarking, 'I'm sending you *Lélia the abominable book*, the scandal of which guarantees its success, even though on my honour I don't see a line there that I couldn't acknowledge before God.'[29]

Smoothly done; and from the distance of two centuries it can look as though a great writer and her work move through the contemporary literary scene like a knife through butter. But close up it's a more granular, messy affair. Dupuy, not the most powerful publisher in Paris, is unable effectually to come to George's aid. Despite the speed and scale of her success hitherto, she's still a young writer, and a young woman with human feelings. The conditional acquaintanceships of new-found celebrity are no replacement for close confidants. She turns back to friends to defend her, telling Sainte-Beuve:

> My friend, I've been very insulted as you know, and am deeply indifferent to this. But I'm not indifferent to the haste [*l'empressement*] and the zeal with which my friends are defending me. You told me that you'll respond to *L'Europe littéraire* in *la revue* [*sic*: *des deux mondes*] and in *Le National*. Do it then, since your heart advises you to, and I won't thank you, but you know that on a similar occasion my words and my life would be at your service.[30]

Gloriously manipulative stuff: *please do this, but only because you want to, so I won't be indebted to you.*

Perhaps noting that he's being manipulated, or perhaps with that languor characteristic of literary gentlemen who have no particular sense that women's writing careers matter in the same way as men's, Sainte-Beuve writes only to *Le National*, and that not till late September.[31] Gustave Planche, on the other hand, has already written in Sand's defence in *Deux mondes*. More energetically – and somewhat astonishingly – he even fights a duel with Feuillide on her behalf. Neither party is injured, but Planche's bullet kills a cow grazing in a nearby field. Sore feelings all round: the editor of the *Deux mondes* is forced to pay for the dead livestock, since Planche with characteristic stubbornness maintains he asked its owner to move it before opening fire.[32]

This whole foolish escapade will be written up by Alfred de Musset in a 144-verse burlesque, his 'Historical and true complaint on the famous duel which took place between several very unknown penmen in Paris, on the occasion of a book which has been much talked about in different ways, as is related in the present complaint (to the tune of "Complaint of the Maréchal de Saxe")'. The joke is even on Sand's distinguished military ancestry: the Maréchal de Saxe is of course her great-grandfather. But the poem will be published only posthumously because it's an intimate form of homage. It's been composed as part of a burgeoning intimacy between de Musset and Sand.[33]

The two writers will become lovers. But before they do, George has things on her mind. This spring she moved Maurice to a quasi-military boarding school in Paris. It's just the sort of establishment in which his father, and his uncle Hippolyte, thrived. But the little boy, who will turn out to be an artist and who is for now a child accustomed to the comforts of life in a country manor, is bitterly unhappy. When George insists he persevere, we'd be wrong to imagine she's eagerly ridding herself of responsibility for the son she adores. Instead we glimpse her as for once simply a prisoner of class, who believes this *just is* the necessary education for a future gentleman.

Odder is the responsibility she assumes for Jules Boucoiran, who, having been the boy's tutor, is now at a loose end. To prevent him marrying a girl from Indre, she installs the young man in Paris and inveigles him into tutoring Solange. He has been a huge support in her parenting of Maurice during recent months, but why is his emotional future her business? And why does she tell Laure Decerfz, back in La Châtre, that Boucoiran 'comes to kiss my forehead with a bedside manner [*d'un air doctoral*] every morning, and closes his eyes when I take off my shirt'?[34] What is the point of offering – flaunting? – this glimpse of such a markedly bohemian way of going on, especially to someone who's part of a whole shared circle of friends back home?

For that matter why when, earlier in spring, she had a one-night stand with Prosper Mérimée, did she blab about that, especially as it went badly? The future author of *Carmen* is a successful writer: an established figure on the literary scene. He regularly publishes travel writing, and a whole series of his novellas have appeared in the *Revue de Paris*; in the six years since it appeared his hoax *La Guzla* has enjoyed particular success. (This collection of fakes is named for the stringed gusle which traditionally accompanies Balkan songs and epics.) It's not hard to understand that after a painful split with Jules Sandeau – 'days of boredom and despair' – Sand should be tempted by a new liaison, especially one with a literary equal. She's feeling 'hideous in my self-involvement and in my isolation'. What better remedy than this worldly lover? 'For eight days I believed he had the secret of happiness, that he would teach me it, that his disdainful insouciance would cure my childish susceptibilities.' And so, she confides to Sainte-Beuve a couple of months after the event, 'I acted at thirty the way a girl of fifteen would not have and committed the most incredible stupidity of my life, I became the lover of P. M.'[35]

Sainte-Beuve is among the mutual friends who had encouraged the two to take an interest in each other. Sand explains herself to him in a panic because she's suddenly become notorious in Parisian literary gossip. At the time, she had confided to another friend that 'I had Mérimée last night. It was nothing special,' and 'Mérimée is five feet, five inches' – remarks which sped around Paris, gathering frisson as they went. In fact (so George will always maintain), that insulting 'five inches' is an embroidery by Alexandre Dumas, the ebullient, gregarious figure whose *Le Comte de Monte-Cristo* is going to appear in the same year as Mérimée's *Carmen*.[36] Easy, perhaps, to imagine the delight in going from table to table in the cafés which are writers' and artists' haunts, and how little actual malice there may be in cranking the rumour mill. But the harm is done. From this point on, the name George Sand is no longer a neutral fact. Forever after, it will imply someone sexually cavalier – disrespectful of masculine fragility – in short, a maneater. Since this is the context of *Lélia*'s publication, it's small wonder the book has been roasted.

Alexandre Dumas is just one of the people to whom George's original confidant passed on this very personal story. And it seems likely her motives are less than innocent. For the culprit is Marie Dorval who, unlike Laure Decerfz, is not an admiring (if intelligent) friend living quietly in rural Indre but a star of the national stage and arguably her century's most successful tragedienne. Like many, George is smitten by her. And so there are a host of possible reasons, most of them freighted with sexual jealousy, for why she boasted to the actor of her conquest, and why the actor may have wished to punish her for it.

Six years older than Sand, a former child star and the

illegitimate offspring of actors, Dorval has been hailed as a great actor since 1827, when she took the female lead in a melodrama called *Trente ans, ou La Vie d'un joueur* (*Thirty Years, or the Life of a Gambler*).[37] She will die in 1849, and there are no photographs of her. But surviving images – an engraving by Paul Delaroche, an 1832 lithograph after Léon Noel, various costumed portraits in role – consistently reproduce large eyes, curls scrunched tightly above her ears, and a slightly plump, oddly blank face with a peculiar quality almost of fleshy nakedness, not so much seductive as vulnerable.[38] The child actor shows through the celebrity.

Perhaps the adult star's loneliness does, too, for Dorval responds to a fan letter George sends her in January 1833 by turning up in person, unannounced. For the next few months the two women are closely involved. In the future, every surviving detail of their closeness will be pored over. It's almost as if a sexual relationship with a woman would prove something about George Sand: some lapse in femininity which could, say, allow another great nineteenth-century figure to be discounted as *not really* a woman writer. Madness, since a lesbian life is if anything not less but more woman-centred.

And a sexual relationship between Sand and Dorval is likely. In Paris in 1833 there's less asymmetry between the social construction of homosexual men and women than in other European countries. Homosexuality was decriminalised in France in 1791, so gay men no longer run the risk of execution; unlike in Britain, where that mortal threat will remain in place for another two years, and legal prohibition will only gradually start to be dismantled from 1967. Unlike the British Queen Victoria, fashionable Parisians understand that women can desire women; their name for this is 'Sapphic'. Indeed, the men in both Marie's and George's lives – Dorval's old friend the poet Alfred de Vigny, Sand's admirer Gustave Planche – warn each about the predatory,

'Sapphic' tendencies of the other.[39] Meaning that each is explicitly aware of this possibility – and neither is scared off by it.

Like George, Marie Dorval is married. Her second husband is Jean-Toussaint Merle, a prolific playwright, theatre director and writer on current affairs. At the start of 1833 he's not long returned from Algiers. The Merles were only married a year when Jean-Toussaint set out in 1830 with the Maréchal de Bourmont on his conquest of what will become modern Algeria, as personal secretary and official recorder. Merle seems to be very much a man's man, though whether this means he is his wife's beard is quite another question. In an era in which marriage is still often arranged, birth control can be akin to magical thinking and childbirth is frequently fatal, female sexual desire is by the by for many marriages. Most unions probably exist somewhere on a continuum of sexual reluctance; and awareness of a lavender marriage, however intentional, is probably easily buried.[40]

Perhaps more significant is how much Marie Dorval and George Sand represent to each other. Both hugely successful, each works almost alone in the interstices of an artistic world run by men. In the interstices, too, of male sexuality; which in an unreconstructed era can be all too nasty, brutish and short. Both are playing roles: the writer is still inventing her persona, while the actor even sits for portraits in dramatic character and costume. How can they not be fascinated by each other? And disguise is their ally. In June, when Marie hurts George by gossiping about the writer's fling with Mérimée, George's letter of reconciliation acknowledges-without-acknowledging that confiding this fling must in turn have hurt Marie. 'In future I'll know to keep quiet,' she says. And it ends with a joke which signals how they use codes in their relationship: 'I'll wear your hat this evening. So you'll see me before receiving my letter. Thus it will be a visit *avant la lettre*. How stupid, my God!'[41] As well as 'before the letter [has arrived]', *avant la lettre* means here, as it does in English borrowing, *before it has been defined*: 'thus it will be a visit *whose nature is not defined*'. More, this whole joke has been crossed out, as if it were riskily explicit. Even the bold must take precautions. And in July, when George has another one-night stand with a man, the exiled Neapolitan writer Alessandro Poerio, she does indeed 'keep quiet'. Neither Dorval nor the rest of Paris get the story.

We can't know what goes on behind a bedroom door unless someone kisses and tells. Biography always runs the risk of voyeurism, and there's something disagreeable about watching future scholars pick over what happens between George and Marie. But neither of this savvy pair denies the rumours around their involvement; and no evidence emerges to disprove the probability that Marie and George desire each other, and likely do something about it. So do six months of intimacy prove George is 'really' a lesbian, rather than simply bisexual? Not so much. Gay women in cultures which prohibit homosexuality often disappear into marriage, whether by force or *force majeure*, for their own protection and economic survival. But George has inherited means of economic and social support, and is already married to Casimir. Her separated spouse would be the perfect beard, if she needed one. And yet there are to be no more women.

George just is unstoppably interested in men. At the end of July she embarks on the romantic entanglement with Alfred de Musset which will continue to involve her one way and another for almost two years. By now a pattern to her sexual taste is emerging. De Musset is, at only twenty-two, six years younger than her. But he already has a double reputation as a poet and a man about town. Perhaps it adds to his swagger that (unlike Sandeau) he's doing his part-time military service with the National Guard. Fiercely good-looking, Alfred has a sexy charisma that shines out of those photos that will survive him.[42] A medal portrait struck by David d'Angers two years before he meets George shows a side parting and a lateral plume of hair which make him look – odd kind of spoiler – remarkably like the pianist Fryderyk Chopin.[43]

De Musset's first poetry collection, *Contes d'Espagne et d'Italie* (*Tales of Spain and Italy*), was published when he was just eighteen. He was then already a regular at the Cénacle, a Parisian literary group led by the writer of gothic fantasies Charles Nodier. Even more precociously, two years earlier the teenager published *L'Anglais mangeur d'opium* (*The English Opium Eater*), a loose version of Thomas de Quincey's *Confessions of an English Opium Eater*. He's since become a user himself. He will be an alcoholic by thirty. Once a brilliant student, in his late teens he toyed with and then dropped various careers, including medicine, law, art and music; in short, very much acting the younger son that he is. And yet he does all this with no family fortune to fall back on. His father worked as a civil servant all his life, and when he perished last year in the cholera epidemic left little in the way of inheritance for his three children.[44]

In his fecklessness Alfred is the antithesis of George, whose writing has at least some of its roots in financial necessity. If painting bibelots for friends had been more remunerative, perhaps we would never have known Sand the novelist. But Alfred resembles her in being recognised as a pre-eminent talent among the young generation of writers. The poetry and drama – and to a lesser extent fiction – that he will produce in the quarter-century of his writing life will transform French literary Romanticism. His poetry resists classicism by maintaining a wellspring of explicit feeling and pleasurable beauty, just as Sand is doing in her fiction. So there is a deep artistic kinship between these two boyish, dark-haired and prodigiously talented writers. They will even joke that their relationship is incestuous: they must be siblings, or else one is the other's parent. In letters they often address each other as 'dear child'.

This courtship is profoundly literary. It's with the poet that the novelist at last becomes fully George: Georges, Georgette, Oiseaulette (Little Bird), but never Aurore. A month after they've been introduced at a dinner party, de Musset writes an admiring letter about *Lélia* which is also a bid for intimacy:

> There are in *Lélia* twenty pages at a time which go straight to the heart, frankly, vigorously, every bit as beautiful as *René* [de Chateaubriand's highly influential 1802 novella] or *Lara* [Lord Byron's narrative poem of 1814]. There you are George Sand; otherwise you would just be Madame so-and-so, who writes books. [...] I could be [...] not even your friend, that's still too moral for me, but a kind of comrade without either consequences or rights, and so without jealousy and without quarrels, able to smoke your tobacco, rumple your peignoirs, and catch a head cold while philosophising with you under all the chestnut trees of contemporary Europe.[45]

He's skirting closer to the truth than perhaps he realises. Ruminating on her entanglements with Mérimée and Dorval, George writes to Sainte-Beuve on what may even be the very same day that 'I am absolutely and completely Lélia.'[46]

Two days later Alfred writes again:

> My dear George, I have something stupid and ridiculous to tell you. Foolishly, I'm writing it to you, I don't know why, instead of having told you coming back from this walk. [...] I am in love with you. I have been since the first day I visited you. I thought I would defeat this simply by calling you 'friend'. [...]

I hope for nothing in telling you this. I can only lose a friend [and] I'm mad to deprive myself of the pleasure of seeing you [...] But the truth is that I'm suffering and I lack the strength [to be platonic].⁴⁷

The new couple enjoy a tender, joking association. They share sketches and puns and Alfred, the lapsed professional artist, draws his lover repeatedly. He writes her poems (though they're not quite as good as the ones he'll write about their break-up). Right from the outset they plan to take a trip to Italy together. But bizarrely, and as if to underline how much the younger partner he is, the twenty-two-year-old cannot get permission from his widowed mother, Edmée, Mme Victor de Musset, to travel out of the country. To make up for this, less than a month after he has made his declaration the lovers take a boat to Fontainebleau, where they book into a hotel for a week.⁴⁸ They're in search of Romantic sensation – and they get it. As they take a moonlit stroll in the famous forest, Alfred is suddenly terrified by an hallucination of meeting himself. He collapses; which is a dramatic and at the same time oh-so-predictable consequence of fashionable toying with extreme sensibility, whether that's through poetry and art, the embrace of an emotional life, or mind-altering drugs. Alfred habitually indulges in all three.

By the time George writes up this incident a quarter of a century from now, in *Elle et lui*, it will all have shrunk to a literary anecdote, long rehashed: first by one of her own *Lettres d'un voyageur* (published in 1834 and then, collected in volume form, in 1837), and then in Alfred de Musset's auto-fiction *La Confession d'un enfant du siècle* (*The Confession of a Child of the Century*, 1836). But actually living this chaotic relationship in the here and now takes up time and space. By the end of August, George has sent Solange back to Nohant – for once, indubitably a selfish move – and in her place moved Alfred out of the parental home and into her own apartment in quai Malaquais. Possession is nine-tenths of the law; before the end of the year she has secured permission to take the handsome young poet to Italy.

She's also writing; her triumph will be that she never really stops. Along with several short stories, in mid-September she produces a short fantasy fiction, *Garnier*, for the editor and advocate for High Romantic literature Urbain Canel. On 2 October 1833 she finishes the novella *Métella* – 'sixty pages of scribbles [*griffonage*]' – for François Buloz. In December she signs a new contract with Buloz: she will deliver her next novel, *Jacques*, by the following May.[49] Four thousand francs of her advance will be paid 'before her departure for Italy', and the remaining 1,000 will be remitted to her in January, 'at Genoa or elsewhere'. It's holiday money: once again, as she did on Jules Sandeau's behalf, George has built a book contract around a man she's involved with. It's as if she sees the substantial commission fee and the freedoms it will allow her, but is so accustomed to her own phenomenal writing speed – or to living continually at stretch – that she dismisses the labour of actually producing the work. Even writing at her speed, it's a reach to complete a novel within five months at the same time as embarking on an Italian odyssey with a lover who, whatever his strengths, certainly keeps her hands full. Yet she will manage to deliver *Jacques* – another story about marriage as a suffocating mismatch – punctually, and to success.

And so on 12 December, three days after she's signed with Buloz and the day after Alfred's twenty-third birthday, George and her lover leave for Italy. From Lyon to Avignon they sail down the Rhône; by chance, on the same boat as Stendhal. No longer a sufferer from the syndrome of paralysing cultural awe that has been named for him, he's travelling under his real name of Marie-Henri Beyle, en route to a posting as consul at Civitavecchia on the Tyrrhenian coast of his beloved Italy. After parting from their senior colleague, the couple spend three days in Marseille before sailing to Genoa on 20 December.

It's a rough crossing, which might have been better avoided at this time of year, and which George stomachs well but Alfred does not. Still, they survive, and continue along the familiar Romantic route, first down the coast by boat to Livorno, and then on to Pisa and Florence before turning north to Bologna, Ferrara, little arcaded Rovigo, Mestre and the heart of Venice. It's not a route an overland traveller would take in the twenty-first century, but it's a way to get to Venice without passing through the great Alpine range which sits like a lid on top of Italy, pretty much cutting off the country from the rest of the continent, especially now the snows have come.[50]

In the end it's Venice itself that proves most taxing for the travellers. Even in midwinter, the city on the lagoon is a health hazard. On New Year's Eve George takes a room right on the Riva degli Schiavoni, that Venetian equivalent of a corniche which looks across the lagoon to the Lido. Regardless of season, the water and light here continually tessellate and shift, as if they were as ornamented as the architectural treasures that surround them. It's a prime waterfront location, and the accommodation isn't cheap. By the twenty-first century, the Albergo Reale where the couple are staying will have become the Hotel Danieli: a tony Venetian institution in a rose-pink, ogee-windowed palazzo. In 1834, however, the lovers take it in turns here to succumb to gastroenteritis and dysentery. Alfred, who may well have contracted typhoid, becomes gravely ill overnight on 4 and again on 7 February.

Perhaps it is George's bad luck, or literature's, that the doctor she summons to attend him is Pietro Pagello. Midway in age between the lovers, with a mop of dark curls and a moustache that's carefully groomed, if a touch too self-indulgently long, Pagello is evidently both competent and intelligent. Despite his youth he has already been a practising medic for almost six years; later in his long life he will become a distinguished surgeon. He's also a cultured figure, who will go on to write three volumes of poetry in Venetian dialect; although so far all he's published is medical research with a highly Romantic sensibility, *Dell influenza delle passioni sul colorito della faccia* (*On the Influence of the Emotions on the Colour of the Face*). For such a man an encounter with artsy bohemia is not unappealing.[51] The hotel room makes it obvious that this is a couple who are sleeping together; and what that implies for George's sexual availability is no mystery to the good-looking young Venetian. He besieges her. By the end of the month she is secretly his mistress.

It's hard not to feel some impatience with George at this point. Despite her experience of being pilloried by gossip, she still doesn't seem to realise that she is her own worst advertisement. But maybe a key to this socially risky, emotionally needy behaviour lies in the way she and Alfred have been playing at being childish siblings. Perhaps, tired of mothering, she longs to be nurtured and understood herself. The competence and practical intelligence of doctoring is reassuring and deeply attractive, as any number of twenty-first-century TV hospital dramas will prove.

Still, when after ten weeks the literary couple leave the Albergo they at first do so together, moving round the corner on 13 March to a cheaper hotel in narrow, palpably medieval Calle delle Rasse. A fortnight later Alfred, finally jealous of Pagello, departs for home. The very next day, 30 March, George leaves with the doctor for a trip around the Veneto. She will remain in the city with him – they move in together first on the Corte Minelli, close to the Teatro Fenice, and then near the Barcaroli bridge – until late July. Even her eventual trip home to Paris will be undertaken with him, and will include extensive sightseeing.

In the Romantic era, elective, recreational travel still contains an element of pilgrimage. Stendhalian rapture is a neo-spiritual experience. Traces of the Grand Tour remain in the renown of certain sites, exceptional landscapes and cultural splendours. Visual and emotional must-sees, they're understood to carry a sort of charge which doesn't simply 'make memories' but changes the witness herself. This is understood to be educational in a particular way: simple art-historical and geographical facts trumped by the lessons of awe. Exploratory travel hasn't been George's particular concern so far; perhaps she's spent too much time on the road shuttling between Nohant and Paris. But now she adds travel writing to her published repertoire, producing the first two of what will become her *Lettres d'un voyageur* for the *Revue des deux mondes*.

Still, her *Lettres* are travelogue as life writing. Packed with anecdote, as well as indiscretions about her relationship with de Musset, they read as a record of personal experience rather than any sort of literary Baedeker. Which is one version, if not quite a perversion, of the Romantic project. The first letter, published on 15 May 1834, is titled 'To a Poet' and cruelly anatomises de Musset, not for his way with map and hotel pillow, but in far more sweeping psychological terms:

> You felt young, you believed that life and pleasure must not be separated. You tired yourself out enjoying everything, at speed and without reflection. You didn't recognise your greatness and you let your life run on at the mercy of the passions that were coming to wear it out and extinguish it [. . .] You wanted to live for your own account, and to murder your own glory with contempt for all things human. [. . .] What love of destruction burned in you?

This is the extinction of one of her ideals. Despite the pleasures, Venice has been no holiday. George is writing as hard as ever for her living: this year, Buzot's *Revue* publishes not only *Jacques* but also *Léone Léoni*, about a Venetian roué, and the shorter *Le Secrétaire intime* (*The Personal Secretary*). Yet, illness aside, it has been a break from her daily life. Back in France, the much-repeated three-day trek between Nohant and Paris – between domestic life as Aurore and literary life as George – is a metonym for the exhausting double shift she continues to put in to free herself from her starting point.

She's been struggling for years, and things are getting no easier. Nohant is by now less her home than Casimir's: to return there is to be faced with the various problems created when she broke open their marriage, on top of all the old difficulties of dealing with someone she finds wilfully intractable. But Paris is still abuzz with gossip about her private life and *Lélia*, though highly praised by writers she admires, has become mired in the related scandal. As if she needs any reminder of how hard she must swim against the normative tide, *Le Charivari* provides one. Since January, the Parisian satirical magazine has been publishing a series of forty lithographs by Honoré Daumier mocking *les bas-bleus*, the blue-stockings: proto-feminist writing women, including George's own followers. Daumier makes sure any woman who can read is portrayed as toothless, fat, bespectacled, bedraggled, hysterical, or any combination of the above: since these are also things women are not allowed to be. *Le Charivari*'s readers are reminded how absurd it is that any of them should want more from life than, as in one of his images, mending their husbands' trousers.

Besides, at the start of July George turned thirty. In retrospect this may be the mildest of the decade milestones. People in their thirties are still young, healthy (all things being equal) and full of creative energy. But those still in their twenties don't know this.

It's a moment for stocktaking, and George does exactly this in response to a letter from La Rochefoucauld asking how she is:

WHOM I LOVE? – My children and my friends.

WHAT I THINK? – Everything and nothing, depending on my health, my mood and the weather.

WHAT I SAY? – Little, because I'm alone three-quarters of the day [...]

WHAT I WRITE? – I've written enormous amounts of foolish things which are now in press, including a novel in two volumes called *Jacques*, entirely stupid and which you will perhaps find less impious and less immoral than the others; but don't believe that this is a conversion, it's just an experiment. [...]

WHETHER I WEAR A CHAIN OR AM UNDER A SPELL? – [...] I live from a memory that will always be dear and sacred to me; but, socially, I live independently and have no ties.

WHETHER MY HEALTH IS GOOD? – No, it's too hot here [...].[52]

It's time for real life to resume. On 8 July 1834, still in Venice, George receives a letter from Casimir telling her that he's had a mini-stroke; and also that Maurice, distressed by her continuing absence, is becoming apathetic. She responds immediately that she will return promptly to Paris and bring the boy home to Nohant for the holidays. She also begs Casimir to cut down his drinking for the sake of his health: their children need him around. Is she feeling guilty? It's hard to tell; but her letter is somewhat defensive. Maurice's depression 'surprises me greatly, since no one's written me a word about this and since according to him, everyone [at the school] is pleased with him. [...] If I had foreseen that my absence would be so prejudicial to him, I would never have left Paris. [Besides,] my mother would never have abandoned him.'[53]

She does not, however, leave Italy immediately. Instead, Romantic traveller to the last, when she eventually winds her way back to Paris in late July, accompanied by Pagello, she visits among other places Verona, Lake Garda and Lake Maggiore, Chamonix, Le Montenvers – where the famous Mer de Glace is the site of the great encounter at the heart of Mary Shelley's *Frankenstein* – and Geneva, birthplace in 1712 of one of Romanticism's most important precursors, Jean-Jacques Rousseau. George knows, of course, that what she's said about Sophie-Victoire's capacity for taking loving care of children is untrue. Yet this tourist itinerary means she won't get back to Paris till 14 August. When she does eventually arrive she gives herself a further ten days in the capital before continuing to Nohant. This turns out to be just enough time to show her face (she has lunch with Balzac) and heal the rift with a desperate Alfred in the course of two emotional rendezvous.

Finally, on 24 August, she sets out for Indre with Maurice, who is by now eleven and beginning to grow into the youth who will so astonishingly resemble her. She's also accompanied by her own mother, though in the event Sophie-Victoire tolerates manor life for just three weeks before hurrying back to the city.[54] Pagello is no longer in tow, but George hasn't exactly broken up with him. One might say she's playing the young doctor. For she and Alfred now start a correspondence in which they rehearse a passionately idealistic version of their relationship. Apparently it's so exceptional it can transcend mere sex. As the poet writes:

> Posterity will repeat our names like those of the immortal lovers [. . .] like Romeo and Juliet, like Héloïse and Abélard; no one will speak of the one without the other. This will be a marriage more sacred than those contracted by priests; the imperishable and chaste marriage of Intelligence.[55]

This kind of talk about sublimely unquestionable love sounds familiar from George's first entanglement with Aurélien de Sèze. Maybe it's once again being deployed to skirt round the fact that she's 'with' two men at once: Pagello, waiting alone in Paris, now takes the place of Casimir as the domestic drag. Or maybe she's simply not interested in sex with de Musset after the bad end in Venice. Typhoid isn't pretty; it must be quite an effective prophylactic.

Whatever the case, she continues to send letters charged with emotion to Alfred, who left Paris on the very day of her own departure for a vacation in Baden-Baden. Perhaps she does so because, although this is her first trip to the country this year, she's clearly restless. She assembles a group of the La Châtre friends to visit the octogenarian statesman Talleyrand, Charles-Maurice de Talleyrand-Périgord, in his magnificent Loire Valley chateau at Valençay, forty-five miles away. (In the event the visit is not a great success.) Only when she returns to the capital in early October does she tell Pagello their affair is over, leaving him little option but to return alone to Italy. (There he resumes his medical career – and writes up a kiss-and-tell, *Da Parigi a Genova* (*From Paris to Genoa*), which he doesn't exactly publish but lodges in a public library, the Bibliothèque Marciana.[56])

This autumn, George brings both children back with her to Paris. She's enrolling Solange in boarding school although, at just six years old, her daughter is even younger than Maurice was when he first entered boarding school so unhappily. There seems no selfish motive for disrupting the little girl's care; the decision smacks of urgency, a salvaging or protecting of both children from life with Casimir, who is drinking heavily. Meanwhile, it's their mother's turn to be desolate. Her on-again liaison with Alfred is off again after less than a month, because a mutual friend has passed on Pagello's boast that he slept with George before Alfred had left Venice.

Life seems to be unravelling. Even the difficult old certainties, like the continual annoyance that is Casimir, seem in doubt. But in late November George finds a surprising new confessor. She has three sittings with Eugène Delacroix for a portrait commissioned by François Buloz; and they become the start of what will prove to be a lifelong friendship between these two prodigiously talented artists.

Delacroix's popular success has been cemented by his *La Liberté guidant le peuple* (*Liberty Leading the People*, 1830), that giant image in which a surging human pyramid is topped by a muscular, Phrygian-capped and flag-waving *Liberté*, who sports a pair of bare breasts that resemble dumplings plated up on a masculine torso. Smart, moustached and bearing a striking resemblance to Talleyrand, whose illegitimate son he's rumoured to be, Delacroix has a reputation as a workaholic. He's also clearly an excellent listener. George quickly confides in him; and in response he captures something of the dishevelment of her life. His 1834 portrait shows her with enormous brown eyes and her glorious dark hair, which she wears abundant and down for most portraits, cut untidily at the collar: she has hacked it all off and sent it to Alfred.[57]

Delacroix captures the truth of her damaged life, but also a fiction: for George will never float passively on a tide raised by others. Even while dramatically acting out the end of the affair with Alfred, she's busy organising her life with characteristic pragmatism. She returns to Nohant in December and continues to visit through the next year. On 13 February 1835 she signs a 'treaty' with Casimir, and a week after that she writes to Alfred that the scenes he's making have to stop:

No, no, it's enough! [. . .] I forgive you everything, but we must stop. [. . .] Saint-Beuve is right. Your behaviour is deplorable, impossible. My god, what a life I am leaving you to! Intoxication, wine! girls, and again, and always! But since I can do nothing to save you from it, must we prolong the shame for me?[58]

'My god, what a life I am leaving you to!' This *cri de coeur* sounds like the lament of mothers over chaotic sons down the centuries. George, whose own son will grow up to be her domestic rock, has become stuck in a pattern of mothering her partners. Earlier this year, she even pretended to sell some indifferent Italian paintings for Pagello in order to bail him out without hurting his pride. Now she's trying tough love – yet still within a quasi-maternal relationship. It seems a strangely restrictive orientation for someone who is making every effort to gain the freedom to be an artist. But boy-men – what a certain section of gay society will call ephebes – offer a paradoxical security. The part of George that remains Aurore will remember what it's like to have no control over her own life as cruel or stupid decisions are made by a brutal husband, a self-absorbed mother. Nor could she forget the bullying force of masculine strength.

Of course, there's also the rescue fantasy: that only an exceptional woman can save the exceptional man. But with Alfred, George has failed. A surviving note from him reveals just how abusive their relationship has become: 'Don't be afraid; I haven't the strength to kill anyone this morning.'[59] It sounds like Romantic rhetoric. But what happens next makes clear that the threat is real. On 6 March George writes to Buloz at *Revue des deux mondes*, asking him to clear her 'small debts' and send her the 500 francs due for her novel *André*, the first instalment of which he will publish in just over a week's time, 'today if you can [. . .]

for I haven't a cent. Or at least send me 200 francs [and] keep secret for me this tentative news of separation and help me to succeed this time.'⁶⁰

On the same day she contacts Jules Boucoiran, by now more a friend than an employee, who lives in nearby passage Choiseul. With him she makes no attempt to disguise the urgency of her situation:

> My friend, help me to get away today. Go to the stagecoach company and reserve a place for me, then come to see me. [. . .] I must avoid disturbing Alfred's suspicions . . . You'll arrive at my place at five o'clock and with a hasty, busy air will tell me my mother has just arrived, she's exhausted and quite seriously unwell, that [. . .] she needs me immediately and that I must go without delay. I'll put on my hat, saying I'll return, and you'll put me into a carriage. [. . .] Come to see me immediately if you can, but if Alfred's home, don't look as though you have something to tell me. I'll go out to the kitchen to talk to you.⁶¹

George isn't making these extreme plans in order to avoid hurting Alfred's feelings, but because she is at risk. This is a textbook escape from an abusive relationship. She's worked out the three things a woman needs to get away from a violent partner: an excuse to escape from coercive oversight (Boucoiran's 'news' about George's mother), money to survive on (from Buloz), and somewhere to go. George goes, of course, to Nohant.

It may feel like a low point; in fact, things finally begin to settle. Slowly, the thirty-year-old starts to live as if her personal resources aren't simply to be squandered; as if she might after all be alive for the long term. Though she will continue to drive herself as hard as ever at work – and though she's still forced to shuttle between Nohant and Paris – she's achieving at last something that almost resembles calm. Which is not to say that romance and heartbreak are finished. Just one month from now she will meet and become involved with the lawyer Michel de Bourges, who lives and works as his name suggests in Bourges, the provincial capital of nearby Cher. In two years' time, he will in turn abandon her. Still to come yet further in the future are both of her arguably most important relationships: the best-known, with Fryderyk Chopin, and the happiest, with Alexandre Manceau.

But her scattergun experimentation is largely over. De Bourges is a significant figure and a moral force, currently acting for the defence in a high-profile political trial. In his personal life what he represents is – himself. He's not a writer; not part of bohemia or the tightly interwoven literary world, all rivalries and alliances. These communities haven't fallen away from George's life, but she negotiates them now less in person and more on the page. Within a month of her escape from Alfred, for example, Buloz is mailing an edition of Plato and a Quran that she's requested to Nohant.[62] She will develop other newly important artistic friendships, including one with the pianist and composer Franz Liszt, by letter.

Even within the great body of George's work, her correspondence is by now bulking large. She doesn't seem as troubled as we are by the distinction between letters and those forms of paid 'professional' writing from which a twenty-first-century author might fret about being taken away. Besides, correspondence plays a central role in nineteenth-century social life, when travel is distant and costly, and all the ways of staying in touch in real time, from telephone to videocall, have yet to be invented. This is an era when indoor entertainment is still, for those with the requisite literacy and the leisure, predominately textual. More than half a century before cinema will even be invented, evenings of leisure and occupations for rainy days broadly come down to music, crafts, reading and writing: including the sending, and reading aloud, of letters.

George uses the same fast, fluent and apparently informal writing style both for her letters and for her books, which are often tonally such close cousins that one has the impression she's simply switched from one sheet of paper to another and kept the pen moving. Perhaps in any case we're wrong to fret about keeping them distinct. Unlike, say, diaries, letters are intrinsically public, written *to be read* by the person they're addressed to; just as fiction is, criss-cross, a kind of correspondence with its editors and readers. This is an idea George's *Lettres d'un voyageur* play with. Though written for the readership of Buloz's magazine, each essay has a nominal addressee.

The sixth *Lettre*, for example, is addressed to de Bourges, who will remain largely a long-distance partner. The couple never formally live together.[63] There are a number of reasons for this. Louis-Chrysostome Michel de Bourges has acquired his sobriquet because of his significance in the provincial city where he's making his reputation. It's hard for a figure of such necessarily public probity to conduct a scandalous affair; almost impossible outside the vast anonymisation of Paris. Besides, the pair are not always free at the same time as each other. In 1835 de Bourges's principles land him in jail for the month of October, and in the spring of 1836 George has another of her overlapping relationships. This time she gets involved with the writer Charles Didier, who has admired her for years. She even moves into Didier's Paris apartment at 6 rue de Regard for a couple of months. Yet another stormy on-off entanglement, her liaison with Bourges ends without seeming to alter the trajectory of her life.

What do alter it, over nine long months from 30 October 1835 to 29 July 1836, are the divorce proceedings George has instigated at La Châtre against Casimir. She will eventually prevail, but his appeal goes all the way to the provincial capital of Bourges. Here, in a packed courthouse, Casimir's lawyer Louis Antoine Thiot-Varnennes argues – in terms that could come straight from a 1950s novelette – that George's writing is full of 'bitterness and regret' and that she will only find happiness by returning to Casimir's side. George is lucky to have the distinguished and gifted de Bourges acting for her throughout. But even his logical response to this attack – that it obviously doesn't make sense for Casimir to blacken his wife's name yet claim he wants her back – only succeeds in dividing the bench. It is ultimately left to Casimir himself to concede.[64]

Is it more truthful to understand the failure of the Dudevants' marriage in moral terms, like Casimir, or fatalistically, like George? Casimir's wife has been unfaithful to him and has abandoned him by stages. But, as her legal submissions will point out, his drunken temper has made him first unkind, and then dangerous. George herself sees the marriage as an insoluble tragedy; her early fiction repeatedly revisits the tragic impasse between a misunderstood, sensitive wife and a husband who is her opposite.

Within the Western canon, these are pioneering accounts of the sorrows of a mismatched yet elective romance. This new subject is not unrequited pursuit (like Goethe's in *Young Werther*), nor the risks of mismatch avoided (as by Jane Austen's heroines), not the perils of seduction (for any number of ruined maids in ballads), nor the prison of arranged marriage, but the unravelling of the romantic dream. Marrying for love is still a recent European privilege; the culture has yet to grapple with what it means when this new compass for a good life fails. Famous explorations like Leo Tolstoy's *Anna Karenina* (which first appeared in instalments in 1875–7), or even *Madame Bovary*, published by George's future friend Gustave Flaubert in 1857, are decades in the future. Besides, both these books written by men ultimately adopt the traditional formula of the individual tragically mismatched with life, a woman engaged in her own self-destruction. George's novels suggest the trouble may be something both more subtle and more existential than a simple question of character flaw.

Aurore and Casimir themselves, for example, became a couple because they genuinely liked and desired each other. As young people in Paris, they seemed to come from similar milieux. Casimir's bluff outdoorsmanship and hearty drinking were forms of masculinity that Aurore, as the orphan of a military hero, was primed to find attractive. Only once they were married did their differences become apparent. Aurore was too clever for Casimir. She must have been bored before she realised she was bored, once the first pleasures of playing house were over. Though not particularly well educated, her mind is fast, insightful and hugely emotionally literate; she herself uses the ideas of the day to frame this as 'sensibility'. Truthfully, the charming sparkiness captured in her portrait by Jean-Baptiste Bonjour was soon running rings round Casimir.

In twenty-first-century France, the principle of serial monogamy will mean that such a growing-apart ends not in tragic impasse but simply with moving on; George's chequered emotional history would be nothing out of the ordinary. But in 1835 her divorce agonises through multiple hearings. Even after he grants it, Casimir appeals the terms first handed down in a May 1836 judgment. These award George custody of her children and the complete return of the inheritance she brought to the marriage, including Nohant, a house at Narbonne, and substantial rental incomes.[65] In the event she prevails, and the very day after her settlement is finalised she returns with Solange to Nohant, in what must be a triumphant act of repossession.[66]

What has swung it for her is another of Casimir's drunken furies. This one took place on 18 October 1835, as we know from the lengthy and meticulous indictment George wrote and sent to de Bourges in the following days. Her letter is evidently a rehearsal for the request for final separation she will file less than a fortnight later.[67] And perhaps its extraordinary fluency comes from being able finally to say what's been building up for years. For at last she has witnesses to the crudely simmering anger and drunkenness of life at Nohant.

As is the way of domestic abuse, what happened was as squalid as it was dramatic. A house party were staying at the manor, and Casimir had already been in a foul temper for two days when, as the Dudevants and their guests were drinking after-dinner coffees, he started shouting at Maurice. The twelve-year-old was reduced to tears. To calm things down, George sent the children up to her bedroom. At this her husband turned on her, first telling her to shut up and then ordering her to her room. When she refused to do either he tried to hit her, and had to be restrained by friends. A struggle ensued. He rushed out yelling, 'You'll see what I will do', only to return and threaten not only George but also their friends with, she records, 'his pistol and an old sword'.

Perhaps they were lucky no one was killed. And, after Alfred's violence, George must have found this outburst not only embarrassing but frightening. Here was another man with whom she had been intimate and who was intoxicated, out of control and threatening her life. She left Nohant the next day. Until the divorce was made absolute and Casimir was forced to leave the manor for good, she would spend much of her time in Indre at La Châtre rather than at home.

In this provisional life, this anxious to and fro, we see a very different George from the flamboyant litterateur-about-town of popular fantasy. We witness a mother who is also still a young and vulnerable woman: she will turn thirty-two just before her decree is made absolute. Apart from talent and a gift for hard work, she has little in the way of certainties on which to build. Her children are her reality – the 'whom I love' of that Venetian letter to La Rochefoucauld – but one cannot build *on* kids: they need to build on their parents. Hippolyte is increasingly absorbed in his own family life – and is drinking. She has relatively little contact with her elder sister; her mother remains a source of complex emotion rather than support. Only Nohant supplies the kind of constant that makes a home. Having the estate returned to her is another turning point. Gradually, as the years go on, the manor will emerge from the background of her literary life until it comes to occupy the foreground – and, eventually, becomes her literary shrine.

Sixth impression: *The soloist*

IN EUGÈNE DELACROIX'S 1838 DOUBLE portrait of Fryderyk Chopin and George Sand, the writer will become a domestic ghost who sits and sews. It's an oddly unrealised image, slipped like a kind of placeholder between two much more vivid renderings: of the musician she will accompany, and of herself in her 1834 solo portrait: distrait, soulful, her hair chopped off at the shoulder.

For in 1834 George is still – like the musician who will become her partner – an individual artist; a *soloist* whose portrait has been commissioned for editorial use in the *Revue des deux mondes*, where she's a star in the literary firmament. Romantic portraiture tries to capture more than just the old, schematic iconography of class and role, costume and setting. It seeks to reveal the emotions and resources of the individual character from which, it believes, life and meaning start. Even a studio portrait, in other words, is somewhere on a continuum with Caspar David Friedrich's iconic 1818 canvas *Der Wanderer über dem Nebelmeer* (*Wanderer Above the Sea of Mist*). That the artist is an individual with responsibility for her self-creation par excellence is a trope of Romantic culture.

So George is portrayed here as an inspired artist – with temperament to match. Delacroix represents her personal artistic resources as a sort of secular spirituality, a tender susceptibility to impressions and emotions. She's dressed boyishly, which only serves – just like future fashions for boyfriend jeans, UGG boots or granddad shirts – to emphasise her feminine fragility; she looks half drowned in a wide-collared jacket. Even the silk scarf knotted loosely round her throat seems to express pathos: the I-can-do-no-more of a young woman about to burst into tears. Those wide eyes could be brimming. The sepia-toned oil, a preparatory work for reproducible engraving, is lit from above and behind us, throwing George's nearer cheek and brow into lit relief. Set against their pallor, her enormous eyes become the focus of the entire image. We follow their gaze as she looks away from us and slightly up, like a Renaissance Madonna at an annunciation.

George is indeed in a highly emotional state as she sits for this portrait. She desperately misses Alfred de Musset, who is punishing her for her affair with Pietro Pagello and has not yet responded to her entreaties to make up. Their *amour fou* will resume in the new year; meanwhile, this is the moment when she has shorn off her own hair and posted it to him like an archaic gesture of mourning. Or as if to say, *If I'm not yours I'm no one's.*

As she poses, she talks about herself. Perhaps the painter encourages her confidences out of kindness and affection; perhaps he half hopes to see her distrait. For he seems in this image to be searching for what a woman writer could possibly be. His George is clothed in the authority of conventional (male) writer's costume, right down to the bohemian gesture of the scarf in place of a neat cravat. But she exhibits a 'feminine' *sensibility* – that other notion from the Romantic vocabulary. He pictures her as if she's registering the passions vibrating in the world around her like the hyper-responsive 'Sensitive Plant' in Percy Bysshe Shelley's 1820 poem, whose 'deep heart is full, / It desires what it has not, the Beautiful.'

In Delacroix's literal brown study, the annunciatory light which falls on his subject's face is surely inspiration 'descending', as the Christian Holy Spirit 'descends on' the girl elected to be the mother of God, or Zeus leans out of the classical pantheon to impregnate the one he chooses. Neither reference is a stretch in a European culture still built upon the twin foundations of Christianity and classical education; which are also the twin traditions through which women of George Sand's generation are understood by the men around them.

Even bohemian men. Delacroix's own artistry in composing this image is neither passive nor accidental. Perhaps it shouldn't shock us that, by the time of the 1838 double portrait, he will place George Sand just a little behind Chopin, and portray her sewing. Like Ariadne, and Athena, and the waiting Penelope. Or like Arachne, after whom spiders are named, who is punished for her hubris in imagining that she could possibly compete artistically with an immortal.

SEVEN

Duet

ONE WAY OR ANOTHER, BY 1838 the die is cast. It's too late for George, as a divorcée with an unusually florid reputation, to seek the conventional protection of a 'good marriage'. But the dream of a great love who understands her is not over. Neither, therefore, are her sexual flings. The next few years will see her embroiled with the actor Pierre-François Touzé and playwright and novelist Félicién Mallefille, among others.

But onlooker's fatigue makes these affairs progressively less interesting. They don't tell us as much about George, or do as much to shape her future, as earlier encounters. Though every life is an experiment in living, her exploratory self-invention has been peculiarly radical. Before she turns thirty-three in July 1837, she has already broken through a whole series of taboos. Extramarital relationships, sex with a woman, infidelity within affairs, initiating first separation and then divorce as a woman: she's done or – what amounts to the same thing – is reputed to have done them all. There are few such conspicuous boundaries left for her to transgress.

This is, after all, still the early nineteenth century. Only two decades ago, even his barony failed to protect Lord Byron from being driven into exile by the scandalous sexual revelations of his divorce trial. When Percy Bysshe Shelley died a mere fifteen years ago, his widow had to battle her in-laws for custody of and financial support for their surviving child, who had been conceived out of wedlock.[1] Admittedly, these fellow writers came from across the Channel, where sexuality is differently policed: for them France, Switzerland and Italy represented political and sexual freedom. (This contrast will only intensify when, on 20 June 1837, that promulgator and doyenne of family values Queen Victoria succeeds to the British throne.)

But other of the choices which are shaping George's life will remain unconventional even in the twenty-first century. For example, there's her pattern of taking as lovers younger men, whom she looks after financially, professionally and emotionally. 'George Sand was a maternal nymphomaniac,' *The North American Review* will huff in the early twentieth century.[2] There's the way she 'mothers' even friends, such as the socialist thinker Pierre Leroux, whom she will subsidise for years, and with whom she will eventually set up a progressive periodical. Her custom of dressing as a man in order to move freely through Paris will look odder two centuries from now – when women will have greater freedom of movement *as* women – than it does in the 1830s, when it's so frequent that the French capital even issued a bylaw against female '*travestissement*' in 1800.[3]

Even among those who love her, George is regarded as an outlier. And so when she first crosses paths with the celebrated Polish pianist-composer Fryderyk Chopin, at the end of 1836, there is certainly no *coup de foudre* between the notorious writer and the delicate, elegant musician. They meet at the Paris home of a mutual friend. The Comtesse Marie d'Agoult lives in the fashionable Hôtel de France at 23 rue Laffitte; since 24 October George has been renting the next-door suite and sharing her salon space. Theirs is a friendly and markedly intimate set-up, and it's during the very first fortnight of this congenial arrangement that her encounter with the man with whom she will have one of the defining relationships of her life occurs.

The countess's principal connection to Fryderyk Chopin is as the lover of his great rival and close peer, the flamboyant virtuoso and composer Franz Liszt. She's also practising that limited form of artistic participation open to monied women of her era, hosting a salon. Artists, musicians and writers meet on evenings she curates, and she now invites George to a series of musical soirées at which Chopin is present and, mostly, performing. The first, on 5 November, is at Chopin's apartment at 38 rue de Mont-Blanc (which will become the chaussée d'Antin). It's followed on 19 November by a second evening at the Hôtel de France, then a recital on 13 December chez Chopin, and finally another concert on an altogether larger, orchestral scale, given by Liszt with Hector Berlioz on 18 December at the Paris Conservatoire. Highlights of this occasion include the kitsch, compelling 'Marche au supplice' ('March to the Scaffold') from Berlioz's still-novel 1830 *Symphonie Fantastique*.[4]

The musical community into which George steps as it moves between these events is not unliterary. Berlioz's writing on music will become well known; within a few years the Comtesse d'Agoult herself will start to publish fiction and works of political history, including a three-volume *Histoire de la révolution de 1848* (*History of the Revolution of 1848*, 1850–53), under the pseudonym Daniel Stern.[5] George helps the cross-fertilisation along with her eleventh *Lettre d'un voyageur*, published in mid-November and addressed to the opera composer and director Giacomo Meyerbeer: 'Maestro [. . .] they played the *March to the Scaffold*. I will never forget your sympathetic handshake.'[6]

But however 'sympathetic' the writer finds these musicians, Chopin's early impressions of her are the very opposite. 'What an unappealing [*antipathique*] woman, this Sand! Is it truly a woman? I'm ready to doubt this,' the composer Ferdinand Hiller will recall him saying as they walk home together at the end of an evening. Chopin writes to his family in Warsaw that 'I've made the acquaintance of a great celebrity: Madame Dudevant, known under the name of George Sand; but her face isn't attractive to me and didn't please me at all. There's something in her that repels me.'[7]

It may not help that George shows up to his chamber concert on 13 December – the 'little get-together, very intimate and made up of very good people [*très bien composée*]', to which she brings the poet Heinrich Heine as her platonic date – wearing a Turkish costume in the national colours of Poland.[8] She's correct, though, in her verdict on the distinction of the gathering. Chopin plays, of course, but there are also Schubert lieder sung by Adolphe Nourrit, star tenor of the Paris Opéra. Liszt and Chopin perform a duet. Eugène Delacroix, Giacomo Meyerbeer, the great Polish Romantic poet Adam Mickiewicz and one of the surviving sponsors of the 1791 Polish Constitution, Count Julian Niemcewicz, are all present, as are a host of lesser writers and musicians. Deeply musical and markedly expatriate in complexion, this is an entire alternative community for George, a different artistic establishment to her own that is nevertheless also at the very heart of cultural Paris. Once again, she's falling in love with a milieu she will go on to make her own.

Though not, for now, through romance with an actual musician. In 1836 Chopin doesn't seem to have his eye in for grown women. This September he became engaged to a teenager nine years his junior – which makes her fifteen years younger than George. In many ways it is an obvious match. Maria Wodzińska got involved with her future fiancé when she was only sixteen. She takes occasional piano lessons from him but has been studying principally with the Irish composer-pianist John Field.⁹ She comes from provincial Polish gentry – the couples' families are friends – and is a talented, arty young woman who has also studied drawing and painting at the University of Geneva.¹⁰ The portrait she made of Chopin this summer, for example, is technically immaculate. It also reveals that she sees her fiancé as a rather weak, ineffectual figure, who sits with arms folded, regarding her anxiously.¹¹ The image is completely without sexual smoulder.

In a self-portrait, on the other hand, Maria herself appears wholesomely brown-eyed, dark-haired and trim-waisted. Like Sand, she has a 'Mediterranean' complexion.¹² Contemporaries describe her as 'brilliant ... striking', and her admirers seem to have included the future Napoléon III. Yet the correspondence which survives from nearly a year of stuttering engagement to Chopin never catches fire. By the end, its dutiful tone is close to insulting. Her brief missives to the man who is taking European audiences by storm sound like a teenager's duty letters. Perhaps this couple initially shared some non-verbal, musical affinity, but Maria seems to have realised she has got tangled up with an older man she doesn't desire.¹³ Perhaps, without understanding it, she's come to sense that he does not desire her either. By the summer of 1837, when the Wodzińskis settle back into their country seat after years spent abroad to avoid a Poland in political and military chaos, the relationship between their daughter and the sickly, possibly tubercular musician has ground to a halt.

He will call their relationship *Moja bieda* – my abjection – as he labels their correspondence and bundles it away. At the keyboard, though, it's a different story. At twenty-seven Fryderyk Chopin is one of the wonders of European culture. His international career started in Berlin and Vienna, and since 1830 he has been touring western Europe on French papers, taking citizenship (and Gallicising his name to Frédéric François) in 1835. Though he performs relatively rarely, he is acclaimed by the greatest living composers, led by Felix Mendelssohn and Robert Schumann. He has already composed his first two sets of Études, two piano concertos, sets of Mazurkas, Polonaises and Nocturnes: all the canonical work up to and including his Opus 27.

But George is one of the few women in the world who has no need to be starstruck. She's Chopin's equal in precocity: 1836 has seen her preparing an *Oeuvres Completes* only five years after she was first published. In preparation for this edition she has removed some of the most revealingly autobiographical passages from *Indiana* and tidied up traces of serial publication, particularly in the *Lettres d'un voyageur*. She's also recently published four shorter historical fictions: *Simon, Poème de Myrza, Mattéa* and 'Le Dieu inconnu' ('The Unknown God') – some of this work is clearly potboiling – and candidly produces *La Dernière Aldini* (*The Last Aldini*) for the money.[14] Eighteen thirty-seven will also be the year that sees *Lettres d'un voyageur* appear in volume form, along with the composition of both *Les Maîtres mosaïstes* (*The Master Mosaicists*) and the somewhat unlikely *Mauprat*. The former, a parable set in medieval Venice, expounds George's ideas about art; in the latter the eponymous anti-hero is transformed by the love of a good woman. And, if this seems an unlikely fantasy for its bohemian author, we should remember how often she has tried to make something of her men.

The links between George's work and her own life can sometimes appear almost schematic. But perhaps drawing force and conviction from what she cares about is the secret both of her tremendous productivity and the idealism that continues to characterise it.[15] In February and March, six *Lettres à Marcie* appear in *Le Monde*. This set of essays in feminist thought and advice addressed to the fictional Marcie, who is in that most vulnerable position of being a woman without money, is written in the persona of a man: that is, it borrows the mask of masculine authority. Borrows and doesn't borrow, since the letters are not pseudonymous – or anyway, no more pseudonymous than any of George's work. Indeed they provoke an attack on Sand in *La Phalange*, a periodical associated with the utopian socialism of Charles Fourier.[16] Before they even appear, *Le Monde*'s editor in chief, Félicité Robert Lamennais, has redacted them heavily: especially the third, which argues in favour of divorce.[17] George's sixth *Lettre* makes the point that by excluding women from education men contrive a self-fulfilling prophecy. Women can be dismissed as 'lesser' because they lack everything that is developed by that education: articulacy, reasoning skills, knowledge. This is a writer who knows from experience how hard it is to find the opportunities a human individual – let alone a woman – least of all a practising artist – needs in order to develop.

And indeed, when it comes to it George will have a good understanding of what a musician's career entails; unlike the Wodzińskis, who expected Chopin to settle down with them in rural Poland. She understands not only from her own experience as a writer: she's already observed a virtuoso's life up close. Since becoming friends in autumn 1834, Franz Liszt and Marie d'Agoult have been frequent guests at Nohant, often staying for months at a time. (Indeed, it was gossip about George's behaviour on their joint holiday to Switzerland in October 1836 that ended her relationship with de Bourges.[18]) Among the trio's 'pranks' are the nicknames they give each other: George adopts Dr Piffoël, while Marie becomes Mirabelle and Franz is *le Crétin*, the Idiot. Sand has an Érard piano especially installed for the summer of 1837, when Liszt comes and goes from Nohant as touring permits while a pregnant Marie stays on at the manor.

Dashingly handsome and Hungarian, Franz Liszt is eighteen months younger than Chopin. In 1837 the first of the three children he will have with d'Agoult is already two years old, and she is pregnant with their second daughter, Cosima. The 'bridge section' of this artistic dynasty, Cosima will grow up to marry the composer Richard Wagner and found the Bayreuth Festival. Such a posterity is symptomatic of the way in which this power couple are building their relationship into the artistic establishment. It must appear enviable to George, who has tried repeatedly to create just such a life: although Marie may recall her having written, a year ago, 'I've had enough of great men [. . .] We hold them in esteem, but we cannot continue to love them.'[19]

The sounds of piano practice and composition show off Nohant as a place where art is made. Liszt and Sand are clearly not sexually attracted to each other, but they become comrades-in-arms who enjoy working side by side. A comprehending friendship has sprung up: they are creative peers who, because they work in different art forms, need never be rivals. D'Agoult's posthumously published memoirs will track her own more gradual comprehension of this relationship. Unease about it is surely understandable, given George's sexual reputation, and would be a good reason for her to give the writer's emerging interest in Chopin every encouragement.

For her own informal liaison is in fact fragile. By the end of 1839, the year in which their third child together is born, she will have stopped living with Liszt; they will separate completely in 1844. The countess, who contracted a marriage of convenience as a teenager, is separated but not divorced from the Comte d'Agoult, who is still alive and by whom she has two daughters. Her peripatetic life with Liszt, celebrated in his *Années de pèlegrinage*, is no Romantic embrace of freedom but something much more pragmatic: a result of the pianist's concertising but also of her own need to keep a low social profile as a figure of scandal.[20]

George's life whirls on even in the country: it would be easy to picture it picking up speed like a mazurka. It's hard to work out when she has time to noodle and reflect the way most writers need to. All through the summer of 1837 Chopin, who is after all engaged to his Polish protégée, resists her repeated invitations to join the Nohant house party.[21] But she keeps busy with her latest conquest, the actor 'Bocage' (Pierre-François Touzé). Sometime in the months that follow, Maurice's latest tutor, the Mauritius-born dramatist Félicien Mallefille (who is three years younger again than Chopin), becomes her lover in turn. It can't have harmed his suit that in the autumn, when Casimir makes an alleged attempt to abduct Maurice and a successful one to carry Solange off for a few days, Mallefille steps up as the man about the manor.

Altogether it's not until the end of April 1838 that, back in Paris, George's musical campaign kicks off in earnest. She spends a week with her friend Charlotte Marliani and, on 25 April, Chopin gives a recital at Marliani's home.[22] Now George takes the initiative, and sends the pianist a four-word note: '*On vous adore. George.*'[23] Chopin will keep this undated, initialled slip all his life; but as declarations go it is both overt and indirect. There is after all no *I* nor informal *you*, no *je* or *tu* (although we shouldn't forget that George writes to close friends, including Charlotte Marliani, with the formal *vous*). Its effect qua declaration is in any case muted by an exclamatory additional message from Marie Dorval, who is also back in town: 'And me too! And me too! And me too!!!'[24] Which apart from anything else tells us that she doesn't realise how serious George is about the musician. More 'We find you adorable' than 'I adore you', then. All the same, the writer has made her advance.

There follows a period of protracted frustration as the musician prevaricates over his response. During these weeks George has two great confidants. Charlotte Marliani is joined on her writing pad by Wojciech Grzymała (Gallicised as 'Albert Grzymala'), an émigré former diplomat and a close friend of Chopin's, whom she now co-opts. On 8 May the pianist performs at another soirée with a distinguished audience, including Victor Hugo; again, George attends. In mid-May she has to break off her romantic pursuit to return to Indre, partly because the family need her – fourteen-year-old Maurice has been unwell – but also because she's embarking impetuously on yet more legal action against Casimir, who has come into an inheritance.

Sometime before she does so, she and Chopin have kissed. She writes to Grzymała from Nohant: 'He would doubtless have distanced himself from my first kiss if he had known that I'm as it were married. We have not deceived each other, we have given ourselves over to the passing wind which has carried us both to another region for a few instants.'[25] At one point, George has sent Marliani a letter which has long been thought to characterise this maddening, confusing period. It clearly does so only by coincidence, since she was not in the same city as Chopin on the date pencilled with a question mark on it. But it is as relatable to her experience now as it is to everyone who's been in this position:

> I've been slow writing back to you because, you know, the weather in the season of *love* is *variable* [. . .] One says a lot of *yes*, of *no*, of *if*, of *but* in a week, and often in the morning one says *this is intolerable* only to say *truly, it's the supreme happiness* in the evening.[26]

She's unable to persuade Grzymała to bring Chopin down to Nohant, so instead she lets him (and therefore Chopin) know that she's returning to Paris. On 7 June 1838 she rents a modest attic set in the rue Lafitte, discreetly using her maiden name.[27]

This romance, if it blossoms, will involve not just one but two celebrities, and it is going to be gossiped about. In the event Grzymała is beaten to the line. When he lets Chopin know about George's return, the musician responds, 'I can't be surprised because yesterday I saw Mar[liani] who told me of her arrival. [. . .] What's going to happen? God only knows. I don't feel very well.'[28]

He may be sick with nerves, but he's also up for what is about to happen. On a Wednesday which can be no sooner than 13 June, in an otherwise undated note to Grzymała, he records: 'The dawn [so he knows George's given name, Aurore] was drowned in mist, yesterday. I hope there will be sun today and I'll write you a word before this evening.'[29]

Evidently, the sun also rises. And more than meteorological metaphors link these two public figures. By July 1838 they have settled into a discreet domestic routine, not at Chopin's well-known address on the chaussée d'Antin but in the mansard attic which a certain 'Mme Dupin' has rented.

In August, this contented interlude is captured in the new double portrait by George's distinguished artist friend Eugène Delacroix. (That it will later be hacked apart means nothing, since it's neither the artist nor the sitters who vandalise it.) The painter poses Chopin at – where else? – a piano specially brought into his painting studio for the purpose, and has George sitting closer to the front of the picture and a little to the pianist's rear. It's a fine, craggily handsome portrait of Fryderyk. But the portrayal of George is even more interesting: like a rebuttal of everything Delacroix's first portrait highlighted. She sits in a low armchair, embroidering, and there's a softness and vagueness to his rendition. In fact her image seems half finished.

Light strikes her lover's face, which is in three-quarters profile, highlighting each riven contour. It's the most heroically masculinising interpretation possible of Maria Wodzińska's shrinking violet, or of that faded, flustered invalid who will appear in Louis-Auguste Bisson's 1849 photograph of Chopin. But George's face and head have become oddly smoothed down, even hieratic. What remains is a statuesque quality alongside the evident intelligence: rather the same unusual combination that a much later literary lioness, Susan Sontag, will make her sexy own. Earlier this year Balzac, who often stays with friends at the Château de Frapesle, twenty-five miles from Nohant, has sketched a similar portrait of an exceptional, handsome woman who is just beginning to thicken up: 'She has doubled the size of her chin, like a canon of the church. She has not a single white hair, despite fearful misfortunes, her tanned complexion remains unchanged, her fine beautiful eyes are just as brilliant as ever.'[30]

In Delacroix's double portrait is the hand that George moves towards us, first finger and thumb together, drawing a needle or gesturing in sympathy with the music? Either way, she's making a sophisticated point, one that feels somehow beyond the viewer. Especially compared to the stress and movement captured by the artist's earlier portrait, this is a study in composure. Something seems assuaged: perhaps the habitual loneliness of the orphan, or artist's exceptionalism? Yet Delacroix has literally positioned her as the 'great woman' who is, in the cliché, 'behind every great man'. Perhaps her friends are eager for Sand to meet her match.

Rites of maturity. By now she is truly orphaned. Though attended by the highly respected Dr Marcel Gaubert, Sophie-Victoire Dupin died of liver failure on 19 August 1837, in the nineteenth-century equivalent of a nursing home at 99 rue du Faubourg-Poissonière.[31] George, who paid for this end-of-life care, arrived in time to give her 'a last kiss which she did not feel', and have her interred at Montmartre cemetery after a service at

Saint-Vincent-de-Paul.[32] And there are other stressors. Félicién Mallefille, finding himself displaced, tries to threaten Chopin to a duel. Worse, up close it's clear that the pianist is seriously bronchial, if not tubercular, and that he desperately needs a warmer, cleaner environment than the Paris of 1838. For though the effects of industrialisation will arrive later in the French than in the British capital, every household here still burns coal and wood in its stoves and fires, and polluted air hangs in its river basin. Crowded on to its medieval street plan, the city also has a particular problem with sanitation.[33]

Worse still, there may be a flaw at the heart of the couple's relationship. Before they became an item, George unburdened herself to Wojciech Grzymała in a lengthy letter which tried to work out the grounds of Chopin's hesitation, and the ethics of romantic connection. At the time of their first kiss she was still involved with Mallefille, and under the misapprehension that Fryderyk was still involved with Maria Wodzińska. But she detected some other kind of hesitation, a check of a more fundamental kind:

> At your place, as we were leaving [. . .] he seemed to disdain, in the manner of devouts, human coarseness, and to blush at the temptations he had experienced [. . .] This way of thinking of love's ultimate embrace has always disgusted me. [. . .] This term 'physical love', used to express what can be named only in Heaven, *displeases* me and *shocks* me, as an impiety and at the same time as a false idea.[34]

A sexual repudiation, in other words. This inhibition so early in their relationship makes George doubt herself, in the great feminine tradition; and she goes on to ask their mutual friend whether 'there could be for elevated natures, a purely physical love and for sincere natures a purely intellectual love?'

In a similar spirit, she examines her own history (it is a very long letter):

> I have greatly trusted my instincts which have always been noble; I've been mistaken sometimes about people, but never about myself. I've lots of stupidities to reproach myself with, no platitudes or mischiefs. [. . .] I've known many kinds of love. An artist's love, wifely love, sisterly love, maternal love, love of a nun, love of a poet [. . .] all this has been perfectly sincere. My being went through various phases, like the sun.

In many ways she's just thinking aloud. But she could also do with knowing what sex means to her new partner. Oddly, when George worries that Fryderyk might be a prude, it doesn't seem to cross her mind that he may not be sexually interested in women at all. Could she really be so naive? Life in Paris's bohemian – and promiscuous – artistic circles means she cannot be unaware of gay men. Surely she must have considered the case of her first, loving friend and mentor Henri de Latouche, even if she hasn't pondered the perpetual celibacy of the dashing Eugène Delacroix?

Fryderyk doesn't hide his very close friendships with men, which involve both effusive correspondence and periods of living together. Letters to the friends of his youth are full of 'kisses' and 'embraces'. But, starting with a high-school friend, Tytus Woyciechowski, he also has a series of intimate, emotional – and flirtatious – relationships. 'I kiss you heartily, right on the mouth, may I?' he greets the youth he calls his 'Dearest life'. Often there's titillatingly more, and the pattern continues across the years. On 27 December 1828: 'You don't like being kissed. Please allow me to do so today. You have to pay for the dirty dream I had about you last night.' Next year, on 3 October: 'Forgive me for sending you the waltz [. . .] I did it to give you pleasure, for I do love you desperately.' And again in 1830, on 5 June: 'What a pity I can't post myself to you instead of this letter. Perhaps you would object, but I want you, and I expect you clean-shaven.'³⁵ Even allowing for the expressive mores of his time, it seems evident that Fryderyk is at least comfortable with bisexuality. As of course is George, whose own famously androgynous behaviour might appeal to someone who is bisexual.

Cohabiting is something else. The copyist-pianist Julian Fontana is another reason for the discreet love nest in rue Laffitte. The latest of Fryderyk's live-in companions, he has been installed in the musician's own apartment in the chaussée d'Antin since 1836. His predecessor, an amateur flautist called Jan Matuszyński who declared of Chopin, 'I have good reasons for staying with him: he is my everything,' shared the apartment from 1834 to 1836. If George has met Fontana – even, for example, at one of those intimate recitals – what does she imagine his role to be? Posterity will also finger the older Grzymała himself as a possible lover of Chopin. But is this likely? After all, both George and Fryderyk have confided the progress of their courtship to him, apparently without inhibition.

The nine years George is going to spend with Fryderyk will be subject to overwhelmingly misogynistic critique. Things are complicated: by human emotion, cultural differences, the passage of time – and secrecy. But this relationship is important – and notorious – enough in the history of European culture that we should at least try to work out what the deal is. Fryderyk Chopin's first reaction to George Sand, shared with Hiller, comes to us at third hand, but there's something authentically campy about 'Is it truly a woman?' Of course, snarky camp isn't a monopoly of gay men. It attracts the brainy or privileged young, and certainly Chopin, accustomed to public adulation and with an adoring close circle, has a robustly narcissistic sense of his own worth. But there is another possibility: that Grzymała and Chopin have worked together to get Sand in place as the pianist's beard. That, even as what she hopes for is true recognition by an equal, she's being intimately deceived, and her idealism about loving understanding being cynically turned against her.

This is painful even to think about: not least because of the effort George will expend in looking after the musician in coming years. Unless any proof comes to light it's also too great a stretch to be more than speculation. We can, though, be certain that the reverse is not the case. Chopin is not Sand's beard, but absolutely her physical type. Younger, boyish, blond and somehow lacking the thumping masculinity of a Casimir Dudevant or a Hippolyte Dupin, he is the emotional descendant of an Aurélien de Sèze or Jules Sandeau.

It is George's comrade and peer Franz Liszt who seems best to understand the loneliness that has led to her sexual adventuring. In a biography of Chopin which he will publish in 1851, he addresses her as:

> Sombre like Lara, torn like Manfred, rebellious like Cain, but fiercer and more pitiless, more inconsolable than they were, for there has not been a man's heart feminine enough to love you as they have been loved, to pay your virile charms the homage of trusting and blind submission, of wordless and ardent devotion, to let your Amazon strength protect his expressions of submission![36]

Which chimes with how another platonic friend and equal, Honoré de Balzac, understands George right now, during the first year of her relationship with Fryderyk. He too is in love with a Pole, and he tells his future wife, Ewelina Hańska:

Her male is rare, that's all there is to it. [. . .] She is a boy, she is an artist, she is great, generous, devout, chaste; she has all the great traits of a man; *ergo*, she is not a woman. I did not feel [. . .] gallantry [. . .] I talked as with a comrade. She has lofty virtues, of the kind that society takes the wrong way. We discussed, with a gravity, good faith, candour, and conscience worthy of [the priesthood] the great questions of marriage and liberty: 'For', as she said [. . .] 'although by our writings we are preparing a revolution for future manners and morals, I am struck by objections both to the one and to the other.'[37]

Like many relationships, the liaison between Fryderyk and George appears knotted by potentially conflicting motives. But there's nothing complex about wanting to get Chopin and his weak chest away to a healthy southern climate for the winter. After much preparation Sand, her children and a maid called Amélie set out for the Mediterranean at dawn on 18 October 1838. The trip is no secret – days before departure see her busily notifying friends – but it is discreet. Chopin will join them in the Midi after travelling separately by mail coach: an accelerated but tiring journey.

Maurice is fifteen but Solange is only ten and the family's progress, via the chateau at Plessis-Picard and then Custine, Chalon, Lyon, Avignon, Nîmes and Perpignan, is steady rather than headlong. They travel several legs by riverboat, enjoying themselves en route. Two days after Chopin meets them, the party set out together for Barcelona and, to avoid crossing the Pyrenees, take a boat for the Catalan city from Port-Vendres. This modest port town at the foot of the mountains is less than two miles from the pretty fishing village of Collioure, which a century from now will be made famous by artists from Pablo Picasso to Raoul Dufy. And here already are the light and colour those modernists will come for: 'I write to you beside the bluest and most pure sea [. . .] the sky is superb, we are hot,' George mails Charlotte Marliani, back in Paris.[38]

It's already 1 November and, though she doesn't reveal any nervousness, in just a couple of hours she will embark on only the second sea voyage of her life. For all that she seems to live in a state of perpetual motion, George, unusually for such a famous cultural figure, has rarely been out of France. Apart from her trip to war-torn Spain as a four-year-old, the only exceptions are those difficult months she spent in Venice with Alfred de Musset and Pietro Pagello and when, two years ago, she took both children along with Liszt, Marie and their brood on a trip to francophone Geneva and Chamonix. Evidently, however, there are no problems with the crossing and on 7 November, after five days in Barcelona, the group embark again. This time they board the paddle steamer *El Mallorquin* for the overnight sailing to Palma, Mallorca.[39]

This too is an easy crossing, during which the worst that happens is that George fails to finish her novel of spiritual awakening, *Spiridion*, on which she's been stuck for months. Not that she's in any way blasé about the trip. Soon she's writing to Christine Buloz, the wife of her publisher, about

> The visits, the dinners, the walks, the curiosities, the ruins, the fountain of Vaucluse, Reboul [the limestone caves, presumably] and the arenas at Nimes, the cathedrals at Barcelona, the dinners on board warships, the Italian theatres of Spain (what theatres and what Italians!), the guitars ~~oh! I'm [never] going to forget the serenades with ad hoc cantatas at Perpignan~~ [George's deletion] the moonlight on the sea, and above all Palma, and Mallorca, the most delicious residence in the world [. . .] with superb ruined convents among palm trees, aloes

and cactus in the middle of broken up mosaics and dilapidated cloisters [. . .]⁴⁰

'Delicious' indeed. But it would take an altogether more experienced traveller to realise how different it is to live in, rather than just visit, another country. Someone, say, like Chopin. As a Pole who's spent much of his life living abroad, in Switzerland and France, he must already understand, as George is about to, 'the inevitable little material disagreements in a new country, the servants who know nothing of the language, windows where panes are unknown, etc.'⁴¹

The language of the Balearics is not French, of course, but Catalan. In 1838, the Mallorcan economy is chiefly agricultural; tourism isn't yet making a real contribution. Landownership on Mallorca is overwhelmingly a matter of large feudal estates called *possessiós* and, for all the mild climate, peasant smallholdings barely offer a subsistence living. A liberal revolution in ownership has been under way for the past five years (though it will ultimately benefit absentee landlords more than the farming peasantry), but meanwhile harvesting costs (especially of olive oil) are rising and producers are facing increased competition from the mainland and abroad. The island's old-fashioned communities, isolated from the Iberian peninsula by the vagaries of marine weather, are undergoing uncertain and unwelcome change.⁴²

Old-fashioned; and strongly Catholic. Hard times don't necessarily make people elastic and forthcoming, able to deal with the new. The arrival of not one but two famous foreign artists, who are unmarried and have brought along another youth (Maurice) and a girl (Solange) whom they dress as a boy, is an occasion not for starstruck celebration but for hostile suspicion. Palma is not Indre. In Nohant, George's standing as the local chatelaine is a given, however radical the anomaly she presents in country society. Besides, France has gained through revolutionary upheavals a sense of its own social modernity. It's among the most progressive and secular places on earth. Mallorca, on the other hand, is governed from a Spain which since 1833 has been convulsed by the First Carlist War, a civil conflict in which the conservative, clerical and anti-liberal Carlists have risen up against their more progressive government. It's the first in the tragic series of iterations of what, in the lead-up to the Spanish Civil War a century from now, the poet Antonio Machado will call 'the two Spains'. Catalonia, including the Balearics, is a Carlist heartland, and the new arrivals represent everything these hard-pressed communities are fighting against.

So perhaps it's only to be expected that, despite several letters of introduction, their first problem turns out to be that

> we have neither hearth nor place. No inns at Palma, no houses to rent, no furniture to buy [...] For four days we were just going from door to door asking not to sleep outside, and [...] a miracle [...] for the first time in human memory in Mallorca, a furnished house is available to rent, a charming country house in a delicious wilderness.

This 'miracle', a pretty, shuttered villa with dormers set into its clay-tiled roof, is called S'on Vent. It stands at the top of a flight of steps above the main through road in the scattered farming hamlet of Establiments, just outside Palma. The rent is 'almost nothing', fifty francs per month.[43] After a grim week spent in lodgings, the household take possession on 15 November.

In fact, it's a double miracle, because before they even move in George has also managed to reserve a suite of three cells in the cloister of the nearly abandoned, and stunningly beautiful,

Charterhouse (Carthusian monastery) up in the hills at Valldemossa, for a peppercorn thirty-five francs a year. 'It's poetry, it's solitude, it's everything that is the most artistic and chic under the sun; and what countryside! We are in raptures.'[44] Meanwhile, with late autumn still in full flower, Maurice captures the picturesque charm of Establiments in a drawing where the house terrace boasts flowers, a pergola with vine and cacti in pots, and plump lizards darting on a sun-warmed garden wall.

Fryderyk finds the place charming too. On the day they move in, he writes to Julian Fontana, back in the chaussée d'Antin

> Here I am at Palma, surrounded by palms, cedars, cacti, olives, oranges, lemons, aloes, figs, pomegranates, etc [...] During the daytime it's hot and sunny, and everyone walks about in summer clothes; at night you hear guitars and singing for hours on end. [...] Everything, including the town, has an African look. In a word, life is marvellous![45]

This early equivalent of a postcard from the sun – which, notably, doesn't mention George – goes on to ask Fontana to 'call at Pleyel's, for the piano hasn't arrived yet. Which route have they dispatched it by?' This piano being sent from Paris by his piano-builder publishers will become a theme of the Mallorca sojourn. It's not just that Fryderyk needs to keep his fingers moving. An instrument is also essential because he composes at the keyboard. By the end of the year George has had to intervene, and 'According to the customs-house people the piano has been waiting in port for a week: they are asking a huge sum for the damned thing. Nature is kindly here but the people are rogues, for they never see foreigners so they never know what to charge for anything.'[46]

In fact S'on Vent has been less a miracle than a last-hope

contact made for George by the French consul, Pierre-Hippolyte Flury. She thinks her new landlord Señor Gomez is Jewish: that is, another outsider. And Señor Gomez's pretty, tiled house, which has no heating stoves, proves as draughty as its windy name suggests. By 3 December George is delighted to get hold of a stove, 'and may Heaven grant us its protection for there are neither doctors nor medicines here'.[47] Coughs, colds and – this being the mid-nineteenth century – perhaps worse besiege the blended family. It's the very opposite of the health cure for Fryderyk's bronchial lungs that has been the primary purpose of their trip. Nor is living in a goldfish bowl of hostile Mallorcan villagers conducive to work, as both artists had hoped.

So after exactly a month (which may suggest these are the terms of their lease) they move out, on 15 December, to

> three rooms and a garden [in an] immense and magnificent deserted convent in the middle of the mountains. The garden is littered with oranges and lemons, the trees are breaking with them. We have cactus hedges twenty to thirty feet high [. . .] a donkey for going to town [. . .] huge cloisters of the most beautiful architecture, a charming church, a cemetery with a palm tree [. . .].[48]

Ever since George found these rooms at Valldemossa, she's been busy buying the furniture that will enable them to move in. ('It's necessary to order beds, tables, mattresses, in fact everything.'[49]) Though Chopin grumbles, even at Establiments he's been managing to work – that is, compose – with or without the assistance of a ropey local piano which George has hired for him. But she herself is once again doing the double shift of domestic alongside creative labour, as she tells Grzymała: 'I cannot get on with my own work yet. We are not yet settled and have neither donkey, servant, water, fire, nor safe means of dispatching manuscripts. In these circumstances I am cooking instead of writing.'[50]

Like his future admirers, the musician seems to take it for granted that even a woman of George's international standing and unconventionality will put the man's work first. Beyond any questions about gender and art, however, this poses an immediate practical problem because, as usual, it's she who has the money: providing she can continue to earn it *by writing*. Before coming away she negotiated with François Buloz for instalment publication of not only *Spiridion* and *Aldini* but, as it turns out, *L'Usoque*, the story of an Albanian freedom fighter, and a short story, 'L'Ocre' ('Ochre'). Next year he will issue three more of her novels, all on conspicuously Sandean themes. *Gabriel* – which she will write on the journey home – asks what would happen if a girl were brought up as a boy; *Pauline* explores the exhausted hopes of a limited, provincial life; while the po-faced *Les Sept cordes de la lyre* (*The Seven Strings of the Lyre*), about which Buloz is unenthused, is a gender-switched reworking of the Faust legend. It's a lot of words and altogether, within a couple of months, George is admitting to her lawyer that 'As usual I'm spending most of the night working on my own account.'[51]

'The little Chop', on the other hand, borrowed funds for his share of costs – cue a number of anti-Semitic grumbles about the banker when this loan becomes due – and needs to complete his next commission, the Preludes, if Pleyel are to pay him the balance of his fee. But when in January 1839 he does finish composing them, he instead asks Fontana to hawk them around to see if he can find a higher bidder. He will end up with a lucrative three-way co-publication between Breitkopf and Härtel in Germany, Wessel in England and Catelin, replacing Pleyel, in France. Altogether, Pleyel do rather badly out of their investment in this work: being made its dedicatee hardly seems recompense. And although George will sell the fine piano they've shipped out to him when she and Fryderyk leave the island, there's no trace of his returning the money this raises, even though the publishers provided it as a form of advance.

This is a young man who, whether or not he really feels that his 'genius' is a sort of sacred obligation, is more than happy to use everyone around him to prioritise his work. What, one wonders, could be more convenient than a woman who has the means and maturity to shower her 'Chip-Chip', 'my Chup', with protective care?[52] But George herself is close to breaking point. In January, as Fryderyk bickers about his own finances, she instructs Alexis Duteil, her lawyer back in Indre, to sell her property near La Châtre at Côte-Noire. She confides to Hippolyte, whom she also urges to sell as much of the estate timber as he can – 'The trees have time to grow back' – that every delay, however well-meaning, will further indebt her. Extending the period over which she has to pay interest, in part to service a loan Casimir took against the property, simply makes it mount up; and it already totals 1,500 francs. The demands on her are becoming impossible to meet:

> The way of life that I'm sustaining can't continue. Until now I've succeeded in nothing except my work and I am exhausted [...] I've created some tours de force in that genre. But this has been going on for six years or more, and I can't keep it up, particularly giving my children at least six hours of lessons a day.[53]

Is the whole Mallorca trip, as George already confided to Charlotte Marliani a day before the move from Establiments, 'in many respects, a distressing fiasco'?[54] Yes and no. The household have arrived in what is always the rainiest month of the

Mallorcan year. Otherwise their plan, which two centuries from now will be imitated by countless thousands of northern European pensioners, is a reasonable one. Their stay may be rainier than usual, but it's all comparative. This is no damp Atlantic eyrie: island winters are usually dry. Average annual rainfall is half that of Paris, and winter temperatures are usually in the low teens. So it's unusual bad luck that for much of their three months on the island, 'It rains here in a way we've never known. It's a frightful deluge, the air is so heavy with it, so soggy, that one can't drag oneself along.'[55]

They'd hoped for a reset in mid-December when they moved up the mountain to Valldemossa, with its stunning views and charming mix of vernacular and ecclesiastical old buildings. The partly disused Charterhouse stands on a residential square at the highest point of this picturesque limestone village. It is historic, inviting, beautiful – in a word, Romantic – and the household's decision to move there is pragmatic (the cheapness, the mountain climate) as well as making complete artistic sense. But the stay here will be used posthumously to misdefine both their relationship and, worse, George's entire life and cultural contribution – though not Fryderyk's. Yet it lasts for less than two months. Their departure, on 11 February 1839, will mark the end of their belief in Mallorca, not only as a solution to the problem of cold and smoggy Paris winters, but as the Rousseauian idyll that may have been lying like a hope at the back of George's mind since she wrote *Indiana*. Mallorca is no Île de Bourbon.[56]

The naysayers are right, though, about the asymmetry of the project. From the outset it has been driven by George's hard work and vision. She has fantasies about settling on the island; at moments she sees herself buying a home in paradise. Fryderyk, on the other hand, wrote to Fontana the very day they moved in to S'on Vent, asking him to let everyone know 'that I will return at the end of the winter'.⁵⁷ And the pattern continues on their arrival at the Charterhouse, when she 'still cannot work' because she needs to sort out their practical situation.⁵⁸

Again, it occurs to no one that Fryderyk might help. He settles to write another letter to Fontana, camply complete with hairdresser and white gloves, and once again redacting any hint of George's presence:

> You can imagine me, between rocks and the sea, in a cell of an immense abandoned charterhouse [. . .] I am there without hairdressers, or white gloves, and pale as usual. My cell, in the form of a great coffin, has an enormous dusty vault, a little window giving on to the orange-trees, palms, cypresses of the garden. Opposite the window, under a rosette of Moorish filigree, a hammock.
>
> Beside the old, untouchable bed, a sort of square standing desk, uncomfortable for writing and on which is placed a lead candleholder with (a great luxury for here) a candle [. . .]
>
> Silence . . . One can shout . . . silence again.⁵⁹

Still, this low mood is for once understandable. Fryderyk remains poorly – 'sick as a dog', as he told Fontana on 3 December – and unable to shake off the cough he has brought with him from S'on Vent.⁶⁰ He hacks up blood, and when George eventually tracks down the island's doctors they propose the debilitating treatments usual for the time: bleeding the patient, limiting his diet and stitching setons (threads, of course unsterilised) through his skin to draw out infection by a kind of ritual magic. Luckily for Fryderyk, George protects him from all of this.

Whether or not, as his posthumous admirers will claim, she's in denial about the gravity of his illness, her protective instinct kicks in once again with its customary energetic practicality. She buys a goat to provide the household with fresh milk in place of the adulterated stuff locals cheat them with, and recruits two local women to help her cook nutritious meals. But it's an uphill struggle. The island is 'at least three centuries behind the times', as she noted in the first flush of enchantment. This conserves a charming folklore: 'there are costumes and customs of which we no longer have any idea in France'. But it also means primitive ideas about hygiene and health, unreliability in the postal service on which both artists rely for their money and work, and a lack of comfortable, efficient forms of transport, all of which make daily life increasingly attritional.[61] Ever the frowning Slav, Chopin puts this succinctly in a note to Grzymała: 'It's a diabolical country in relation to the post, people and comfort.'[62]

And yet among the struggle and disappointment there is something important. This brief winter does see Fryderyk, who is now almost at the midpoint of his professional life, produce compositions that will remain significant in his oeuvre, and in the history of Western music.[63] He completes the Ballade in F major, Op. 38, and composes the Scherzo no. 3 in C# minor, Op. 39, and the Polonaise in C minor, Op. 40 no. 2, which he dedicates to Fontana. It is worth remembering that he never dedicates any of his work to George. And then there are twenty-four Preludes themselves, one in each of the twelve major and twelve minor keys, like J. S. Bach's famous set of Preludes and Fugues, published over a century ago as the *Das wohltemperierte Klavier* (*The Well-Tempered Clavier*). Chopin has this score with him in Mallorca.[64] Like Bach, he arranges his pieces in key order, starting with that fundamental of Western art music, C major, and following each key with its relative minor. While Bach ascends the scale stepwise by semitones, Chopin modulates up the circle of fifths, passing from C to G to D, and so on. Like Bach's canonical work, therefore, the Preludes are no pick-n-mix scrapbook but a serious exploration of the palette of major-minor tonality: of range but also of relationship.

In juxtaposition, musical keys exert an often plangent pull on each other. This pull of harmonic relationship is what creates a tonal world; a systematic cycle through all twenty-four keys of Western tonality reveals how mutability is the sound of chromaticism. The ear is destabilised, for example, when a phrase stretches to an unexpected pitch, or modulation lifts or lapses. This push and pull is the feelingful give at the heart of Chopin's otherwise comparatively formal music. It mimics – and then creates – the quick intake of breath that expresses feeling: it finds space for expression *within* the technical fluency of both composer and performer. Chopin's use of rhythmic delay – dotted notes held over a beat, harmonic suspensions – works in the same way, deferring and modulating gratification for all the world like a sexual tease. His is a music of nuance and sensibility, something that a comparison with the *Sturm und Drang* of his contemporary and alter ego Franz Liszt makes all the clearer. It's even there in the titles: while Liszt's will become flamboyantly narrative, Chopin's almost always simply name a musical form.

George's own work is narrative, of course. But she shares with Fryderyk a belief in sensibility. Romanticism lays almost definitive store on the discerning reactions of a highly developed sensitivity as a kind of spiritual weathervane. Yearning hyper-attunedness has become the mark of a great soul; and both novelist and musician are at the forefront of the late-Romantic search for meaning through feelingful reaction. Romanticism takes art not as inert cultural artefact but as a conduit for emotion and other, perhaps spiritual, experiences. When music arrives in George's fiction – for example in the novel *Consuelo*, which she will publish in 1842–3 – it is as an experience her characters have.[65] As she will write of Fryderyk after his death:

The genius of Chopin is the most profound and the most filled with feelings and emotions that has existed. [. . .] Chopin experienced his power and his weakness. His weakness was in the very excess of this power that he could not regulate. He could not, like Mozart, make [. . .] a masterpiece with a level hue. His music was full of nuances and of the unexpected. Sometimes, rarely, it was bizarre, mysterious and tormented. Though he had a horror of what is incomprehensible, his excessive emotions carried him, without his knowledge, into regions known only to him.[66]

The whole unhappy expedition to Mallorca, which she will write up under the eventual title of *Un hiver à Majorque*, may after all demonstrate what that early great Romantic Goethe has called *die Wahlverwandtschaften*, elective affinities.[67] But this winter, once she's finished grappling with the knotty religious ideas *Spiridion* explores, George is chiefly absorbed in rewriting *Lélia*. Its second, 1839 edition sees her baulked and tragic heroine no longer murdered but (arguably worse) defrocked and incarcerated. This quieter, more realistic narrative turn is perhaps the first inkling of a dawning attention to politics and the legislature, which will grow to be one of the writer's central preoccupations by the time of the Revolution of 1848.

In the short term, however, even getting home to France will be no mean achievement. Fryderyk's possibly tubercular cough sees their household increasingly spurned by anxious Mallorcans. As they leave the island, authorities force them to destroy rather than sell their furniture and belongings, in line with quarantine regulations. When they arrive in Barcelona on 14 February the captain of *El Mallorquin*, who must do the same with the bed in their cabin, takes the opportunity to overcharge them on replacement costs, as George tells Charlotte Marliani in a desperate letter.[68] The family have had enough. When they finally board a French steamer for Marseille a week later, George and the children shout '*Vive la France!*'. But relief is short-lived. By the time they dock, after a rough thirty-six-hour crossing, Chopin is so unwell that he's forced to pause at the port city to recuperate.

All the same, recuperate he broadly does, especially with the help of François Cauvière, a doctor with whom Charlotte Marliani puts George in touch. In the first decades of the nineteenth century, all pulmonary symptoms tend to be regarded as tubercular; and tuberculosis, being both infectious and often fatal, is treated with a mixture of superstitious dread and rational quarantine measures. But it's perfectly possible, in this era without antibiotics, steroid inhalers or chest X-rays, that Fryderyk is simply suffering from bronchitis, like Elizabeth Barrett Browning, another contemporary artist whose life is restricted and eventually curtailed by pulmonary disease. Cauvière, who even lets the pianist stay in his own home, evidently agrees with the ship's doctor of *El Mallorquin*, who examined him for contagious disease before letting him board, that Chopin is not actually consumptive, reassuring George 'that this is an excessively weak chest, but there was nothing hopeless there, that with rest and care he would soon recover his little health'.[69]

After four months in Marseille under Cauvière's care – a convalescence perhaps extended by their unwise decision to take a side trip to Genoa at the start of May – the party make for Nohant. They arrive on 1 June for the first of what are to be seven productive summers of work at the country manor. Adding to a sense of things stabilising, George's old La Châtre circle includes medics: she's able to call on her long-term friend Gustave Papet for clinical reassurance about her partner's health.

Quick quick slow. A calmer way of life is coming into focus. The education of George's children is coming into focus, too. It is, she notes to Charlotte, 'the most noble, the most important, the most holy of functions to raise the young'.[70] Fryderyk gives Solange piano lessons; the proud mother boasts that her daughter is already reading Shakespeare with genuine insight. But working a double shift as family tutor remains exhausting, and it will only finally end, after another Nohant summer, in the autumn of 1840. That November Maurice joins Delacroix's atelier to study art, while in October George again places Solange in a Paris boarding school.

Maternal pride notwithstanding, she feels her daughter is becoming chaotic and wilful. Like her own grandmother, faced with the onset of girlish adolescence George panics, evidently feeling she doesn't know how to cope. It seems there's something peculiarly alarming about the chaos a rather wild young woman might cause. Maman's response to what she saw as incipient rebellion was boarding school and, since in the end this allowed George herself to thrive, it now appears to her the ideal remedy. There will be a false start at Michelle Héreau's establishment, where twelve-year-old Solange plays up because, as her mother – astutely or foolishly? – observes, 'she truly loves Mme Héreau. But she never obeys those she loves, because she flatters herself that she is loved too, and has the upper hand.'[71] In April 1841 George will withdraw her daughter, rather unassertively on the pretence that she needs her at home 'for some days that I'll be spending in the countryside', and deliver her to an altogether smarter and more demanding establishment.[72] This boarding school for girls, directed by Sophie Lagut Bascans at 70 rue de Chaillot, sits in an elite location, halfway between the Tuileries and the Bois de Boulogne. Mme Bascans runs it with her husband, a teacher of history and literature and, as an editor involved in progressive politics, no stranger to George's own world.

But back in 1839, as she arrives with Fryderyk and the

children at Nohant after the trials of Mallorca and Marseille, the writer is still juggling family obligations along with the level of literary productivity necessary to keep the household's financial show on the road. It's at this early stage in their relationship that George seems to conclude that Fryderyk, though many years her junior, will never equal her own prodigious strength and energy: 'Chopin is always somewhat better, somewhat less good, never precisely either ill nor well. I truly believe that the poor child is destined to a perpetual slight languor.'[73] It's probably also now, on 19 June, that she decides – or rather more likely, accepts – that they will never be lovers again, and she is now the 'mistress of her own bedroom', in the words she will use, in the waning years of the relationship, to Grzymała.[74] She even carves the date into the window frame of that room.

But in a way this solves nothing. Years from now she will still find Chopin's feelings for her to be 'a jealous and exclusive passion. It's a little fantasised and sickly like him, the poor angel.'[75] Whereas for herself, as she will recall in *Histoire*: 'A sort of fear squeezed my heart before a new duty to be contracted. I was not deluded by a passion. I had for the artist a sort of intense, very real maternal worship which could not for a moment contend with instinctual love.'[76] 'A very real maternal worship . . . for the artist': this image of an only-just-secular Pietà will speak to her readers in still largely Catholic France. Yet it also signals the atheist Romantic belief in art as something elevated, even transcendent.

Her 'poor child' 'Chopinet' needs routine. The least change disturbs him. But the musician also wants more than one mutually irreconcilable thing at once. In the coming years, George helps him alternate between quiet downtime in the Indre countryside, where he can compose without interruption, and the more sophisticated pleasures of Parisian artistic milieux where he can shine. But he seems irresolute, tetchily unable ever to be content in either place: 'Chopin always longed for Nohant, and could never bear Nohant. He was a man of the world par excellence [. . .] but of the intimate world [. . .] of the hour when the crowd leaves and the habituées crowd round the artist.'[77] For the rest of their time together, George's financial support will allow him to avoid the touring and concertising which he claims to detest, and to concentrate on producing the extraordinary body of compositions which will be his legacy.

But her generosity remains discreet. In the city Fryderyk continues to live semi-separately, first at 5 rue Tronchet and then, when that proves chilly, in the 'other' of a pair of garden pavilions which George has taken at 16 rue Pigalle. Pavilions and garden will have disappeared by the twenty-first century, but Balzac, visiting her there, captures her:

> living in a garden [. . .] Her snug is the colour of milk coffee, and the salon is replete with Chinese vases full of flowers [and] a buffet with all kinds of curiosities, paintings by Delacroix, her portrait by Calamatta [. . .] A magnificent piano [. . .] Chopin is always there. *She smokes just CIGARETTES* [Balzac's emphasis: no opium, in other words] and nothing else. [. . .] Her bedroom is brown, her bed two mattresses on the floor, Turkish style.[78]

Picturesque maybe, but one winter in a garden is enough. In September 1842 the entire blended family move to more appropriate accommodation at the square d'Orléans, where Charlotte Marliani and her family already live at number 7. Fryderyk is installed on the raised ground floor of number 9, where he will remain till the year of his death, George in one apartment at number 5, and Maurice and Solange each in studios on a higher floor. Proximity with breathing room: it's a recipe for stability.

Meanwhile, summers at Nohant continue to be creative. Sometimes the whole household gets involved as the composer delightedly discovers Berrichon folk music and traditional dances. Especially characteristic of the region are *bourées* – fast three-time gavottes – with which he will be familiar: and *branles*, with which he won't. The *branle* is the hypnotic, four-time, four-square Western equivalent of the Balkan *kora*; it can be danced slow, fast, or slow-becoming-fast, by lines of dancers holding hands. Excitingly for these amateur ethnomusicologists, unlike the *bourrée* it has not been gentrified and incorporated into art music.

In the event Chopin will compose neither *bourrées* nor *branles*. But, like many Romantic composers, he will use traditional dance forms from his own country: mazurkas and polonaises. His time with George will see him compose all the rest of the work published in his lifetime, from the Ballades in A♭ major, Op. 47, and F minor, Op. 52, to the Cello Sonata, Op. 65, including the Polonaises in F♯ minor and A♭ major, Opp. 44 and 53, three sets of Nocturnes, Opp. 48, 55 and 62, the Mazurkas, Opp. 50, 56, 59 and 63, the Fantasie in F minor, Op. 49, and the Sonatas in B♭ minor, Op. 35, and in B minor, Op. 58.

For George, these Nohant summers are also key. This period marks a turning point in her relationship to her surroundings – her literal patrimony. From now on the countryside, both the people who live in it and the natural environment itself, will come progressively to the fore in her writing and thinking. But once again she is not to be granted a Rousseauian idyll. Her years with Fryderyk are both personally and professionally complex and the costs of maintaining this semi-domestic stability are high. By August 1843 she is confiding to Delacroix in a passionate outburst:

a huge exhaustion of all the personal satisfactions that seem so great when one is young and chases them, and then seem such a small thing when one no longer hopes for them and has no more strength to run after them. In brief, I no longer exist, as I told you. I have been dead for three years, precisely calculated [in other words: since the summer of 1840], having voluntarily killed myself to escape dying and dragging around a ridiculous agony. My ideal is no longer in my real life. It's in another world, in another century, in another humanity.[79]

As if this weren't enough, for the first time in her life work, traditionally her escape route, is proving problematic. In the spring of 1840 her first play, *Cosima, ou La haine dans l'amour* (*Cosima, or Hate in Love*), staged for three weeks at the Théâtre Français and in part a vehicle for her old love Marie Dorval, will be an embarrassing flop.[80] Worse, in 1841 her long-term editor and literary wingman François Buloz – since autumn 1838 comfortably tenured as the chief administrator of the Comédie-Française – will refuse to publish her latest novel, *Horace*. He finds it skirts too radically close to communism.[81]

Buloz has a contractual commitment to print everything George writes. But he's already rehearsed similar concerns over her previous novels of ideas, *Spiridion* and *Les Sept cordes de la lyre*. George's more think-y books aren't as popular as her feelingful fiction about human relationships. She may be the *Revue*'s golden goose, but now that he doesn't rely on his salary from the periodical her long-time editor can afford to be picky. George, though, *does* still have to rely on her writing, and in the autumn of 1841 she's forced to break with him and find other places to publish. Breaking up is hard to do. This working partnership has been formative for both of them, and their painful rupture will last until 1858, the span of an entire literary generation.

One result of this falling-out is that October 1841 sees George found the mordantly titled *La Revue indépendante* with Pierre Leroux and Louis Viardot. Clubbable in the way of periodicals, its first volume includes their own writing alongside work by Eugène Pelletan, formerly secretary-tutor at Nohant, and Étienne Aragon, co-founder of *Le Figaro*. Initially published monthly, then after a year every two months, the *Revue* will continue to appear until the tumult surrounding the foundation, and dissolution, of the Second Republic in 1848. But its founders' names will disappear from the masthead in January 1843, and in 1845 they will dissociate themselves completely, paradoxically because they feel the periodical has become too political. Leroux and Sand will then found *La Revue sociale*: whose title indicates political leanings of its own. It too will be interrupted by the events of 1848.

For George, these are years of gradually increasing political activity of several kinds. In 1843 she's shocked by the story of Fanchette, a teenager with learning difficulties, who is abandoned in the middle of nowhere by the nuns of a La Châtre convent and, by the time she's found weeks later, is pregnant despite lacking capacity to consent. (As the case of Gisèle Pelicot will demonstrate two centuries from now, absence of consent is not part of France's legal definition of rape.) First George gives this story oxygen by writing about it in *La Revue indépendante*, then she reprints her articles in a limited edition of which half are given away to workers and half are sold to raise funds for Fanchette herself. It's her first piece of political direct action.

The tremendous literary production continues apace. During the years of her involvement with *La Revue indépendante* she used it to publish not only *Horace*, the work Buloz rejected, but other novels, notably *Consuelo* and its sequel *La Comtesse de Rudolstadt*. The eponymous heroine of both of these, a Spanish orphan whose beautiful singing voice leads a famous maestro to take her under his wing, has been inspired by George's friend Pauline Viardot.[82] She's someone to whom George and Fryderyk have become increasingly close: a hugely distinguished mezzo-soprano and pianist, who is of Spanish descent like George's character Consuelo, and is married to George's co-editor at *La Revue indépendante*. Louis Viardot is both the singer's agent and the father of her child. A former child prodigy, who will go on to produce a body of distinguished compositions when she retires from singing, Pauline Viardot may not be entirely flattered to have her achievements trivialised and sentimentalised by George's fiction, even in the cause of exploring women's artistry. But the friendship survives the novel.

It will also survive the tricky summer of 1844, when the twenty-four-year-old Pauline, whose husband is a whole generation her senior, has a dalliance with George's own twenty-one-year-old son. Maurice, too, seems altogether unabashed about pursuing his private life under his mother's nose. Not long after his summer with Pauline, he brings a distant cousin back with him from Paris to Nohant. This is another musician, the 'young and charming' Augustine Brault, who is studying singing at the Paris Conservatoire with Pauline's cousin. Nohant approves. Maurice enjoys a romance with her; George places her on a retainer, and in January 1846 will formally adopt her. Only Solange, perhaps feeling displaced, is resentful.[83]

La Revue indépendante also publishes pseudonymous reviews by George, including some under the byline Blaise Bonnin.[84] Although neither the *Indépendante* nor *La Revue sociale* will become among the great fixtures of French public life, her work on these periodicals reminds us how seductive George finds the intellectual social life of collaboration. This is also the period when she starts to work with Pierre-Jules Hetzel, the entrepreneurial writer, artist, publisher, and future discoverer of Jules

Verne. He becomes her literary agent; an arrangement that will run smoothly until the coup of 1851 forces him into exile.

In 1845 alone, he oversees the appearance of four of her novels which explore socialist ideas. In *Le Meunier d'Angibault* (*The Miller of Angibault*), social class defines life choices, though landscape offers consolation and models a redemptive freedom. (The watermill at Angibault, which will still be standing in the twenty-first century, is less than five miles from Nohant manor.) In *Le Péché de M. Antoine* (*Mr Antoine's Sin*), a young couple, married across class and the urban/rural divide, carry out social reforms. *Isadora* unpicks the virgin/whore dichotomy, showing how women become prostitutes, contrary to male fantasy, largely through economic necessity. They work not beyond but within the socio-economic network we call community. *Teverino* is, like *Le Meunier d'Angibault*, a transitional work, which shifts its familiar romantic choreography to the countryside and introduces a kind of wild innocent called Madeleine. Young and female, she subverts traditional personifications of the natural order as green men, or peasant sages. But the novel which is the precursor to George's famous 'rural fiction', as she herself acknowledges, is *Jeanne*, which was published a year earlier. Here for the first time we find landscape offering the writer the conceptual space in which to simplify and distil moral clarities. Jeanne 'of Arc' is another young woman as outlier: an exception within her rural community yet paradoxically created, in all her virginal idealism, by that very community and its religious values.

Life in the countryside doesn't preoccupy George Sand simply for aesthetic reasons. Neither in these novels of the mid-1840s nor in her celebrated pastoral trilogy – *La Mare au diable*, *François le Champi* and *La Petite Fadette* (*Little Fadette*) – does she indulge in the Romantic picturesque. Nor is her Indre merely the setting for the kind of sentimental, if well-intentioned, portrayals of poverty that have by now made Charles Dickens famous. Instead, these stories identify in rural life a kind of depth charge of long-held values and meaning. They also acknowledge how often idealism can be – as revolutionary history has repeatedly reminded French society – passionately working-class. *Jeanne*, for example, explores a profound radicalism disguised as peasant naivety.

A century and a half from now, the Marxist anthropologist Michel Dion will use the phrase '*la France profonde*', deep France, to mean not only what is unmodernised – that is, both rural and historic – in the nation's territory, but traditions at the roots of France's understanding of itself. Dion will align this with principles of reformed Catholicism and decentralised socialism. By 1844, George has already come to the same conclusions.[85] This new turn towards the locality of Indre in her fiction is also reflected in her founding one more newspaper in the September of that year. A local progressive weekly, *L'Eclaireur: Journal des départements d'Indre, du Cher et de la Creuse* will run until 1848.

The events of that year won't be the first revolutionary upheaval through which George has lived, but they are the first in which she's politically active. In this season of pan-European uprising, the 'springtime of the nations,' a provisional French government which calls itself the Second Republic is formed in Paris on 26 February, two days after King Louis-Philippe has been forced to abdicate. It immediately founds a national bank, enacts universal male suffrage, abolishes slavery and counters mass unemployment with National Workshops that offer ordinary people jobs and wages. George supports this work. Dedication to a cause – this time, one larger than a single man of genius – suits her fundamental intensity. Moving between Nohant and Maurice's Paris apartment at 8 de la rue de Condé, in March she publishes two *Lettres au peuple* (*Letters to the People*). Each pamphlet sells for ten centimes and offers a dose of populist rhetoric: 'You are going to be loved, because you are worthy of it.'[86] She is perhaps more within her comfort zone addressing the readers of her 'A word on the middle class', in *Journal de Loiret*, while adopting a (double) pseudonym may help with the composition of *L'Histoire de France écrite sous la dictée de Blaise Bonnin* (*History of France dictated by Blaise Bonnin*) and five instalments of *Paroles de Blaise Bonnin aux bons citoyens* (*Speeches of Blaise Bonnin to Good Citizens*). She publishes almost daily articles in the optimistically titled *Bulletin de la République* and *La Vraie République* and in April founds a short-lived weekly, *La Cause du peuple*.[87] Even Maurice, now twenty-four, gets involved, becoming the Republican mayor of Nohant in March.

But democracy isn't necessarily accompanied by astute democratic literacy, and April sees the election of an Assembly that's largely conservative in character. On 23 June this anti-socialist body abolishes the National Workshops. Their closure after just four months of optimism and opportunity tips the people who were relying on them into desperation – and the June Days Uprising, which is violently suppressed. One and a half thousand citizens are mown down by troops and 15,000 deported to Algeria. The scene is set for a reactionary, replacement Second Republic and the swearing-in of Napoléon III as the country's first president, soon to be its emperor and last monarch. It's the end of hopes for a more socially inclusive France. It also draws a line under the political activity into which George has poured much emotional energy.

Eighteen forty-eight also ushers in life after Fryderyk. A year of pan-European upheaval, when no one is much concerned with one ailing golden boy, is not the best time for the musician to find himself suddenly cut adrift from George's financial and emotional support. Though he survives until October 1849, he will prove unable really to put his life back together. His health failing, he gives his final Paris concert at Pleyel's salon on 16 February 1848.

What in the end has gone wrong between the partners? It involves all the family, which has undergone a two-year implosion precipitated by the arrival of a son-in-law, Jean-Baptiste (Auguste) Clésinger. It is George herself who introduced this chaotic, impecunious – and dashing – sculptor to her then eighteen-year-old daughter. When the women turned up to pose for him in February 1847, Solange was engaged to Fernand de Préaulx, a young member of the local gentry. All seemed set fair; the storms of adolescence weathered. But as the resulting formulaic bust in antique style of George – no portrait at all – would make abundantly clear, Clésinger's attention was from the outset not on the great writer but on her nubile daughter.[88] Though already thirty-two, he had only recently emerged as a sculptor specialising in sexy marbles of writhing women, whose signature breasts were set usually akimbo. Dark-haired, vulpine and with a shady past, he now swept Solange off her feet, broke her engagement, and within three months had married her. She was swiftly pregnant.

Passionate indeed. But it transpired that Clésinger had debts, and was counting on a substantial dowry. Within five months, in July 1847, he was at Nohant, demanding money and threatening George with first a hammer (which he used) and then a pistol (which he did not). For it turned out that his new wife had already received her settlement from her mother as a coming-of-age gift. Undeterred, the artist commanded George to conjure further funds by mortgaging Nohant for him. But for his mother-in-law, of course, male domestic violence is an absolute taboo. Even though she was not seriously injured, Clésinger's hammer and pistol were like a replay of Casimir's sword and pistol. She refused the couple's demands and threw them out.

As it turned out, Solange's first child, Jeanne-Gabrielle Clésinger, lived for only a week, and she and the father will separate within seven years.[89] But when the violence erupts Fryderyk, for years another unquestioning beneficiary of George's generosity, suddenly pays attention, identifying with Solange and accusing George of heartlessness. You couldn't make it up. In an exhaustive account of the affair to her friend Emmanuel Arago – the gifted lawyer, playwright and future Republican man of affairs – George finally admits just how much of a burden Fryderyk has been: 'What a relief! What a chain broken! Always resisting his narrow, despotic ideas, but always tied down by pity and fear that he would die of grief. For nine years, while full of life, I have been tied to a corpse.'[90]

It's as if she's been existing less as a real person than as a resource for others. 'Chopin was never a refuge for me in my sadness,' she will write.[91] Still, two days later she has the satisfaction of sending him a magnificent in-sorrow-not-anger letter ending the relationship:

> Well my friend, do what your heart now tells you and take this instinct as the voice of your conscience. I understand perfectly.
> As for my daughter [. . .] Look after her then, since it's to her that you believe you must devote yourself. [. . .] Enough with being a dupe and a victim. [. . .] Farewell my friend [. . .] and I will thank God for this bizarre outcome to nine years of exclusive friendship. Give me your news from time to time. It's useless to go over the rest again.[92]

George's last meeting with Fryderyk in March 1848, hasty and accidental, takes place just before he embarks on a gruelling seven-month tour of Britain. The couple bump into each other one last time, on the staircase at Charlotte Marliani's. Standing there, he gets to break the news to George – because he has stayed close to Solange – that she has become a grandmother. This grubby spite does little justice to what has been one of the great artistic partnerships of nineteenth-century Europe. But the loss is all his. George had looked after the musician's health and well-being, creating a domesticity that allowed him to achieve his work. He turns out to be literally unable to live without her. In a final irony, the magnificent sculpture of a downcast Euterpe, muse of music, that will decorate his monument in Père Lachaise cemetery less than two years from now is created by the very man who destroyed that domesticity, Auguste Clésinger.[93]

Seventh impression: *Fame in a black lace mantilla*

In August Charpentier's portrait of George Sand, painted in the spring of 1838, the thirty-four-year-old's face has a softness and heaviness that's both sultry, with its suggestion of fleshliness, and powerful. In these years of her prime, she has none of the spidery braininess of, say, a Simone Weil, nor the pallor of the Brönte siblings.[94] The enormously dark eyes which Alfred de Musset enlarged and orientalised in his portraits five years ago still dominate her face; as they will do even when she becomes a grande dame in her seventies. Portrait after portrait shows them heavy-lidded, set so deep that there's shadow beneath them. Now they stare back at Charpentier, their expression neither acquiescent nor withheld, with the same very faint asymmetry that later photographs will capture.

George's left eye is just a touch steelier, her right a touch larger and more quiescent. But this inflection of the left side of her face, the way that eye seems to look straight back at us, is muted by her coiffure. This is Big Hair, brushed up to bulk thickly round her head. Though she's wearing it loose and ringleted, there's nothing casual about the arrangement, which includes a dazzle of flowers above her left ear. That home-made fascinator of poppies and what looks like edelweiss could not possibly stay in place if she were to move. But, pinned against her cheek and trailing a pendant garland, it catches the light so as to turn her curls into the dark of a chiaroscuro.

Chiaroscuro in turn lifts the skin tone on forehead, cheekbones and neck, brightening her complexion, which keeps its golden-olive tone. The brightness of white flower petals is caught again by a crucifix of pearls – a highlight perhaps as deliberate as Delacroix's heavenly light in his 1834 portrait of the writer as soul-in-torment – and the hooked white stripes within a large onyx at George's waist; drawing the eye across and down like a diagram of how to look at the picture.

One thing there's no sign of is the premature greying characteristic of unusually dark European hair. But then, Auguste Charpentier is a celebrity portraitist, and it's his job to capture his wealthy and powerful subjects' best selves. This, though, is the moment at which his entire professional context is about to change, and the shadow of obsolescence passes over this fashionable artist, still only twenty-five years old. Louis Daguerre is even now developing the daguerreotype process which, when it's made publicly available next year, will transform portraiture.

Unsurprisingly, given her celebrity, there does seem to be an early daguerreotype of George Sand herself.[95] A blotchy image pictures her once again wearing an oval brooch, this time where her bolero meets over a lacy blouse (there's another at her collar). Her hair is not only fiercely dark – dark enough to suggest a little help from a friend – but scrunched into the vertical barley curls that will soon become the signature style of her English near-contemporary the poet Elizabeth Barrett.[96] George has a tiny waist, again, and is wearing a pretty floral skirt as well as what appears to be a sort of lace mantilla off the shoulder. She leans her chin on curved fingers in a pose that is to become a cliché of the twenty-first-century author photo (but it's probably helping her to keep still while the image takes).

Who made this picture of George, if it is indeed of her? It can't be earlier than 1839, the year the technique becomes available, nor can it date from many years after and still be of George, since in it she appears comfortably less than forty. One possibility is Louis-Auguste Bisson, who will open a collodion (that is, reproducible image) process studio in Paris's Madeleine neighbourhood with his brother, also called Auguste, in 1841. An early Bisson coup will be a dashing portrait of George's friend Honoré de Balzac – open shirt neck, hand on heart. This in 1842, the year that Balzac dedicates his *Mémoires de deux jeunes mariées* (*Letters of Two Young Married Women*) to his fellow novelist. Could he also have introduced her to the Bisson brothers?

The Frères Bisson will only trade at the Madeleine address for four years, but they'll continue to go from success to success, reopening a studio with up to thirty assistants in the grand seventeenth-century Hôtel de Sourdéac in the rue Garancière between 1852 and 1863, and even accompanying Napoléon's military expedition to Savoy in 1860 as official war artists. Among future photographic subjects will be Fryderyk Chopin in 1849, the year of his death. (Possibly he also poses for them in 1847, the year he and George split up.) The famous brothers' astonishingly crisp, confidently composed outdoor and landscape photography is to prove pioneering. But they have an eye for sumptuous interior detail too, posing portrait subjects before a silk curtain, or next to tables piled with handsome leatherbound volumes. In the daguerreotype which appears to be of George, she rests her elbow on a table covered with a lavishly patterned silk that seems to offer itself like a clue of where and when she is being photographed.

Eighteen thirty-eight, the year of Charpentier's portrait, is the year that George's pursuit of Fryderyk Chopin finally pays off, as Eugène Delacroix's great, if unfinished, double portrait, for which they sit together that autumn, records. The Charpentier oil, on the other hand, sits both within and beyond the context of that relationship: it's to *her*, as she is *now*, that Chopin commits. We may or may not be able to look at her through the Bisson brothers' eyes, but we can stand alongside the musician, and her public, in witnessing the famous novelist in her prime. Next year, when Charpentier hangs this portrait in the 1839 Salon, it will be, as George Lubin will quaintly put it, '*beaucoup lorgné par les visateurs*', 'much eyed up by the public'.[97]

EIGHT

Dear master

'HAPPINESS WRITES IN WHITE INK on white pages,' Henry de Montherlant's decadent version of *Don Juan* will declare, more than a century after Fryderyk Chopin's death.[1] But in the new Europe then emerging from two shattering world wars, the morbid excesses of this kind of bohemianism will be understood as nostalgic rather than radical. By the time she's in her forties George Sand, whose radicalism has become notorious, knows first-hand how often decadence is, as the word literally denotes, a kind of collapse.

As she recovers from the wounds to her idealism caused by the political defeats of 1848 – as well as that other more personal defeat which is the failure of her relationship with Chopin – George is no longer in the avant-garde of sexual and social change. Now hers is 'the middle generation', populating the intellectual and cultural establishment. Michel de Bourges is about to be reappointed as a deputy; he has become a leading *avocat*, or barrister, who defends possible revolutionaries in high-profile trials. Alfred de Musset was awarded the Légion d'honneur in 1845 and, although dismissed from his post as Librarian of the Interior Ministry in the upheavals of 1848, will become a member of the French Academy in 1852 and be reappointed to another public librarianship a year later. Honoré de Balzac, awarded the Légion d'honneur at the same time as de Musset, will leave his great *Comédie humaine* unfinished at his death in 1850; but it will still run to more than ninety novels and other writing, and change the course of European fiction. Fryderyk Chopin and Franz Liszt are international celebrities and, though Marie d'Agoult's friendship with George won't outlast her split with Liszt, the countess is publishing her own first stories: *Hervé, Julien, Valentia*. Eugène Delacroix is deep into his years of major commissions for murals in the churches and public buildings of Paris. François Buloz is still running the Comédie-Française. Even Jules Sandeau is finally publishing fiction of his own, including 1839's *Marianna*, with its portrayal of George as a headstrong seductress; the 1850s will see him, too, receiving public librarian appointments and elected to the French Academy.

It's a time of professional plenitude. George is part of the 'village' of interconnected people at the pinnacle of the national artistic establishment. Indeed, she's turning into a literary institution. By a kind of synecdoche Nohant will become part of that institution; one of those necessary destinations of the cultural imagination, a combined salon and retreat to which artists, writers and thinkers will make their pilgrimage. Since 1847 the new railway connection to Châteauroux has shrunk its distance from Paris: the three-day expedition of George's youth has become a more realistic eight hours by train, followed by three in a diligence. Among the first such pilgrimages, however, is the one made earlier, in 1846, by a twenty-four-year-old British Europhile, Matthew Arnold. Throughout his long future as an immensely influential British poet-critic, Arnold will admire Sand's idealism about human nature and society. The terms he will use in his eventual obituary sum up what is by now the consensus about her work:

The immense vibration of George Sand's voice upon the ear of Europe will not soon die away. Her passions and her errors have been abundantly talked of. She has left them behind her [. . .] There will remain of her the sense of [. . .] that large and frank nature, that large and pure utterance, [. . .] the greatest spirit in our European world from the time that Goethe departed.²

From Feuillide's 'prostitution of the soul and body' in 1833 to 'large and pure utterance' in around a dozen years. Becoming an authority figure gives George a different set of opportunities to transcend gendered expectations. In 1848, the diplomat and political philosopher Alexis de Tocqueville, already celebrated for his *De la démocratie en Amérique* (*Democracy in America*, 1835), sits next to her at a lunch and has his prejudices overturned:

I detest writing women, especially those who systematically disguise the weakness of their sex [. . .] despite this, I liked her. [. . .] What especially struck me was finding in her something of the natural bearing of great minds. [. . .] Mme Sand was a sort of statesman; what she told me truly impressed me.³

In April of the same year, the editor of *La Voix des femmes* (*The Voice of Women*) proposes her as the first woman to stand for the Chamber of Deputies – though George hastily demurs – in similar terms: 'Her mind makes her a man, she remains a woman through motherhood.'⁴

In the twenty-first century, these mannish identifications will sound complex: either turning George into a kind of sacred monster or else identifying some 'essentially' transitional gender identity. But in the 1840s the attributes of a (white) man are seen as the height of human development just because they're his. And therefore intelligence and wisdom, so deeply interlinked with a quality of education men allow only themselves, are viewed as not just masculine qualities but male attributes in some essential sense. Why wouldn't a talented, energetic woman, knowing from her own experience that this is untrue, want some of that action? For a long time George herself associated her apparently unstoppable literary talent with boyishness – *garçon*-hood – until this persona shattered under the burden of caring for Chopin as well as her kids. 'I am no longer a boy [*garçon*], a family is singularly incompatible with frequent travel,' as she confided to Charlotte Marliani in 1839.[5]

But this idea of herself as a boy must go some way towards explaining why she's spent her youth falling for men who are even younger than herself. There's a sense of the emotional and existential freedom of being two guys at play together. Her 'type' – slim, unmuscular, lacking the traditional confidence of adult masculinity, and in the case of Fryderyk Chopin possibly not just bisexual but gay – is androgynous. More physically and emotionally androgynous, in fact, than she is herself.

George's own androgyny – though fiercely exceptional – is almost entirely of the mind. Not, that is, in the sense of a sexual fantasy, but as an understanding of herself as thinking, writing and earning a living like a man. She is much closer to living as a gay man than as a lesbian woman; as for sexual desire, she has only one pretty much confirmed affair with a woman. George knows, of course, intimately and intensely, that she *is* a woman. She doesn't need literary policemen to remind her of a lived experience which after all includes domestic violence, motherhood and possibly abortion. The vast majority of her fiction is written from the viewpoint of women, whose experience is elsewhere routinely ignored in this first half of the nineteenth century by the culture and society around her. Her work repeatedly asks what these often visible yet apparently inaudible women themselves want. It explores the social injustices they suffer. It reverses the gender roles in familiar stories to ask *what if it were a woman who . . . ?* Yet in order to write these stories she has had to refuse to be shut out of things only men conventionally get to do.

They happen also to be things she's profoundly attracted to: from the impersonal excellence of life in a fast-paced newspaper office to participation in the smoke-filled rooms of literary criticism, editing and gossip. Her intimates embrace this 'masculinity' within her femininity. In 1833, Alfred de Musset addressed her in their living intimacy, '*Ô mon George, ma belle maîtresse*': 'Oh my [taking the masculine form] George, my beautiful [feminine form] mistress.' In her fifties she will embark on a great literary correspondence with the younger novelist Gustave Flaubert, which will last the rest of her life. No flirtation will be involved in what develops into a profound friendship between equals. Yet he too will almost immediately start to address her as '*Chère maître*': 'Dear [feminine] master'; sometimes adding another joking endearment, such as 'good [masculine] like good bread' – an echo of her school nickname, *du pain*.[6]

In her forties, living a lull between these different relationships, is George content? She has plenty to make her so. Maurice has become a source of happiness rather than a responsibility; he's turning out to be fine, like-minded company. She's leaning into her understanding of the rural Berrichon way of life. As an established literary figure she can increasingly explore writing in new forms and on a variety of topics – political, non-fictional, personal – so long as she keeps on producing work.

But on the other hand, it must sometimes be hard simply to put her head down and do so. France's habitually violent politics show little sign of calming down. On 2 December 1851 President Louis-Napoléon Bonaparte, who is due to complete his term in power next year, stages a self-*coup d'état*. Despite violent resistance, violently supressed, within less than three weeks a new constitution concentrating power in his hands has received allegedly widespread electoral endorsement. On 2 December the following year he has himself crowned emperor. These events generate a fresh wave of political exiles: Victor Hugo and George's friend and agent Pierre-Jules Hetzel are both among those now forced to leave France.

Though Napoléon III is wrong to fantasise that only he could lead the country in the direction it needs to travel, in the event some of his reforms prove excellent. He appoints Georges-Eugène Haussmann, who will reshape Paris in the 1860s; and also commissions Eugène Viollet-le-Duc's major restoration programme for medieval built heritage, from Notre-Dame de Paris to fortified Carcassonne. He initiates the tremendous flowering of contemporary painting when in 1863 he ordains the famous Salon des Refusés, an exhibition, showcasing the emerging avant-garde, of work rejected by the increasingly conservative Salon de Paris. It includes work by Paul Cézanne, Henri Fantin-Latour, Camille Pissarro, James McNeill Whistler – and Édouard Manet, whose *Le Déjeuner sur l'herbe* becomes a symbol of the show and its new artistic freedoms. The emperor tightens press censorship, but at the same time increases worker rights, including the rights to strike (1864) and to organise (1866), and initiates public worker insurance funds. With his wife Empress Eugénie he will gradually reform French education, distancing it from the Catholic Church so that the curriculum modernises. He will encourage the first women to pass the baccalaureate (in 1861) and to enter medical school (in 1862).

Above all, in 1863 he will appoint as Minister of Education Victor Duruy, an historian with a working-class background, who founds 800 new schools for girls – one in every commune with a population of more than 500 – and 1,500 school libraries. The impact on literacy rates is immediate, and that on the curriculum striking. For the first time all state schools, although they're still fee-paying, will teach history and geography in primary school (*école élémentaire*), and philosophy, modern languages, gymnastics and the arts in the high-school years (*collège* and *lycée*).[7] For every writer this means the transformative rise of a wide middle-class readership. For George, the number of new women readers it creates – and their increasingly educated minds – is to prove especially significant.

Decades after the last century's bloody Revolution, a modernised state is at last emerging. But this is still a paternalistic model of government, and inevitably it loses its head to hubris. Napoléon III's restless foreign policy is militarily costly and makes the state an increasing burden on its citizens. It includes fighting the Crimean War with Britain, helping defeat Austria in the Second Italian War of Independence, doubling the size of France's colonial empire and supporting the construction of the Suez Canal. Then there is the long national descent through his domestically unpopular embrace of free trade, a failed intervention in Mexico, and eventually defeat by Otto von Bismarck in the Franco–Prussian War of 1870.

George Sand will outlive Napoléon III. Half a dozen years after he has disappeared into exile in suburban Kent, she will still be living and working at Nohant. Since, luckily, Maurice has not followed his grandfather into a career in the cavalry, these national martial adventures may sometimes feel far removed from daily life in the backwaters of Indre. But it would be impossible altogether to ignore the busy times she is living through.

Hippolyte, of course, did take his father's path. But he dies at the end of that year of transitions, 1848. He's just forty-nine, and alcoholism has reduced him to something 'between idiocy and madness'.[8] Perhaps it's symbolic that he dies in a chateau he forcibly expropriated from his father-in-law as dowry; the crenellated castle of Montgivray, close to Nohant. It's an ugly end for George's half-brother; someone whose boyish high spirits could perhaps never in the end be enough to allow him to secure an equal place in legitimate society.

He's survived – perhaps in every sense – by his widow Émilie de Villeneuve, his married daughter and two (eventually three) grandsons.[9] But for George this is a loss both complex and real. Hippolyte surely represents for her something of the tenuousness of her own good fortune. If their father had not done the decent thing by Sophie-Victoire, a month before her own birth, it is probable she herself would have been disinherited – perhaps in her half-brother's favour. And new bereavements reopen the wounds of earlier ones. There must be ways in which her older brother's rough-and-ready soldiering masculinity, arriving in her life just days before she lost her similarly boisterous, cavalry-riding father, has worked for her as a kind of continuation of that paternal presence.

By the time her mother died, Sophie-Victoire's lifelong self-involvement seems to have reduced her to little more than a cypher for George, who took no active part in the end-of-life nursing she financed. But Hippolyte has been part of George's family since she was four, and has never left it. True, the siblings were closer at some times than at others: he lent her money to pay off the final parts of her settlement with Casimir, yet took Solange's side in the rift of 1847. Bluff and provincial, he has been protective of his sister while unable to accept her nonconformity. Like Casimir, he could become violent in his cups:

> Poor Hippolyte! How charming he was on his good days, and how unbearable in his bad times [...] his ramblings, his tears

and his anger [. . .] Besides, when he recognised his faults, he accused himself so wholly, so amusingly, so energetically, uttering a thousand spiritual naivites while swearing and weeping copiously [. . .] but [. . .] that was him!¹⁰

But in *Histoire* George has the completely modern insight that Hippolyte battled all his life with the deletion of identity that nineteenth-century illegitimacy entails. Hippolyte is not legally or emotionally that which he is biologically: his father's son. Though he got to know Maurice Dupin, it was never as his child. He must have felt fundamentally cheated when he later found out their relationship. Instead he was brought up fatherless, and more painfully still motherless, even though Catherine Chatiron was living just five miles away in La Châtre:

> The most enterprising and independent member of the family, the one who dares everything and whom one denies nothing, because his gut sense [*entrailles*] needs to compensate him for society's abandonment. In fact, being nothing officially [*n'étant rien officiellement* literally means the much more painful 'being officially nothing'], and being unable to claim anything legally in my home, Hippolyte always let his turbulent character, his good heart and his bad head, dominate.¹¹

It's hard not to compare how understanding George is of her brother's behaviour with how she reacts to her troubled daughter. Solange may have been an accident too. But then, so were both her parents. Unlike George, however, she was born into a marriage which had already failed; a home from which her mother was repeatedly leaving. When she became an adolescent, that same mother expressed anxieties about the precocity of her physical development with clumsy 'pet' names like '*grossière*'. It's true that she was big for her age. When she started her periods, in August 1840, she was a month short of her twelfth birthday, which was at the time a 'precocious puberty'. In the mid-nineteenth century, sixteen or older is the norm for the onset of menarche.[12] George rather sweetly worried that it had been brought on by horse-riding. Less sweetly, she links it to an emerging teenaged storminess in highly judgemental terms: 'I believe she's undergoing a physical crisis which influences her moral character.'[13]

For George is every bit as demanding a critic of her daughter as her 'two mothers' were of herself. She sends a damning assessment of her twelve-year-old to the boarding school in rue de Chaillot:

> She has a very good heart and you'll see [. . .] that she has the most organised of heads. It's just the character that errs. It's whimsical, unmatched, *dominating, jealous and carried away* [George's emphases]. These are the tendencies. To combat these unfortunate instincts are much intelligence, generosity, a certain innate grandeur, the total absence of resentment, even tenderness and an elevated feeling for justice.[14]

Yet in 1847, when she looks back at Solange's upbringing in a long, analytical letter to Emmanuel Arago, George sees herself not as a martinet but as the soft touch: 'I yielded to everything; I was her attendant, her dressmaker, her jockey, her hairdresser, her companion on walks [. . .] paying, sewing, working day and night, being enslaved to her whims, and never knowing how to refuse or to punish.'[15] Solange herself probably understands best what went wrong between them. In 1849 she will tell her mother's close friend Charlotte Marliani – presumably knowing that the insight will be relayed – that 'It wasn't a horse or dresses I needed, it was affection.'[16]

The mother–daughter relationship is still knotty. Solange names her own second daughter, born this year, Jeanne-Gabrielle, after her lost firstborn. Jeanne-Gabrielle Béatrice, known as Nini, carries none of George's names (Amantine, Aurore, Lucille); pointedly, she's named for her father, whose first given name is Jean, and his mother, Gabrielle-Anne.[17] Perhaps the point being made is the one George herself made in not naming Solange after her own mother. Nevertheless, in August 1852, the very month her separation from Auguste Clésinger is legalised, Solange leaves the three-year-old in her own mother's care. History seeming to repeat itself, Nini will be raised by her grandmother for nearly two years. It's surely no coincidence that during this period George publishes two forensic examinations of daughterhood both biological and adoptive: *Mont-Revêche* and *La Filleule* (*The Goddaughter*).[18]

A pretty daguerreotype survives of Nini at around four years old. She poses with a watchful, intelligent expression but relaxed posture, leaning one childishly chubby arm on a prie-dieu. Her Nohant childhood is a small idyll. When she's four, George creates a secret garden they christen the 'Trianon' for her in the woods. A rockery with 'moss, ivy, tombs, shells and caves', it's half ornament, half miniature adventure playground. But in the month she turns five her stormy, threatening father turns up at the manor and demands custody even though, or perhaps because, he is estranged from Solange. It's a startling echo of how Solange's own father tried to abduct her while he and George were divorcing.

Casimir's attempt lasted only a few days, but Clésinger gains de facto custody of his daughter for nine months. Just as George wins the legal case to get Nini back, horrifyingly, the little girl dies. She may be in her father's care but she is not being sufficiently cared for. On 14 January 1855, poorly nursed, she succumbs unexpectedly to scarlet fever. She sickens and passes away in Paris, far from her home at Nohant and without the mothering comfort of either Solange or – another echo, of another childhood – her grandmother.[19]

George has the small body brought back to Nohant. Nini is buried beside her grandfather and great-grandmother in a corner of the modest village cemetery, close to the manor wall, which her grandmother now negotiates to retain as a family plot. Even if too little, too late, it's a kind of symbolic safekeeping. But, a couple of months later, when the rest of the Nohant household go to Rome for a three-month trip, Solange does not join them. Not even bereavement has healed the family rift. Since splitting from Clésinger, she has continued to demand money from her mother, who continues to respond reluctantly. In 1861, in the course of one resulting row, George declares that her daughter, who takes lovers and who has no profession with which to pay the bills, has become a kept woman. Which puts an immediate end to contact, and for four years the women are not in touch at all. Perhaps it was a momentary outburst, at a moment when George was feeling harassed, but it remains an extraordinary accusation. Especially from a woman who once upon a time endured the shame when her own grandmother made a similar accusation about her mother. Not to mention the writer who, nearly three decades ago in *Lélia*, exposed how, if society expects women to be economically reliant on men, even the most respectable are in a sense 'kept', first by fathers and then by husbands.

It's surely a bruising crystallisation of some deep-seated mutual resentment. Is George, in mothering her daughter, repeating Sophie-Victoire's behaviour by envying the next generation their greater ease? If so, what sort of overidentification, say, is she repeating? It's hard not to look back and see in the three-year-old Solange her mother brought to Paris in the middle of a cholera epidemic something of the three-year-old *poupée* Aurore's mother took to war-torn Madrid in 1808. Whatever the case, the same George Sand who on the page dissects human motive and emotion with such perceptive delicacy seems unable to resolve this personal impasse. Unable, or anyway unwilling.

Solange will have no more children, and so leave no descendants. But in 1870, as Solange Clésinger-Sand, she publishes a novel, *Jacques Bruneau*, with the reputable Michel Lévy Frères, who are then in the middle of issuing George's *Oeuvres Complètes* (from 1860 to 1878). In 1889, when she's sixty, she publishes a second, *Carl Robert*, with the successor firm, Calmann-Lévy. From 1873 she lives in comfortable style at the chateau of Montgivray, where her uncle Hippolyte died a quarter-century earlier. After his widow sells it to her in 1875 she adds, among various decorative refurbishments, an elegant 'salon of twenty-nine mirrors'.[20] She will die of flu at seventy, in the eighth arrondissement of Paris on 17 March 1899, just months short of the twentieth century.[21]

For all Montgivray's proximity to Nohant, this is a very different life from the one unfolding for her brother Maurice. After his studies with Delacroix he returned to live with George, and gradually developed a life of his own in the arts. His famous mother helps him. In 1852–4 Hetzel will bring out the multi-volume *Oeuvres illustrées de George Sand* (*The Illustrated Works of George Sand*). George ensures it's Maurice who is commissioned to provide – alongside work left by the great illustrator Tony Johannot, who dies during production – the illustrations Hetzel liberally includes.[22] Engraved by Henri Delaville, the images Maurice creates are sensitive and charming – and he signs them 'M. Sand'. Throughout his career he will be Sand, rather than Dudevant. A few years later, his illustrations for his mother's 1858 potboiler *Légendes rustiques* (*Rustic Legends*), a compendium of folksy storytelling, pass through the smudgy hands of a lithographer, but include a cheerfully uncanny line of werewolves hanging around by a cemetery wall, hands in imagined pockets: a witty rendering of country youths with nothing better to do.[23]

As part of her support for this work, in 1852 George converts half the main range of the attic at Nohant into a studio for her son. It's a beautiful room, lit by huge gable windows facing south across the park and (de rigueur of course for artists) north over the village square and church. But the expectations of such a distinguished mother are difficult to live up to. Rather like other offspring of great writers, Pen Browning or Percy Florence Shelley, Maurice emerges as a delightful young man, keen to be agreeable, and over time his mother's greatest fan. Like Pen Browning, he never quite becomes a leading artist himself. Yet he's full of gifts which, in a less exceptional family, would have been quite enough for him to shine.

The paintings which survive include delicate, atmospheric landscapes. But as an illustrator, Maurice enjoys perhaps his greatest success with *Masques et bouffons*, a double album of commedia delle'arte figures published in 1862. It includes an introduction by his mother; the plates are engraved after his original paintings by the man who will by then be his mother's lover, Alexandre Manceau. Playful delicacy is Maurice's signature style. By the time he dies in 1889, thirteen years after George, he will have published more than a dozen books, a number of them with prefaces by his mother. They include novels, volumes about George and about Delacroix, and travelogues (*Le Québec – lettres de voyage*; *Quebec: Travel Letters*, 1862) and *Six mille lieues à toute vapeur* (*Six Thousand Leagues at Full Steam*, 1873). There are also two studies of butterflies: *Le Monde des papillons, promenade à travers champs* (*The World of Butterflies: A Field Walk*, 1867) with fifty colour plates by Maurice, which he must surely have expected to become a library essential, and the altogether drier *Catalogue raisonné des lépidoptères du Berry & de l'Auvergne* (*Catalogue Raisonné of the Lepidopterae of Berry and the Auvergne*), a 210-page list of sightings published in 1879. By the time this appears, Maurice is able to describe himself on its title page as a 'knight of the Légion d'honneur and a member of the entomological and geological societies [*sic*] of France'.²⁴

He receives the Légion d'honneur in March 1861. Perhaps this is in no small measure because his mother has sent in his biography to Alfred Arago, the Inspector-General of Fine Arts and – that establishment village in action – brother of her old friend Emmanuel. (Very sweetly, in her 'Note on Maurice Dudevant', Sand gives his age as 'thirty six and a half' and she starts with the kind of flourish familiar to anyone who's had to write an author puff: 'Pupil of Delacroix, writer and distinguished painter, he has produced many genre paintings and pictures which have been noted in the latest exhibitions of painting.'²⁵) When, the same year, Maurice returns from an extended two-continent trip under the auspices of his friend Prince Napoléon-Jérôme, first cousin of Napoléon III, this too is partly down to his mother's connections.

Maurice gets to travel to Algeria, via the Iberian peninsula and on to North America, first by the prince's yacht and then on board a steamship of the Imperial Navy named for the prince. He clearly has a whale of a time, though his mother is understandably torn. 'I'm tormented because Maurice wants to go and make a trip in Africa,' she tells Pauline Viardot: 'I'm afraid he doesn't want to wait for these storms to end and that's going to stress me atrociously. But I can't tell him this because one mustn't make children cowardly [. . .] nor spoil their pleasures.'²⁶

These imperial connections had started almost a decade earlier and in less nepotistic style. In January 1852 George met and negotiated with the Emperor Louis-Napoléon Bonaparte himself for clemency for some of his political opponents. That December, 'N Bonap' is, remarkably, recorded among the figures making the pilgrimage to see the great writer in her home territory. (Other visitors to Nohant in the same month include Robert and Elizabeth Barrett Browning.[27])

Is George guilty of maternal nepotism? Of course she is; and this seems part of the dismaying polarisation in the way she treats her children. It's inexcusable; but some of it might be down to a deep-seated vocation which prevents her understanding those people, like Solange, who don't want to be artists. She herself has always particularly enjoyed collaborating and being part of a community of writers and artists – those early months sitting in the open-plan offices of *Le Figaro* are still with her – and by now Maurice's enthusiasms are feeding her own work. Influences go in both directions. As her son develops as a botanist and lepidopterist, slowly building his comprehensive specimen collections, he is engaging more and more deeply with the environment of rural Indre.

And so is her own writing; although for George this landscape is always *inhabited*. Her great trio of Berrichon novels frame this time of transition. When the first, *La Mare au diable*, appeared in instalments in 1846, it overlapped with the instalment publication of *Lucrezia Floriani*, her portrait of life with a great artist which will be widely read as a satire on Chopin's self-absorption. The next two, *François le Champi* and *La Petite Fadette*, both appeared in 1848. In each story, marriage and love are hedged about by custom and duty. Within the impoverished, deeply interdependent rural lives they portray, the choice of a spouse is a matter both of individual responsibility and collective concern. All three books distinguish morality as custom – what we might call respectability – from the kind of morality that springs from a traditional community's most deeply held values. Each novel is a kind of parable: appearance opposed to reality, integrity versus obedience, internal rather than external imperative. Yet each has a tender respect for agricultural communities – still in the 1840s poorly educated and quite simply poor – which make something collective and ethically meaningful out of a life of physical labour.

In *La Mare au diable*, the widower Germain needs to find a new wife to help out his elderly in-laws. He chooses a penniless but virtuous waif who, like the Madeleine of *Teverino*, is associated with all that is natural and spontaneous.[28] The orphaned *Petite Fadette* and her brother, wretchedly brought up by a wicked grandmother, are village untouchables – until Fadette's return, transformed by money into a respectable member of society, to marry the boy who once spurned her.[29] *François* is another waif, known as *le champi*, 'of the fields', because he was found abandoned in a ditch. Being a foundling makes him the lowest of the low in rural Berrichon society: the very communities that so brutalised the real-life foundling Fanchette for whom George advocated five years ago. But this is also a story about maternal incest, in which the youth grows up to marry his foster mother. As well as a darkly shadowed vision of the distance between respectability and compassion, it affords a revelatory glimpse into the author's own sexual and emotional dynamic. Her relationship with her son appears straightforwardly merely proud, loving, possessive: the usual maternal virtues, even if perhaps brought to an unusual pitch. But the boy-men she has taken as lovers since her marriage seem, like the figure of François, to repeat a fantasy of sexualised maternity. (We should remember that this novel itself is the leitmotif in Marcel Proust's own literary fantasy of maternal incest. It's the book the beloved mother reads to the little boy, and the one that, stumbled upon in adulthood, unlocks for him the secret of time regained.)

Sand is neither writing peppy social realism nor sentimentalising peasant life. She doesn't describe the countryside's visual splendours as if they were somehow affectless, like pictures hanging in a gallery; she ignores the late-Romantic sensationalisation of aesthetic pleasure. Instead she pays attention to *how things work* in the woods, fields and rivers around her, and the ways people act in and on the landscape. It is at the very least a reclamation of the pastoral tradition of Hesiod and Virgil, in which the country calendar portrays a working year. In the mid-nineteenth century, this is a pioneering repudiation of the Romantic corruption of pastoral as mere picturesque. It's not only the last Queen of France, in her faux-rustic Hameau, who has been guilty of treating rural scenes as mere background to more privileged lives. The backcountry Indre George reveals to her readers is not an affair of charming style but of demanding content: hard labour, tough conditions, modest reward. And she herself is a pragmatist who must run her estate to feed herself and her dependants; an active kitchen gardener who installs the best modern stoves and sinks for her cooks.

All the same, her position as chatelaine of Nohant makes her an unlikely witness to rural hardship. The tall windows which punctuate the facades of her manor are evenly spaced and elegantly eighteenth-century. They observe the traditional proportions of classical good looks: four panes tall on the ground floor, three on the first where the writer has her study. When George has the shutters opened, they give on to raked gravel at the front of the house, the gardens and park behind. Everything on this side is honey-coloured or tawny: pinky-gold limestone and red clay tiles on the working stables that rather informally frame the entrance courtyard. There's more gravel in the parterre to one side of the manor, where she's overseen the planting-up of flower beds since she regained possession of the house on her divorce. Green clouds of tree canopy – walnut and yew, plane and elm – fill the interstices of the views from the first floor, where the writer's study overlooks a grassed cedar garden and the orangery that even yields a rare pineapple. All is curated, traditional and calm.

Yet the eye that looks out from these windows has a radical take on this apparently timeless scene. It sees how the front *cour d'honneur* gives directly on to the main square of the working farming hamlet, while to the south and east – the direction in which the writer's study faces – an 'English' parkland created by George's grandmother at the start of the nineteenth century opens on to a wide landscape of fields. The manor grounds are just an island of leisure in the midst of a working environment.

The Bonne Dame Nohant has learnt to read how these rural vistas are shaped by tough, under-remunerated peasant labour. She's earned her sobriquet by offering hard-pressed local communities help in the form of herbal remedies and health advice. The twenty-first century may note her personal profit from the class system's still-huge divisions. George knows it. Both in her overtly political activity – writing and lobbying – and through her fiction she campaigns for solutions to rural destitution that are not merely moral or personal but political and economic. But meanwhile, practical assistance can make a material difference, and so she offers it.

At the same time, her writing articulates the twin insights that the natural world exists independently of human need or understanding, and that it's malleable, and so susceptible to human intervention and damage. She writes about 'the recognition [*salut*] between the planet and its inhabitants [. . .] the necessity of what is good and fine: if the planet deserts this order, it will perish'.[30] This is pioneering, proto-ecological stuff. The German naturalist Ernst Haeckel (1834–1919) won't coin the term 'ecology' (*Oecologie*) or elucidate the concept until 1866, in his *Generelle Morphologie der Organismen* (*General Morphology of Organisms*).[31] But George already understands what Haeckel will call 'the relationship of the organism to the surrounding external world, which in a broader sense can include all "conditions of existence"'.

In looking at the natural world in its own terms, rather than by way of how it affects humans (whether practically or emotionally), George is adopting the newly fashionable approach of gentlemen scientists like her lepidopterist son. But Maurice is influencing his mother in another way too. He's gradually becoming a brilliant marionettist. What starts as entertainment for his mother's guests develops at first in a *castelet* rather like the traditional English Punch and Judy booth. But eventually he has a marionette theatre purpose-built at Nohant. He designs spring rods, glove manipulators that allow him to work several puppets at once, lighting systems and even motionless 'extras' on lateral sliding rods. Over time he moves on from glove puppets to marionettes, amassing a collection of hundreds. He improvises scenarios and produces dramatic adaptations, parodies and his own scripted puppet plays. After George's death he will create the puppetry Théâtre des Amis in the home he moves to at Passy. After his own death in 1889, his *Le Théâtre des marionettes*, the magisterial illustrated volume in which he collates this passionate expertise, will appear posthumously from the loyal Calmann-Lévy.[32]

This is joyous stuff; George enjoys the ways in which Maurice has become a constant in her life at Nohant. But eventually, at thirty-nine, even he marries – though he doesn't exactly cast his net wide. Lina (Marcellina Claudine Augustine) Calamatta is the daughter of family friends, and she's still a month shy of twenty when she weds this man twice her age and moves in to the family manor. Her father, Luigi Calamatta, is the well-known artist whose portrait engraving of George was noted by Balzac in the writer's rue Pigalle garden pavilion two decades ago. Artist and writer have been friends since 1834: 'Italian in manner, that's to say more trusting and expansive, [he] quickly became attractive to me and little by little our mutual friendship was established for life.'[33] In 1837, Calamatta was the model for a character in *Les Maîtres mosaïstes*, George's story about Renaissance artists.

Yet Lina is herself a presence. With her Italian colouring and distinctively intelligent cat's face, she survives in photographs as a smiling, relaxed and slightly bohemian young woman. At first, she wears a folksy two-piece and her curly hair is too thick to force into a chignon. By the time she's a young mother, in a photo taken by Placide Verdot at his Châteauroux studio in 1871, the wildness has been tamed by a braid band, and her dress is decidedly formal. She has gone through the death of her first child, Marc-François, at one year old, and given birth to her two daughters, with whom she now poses. The elder, Aurore (Jeanne Claudine Aurore) – named, unlike Solange's daughters, for her grandmother – was born in 1866; and Gabrielle (Jeanne Lucile Gabrielle) two years later.[34]

Both girls will grow up to be artists. Aurore will paint. Gabrielle, whose family nickname is Titite, will become a gifted and pioneering topographical photographer. Like their mother, the sisters will remain in love with Nohant and its mystique all their lives. When they eventually inherit, early in the twentieth century, they will attempt to safeguard the manor by leaving it to the nation; something that's finally achieved in 1952.[35] Aurore, who survives her grandmother by eighty-five years, will live on at Nohant until her death in 1961.

It is the house itself that will be George Sand's physical posterity.

None of her adored granddaughters is survived by children. Not, of course, little Nini, dead from scarlet fever at only five (nor her elder sister, Solange's first child, who lived just days). Aurore and Gabrielle will both marry around the time of their father's death. But Aurore's marriage, to the painter Frédéric Lauth, produces no surviving children, and Gabrielle's Italian husband, a drawing teacher called Roméo Paluzzi, will prove so stormy – and perhaps violent – that she leaves him after only four years, and has no children.

When the great novelists of a future generation, Henry James and Edith Wharton, visit Nohant reverentially together in 1907, thirty years after George's death, they find only a 'plain old house [. . .] so shy and remote [with its] row of closed shutters'. But while its chatelaine is still alive it resembles a stage set for scenes from the ideal life of a writer, in which the formerly scandalous George Sand plays her role as the Good Lady of Nohant surrounded at last by a sympathetic and appreciative household. Almost as if the manor itself were the marionette theatre that it contains, and the family hung ready to play their parts like 'Maurice's marionettes, which still dangle', Wharton will note, 'wistfully from their hooks in the little theatre downstairs'.[36]

In fact the way of life which characterises George's last quarter-century came into being, like every period in a life, because of what went before. In 1849, when she was on the threshold of her fifties, two of her most distinguished former lovers died. Fryderyk Chopin and Marie Dorval have both represented something important about artistic fellow feeling; each relationship a kind of watershed. George may have been estranged from Fryderyk but she's still shocked when he dies, on 17 October. Solange, actually present at his death, had not warned her how gravely ill he was.[37] There has been no such estrangement from Marie, and after her death in March George provides a financial safety net for Dorval's grandchildren, welcoming them to Nohant each summer for years to come.

The losses continue. In August 1850 her old comrade Honoré de Balzac dies at fifty-one, just five months after finally marrying Ewelina Hańska. Unsurprisingly, in 1857 Alfred de Musset will also die young, at forty-six, of alcoholism and heart failure. But life – and sex – also continue. George has not been wholly faithful even during the Chopin years.[38] In 1844, a fan letter to the influential radical writer and future deputy Jean Joseph Louis Blanc about his leftist periodical *La Réforme* led to a brief entanglement that was at the very least emotional, and quite probably sexual. It's always a giveaway when George starts calling a prodigiously gifted younger man 'My dear child'.[39] But by 1849 she is absolutely free to install Victor Borie, a thirty-year-old aspiring journalist and future agricultural specialist, in Fryderyk's old room, between the library and her own bedroom, at Nohant. When Borie flees to Brussels at the end of the year, after being sentenced *in absentia* for publishing socialist literature, he is replaced on-site by a German musicologist, Hermann Müller-Strübing. This affair barely lasts into the spring. Müller-Strübing is soon resettled at the Château de Coudray as tutor to Charles Duvernet's children: among friends, but safely off-site.

All the same, he will prove useful in years to come as the translator of the first volume of *Histoire de ma vie* into German. George's autobiography was commissioned at the very end of December 1847 by the entrepreneur and industrialist Charles Delatouche, who signed up for five instalments to appear at two-monthly intervals. The advance, negotiated by Hetzel, is generous. But the work will take George an uncharacteristic seven years to produce, and when it finally appears is published not by Delatouche but in the popular daily *La Presse*, which serialises it between 5 October 1854 and 17 August 1855.[40]

For the next two centuries, *Histoire* will be celebrated as among the most engaging of George's works. It has all her hallmark emotional intelligence: being memoir it must, ostensibly at least, manage without invented characters, instead experimenting with a much riskier analysis of real people and their possible motives. The writing lays out the author's thinking and the connections she makes in ways that prefigure psychoanalytic insight. Though of course George doesn't work out a systematic theory of ego, superego and id, *Histoire* suggests that people don't always know why they behave in ways they do, and explores how character is influenced by circumstance.

Twenty-first-century critics will compare the late-Romantic self of George's *Histoire* with the one Jean-Jacques Rousseau famously portrayed in his *Confessions*, first published in 1782–9 at the other end of the Romantic era. They will contrast Rousseau's quasi-heroic individualism – all self-observation, to say nothing of self-dramatisation – with a Sandean version of selfhood that they will argue works the opposite way, contracting into a purely grammatical first person which is all narration and never takes the space to define the narrator herself. Perhaps predictably, many who read it this way will decide her technique is (that reductive term) feminine.[41]

George herself anticipates the comparison with Rousseau, writing to Charlotte Marliani at the time Delatouche signs her that 'It is a *story of my life, (not* CONFESSIONS*)*, the public is too ignoble for me to do it the honour either to accuse myself or to justify myself about anything before it.' Nor does she intend to implicate other people:

> Jean-J Rousseau demonstrated this, and I admire his book but disapprove of it as a fairly bad action. So I won't wrong or injure *anyone*. I've enough to say about my (*artistic*) and

intellectual inner life, without making the public my intimate confidant [. . .] I conceive of [my book] as very clear, very calm and quite fun.⁴²

Not quite so clear and calm in fact. While on the page Rousseau's fixed, unitary self is unchanging – we meet him again in each set piece – Sand's is a modern subject-in-process, constantly being formed and re-formed by what happens to her. Rousseau's *Confessions* use memory as a mirror in which the narrator expects to see his self reflected. Sand understands that the remembering self who narrates *Histoire* is out of sync with the self glimpsed within those memories. After Marcel Proust's monumental study of memory and its storytelling abilities in *À la recherche du temps perdu*, this recognition of out of sync-ness may seem passé, or at least obvious, to twenty-first-century readers. But Sand remains ahead of her own literary and social times.

Her *Histoire* appears over half a century before Proust's seven-volume masterpiece. And it is, at least in part, an uncovering of – and a homage to – the complexity of human nature. George's memoir has a glorious thickness of texture: she quotes long-forgotten conversations verbatim, and describes long-lost rooms in detail. Posthumous historians will grumble that this makes the author an unreliable witness to her own life, but such purism is anachronistic. Her own era has an altogether more relaxed attitude to creative reconstruction. For influential architects like Eugène Viollet-le-Duc, the preservation of historic buildings means partial rebuilding; his ever so slightly kitsch reconstructions at Notre-Dame de Paris, or of the Carcassonne battlements, are not judged inauthentic by his contemporaries. *Histoire* works in the same way. George's storytelling is anecdotal – emotional, incomplete, inconsistent – and this very informality gives the reader a feeling of greater intimacy with the writer herself than any number of facts could supply. More intimately still, its bumpy, repetitive surface even feels like a record of the laborious process of its composition.

There may be lived as well as literary reasons for the time it takes to complete the work. An additional reason why Müller-Strübing's move to Coudray in the spring of 1850 is so convenient is that by April George has started a new relationship, this time with a friend Maurice made at Delacroix's studio. Alexandre Damien Manceau arrived in Nohant at the same time as the youth he now displaces. The son of a lemonade-seller, he is no social sophisticate. But he is a well-known engraver, by now in his early thirties. The golden boys are getting a little older as George herself gets older, but Manceau (who was born in 1817) is still her type: physically a little frail, her junior both chronologically and professionally, and yet exceptionally gifted.

Against type, however, he is also kind and loving:

> He has all the care of a woman, and of a skilful, active and ingenious woman. When I am ill, I am cured just by seeing him prepare my pillow and bring me my slippers. I who never ask for or accept care, need his as if it were my nature to be pampered. Finally, I love him, I love him with all my soul, with his faults, with the ridiculous things that others find in him [...] and there is an astonishing calm in my love despite my age and his.[43]

Alexandre Manceau will prove to be George's rock. But despite his comparative youth he will predecease her by more than a decade. When he dies on 21 August 1865 he is only forty-eight, but resembles an old man. Like Chopin at the end, he has tuberculosis. If the portraits of the musician taken by Louis-Auguste Bisson in 1847 reveal someone shockingly drawn and blotched by illness, those Félix Nadar takes of Manceau in the last year of his life are solemnly tragic. They show an ageing figure with black rings under his eyes, supporting his head in a gesture that might be formal if it were not simply exhausted. His cheekbones look as though they could slice through his skin; only the heavy-lidded eyes are alive.

These pictures have been taken at a double sitting. The portrayal of George which emerges from the session is perhaps our most iconic image of her as a literary grande dame. She wears a sort of striped poncho with a tassel tie and matching skirt. Her hair is scraped aside from her centre parting, where it looks whiter than it does in the pyramidal arrangements on either side of her crown. And since after all she's now sixty we learn from this that, like many women before and since – with and without younger partners – she helps her hair colour along, even if only with walnut juice. In Nadar's most successful plate, for which the photographer has plainly posed her, the chin lifts and tilts as she half turns towards her left shoulder. Her Roman nose and wide lips, her huge dark eyes, look as strong as ever. Even the formal arrangement of her hair settles into a generous sideways swirl.[44]

Perhaps the most concrete proof that Alexandre Manceau really cares for George, rather than simply relishing the comfortable life she provides him with, is that he buys a home for them to enjoy as a couple. Houses matter: symbolically, practically. This one is, perhaps, a retreat from quasi-public life as a literary institution at Nohant. It's also a way in which, though far from wealthy, he can literally give his partner a home. In this sense the minute cottage he purchases at Gargilesse, with its thick-set masonry walls and vernacular tiled roof, is a traditional, masculine gesture. Perhaps it's also a way gently to indicate how little manors and chateaux, those traditional identifiers for gentry like George, matter to him.

Gargilesse is a pretty limestone settlement on the meandering River Creuse, little more than twenty miles from Nohant. The bulwarked, medieval village street rises steeply from the valley bottom to a turreted chateau. The crypt of the Romanesque church glows with medieval frescoes. It's like a tiny, local version of Valldemossa. George and Alexandre fall in love with the place on a country walk in June 1857; by the next month he has bought a tiny end-of-terrace cottage that sits below the church. As if to underline that there's no split from their life with Maurice and his family, they name the place Villa Algira after a lepidopterist's delight: a rare sighting of *Dysgonia algira*, known as 'the passenger', a moth usually found in North Africa and southern Europe. And perhaps also because the name carries with it some sense of *allegro*, the Italian form of lightness and delight.

A writer's retreat can also be a writing retreat: this year George produces the whole of *Elle et lui*, her *roman-à-clef* about life with de Musset, in just three weeks at Gargilesse. This private home is as useful as it is delightful, though neither she nor Alexandre has come to dislike their more public existence at Nohant. On the contrary, when he leaves the manor seven years later, in June 1864, Manceau will record, 'Final evening at Nohant. [. . .] I think in spite of myself that during the fourteen years I spent here, I laughed more, cried more, lived more than during the thirty-three that preceded them.'[45]

But he will be forced out. With a show of hitherto unsuspected strength of will, Maurice claims to be worried by the tuberculosis which is by now becoming painfully evident. Married to Lina for two years and with a boy of his own who's nearly a year old, George's son now has his own little family to be responsible for – and with whom he may relish private downtime. Yet there's a silver lining to this, in the shape of privacy for the older couple, too. As Alexandre's diary continues, 'Here I am now alone with her, what a responsibility, also what an honour and what a joy!' For George, much as she loves Maurice and Lina, has chosen Alexandre. She buys a property at Palaiseau, near Paris, and lives with him there for the brief remainder of his life.

This rather quotidian villa at 5 rue de Gutenberg is heavily shuttered under a mansard roof; it sits in a garden of gloomy mature trees. Despite the good auspices of an address named after the father of printing, it is not a lovable house like Nohant – or indeed Gargilesse, which Alexandre is rather sadly compelled to sell to Maurice this year. But Palaiseau is only a dozen or so miles from central Paris, with its doctors, friends and literary and artistic colleagues. To capitalise on these benefits, George also takes a pied-à-terre in the capital itself.

The mezzanine apartment she finds is at number 97 on the appropriately named rue des Feuillantines (which will become 90 rue Claude-Bernard), a charmless block on a wide, bare street. It's cheap but, like most compromises, turns out to be a mistake. George herself soon calls it a 'little slum', telling Emmanuel Arago that it's 'so small and so cold that I dare not meet you there'. The great photographer Félix Nadar, who does make it to the apartment, describes 'student accommodation' with cheap Algerian-style furniture. He insists to the writer, 'You must not stay here.'[46]

This hiatus in her Nohant life is to prove a sobering passage altogether. Choosing Alexandre is not exactly choosing life. His long, ultimately terminal illness asks even more of George as nurse and companion than either Fryderyk Chopin's frailty or Maman's decline. Five weeks after they leave Nohant her grandson, little Marc-François, is dead anyway, succumbing suddenly to dysentery. Fourteen months later, on 21 August 1865, Alexandre dies too. George is back at Nohant within three years of leaving the manor. After another couple of years she sells Palaiseau, which, for all its proximity to the capital, is both a practical burden and a repository of sad memories. Finally, in 1868 she changes her Paris address to 5 rue Gay-Lussac, which she will retain until her death.

But through all this upheaval she has been working. Her loving years with Manceau encourage the publication of numerous novels and prolific work for the stage. These genres leak into each other: dramatic adaptations of novels, published playscripts. The spirit of Nohant theatricals runs through prose fictions like 1850's *Histoire du véritable gribouille* (*The Story of a Real Naif*), a joyous tale about a muddle-headed boy in a fantasy world where plants and insects can speak. George's life with Maurice and his Nohant atelier makes a more literal appearance in 1851's *Le Château des desertes* (*Wilderness Castle*), which joins *Les Maîtres mosaïstes* and *Lucrezia Floriana* in exploring how art sits in an artist's life.[47]

Adriani, published in 1854, is an almost premonitory novel about widowhood, while in 1855 George picks up pace again, signing a ten-book deal with Hachette for their *Bibliothèque des chemins de fer* (*Railway Library*), still a novel institution.[48] In 1856 she issues *Evenor et Leucippe: Les Amours de l'Âge d'Or; Légende antidéluvienne* (*Evenor and Leucippe: The Loves of the Golden Age; an Antediluvian Legend*) – a mixture of myth-making and philosophy set in a prelapsarian past – and, ever the professional pragmatist, changes her handwriting to make composition quicker and editorial transcription easier. Next year sees *Les Dames vertes* (*The Green Ladies*) and *Les Beaux Messieurs de Bois-Doré* (*The Fine Gentlemen of Golden-Wood*), both set in country chateaux.[49]

By now George is exploring historical fiction. Her third novel to appear in 1857 is *La Daniella*, which like *Le Château des desertes* and next year's *L'Homme de neige* is a *Künstlerroman*. *The Snowman*, her return to the *Revue des deux mondes* after a long-delayed reconciliation with François Buloz, is dedicated to Maurice, perhaps because its protagonist is a puppeteer. It's followed by *Narcisse*, a retelling of the classical myth. There's no let-up in her almost manic rate of production: she seems pursued – by what? Financial obligations? Workaholism? The freelance imperative to stay visible at all times? Eighteen fifty-nine sees *Jean de la Roche*, set in another Loire chateau, *Constance Verrier*, a further story of mismatched marriage, and *Flavie*, whose eponymous heroine marries a man because she adores his mother – just as, in real life a couple of years from now, Lina Calamatta will claim to do.[50]

Life and art do busily intertwine. George falls ill in the autumn of 1860, with typhoid fever somehow interleaved with gallbladder disease. She's fifty-four, and it's the first grave illness of her life. She spends the whole of the spring of 1861 convalescing among pines, cactus and picturesque limestone coves at Tamaris, a pretty fishing village just outside Toulon. Even so, 1860 sees the instalment publication of *La Ville noire* (*The Black Town*) and *Le Marquis de Villemer*, and 1861 of *Valvèdre* and *La Famille de Germandre*.[51] In 1862, the year Maurice and Lina marry, she publishes two volumes of essays and two novels. *Tamaris* follows a doctor's life in that pretty coastal settlement while, like a sort of thematic greatest hits, *Antonia* asks questions about the respectability of artists, loveless marriages and class conflict. In 1863, George's critique of Roman Catholic confessional practices results in her entire corpus being placed on the *Index Librorum Prohibitorum*. But even in 1864–5, the difficult years of Alexandre's illness and death at Palaiseau, she produces three novels – *Laura*, *La Confession d'une jeune fille* (*A Young Girl's Confession*) and *Monsieur Sylvestre* – as well as a short fantasy, *La Coupe* (*The Cup*).[52] Given this astonishing rate of production against the grain of life events, it's perhaps forgivable if some of the work is a touch formulaic.

There are still more novels and non-fiction prose works to come. But 1865 is notable as the last year when George's diary is crowded with regular performances of her work on the professional stage. She's proved to be as hard-working a playwright as she is novelist. Since the break with Chopin she's written more than a dozen original dramas, as well as adaptations of her own novels, and in 1851 she inaugurated a parlour theatre literally alongside Maurice's marionette theatre at Nohant, its stage taking up a second wall of this intimate chamber. It was the kind of playful but useful try-out space where, for example, a housemaid could become a a kind of star, garnering compliments from cultural leaders down on a visit from Paris. Up in the capital, 1851 also saw plays by George open in not one but three major Paris theatres: *Claudie* at the former opera house Théâtre de la Porte-Saint-Martin, on the boulevard Saint-Martin; *Le Mariage de Victorine* at the Théâtre du Gymnase, smaller but just as pretty and also in the tenth arrondissement; and her *Molière* at the huge Théâtre de la Gaité, currently on a site which will soon disappear under Haussmann's place de la République.

Although commissions like these have been a financial lifeline for George, work for the stage also just *is* creatively collaborative in a way she's always enjoyed. Writing books can be tediously isolating: she must sometimes feel like a fiction machine. The theatrical incubator at Nohant, on the other hand, has drawn the household into an ever-stronger sense of artistic collaboration while also strengthening her hand as a dramaturge in the professional theatre. When she and Alexandre are forced to move out to Palaiseau, therefore, two things happen. George publishes *Le Théâtre de Nohant* (1864), a selection of her work written for that chamber space during thirteen years of happy experimentation, and professional theatre work dries up within the year.

She will fret in letters to friends about the economic consequences of this falling-away. But lives do change. Perhaps George has spent enough time and energy on drama. Or perhaps it's all just muddle and coincidence, and only from a distance does the illusion of pattern appear. What is true is that she's about to embark on another kind of literary rehearsal, or collaboration: there are many ways to describe what is unarguably a highlight of her final decade. The extraordinarily rich correspondence with Gustave Flaubert is now gathering pace and will last until her death in 1876.

Theirs is and is not an obvious friendship. Flaubert, seventeen years younger than Sand and therefore also the junior novelist, is a writer whose stature Sand recognises from the outset. Indeed, their acquaintance is built on that recognition; which includes a small psychic rescue service she performs after Flaubert has been prosecuted for *Madame Bovary*. When she reads his novel on its first serialisation in the *Revue de Paris* at the end of 1856, the work gives her so much pleasure that it even merits a mention in Manceau's diary. In February 1857 Flaubert, the *Revue*'s editor and its printer are all prosecuted for obscene publication. The trial collapses but the process is, as it's designed to be, both emotionally and professionally costly. Sand, qua establishment figure, hasn't yet commented publicly. But April sees an exchange of courtesies: the novel now appears in volume form and Flaubert sends Sand a copy, inscribed 'To Madame Sand, the homage of an unknown'.

A few days later the writers' paths cross at an opening night at the Théâtre de l'Odéon. Neither leaves a record of first in-person impressions, but in September Sand defends *Bovary* in her influential weekly column in the *Courrier de Paris*.[53] Writers do not, unless they're very stupid, forget such favours. Two years later, Flaubert calls on Sand when she's in Paris; and when *Salammbô* appears in November 1862 she receives an author copy and responds with a rave review, which *La Presse* publishes on

27 January 1863. Finally, on another visit to Paris, George attends her first Magny dinner on 12 February 1866, and there she and the younger novelist meet up properly for the first time.

This Monday-evening literary club has been meeting monthly at the Restaurant Magny in the rue Contrescarpe-Dauphine (later rue André-Mazet) in the sixth arrondissement for more than three years (by coincidence commencing in the month that *Salammbô* appeared). It's a rumbustiously masculine talking shop convened by George's old friend Sainte-Beuve, the brothers Edmond and Jules de Goncourt, and her old acquaintance the illustrator Paul Gavarni who, three decades ago when he was a coming man, caricatured George in his series on Parisian mores.

The writers manage the invitations, but George knows Modeste Magny himself from the time, three decades ago, when he was a waiter at Chez Philippe in the rue Montorgueil. Indeed, their friendship is established enough that, last August, he was among the mourners at Alexandre's funeral.[54] In rue Contrescarpe-Dauphine he's the proprietor of his own large establishment offering 'salons, cabinets' and more: four floors and a double mansard storey, according to the contemporary photo by Félix Nadar. It's all very smart, and the evening ought to be immensely enjoyable; a celebration of all kinds of coming good.

But perhaps George is finally weary of being the only woman in the room, however hard she tries not to be treated as one. The Goncourts' journal entry for the dinner manages to include a racial slur:

> Mme Sand comes to dine at Magny today. There she is, beside me, with her beautiful and charming head, in which is revealed with age, day by day, a little more the type of a [Black biracial] woman. She regards the world with an intimidated air, blurting

in Flaubert's ear: 'You're the only one here who doesn't embarrass me!' She listens, does not speak.⁵⁵

Which makes uncomfortable reading for any woman who has braved male-dominated literary spaces and knows their sometimes braying, barnyard atmosphere. Still, it's good to see that George, forcing herself to go out and about in the literary capital after Manceau's death despite her bereavement, already feels confident in Flaubert's friendship. Soon, the pair are exchanging jokey letters signed 'Goulard' or 'Jorje Sens' ('George Sand' with a comedy accent) – and it's this spring that Flaubert finds the perfect term of address for George, *Chère maître*.

Dear [female] master: what follows is one of the most illuminating exchanges in writing history. These are two writers at the top of their game, both knowing themselves to be so but both as full of the difficulties of the métier as any other literary professional. Each is primarily a novelist; each utterly dedicated to their vocation. Yet how they work could not be more different. In the midst of a life of responsibilities and commitments, George Sand is hugely productive; as a result the quality of her work can be uneven. Perhaps more costive, Gustave Flaubert is unremitting in his search for what he is the first to term *le mot juste*. Posthumously celebrated as the perfectionist master of realist fiction, his resistance to lazy writing, and cliché in particular, creates a realism so crispy it's almost hyper-real. This also means that he writes very slowly. He spends much of his time not in the hurly-burly of Parisian literary life, but at his writing desk at Croisset, a hamlet outside Rouen, where the family home stands on the banks of the wide, winding Normandy Seine.

By the time he's become George's 'cherished old troubadour' all Flaubert's adventurous youthful travel, including the trip to Carthage when he researched *Salammbô*, is behind him.⁵⁶ He's been settled at Croisset since ill health – or possibly temperament – caused him to abandon legal studies in the capital when he was twenty-five. And it's good for Sand's admirers to be able to picture this house above the river, and its writing pavilion, let into the roadside wall, where so much thinking about and writing to her will go on. The property belongs to Flaubert's widowed mother, with whom he is genuinely close. When she dies in 1872, he will tell George that 'my poor dear mother was the being I loved most. I feel as though part of my entrails had been ripped out.' Perhaps because he lives with venereal disease, probably contracted before he was thirty – though luckily he'll never succumb to syphilitic dementia – the flamboyantly moustached 'Goulard' is something of a homebody; possibly he also needs a great deal of mental space in order to work. And perhaps his literary friendship with George also helps this choice seem less eccentric: both are creating cutting-edge excellence in the provinces. As he mourns his mother he will write that 'Mme Sand is now, with Turgenev, my only literary friend.'[57]

Ivan Turgenev, part of the exodus of Russian intelligentsia under Tsar Nicholas I, is a simpatico mutual friend. He too is writing at one remove from Paris gossip: always on the move while he follows his married lover, George's old friend Pauline Viardot, around Europe as she tours its concert halls and opera stages. Indeed, in this company Turgenev sees more of George than Flaubert ever will. He and the Viardots visit Nohant in autumn 1872 and again, twice, in 1873.[58] It helps that the four Viardot children overlap in age with George's granddaughters, whom she is by now busy tutoring. And in 1872, when Aurore and Gabrielle are six and four respectively, George publishes her first stories for children, which will be collected the next year as *Contes d'une grand-mère* (*A Grandmother's Tales*).

By contrast with this messy and cheerful domesticity, it may be that the perfectionist in Flaubert thrives on a primarily epistolary intimacy. Perhaps a written relationship feels more continuous with a life lived largely on the page. Or perhaps it's more perfectible than other kinds of friendship. There's time, in letter-writing, to stretch for *le mot juste*; less risk of clumsiness or regret. In writing, unlike in life, there need never be *esprit d'escalier*: you simply redraft. Besides, the deeply fraternal affection he shares with 'Jorje Sens' has palpably safe limits. Like her earlier artistic comrades-in-arms – Honoré de Balzac, or Franz Liszt – he understands that when George sends him 'a thousand tendernesses' there's no need for him to worry that she might seek to embody them. This guardedness is nothing personal. Despite a predilection for prostitutes of both sexes, he's not known for certain to have ever had more than one deep romantic affair, and his eight years with the poet Louise Colet ended in 1854, two years before *Bovary* and George's first encounter with his work.[59]

For her part, George has been passionately epistolary all her life: as promiscuous a letter-writer as she is a writer for publication. For her, too, writing is a way to 'live her best life'; but it allows her a different kind of freedom from the one it offers Flaubert. The page can be occupied by an authorial *I* that doesn't need to fret about its own gender, acceptability or identity. It can emerge with a kind of pure singularity from the page – on which the person writing it might ideally cast, as it were, no shadow. Perhaps this makes George and Gustav each other's ideal readers; sublimated confessors of their work and of their lives. And, for the former convent girl, the figure of the spiritual confessor must surely linger as some sort of precursor to the ideal reader: a memory of the kind of sensitive moral understanding that can trump mere romantic involvement.

Maybe this is why, although George repeatedly invites this 'dear friend of my heart' to visit Nohant, his repeated failures to do so create no bad feeling between them. (He does manage one visit, in late December 1869.[60]) Their friendship also survives pummelling circumstances. On 16 July 1870, during a smallpox epidemic which prompts George to move her household deeper into rural Creuse, France declares war on northern Germany. The ensuing Franco–Prussian War sees the collapse of the Second Empire after French defeat in the Battle of Sedan. The empress regent flees the capital, which is besieged for more than four months. A Government of National Defence takes over until shortly after Paris falls on 28 January 1871.

In Croisset the Flaubert home is among many requisitioned by the Prussians occupying Normandy. The peace negotiated by the Government of National Defence involves such financially punitive remunerations to the newly unified German states that worker-led revolts across France lead, after a month, to the formation of the Paris Commune. For two months, in the spring of 1871, the Commune promotes progressive reforms, such as the abolition of child labour, rent relief and the separation of Church and State. But in May it carries out a spate of political executions. The army intervenes, overthrowing the Commune and arresting thousands.

Yet by a miracle nineteenth-century France does not go the way of twentieth-century Russia or China. Under the Third Republic, normal political life and civil society by and large resume. Life resumes for George too. She continues literally to cultivate her garden. The twin cedars she planted for the births of her children are by now tall trees shading the lawn at the back of Nohant manor. In the copse to its west, grass paths replace gravel and the understorey, 'soil rich in local plants [which] allows parts to be completely abandoned', is thick with periwinkles and violets.[61] This covert allows wildlife – roe deer, foxes, even coypus and herons from the Indre, whose nearest tributary is just 300 yards away – to come unusually close to the house.

Elsewhere, the mild Berrichon climate and the garden's sheltering stone walls, which George had restored in 1844, create ideal growing conditions. She has an orchard, a potager and the parterre generously planted up with lavender, roses and mixed herbaceous borders. And although her literary productivity is slowing to an almost conventional rate, she continues to publish novels, including *Cadio* (1867), *Mlle Merquem* (1868), *Pierre qui roule* (*A Rolling Stone*, 1869), *Francia* (1871) and, in a flurry in her last full year of life, *Flamarande, Marianne Chevreuse, La Tour de Percemont* (*The Tower of Percemont*) and a set of short stories. This late burst of activity in 1875 will also see her arrange her complete works for publication by Michel Lévy.[62]

She's turning back to non-fiction, too. Her *Promenades autour d'un village* (*Walks Around a Village*), explorations of the Indre countryside in the contrasted, fictional company of a naturalist and an artist, were collected in book form in 1866. In 1868 she publishes *Nouvelles lettres d'un voyageur* (*New Letters from a Traveller*), and in 1871 *Journal d'un voyageur pendant la guerre* (*Journal of a Traveller in Wartime*), both state-of-the-nation instalment essays. In 1871 she becomes a regular correspondent of the daily *Le Temps*, and in 1873 publishes *Impressions et souvenirs* (*Impressions and Memories*) in that paper. This increasing engagement with literary non-fiction seems to reflect a new freedom to explore her own preoccupations in her writing. Novels sell better than non-fiction, but George has become the kind of national treasure who can write what she wants.

All the same, lived experience remains the bridge between the social preoccupations of her political texts and the personal, emotional realm which has marked so much of her fiction, and of her own life. Reflection spills into her correspondence. October 1871 sees her writing to Flaubert:

> 'My roots' – one can't change them. [...] I lived through the revolutions [of 1848] and had a close view of the major participants. I saw [...] into their depths [...] no principles, and therefore no genuine intelligence or strength or perseverance. [...] Among artists and writers I haven't found anything of substance. You're the only one with whom I've ever been able to exchange anything but professional ideas [...] at Magny's one day I told them they were all 'gentlemen'. They said one shouldn't write for the ignorant, and shouted me down because the ignorant were the only people I did want to write for, since they are the ones that need it. [They] have nothing, and I pity them. Love and pity go together.[63]

She doesn't mean readers who misunderstand or reject her books, but the Berrichon peasantry she has by this time placed at the centre of her work, and of her life. 'Ignorant' is no insult, but simple acknowledgement of the extent to which they are excluded from education.

'Love and pity go together': the quasi-maternal tenderness which George now directs towards her country neighbours has marked her life. It emerged when, as a teenager, she found herself nursing her formidable grandmother. She demonstrated its extraordinary extent in the many romances with which she tried to break the mould of her marriage. Whatever her failings by Solange, it found expression in her years as a mother and then a deeply involved grandmother. Now it colours her last long friendship with Flaubert, even though theirs is an elective affinity between writerly equals.

This is not a perversion, in other words, but protectiveness as the active recognition that something is of value. And in this friendship at least the mother–son pattern is reciprocal. Flaubert, who has such respect for George, is both emotionally and practically dependent on his own mother, at whose death he is left not only impoverished and bereft but unable properly to look after himself. A slow, depressing descent commences, and in 1880 he will die of a cerebral haemorrhage at the age of just fifty-eight.

Yet it's George who will die first, of bowel cancer. It seems a cruel irony that someone who has been so prolix, both as a writer and in her emotional life, should become literally, and fatally, costive. But illness is, as that other culture-shifting woman writer Susan Sontag will point out a century from now, no metaphor.

By the summer of 1876 George has been ill for months, perhaps even years. Her digestive system has never fully recovered from the bout of typhoid and gall-bladder disease she suffered in 1860. (Did the typhoid she and Alfred de Musset caught all those decades ago in Venice weaken her system even earlier?) At the end of May she writes to her most trusted doctor in Paris, Henri Favre, that she has virtually ceased to have bowel movements. But she does so without much practical hope. She's already realised that things aren't likely to get better. Her old doctor friend Gustave Papet confirms it to witnesses: 'She is doomed,' and on 30 May two local doctors from La Châtre back up his verdict.[64] Though on 2 June they try a futile enema: a bizarrely gestural and cruel resort since it only makes her suffering worse, as they must have known it would.

George has an agonising ending, which goes on for days. Attended turn and turn about by Lina and – proximity overcoming emotional distance – Solange, as well as a doctor and a maid, she screams and begs for death. It's not at all clear why she is offered neither wine nor morphine to take the edge off the excruciating pain; or at least, not offered it in remotely sufficient quantities. Nearly a century earlier, for example, in 1797 Mary Wollstonecraft was kept in the merciful haze of a 'wine diet' – that is, inebriation – during her own agonising death from post-partum sepsis. No screams were recorded at her London deathbed.

But perhaps, as with that unnecessary enema, the consciences of George's attendants prefer the clean hands of probity to compassion; doing nothing instead of helping ease her end. She finally dies, early on the morning of 8 June, in the presence of Lina, Solange and her two much-loved nephews, Hippolyte's grandson René Simmonet (actually her great-nephew) and Caroline's son Oscar Cazamajou.

This seems the most sanctimonious moment of all, more like the tableau carved on a monument than a crisis of shared family emotion. For they are all kneeling at the foot of her bed. Why is no one brave enough to hold her hand? Maurice, her adored son and perhaps the person to whom she's been closest in her life, is sleeping between stints at the deathbed. No one wakes him to offer the unique comfort of his presence as she slips away. Why not? When he does wake, he exclaims again and again, in a rapture of despair, 'Our life is over.'[65] And so, in a way, it is. The shared life of rewarded and rewarding creativity in, and deeply informed by, a much-loved *paysage* is over. So is the extended family which George has, eventually and against the odds, patched together.

She has, characteristically, died pen in hand – or at least with a novel, *Albine Fiori*, left unfinished. Flaubert, finally making the trip to Nohant again, is one of the many dignitaries from her literary life who come to mix with villagers at her funeral. Victor Hugo sends a pronouncement: 'I mourn a dead woman and I salute an immortal one.' Prince Jérôme Napoléon arrives by night train to join writers including Alexandre Dumas fils and Ernest Renan, the publisher Calmann-Lévy, journalists from the national press and others at the ceremony, which is – controversially – held in the parish church of Sainte-Anne. The convent girl has been, in the end, gathered back in by the Catholic communion. She's interred in the village cemetery across from the church, in the family plot against the manor wall.

Flaubert tells Turgenev he 'wept like a calf at her funeral':

> The first time when I kissed her granddaughter Aurore (whose eyes, that day, were so like hers as to be a kind of resurrection); the second, when I saw her coffin carried past [...] The good country people wept copiously around the grave. We were up to our ankles in mud in the little village cemetery, and a gentle rain was falling. Her funeral was like a chapter in one of her books.

If interment is a final homecoming, George's final home is Nohant. And after all, as Flaubert tells Turgenev, 'why pity her? She had everything life had to offer, and will remain a very great figure.'

But 'love and pity go together', and even as he writes this it's as if he's still standing at the graveside in the rain, hat in his hands, with his coat wet and his hair drenched, to ruminate on and honour his old friend. It was to 'her old Flaubert' that the living George wrote, in October 1871, what stands as an explanation of her life and work. It's both an *ars poetica* and an *ars amatoria*:

> One fine day I [...] found myself with [...] don't laugh [...] childish, innocent principles that have stayed with me through everything – through *Lélia* and the romantic period; through love and doubt, enthusiasms and disillusions. To love, to sacrifice oneself, never to withdraw unless the sacrifice comes to harm the people it's meant to benefit, and then to sacrifice oneself again in the hope of serving a true cause – love. I'm not

talking now of personal passion but of love of the human race; of an extension of self-love that abhors concentration on the self alone [...] for if a natural society is to survive, its first law must be mutual service, as with the ants and the bees. [...] Human instinct is love, and whoever omits love omits truth and justice.[66]

Ars longa. Proving that point in the most ironic of ways is Auguste Clésinger, George's hated former son-in-law. He's still a mover and shaker and now, opportunistically, he profits once more from his sometime mother-in-law. His full-length marble statue of the writer, which had been commissioned in 1854 by a group of her influential admirers, is bought by the Department of Fine Arts as a memorial and unveiled at the Comédie-Française on 4 June 1877, the night her *Le Marquis de Villemer* opens in their repertoire. But this blank-faced, formulaic figure can stand as no more than a place-marker for the immense liveliness of George's actual presence. Soon enough, it gets consigned to a provincial museum at the chateau of Compiègne; in the twenty-first century it stands in the renovated stables at Nohant: blank-eyed, frowning and immovably classical.

It's in her own words, after all, that the posthumous George Sand is to be found. She finishes the story of her life, in *Histoire*, on an idealistic note:

And we too have our moments of dejection and despair when it seems that the world is marching madly towards worship of the gods of decadence [...] But if we test our heart, we find it rapt with innocence and with charity as in the first days of our childhood.[67]

Innocence, some original way of understanding the world that is aligned with the truth of things, is the touchstone. Its freshness creates the 'rapture' of childhood; perhaps, too, of writerly imagination. It comes before, and is more whole-hearted than, social convention; its principles aren't blunted by circumstantial compromise, but deal in the absolutes of idealism. The 'childish innocent principles' of a lifelong idealism, repeatedly articulated and acted upon, remind us that, even when she dies just short of seventy-two, George is at heart the tender, emotional child who was born Aurore Dupin soon after the turn of the nineteenth century. Who lived through revolution, war and epidemics and who, like the foundling in a fairy tale – or one of her own stories – had to outwit circumstance in order to survive. Who sometimes covered up that touchstone innocence with worldly sophistication: much as she borrowed men's clothes and a man's name to pursue her vocation. And who grew up to become a literary giant on whose shoulders women will still be standing a century and a half after her death.

As Flaubert tells Marie-Sophie Leroyer de Chantepie, a wealthy writer from Pays de la Loire and a mutual friend:

> One had to know her as I did to know how much of the feminine was in that great man [*sic*], the immensity of tenderness in that genius. Her name will live in unique glory as one of the great figures of France.[68]

Final impression: *Of mastery*

ON THE CUSP OF SIXTY, George Sand is posed as Molière by the famous Paris photographer Félix Nadar. To dress her up as this great seventeenth-century playwright, Nadar has used a velvet throw and Louis XIV wig that he keeps in his studios at 35 boulevard des Capucines.

We recognise these studio props from some of his other photos: a luminous study of the twenty-year-old Sarah Bernhardt, portraits in fancy dress of his son Paul as a Renaissance page and of himself in Indigenous American costume. Items from a theatrical wardrobe, they're probably a bit dusty, maybe not perfectly clean. And they're just accessories, not a disguise. When Nadar uses them, he does so not to mask but to highlight his subject's unique identity.

In self-portraits, for example, the tumbling curls of the Louis XIV *perruque* give Nadar himself a touch of Glam Rock excess. But he has braggadocio even without this: heavily moustached, and sporting the side parting which in 1860s Paris denotes *art*. His studios dominate the extraordinary four-storey, four-bay building at their fashionable address in the capital. Its facade appears to be constructed entirely of glass and steel, like Europe's latest architectural wonders – Joseph Paxton's Crystal Palace in London, Jacques Ignace Hittorff's Gare du Nord in Paris – and here all that steelwork is painted crimson. Bolder still, Nadar's own signature is scrawled across the upper storeys in an incandescent gas fixture designed by Antoine Lumière.

It's the building as showman. Everything's blown open and visible; in your face. So you might not choose Nadar to do your portrait if you were at all retiring. But George Sand – notorious almost from the moment, more than three decades ago, that she burst on to the Paris scene – is used to being in the public eye. And when she arrives at his studios, at eleven on the morning of 4 March 1864, she's full of a fresh triumph as a playwright. Last month, the dramatisation of her novel *Le Marquis de Villemer* premiered at the Odéon theatre in the presence of the emperor and empress. On opening night she was mobbed in the streets of Paris by a crowd of admiring students – chaos and glamorous spontaneity. Imagine being picked up, chair and all, like an old-fashioned bride at her wedding. A kind of rapture of lights and darkness, hubbub. Out into the streets: maybe the boys aren't quite sober. Excitement, nervousness. Things splash and break on cobbles.

Being chaired from the theatre by Paris students, those notorious bellwethers, is a triumphant affirmation of George's ability to cross genres as a writer; and of an enduring appeal across generations and over decades. She must feel like a national treasure, if not quite yet the timeless icon Molière himself is. And even though the tone of their actual writing couldn't be more different, her famous predecessor matters particularly to her. Her own full-length drama *Molière*, about the last years of the dramatist's life, premiered in 1851, and this material was given a first airing in a theatrical sketch, *Le Roi attend* (*The King Is Waiting*), which she wrote in 1848 to support the movement for theatre free to audiences. Earlier still, one of the theatrical productions she mounted while at school in the convent of the

Dames Augustines Anglaises was Molière's *Le Malade imaginaire* (*The Imaginary Invalid*).

As she sits for Nadar on this spring day, George is recovering from the flu and from having had four teeth pulled.[69] Her partner, Alexandre Manceau, is showing worrying symptoms of tuberculosis, though all doesn't yet seem to be lost. She may be feeling her age, just a little. But also her power. She's one of the most famous writers in the world. Admired by all the great artists of the day, from Honoré de Balzac to Matthew Arnold, from Eugène Delacroix to Franz Liszt, she has huge cultural influence. She's also a political commentator and literary advocate of genuine reach. That the 'master' who has achieved all this happens to be a woman is by the by. And at the same time it's extraordinary.

The paradox of gender in writing. We're wary of being reductive, yet feel endlessly involved in the subject. As the American writer and novelist Elizabeth Hardwick – another woman writer posthumously shrunk down to her private life – will write, more than a century after the March day on which George Sand poses for this photo: 'And women writers, of course, interest me more *since I am a woman*. Remember what Sainte-Beuve said about George Sand: "A great heart, a large talent, and an enormous bottom" [my italics].'[70]

Authorship and authority are all tangled together in the person of the writer, as George Sand knows all too well. Who cares, is Hardwick's point, what size a male author's bottom is. Félix Nadar, master impresario, knows this too, and that's why he digs out the *perruque*. That this palimpsest portrait of the Great Writer is both Molière and Sand, both then and now, both male and female, is both beside the point of his photograph – and at the same time the whole of it.

By the twenty-first century, George Sand will have been reduced to anecdotes about her gender and sexuality, especially the false allegation that she placed Fryderyk Chopin in jeopardy: a literal femme fatale. The actual writing work that made her famous – hugely influential, pioneering in its forensic, proto-psychoanalytic emotional intelligence, and in its ecological awareness – will be routinely overlooked. Worse, because she is a woman and thus peculiarly embodied, the terms used for this reconfiguration are crudely bodily.

The process started in her own lifetime. In 1852, even her future confidant Gustave Flaubert was admonishing his lover Louise Colet, probably because she was herself a writer, 'In G. Sand one smells the *fluor albus* (mucus): everything oozes, and ideas trickle between words as though between slack thighs.' Before the end of the century, in the posthumously published *Mon coeur mis à nu* (*My Heart Stripped Bare*), Charles Baudelaire, himself no stranger to promiscuity or decadence, would opine of her, 'That men have been able to fall in love with this latrine, is the proof of the abasement of this century's men.' By 1889, in *Götzen-Dämmerung* (*Twilight of the Idols*), the (since we can all play this game) syphilitic philosopher Friedrich Nietzsche was labelling her 'An abundance of milk, [a] dairy cow with a "beautiful style".' In the mid-twentieth century even one of her own biographers would record with approval the verdict of an anonymous librarian that she was a *pisseuse d'encre* (ink-pisser).[71]

As false as they are offensive, these *ad feminam* 'literary' slurs demonstrate exactly why, even had there been any truth in their dismissal of the quality of her work, the writer who is their object still matters over 150 years after her death. For in allowing herself to be *seen* as this much-mocked figure, a writing woman, she makes things that bit easier for everyone who will come after her, whether or not we have her grandeur of talent and energy. George Sand absorbs and shields us from much of the visceral disgust directed at her for daring to write. And by having the courage to do so she makes herself visible in the very same gesture with which she tries to fit into male literary Paris.

Men's clothes with a sexy and very gendered cinch at the waist, and curls tumbling from under the brim of a top hat, are not a disguise but a woman wearing the writer's uniform of her day. She is a child of the French Revolution, whose *Liberté, egalité, fraternité* articulated the Romantic era's great turn towards a belief in the intrinsic value of every human being. In practice, like most revolutions, this one takes too long to notice that women also fall into the category of equal human beings; it doesn't happen in time for her. In such a context, what could a woman's own authority possibly look like?

The face in Nadar's portrait has a shot at an answer. It's heavy-set and wise, with humorous, intelligent eyes. Framed as Molière, it fits comfortably, even 'naturally,' into the Great Tradition of male authors. Nadar has created a portrait, not of a man or a woman, nor even of a woman dressed as a man, but of literary authority itself. If it seems to oscillate – like Ludwig Wittgenstein's duck-rabbit drawing – between its palimpsest subjects, male and female, it does so without changing. Only the eye of the beholder changes. Authority, as Félix Nadar helps George Sand to show us, is ambidextrous.

On language and sources

GEORGE SAND WENT BY SEVERAL names before she arrived at the one she's known by, sometime around 14 February 1833. By then she was already twenty-eight. Since, as she knew, names are a foundation of personal identity, in each chapter I've tried to use the one she was most likely using to think of herself at that time.

Unless otherwise specified, translations are my own.

My references cite Georges Lubin's authoritative, twenty-five-volume edition of *George Sand: Correspondance* (Classiques Garnier, 1964–91), which is of course in French. In keeping with my aim to make this material entirely accessible to anglophone readers, I've translated this title, and I give volume number and letter reference information (Lubin's numbering, the correspondents and, in translation, the date) rather than an uninformative page number which may be superseded by digitalisation. Letter dates in square brackets are Lubin's informed conjectures; those unbracketed appear in the original letter. The very occasional italicisation of dates in square brackets indicates that an alternative scholarly source presents what seems to me a more convincingly argued alternative.

Sand was prolific as a writer, and as a correspondent. The other major primary source she herself offers us is her autobiographical writing, in particular her *Histoire de ma vie*. However, there isn't a complete edition of this multi-volume work in English; nor is there a recent, even partial, translation. I've used the Project

Gutenberg scan of the first, 1855 edition (which is in French of course), and for references its pdf pagination (rather than numbering of the lengthy chapters, which don't 'find the place'). I use the title *Histoire* throughout.

George Sand's own work is best read in French in the Folio Classiques Gallimard editions where possible. It also survives – particularly the minor works, mainly but not exclusively in French – in print-on-demand and digital scan resources, including Gallica BNF of the Bibliothèque nationale de France, HathiTrust and Project Gutenberg. For English-language readers I'd recommend Sacha Rabinovitch and Patricia Thomson (trans.), *Lettres d'un voyageur* (London: Penguin, 1987) and Sylvia Raphael (trans.), *Indiana* (Oxford: Oxford University Press, World's Classics, 2008) before venturing off-piste with other, sometimes abridged English-language editions.

Claude Malécot's *George Sand / Félix Nadar* (Paris: Monum, Éditions du patrimonie, 2004; French, but with stunning original images), a scour through the photographic record held in the nation's archives from the Centre des monuments nationaux, is hugely exciting and inspiring. Belinda Jack, *George Sand: A Woman's Life Writ Large* (London: Chatto & Windus, 1999), Michelle Perrot, *George Sand à Nohant: une maison d'artiste* (Paris: Éditions du Seuil, 2018), and Martine Reid, trans. Gretchen van Slyke, *George Sand* (University Park, PA: Pennsylvania State University Press 2018, French original Paris: Éditions Gallimard, 2013) are all useful biographies. A good introduction to Sand's ecological thought is an anthology introduced by Patrick Scheyder and Gilles Clément, *George Sand, Écrits sur la nature* (Paris: Le Pommier, 2022). Francis Steegmuller and Barbara Bray (trans.), with a foreword by Francis Steegmuller, *Flaubert-Sand: The Correspondence* (New York: Alfred A. Knopf, 1993) offers readers this correspondence in both directions and does so in a smart, scholarly edition. Alan Walker, *Fryderyk Chopin: A Life and Times* (London: Faber, 2018) adds context to Sand's relationship with the musician.

Last but not least, of course, is an extraordinary resource: the Maison George Sand museum in her home at Nohant-Vic, where much of this material is held.

Acknowledgements

I'm exceptionally grateful to my editors, Alex Christofi and Jill Bialosky, as well as to everyone at Penguin Random House/Transworld and W. W. Norton who has worked so generously and with such good humour on this book. Thank you particularly to Linden Lawson for an immaculate copy-edit (any errors are my own) and to Katherine Cowdrey for securing the rights to such a fine gallery of portrait images. I'm deeply grateful to the rights holders of these pictures, without which this would be a volume without its spine.

My first and most profound debt is to the brilliant Jessica Bullock and Sarah Chalfant at the Wylie Agency, without whom this book would never have come into being. And most of all, and as always, my heartfelt gratitude goes to Peter Salmon, first reader and fellow explorer of bookshelves and psyches, identities and ideas.

Picture credits

Page 38: *Nohant, facade on the garden*, Placide Verdot, 1875, from the Centre des monuments nationaux © Reproduction Benjamin Gavaudo / CMN (https://regards.monuments-nationaux.fr/fr/recherche)

Page 74: *Portrait of Maurice Dudevant*, Joséphine Calamatta, c.1845, Bibliothèque nationale de France, Château de Nohant. Public Domain (https://en.m.wikipedia.org/wiki/File:Maurice_Dudevant-Sand_(1823-1889).jpg)

Page 110: *Portrait de George Sand à 17 ans*, Jean-Baptiste Bonjour, c.1849, Private collection. Image credit: Zuri Swimmer / Alamy Stock Photo

Page 146: *George Sand dressed as a student, and her lover Jules Sandeau in Paris, c. 1831*, engraving by Paul Gavarni. Image credit: PVDE / Bridgeman Images

Page 176: *Sketch of George Sand* by Alfred de Musset, 1833, Bibliothéque de l'Institut de France, Collection Charles de Spoelberch de Lovenjoul. Public Domain. (https://commons.wikimedia.org/wiki/File:George_Sand_par_Alfred_de_Musset_(05).jpg)

Page 224: *George Sand*, Eugène Delacroix, 1834, Musée national Eugène-Delacroix © Fine Art Images/Heritage Images via Alamy

Page 272: *George Sand* by August Charpentier, 1838, Museé de la Vie Romantique, Paris. Image credit: incamerastock / Alamy Stock Photo

Page 322: *George Sand in a Molière wig,* Félix Nadar, c.1864. Image credit: Science History Images / Alamy Stock Photo

Notes

INTRODUCTION

1 Georges Lubin (ed.), *Correspondance de George Sand* (Paris: Classiques Garnier, 1964–91) (*Corr.*), Vol. 1 (*Corr.1*) #366, GS (Aurore Dupin/Dudevant/Georges/George Sand) to Jules Boucoiran [7 March 1831].

CHAPTER ONE: DAWN

1 Amandine became Amantine at the Hôtel de Ville, where her birth was registered.
2 *Histoire de ma vie* (*HMV*) (Paris: Victor Lecou, 1854–5). Project Gutenberg transcription by Hélène de Mink. Gutenberg book and pdf page numbers: Book 1 of 3, pp. 7, 129. Marriage certificate of Aurore's parents https://www.ancestry.co.uk/imageviewer/collections/62058/images/62058_b998715-00415?usePUB=true&usePUBJs=true&pId=10083989 (retrieved 20/11/24).
3 *HMV1*, p. 46.
4 Rather, in fact, as that monument in Bruère-Allichamps is itself a reused Roman way-marker and sometime sarcophagus.
5 Unlike the hymn-writer Dorothy Frances Gurney, the Victorian Londoner who wrote, 'One is nearer God's heart in a garden, / Than anywhere else on earth.'
6 *HMV1*, pp. 209–10.
7 *HMV1*, p. 130. In this first account, Sand gets her own birthday wrong: she says it was 5 July, though later she corrects this to 1 July.
8 https://ordinaryphilosophy.com/2015/08/30/fifth-day-in-paris-following-thomas-paine-mary-wollstonecraft-and-thomas-jefferson-aug-19th-2015/ (retrieved 14/9/23).
9 To quote from the title of his 18 October 1789 'Address to the National Assembly'.

10 The house belonged to Aline Filliettaz, whose mother had been headmistress of a school where Wollstonecraft's sisters taught.

11 Popularised by Henri Murger's collection of short fictional 'Tales from the City', *Scènes de la vie de Bohème* (1851), whose dramatisation by Théodore Barrière made both him and the culture he was writing about famous. https://www.britannica.com/topic/bohemianism (retrieved 11/11/24).

12 *HMV1*, p. 8.

13 *HMV1*, p. 409, cited in André Maurois, *Lélia ou la vie de George Sand* (Paris: Hachette, 1952).

14 'Monde de mœurs équivoques': earliest citation of 'demi-monde', Mme d'Arblay, *Evelina* (1789), Vol. 1, p. 34. Centre National de Resources Textuelles et Lexicales https://www.cnrtl.fr/definition/demi-monde (retrieved 20/9/23). 'Naguère, milieu constitué autour de femmes légères, souvent vénales ou entretenues, en marge de la bonne société, mais fréquenté par les hommes de celle-ci.' Dictionnaire de l'Académie Française https://www.dictionnaire-academie.fr/article/A9D1211 (retrived 20/9/23).

15 *HMV1*, p. 145.

16 *HMV1*, p. 40.

17 https://www.wikitree.com/wiki/Delaborde-3 (retrieved 20/9/23). Caroline's birth and marriage certificates have been destroyed. Her marriage certificate has been reconstructed in summary. She married 'Pierre-Jean-Nicolas Cazamajou, contrôleur d'armes, fils de Jean-Baptiste Cazamajou et Anne-Marie-Nicole Lesage', 12 December 1821 in Paris. Source: Acte de mariage (reconstitution): Reconstitution chronologique des actes de mariage (série V.2E), 1568–1859 Mariages décembre 1821–20 avril 1822 N° de film 007839772 image 179. FamilySearch, avec l'autorisation des Archives de Paris. The full entry of her death at three in the morning on 2 October 1878 at the house of her son Oscar Cazamajou on rue Bourbon, Châtellerault has survived, in the Archives of Vienne https://archives-deux-sevres-vienne.fr/ark:/28387/vta3e2a7ffa9c614668/daogrp/0/78 (retrieved 13/10/23). It states that she was seventy-nine at the time of her death, so she must have been born – in Paris, as it also records – in 1799 or late 1798.

18 *HMV1*, p. 92.

19 *Corr.6* #2778, GS to Charles Poncy 23 December 1843.

20 *HMV1*, p. 98.

21 *HMV1*, p. 57. These expenses would accelerate through his twenties: after fighting the Jena campaign of 1806 and a winter campaign in Poland, he had been further promoted to the rank of *Chef d'escadron* – squadron leader or major – of the 1st Regiment of the Hussars. *HMV1*, p. 151.

22 *HMV1*, p. 98.
23 *HMV1*, p. 106
24 Population of La Châtre in 1800: 3,357. *Des villages de Cassini aux communes d'aujourd'hui*: Commune data sheet La Châtre, EHESS (retrieved 18/9/23).
25 *HMV1*, pp. 106-7.
26 Or so GS believed: *HMV1*, pp. 106-7.
27 One wonders what the Chatirons made of Maurice Dupin's new lover.
28 *HMV1*, p. 29. 'During the revolution, which soon came to quibble over all kinds of titles, Abbé Deschartres prudently became Citizen Deschartres. Under the Empire, he was Mr Deschartres, mayor of the village of Nohant.'
29 '*Cuistre*' in Centre National de Ressources Textuelles et Lexicales, *Ortolang: Outils et Ressources pour un Traitement Optimisé de la Langue* https://www.cnrtl.fr/definition/cuistre (retrieved 17/10/23).
30 *HMV1*, p. 29.
31 *HMV1*, p. 107.
32 George understands these implications when, elsewhere, she rounds up her mother's age to thirty. Institut National d'Études Démographiques (INED) https://www.ined.fr/en/everything_about_population/graphs-maps/interpreted-graphs/life-expectancyfrance/#:~:text=In%20the%20mid%20eighteenth%20century,reaching%2045%20years%20in%201900 (retrieved 13/10/23).
33 His own illegitimate status is reinforced on their wedding certificate, dated '16 Prairial year 12' (5 June 1804), location 'old 2nd arrondissement' where he is recorded as 'Maurice son of [fs] Elizabeth Dupin' https://www.ancestry.co.uk/search/collections/62058/records/10083989 (retrieved 21/11/24).
34 *HMV1*, p. 165.
35 *HMV1*, p. 168.
36 *HMV1*, p. 168.
37 It takes up plenty of room in her *Histoire*.
38 *HMV1*, p. 172.
39 *HMV1*, p. 172.
40 *HMV1*, p. 173.
41 Sand tries to calculate when she arrived in Madrid using the encounter as a marker. We can work out that it could have occurred no sooner than 7 May if their paths crossed in the Basque Country. Even from Madrid to the closer city of Burgos is a distance of some 160 miles; which means that if Aurore saw the infanta there, just before the midpoint of the royal progress, the

queen would have been travelling for three or more days, and the date would have been around or shortly after 5 May. Allowing for the slower progress of Mme Fontanier's calèche making the same journey in reverse, the earliest date for her arrival must be 8 May.

42 Today the externally rather austere building on Plaza Marina Española, of pale brick with stone facings, is in public hands. Currently it houses the Centre of Constitutional Studies.

43 Fondation Napoléon https://www.Napoléon.org/en/young-historians/napodoc/joachim-murat-king-of-naples/ (retrieved 2/11/23).

44 That's the subtitle of the painting, which was painted six years later and is today at the Prado. Twenty-first-century Príncipe Pío is a Madrid district and a metro stop.

45 In a letter Sand transcribes and dates to that day. *HMV1*, p. 180.

46 *HMV1*, p. 181.

47 *HMV1*, pp. 182–3.

48 *HMV1*, p. 181

49 *HMV1*, p. 152. Sand transcribes the letter as sent from 'Rosemberg, 10 mai 1807, au quartier général du grand-duc de Berg' and adds the note: 'These three children were me, Caroline, and a son born in 1806, who did not survive.'

50 *HMV1*, pp. 168–9.

51 *HMV1*, p. 168.

52 *HMV1*, p. 170.

53 *HMV1*, p. 132.

54 She had not asked while her mother was alive because informants had assured her that her parents were lying.

55 Aaron O'Neill, 'Child mortality rate (under five years old) in France, from 1800 to 2020' (21/6/22) Statista https://www.statista.com/statistics/1041724/france-all-time-child-mortality-rate/#:~:text=The%20child%20mortality%20rate%20in,it%20to%20their%20Fifth%20birthday (retrieved 10/10/23).

56 There's something odd about this date: Edmond Plauchot says that Marie-Aurore de Saxe bought Nohant swiftly after being saved from the scaffold by the Thermidorian Reaction, which brought an end to Robespierre and his Reign of Terror. But that was to occur a year later, on 9 Thermidor Year II: 27 July 1794. Edmond Plauchut, *Autour de Nohant* (Paris: Calmann-Lëvy, 1897), p. 14. As a young man the journalist and travel writer Edmond Plauchut (1824–1909) had been encouraged by generous letters from Sand;

these letters had survived shipwreck on the Cape Verde islands, where they proved his standing so that he was given shelter by a wealthy Portuguese settler. Sand called him 'the cream of the shipwrecked'. He stayed at Nohant frequently from 1868 until Sand's death. Marie-Aurore de Saxe bought Nohant at a time of runaway inflation, as the government (and Swiss pirates) printed unregulated amounts of paper *assignats*, a kind of halfway house between paper currency and paper cheques whose value was assured against the government's vast holdings of newly confiscated lands. Within two years the livre would be abolished and a new currency, the franc, introduced. In November 1793, after a series of attempts to make staples such as bread accessible to all, the government even attempted to calm the chaos by imposing maximum price legislation: three sols, or 15 per cent of a livre, was then the maximum price of a standard small 1lb loaf. The price she paid for it would, even by the following November, still have bought one and a half million loaves of bread. As I write, that's equivalent to around £2.25 million: not cheap for a French *manoir*. Value of the livre https://en.wikipedia.org/wiki/French_livre#:~:text=The%20livre%20was%20established%20by,)%2C%20each%20of%2012%20deniers (retrieved 24/10/23). Value of bread https://chezjim.com/18c/breads/Bread_18_4pe.html (retrieved 24/10/23).

57　Serennes had bought Nohant for just 78,600 livres on 10 November 1767. Plauchut, p. 8 https://babel.hathitrust.org/cgi/pt?id=uva.x000009149&seq=30 (retrieved 4/11/23). The extent of Nohant estate https://www.bude-orleans.org/dossier-Sand-Nohant/Nohant-Sand.html (retrieved 24/10/23).

58　'Madame Dupin [. . .] had the ditches with which M. de Serennes had surrounded the castle filled in, then she raised the ground so that it formed a terrace on the west side. Four grey walls, of a forbidding appearance, surrounded the dwelling on all sides; she had the part facing south thrown down, and from then on, from her windows opening in that direction, she was able to embrace at a glance the wooded hills from which stand out the red roofs of the buildings of the village of Laleuf and the hills behind which rise the beautiful ruins of the keep of Sarzay.' Plauchut, pp. 10–11. For other studies of Nohant https://www.bude-orleans.org/dossier-Sand-Nohant/Nohant-Sand.html (retrieved 24/10/23).

CHAPTER TWO: THE VERY RICH HOURS

1　*HMV1*, p. 181.
2　*HMV1*, pp. 184–5.
3　*HMV1*, p. 15.
4　*HMV1*, p. 130.

5 'Aurore' was effectively a patronymic, as well as a way to trace the anchoring power of grandmothers.

6 Though the liaison didn't last, after undertaking diplomatic errands she attained security and prestige as coadjutor abbess and lady provost of Quedlingburg Abbey in Saxony, a tenth-century foundation and Imperial Estate of the Holy Roman Empire.

7 'Königsmark, Maria Aurora, Countess of' in *Encyclopaedia Britannica* (1911), Vol. 15, p. 895. The entry references: 'F. Cramer, *Denkwürdigkeiten der Gräfin M. A. Königsmark* (Leipzig, 1836); *Biographische Nachrichten von der Gräfin M. A. Königsmark* (Quedlinburg, 1833); W. F. Palmblad, *Aurora Königsmark und ihre Verwandte* (Leipzig, 1848–1853); C. L. de Pöllnitz, *La Saxe galante* (Amsterdam, 1734); and O. J. B. von Corvin-Wiersbitzki, *Maria Aurora, Gräfin von Königsmark* (Rudolstadt, 1902).'

8 Uta Dorothea Sauer, 'Dance and poetry in the works of Maria Aurora von Königsmarck' in *New College Oxford*, https://www.new.ox.ac.uk/node/1736 (retrieved 28/10/23).

9 'Det Qwinliga Könetz rätmätige Förswar'. None of this was seen as overstepping the gender mark: Brenner was actively encouraged by her husband's circle.

10 To become a Marshal of France, as he did in 1743, is to be granted not a working military rank but a title; though in his case this honoured military exploits. Among other feats, in 1741 he had used a surprise night attack to seize Prague just as his maternal great-grandfather, Hans Christoff von Königsmarck, had done almost a century earlier. In 1747, three years before his death in the gloriously many-towered Renaissance Château de Chambord – of which the king had given him lifelong use – Maurice de Saxe became Marshal General of the King's Camps and Armies.

11 She was given a fictional father with the punning name Jean-Baptist de la Rivière (John the Baptist of the River). Her formal submission to be recognised as her father's daughter survives at Archives Nationales Cote: X1a 4533, folio 110 verso, 111 et 112 recto, Registre en date du 11 au 28 mai 1766. https://en.wikipedia.org/wiki/Marie-Aurore_de_Saxe#/media/File:Marie-Aurore_de_Saxe_(1748–1821)_Reconnaissance_A.jpg (retrieved 11/3/24) . The petition survives and is in the name of 'Mlle Aurore, the only natural child of the Marshal de Saxe'; though the handwriting is exquisite for a child of that age.

12 She was there for a little over a year. When the couple wed on 14 January 1777, they did so in London, at the chapel of the French Embassy, in order to sidestep family resistance. That April they confirmed their marriage at the church of Saint-Gervais-Saint-Protais in the Marais.

13 *HMV1*, p. 186. This change is reflected in *Histoire*'s altered perspective. Up to this point in her story, Sand explores a child's understanding, even of ideas as big as life, when she animates her dolls, or death, as she weeps for a pet pigeon. Now attention shifts to the external realm where people act and interact.
14 *HMV1*, p. 186.
15 *HMV1*, pp. 186–7.
16 *HMV1*, pp. 187–9.
17 'He said to her ...' 'I heard ...' *HMV1*, pp. 190–92.
18 *HMV1*, p. 191.
19 'Is my daddy ...' 'some burglar ...' *HMV1*, p. 192.
20 *HMV1*, p. 192.
21 *HMV1*, p. 188.
22 *HMV1*, later discovery, p. 189; Sophie-Victoire as source, p. 187.
23 *HMV1*, p. 195.
24 *HMV1*, p. 196, Ursulette tells her mother: 'I'm in my "golden age" and I'll take *riches* while I have some.'
25 *HMV1*, pp. 197–8.
26 She will remain in La Châtre, marrying Jean Jos in 1825; her son Eugène, born on 11 April 1831, will inherit his mother's brains, becoming a teacher. *Corr.8*, Index des Correspondants, p. 788. She was born on 17 January 1804 (26 Nivôse Year XII); later officials seem to have been unable to convert accurately and her marriage and death certificates give her birthdate, inaccurately, as 16 January 1803 https://www.ancestry.co.uk/discoveryui-content/view/86447624:62269?tid=&pid=&queryId=3c733725-f69b-46d4-8cec-8813bd41a940&_phsrc=EvG37&_phstart=successSource (retrieved 23/2/24).
27 *HMV1*, p. 195.
28 *HMV1*, p. 196.
29 *HMV1*, p. 214.
30 In her memoir she attributes this realisation to Ursule's family. *HMV1*, p. 195.
31 Though Sophie-Victoire also received 1,000 francs per annum from an estate left her by Maurice senior.
32 *HMV1*, p. 219.
33 *HMV1*, p. 216.
34 *HMV1*, on taste, pp. 216–17, à la Chinoise, p. 217.

35 *HMV1*, p. 214.
36 *Corr.1* #1, GS to Mme Maurice Dupin 1812.
37 In the collection of the Paris Museums. Dated in Belinda Jack, *George Sand: A Woman's Life Writ Large* (London: Chatto & Windus, 1999), plate 5.
38 *HMV1*, p. 210.
39 *HMV1*, pp. 192–3.
40 Mayo Foundation for Medical Education and Research (MFMER), 'Mayo Clinic: Absence seizure' https://www.mayoclinic.org/diseases-conditions/petit-mal-seizure/symptoms-causes/syc-20359683 (retrieved 20/2/24). For example, *Epilepsy Behaviour* 2010 May; 18(1-2):13-23. doi: 10.1016/j.yebeh.2010.03.006 archived at National Library of Medicine https://pubmed.ncbi.nlm.nih.gov/20483670/ (retrieved 20/2/24), which offers a bibliography of 'similar articles' and citations.
41 As if itself caught daydreaming, the *Histoire* here confuses chronology, claiming that Aurore was seven when she first followed her mother to Paris, after 'two or three years' of vacillation on the adults' part: a claim refuted by the dates of Sophie-Victoire's agreements with Aurore de Saxe.
42 *HMV1*, p. 179.
43 'À Charles Edmond', *Impressions et souvenirs* in *Le Temps*, 22 August 1871, cited in Patrick Scheyder (ed.), Gilles Clément (intro.), *George Sand, Écrits sur la nature* (Paris: Le Pommier, 2022), p. 25.
44 *Impressions et souvenirs* in *Le Temps*, 19 September 1872, cited in Scheyder, p. 33.
45 *Impressions et souvenirs* in *Le* Temps, 13 November 1872, cited in Scheyder, p. 77.
46 GS to Gustave Flaubert (GF), Francis Steegmuller and Barbara Bray (ed. and trans.), *Flaubert-Sand: The Correspondence* (New York: Alfred A. Knopf, 1993), #289, 25 October [1871].
47 Fosses, the Latin term for fortified ditches, were the medieval city ramparts, here at their highest point. The convent, not to be confused with the Benedictine convent of a similar name, moved to Neuilly-sur-Seine in 1862. The pencil drawing by Léon Leymonnerye is at the Musée Carnavalet Histoire de Paris, inventory number D.8021(1034) https://www.parismuseescollections.paris.fr/fr/musee-carnavalet/oeuvres/st-victor-rue-des-fosses-communaute-des-jeunes-anglaises-demoli-1861#infos-principales. For more primary sources on 'Early Modern Exiled Nuns' see https://emen.hypotheses.org/primary-sources (retrieved 6/3/24).
48 *HMV2*, p. 164.
49 *HMV2*, pp. 162–3.
50 *HMV2*, p. 165.

51 All French religious orders were dissolved on 13 February 1790. Many had anticipated instead being adopted by the Revolution because their teaching and health care were such useful community work, a point made in Corinne Gressang, 'Breaking Habits: Identity and the Dissolution of Convents in France, 1789–1808', University of Kentucky Thesis, 2020 https://doi.org/10.13023/etd.2020.257 (retrieved 6/3/24).

52 According to Sand, Marie-Aurore de Saxe was arrested on 5 Frimaire Year II (26 November 1793), and released on 4 Fructidor Year II (21 August 1794). M. l'abbé F. M.-Th. Cédoz, trans. Roger Peters, *Un couvent de religieuses anglaises à Paris de 1634 à 1884* (Paris and London: Lecoffre and Burns and Oates, 1891), Ch. 8, note 15 https://www.wissensdrang.com/dcon8fr08.htm#15 (retrieved 5/3/24).

53 *HMV2*, p. 154.
54 *HMV2*, p. 159.
55 *HMV2*, p. 156.
56 *HMV2*, p. 162.
57 *HMV2*, p. 203.

CHAPTER THREE: REVERIES OF A SOLITARY WALKER

1 *Oeuvres Autobiographiques* (Paris: La Pléiade, Vols. 1 and 2, 1970 and 1971) (*OA*), pp. 861–8.
2 *HMV2*, p. 271.
3 *HMV2*, pp. 274–5.
4 One could imagine his killing was a *crime passionnel* by a jealous husband. A measure of the significance of this assassination is that the king demanded the Salle be flattened, and a new Salle, completed a year later, was built for the Opéra company on the rue Le Peletier.
5 *HMV2*, Ch. 15.
6 For example the visit recorded in *Corr.1* #11, GS to Marie-Émilie de Wismes [18 August–28 September 1820].
7 It's hard not to feel that Hippolyte may have lived with some form of ADHD, as well as the unassimilable sense of his intrinsic 'wrongness' as an illegitimate son.
8 *Corr.1* ##8, 9 and 10, Jane Bazouin to GS [August, September and September 1820]. All the same, Aurore kept Jane's letters, although her own to Jane have not survived. Is this evidence of some underlying asymmetry in their affection, or just a result of the unusual security enjoyed by documents of all kinds at Nohant, in what will after all eventually become a museum?

9   *Corr.1* #10, summary Jane Bazouin to GS [September 1820].
10 *Corr.1* #11, GS to Marie-Émilie de Wismes [18 August–28 September 1820].
11 'there is some time ago' in English in the original.
12 *Corr.1* #12, GS to Marie-Émilie de Wismes [October 1820].
13 *Corr.1* #18, GS to Apollonie de Bruges 31 December [1820].
14 *Corr.1* #23, GS to Apollonie de Bruges [spring 1821]. Though in a note Lubin thinks an intervening letter has been lost.
15 *Corr.1* #20, GS to Marie-Émilie de Wismes [January 1821].
16 *Corr.1* #20.
17 *HMV*2, p. 104.
18 *HMV*2, p. 287. However little such a crossing of generations traditionally worries older men, it confuses young women who discover that older men are very rarely 'father figures'.
19 His wife Isidore Eugénie will live on for almost another half-century https://fr.wikipedia.org/wiki/Louis_Pierre_Alphonse_de_Colbert (retrieved 23/4/24).
20 In *HMV*2, p. 287 Sand sets the evening among 'the last evenings in February', and on p. 288 the planned trip to Paris 'in March' is to be in 'eight days" time.
21 Two to three months after the stroke 'the paralysis has almost entirely dissipated, ideas have become healthy again, and although the moral faculties are much weakened, she's as good as one can be at her age'. *Corr.1* #27, GS to Marie-Émilie de Wismes [April or May 1821]. But in *Histoire*, the adult Sand is more honest about what 'moral faculties are much weakened' actually means, *HMV*2, pp. 293–4.
22 *Corr.1* #23.
23 *HMV*2, p. 287.
24 *HMV*2, p. 287.
25 *Corr.1* #20. Lubin dates the letter to the second half of January; even were his arguments for this to be disproved, the letter is clearly written before Aurore's grandmother has fallen gravely ill. Earlier still, in #19, GS to Jane Bazouin, to which Bazouin replies on 16 January 1821, GS announces a visit to Paris; Bazouin responds that the rumour in the convent is that it will be 'next month', that is, in February.
26 *HMV*2, p. 296.
27 *HMV*2, p. 294.
28 *Corr.1* #23.

29 *Corr.1* #34, GS to Mme Maurice Dupin 18 November 1821.
30 *HMV2*, p. 293.
31 *Corr.1* #30, GS to Marie-Émilie de Wismes [July [responding to letter of 17 June] 1821].
32 *HMV2*, p. 293.
33 *HMV2*, p. 293.
34 *HMV2*, p. 295.
35 https://premium.weatherweb.net/weather-in-history-1800-to-1849-ad/ (retrieved 24/4/24).
36 *HMV2*, p. 299.
37 *HMV2*, p. 317.
38 *HMV2*, p. 312.
39 *HMV2*, p. 309.
40 *HMV2*, p. 331.
41 *HMV2*, p. 332.
42 *HMV2*, p. 355.
43 Perhaps explaining the later confusion in Sand's memory, the bells would also have been chiming on Christmas morning, for the dawn Shepherds' Mass of the Nativity.
44 *HMV2*, p. 355.
45 *HMV2*, p. 391.
46 *Corr.1* #38, GS to Hippolyte Chatiron [May 1822].
47 In her notebook B.N., N. a fr 13641 fol. 7 recto (note 2 to *Corr.1* #39, GS to Casimir Dudevant [June 1822]).
48 *HMV2*, p. 332.
49 His mother was Augustine Soulé and he was born François Dudevant on 17 Messidor Year III at his father's home and registered by him the next day. Archives de Lot-et-Garonne, Naissances Pompiey an. III, c4, E211, 42–3.
50 After working on the new Penal Code and being made a Knight of the Empire in 1810.
51 https://tomaselli-collection.com/artistes/jean-baptiste-bonjour (retrieved 27/11/24) https://www.invaluable.com/auction-lot/jean-baptiste-bonjour-le-landeron-1801-1882-paire-177-c-3c840c1ab1?srsltid= AfmBOorQX59ojHTtAE7Xoxx-9AQTsWmxTyxEqTLXPien9vXgYxg_ OgvO (retrieved 30/7/24).

CHAPTER FOUR: ENTERING ON TIPTOE

1 Note to *Corr.1* #47, GS to Casimir Dudevant [29 July 1823]. Article 217 of the Napoleonic Code states: 'The wife, even when she is separate in estate from her husband, cannot grant, alienate, mortgage, acquire, either by gratuitous or encumbered title, unless her husband concurs in the act, or yields consent in writing.' LA. Crv. CODE ANN. art. 122 (West 1952). Cited in André Tunc, 'Husband and wife under French law', *University of Pennsylvania Law Review*, Vol. 104 (1956), pp. 1064–79. Tunc personalises: 'Bonaparte [. . .] clearly believed that women were very inferior creatures. His life as a soldier – and probably his shyness and ambition – had reinforced the ideas that he had inherited from his birthplace, Corsica.' p. 1068.
2 Deschartres leaves Nohant on 15 August 1823.
3 Probably on 2 June 1822, when GS wrote in her notebook: 'Happy as I have never been.' *Corr.1* 814.
4 https://gw.geneanet.org/gchatillon?lang=en&iz=116&p=ange+-justine&n=melin (retrieved 9/6/24).
5 Hippolyte's bequest from his grandmother, comprising 'an annuity of 1,000 francs annually and for life', is itemised in his marriage contract of 17 January 1823. *Corr.1* #46, GS to Marie-Émilie de Wismes 30 January [1823], note 1, p. 107. It was equivalent to roughly half a year's wages for a skilled labourer in Britain https://www.quora.com/What-is-the-equivalent-of-half-a-crown-from-Victorian-times-in-modern-money-England (retrieved 18/6/24).
6 The marriage contract is drawn up on 24 August 1822. Baron Dudevant dies on 20 February 1826. *Oeuvres Autobiographiques*, Vol. 2, pp. 1311–12. Casimir's stepmother will be left the lion's share of his father's estate.
7 Aurore is at most a fortnight pregnant, and quite possibly unaware of the fact, when her old friend Marie-Émilie de Wismes responds to her letter announcing her marriage on 26 September 1822. *Corr.1* #42, GS to Marie-Émilie de Wismes [September 1822], note. An exact forty-week pregnancy would have been conceived on 24 September 1822, one week after the wedding. The account of Maurice's birth is in *HMV*3, p. 4.
8 *Corr.6* #2575, GS to Hippolyte Chatiron [mid-February 1843].
9 *Oeuvres Autobiographiques*, Vol. 2, pp. 1309–10.
10 Their nationally set syllabus includes 'ancient languages, history, rhetoric, logic, music and the elements of mathematical and physical sciences' https://en.wikipedia.org/wiki/History_of_education_in_France (retrieved 17/6/24).
11 EBB 'Untitled Essay', *c.* early 1840s, Philip Kelley and Ronald Hudson (eds), *The Brownings' Correspondence* (Winfield, KS: Wedgestone Press, 1984), Vol. 1, pp. 360–62 and at www.browningscorrespondence.com.

12 Each will combine the years of fame with being the doting mother of an equally devoted son. Mary Shelley, born seven years before Aurore, broke off her studies when she began repeatedly to fall pregnant – and also in order to write her first novel, *Frankenstein*, when she was the age Aurore is now.

13 The two stops are Barrett Browning's characteristic punctuation. EBB to John Kenyon, 15–16 February 1852, *The Brownings' Correspondence* #3005.

14 *Corr.1* #47, GS to Casimir Dudevant 'Tuesday evening' [29 July 1823].

15 *Corr.1* #49, GS to Marie-Émilie de Wismes 4 November [1823].

16 According to *Corr.1*, note 1, p. 107, the religious ceremony was in the fashionable church of Saint-Étienne-du-Mont, though not till 22 March. (So was the Nohant household really awaiting the newlyweds' arrival? Or was this a way of saying that they would not be attending?) The civil marriage contract had indeed been drawn up on 17 January by a Parisian notary, Jean-Louis Lambert – https://www.archivesportaleurope.net/advanced-search/search-in-names/results-(names)/?repositoryCode=FR-FRAN&recordId=FRAN_NP_011328 (retrieved 17/6/24) – although no record of a marriage certificate survives.

17 *Corr.1* #46, GS to Marie-Émilie de Wismes 30 January [1823]. 'You have to love your husband, and love him a great deal, to come to get to this point and know how to make *the honeymoon* last. Like you I used to have a sad opinion of marriage up to the moment when I attached myself to Casimir, and if I've changed that, it's only in my own regard.'

18 Hippolyte to GS 3 April 1827, cited in *Corr.1* #148. Besides, their grandmother was wealthy enough to have been able to leave a more generous bequest to Hippolyte and still ensure Aurore's security.

19 *Corr.1* #51, GS to Marie-Émilie de Wismes 28 July (misdated for November) 1823.

20 *Corr.1* #58, GS to Marie-Émilie de Wismes 28 April 1824.

21 *Indiana* (Paris: Edition Béatrice Didier, 1984), p. 50.

22 *HMV3*, p. 8.

23 Future biographers will cite circumstances as if they were (just) cause. Aurore was playing with the children, some sand got in her husband's coffee, she did not move the play away quickly enough for his taste. Of course, this is not a cause. Domestic violence is caused by men's attitudes to their own potential for violence, not by what a woman does.

24 *Corr.1* #72, GS to Zoé Leroy 5 Sept[ember] 1825.

25 *Corr.1* #72.

26 Cited in *Corr.1* #117, GS to Louis-Nicolas Caron 9 April [1826], note 1, p. 326.

27 *Corr.1* #104, GS to Casimir Dudevant [15] November 1825.
28 Cited in Curtis Cate, *George Sand: A Biography* (London: Hamish Hamilton, 1975), p. 126.
29 Casimir finds the notebook on 6 November; he will return from Nohant on the 20th. Jack, p. 138.
30 *Corr.1* #94, GS to Casimir Dudevant Monday, 7 [November 1825].
31 *Corr.1* #104, GS to Casimir Dudevant [15] November 1825. The date calculated by Lubin.
32 *Corr.1* #94, GS to Casimir Dudevant Monday, 7 [November 1825].
33 Pouradier-Duteil https://gw.geneanet.org/wikifrat?lang=-fr&n=pouradier+duteil&oc=1&p=alexis (retrieved 22/6/24).
34 Costume: https://www.mimimatthews.com/2015/11/23/the-1820s-in-fashionable-gowns-a-visual-guide-to-the-decade/#:~:text=1825,the%20Fashionable%20world%20as%20well (retrieved 22/6/24).
35 *Corr.1* #34, GS to Mme Maurice Dupin 18 November 1821.
36 *Corr.1* #137, GS to Zoé Leroy [10 October 1826].
37 On 29 December she writes, 'Your letter of 10 October reached me . . .'. *Corr.1* #137, GS to Zoé Leroy [10 October 1826], note 2, p. 362.
38 The next surviving letter. Of course, one could have gone astray . . . *Corr.1* #145, GS to Zoé Leroy 3 March [1827].
39 *Corr.1* #172, GS to Casimir Dudevant Saturday evening [15 December 1827].
40 She tells Casimir they need seats, plural: these might just be for herself and her manservant André, although it seems likely Jules de Grandsagne would also be making the return journey. Was Stéphane coming home too, perhaps for Christmas, as biographers have assumed? We have no proof.
41 On 10 December, for example, she tells Casimir all about Jules Nehaud's behaviour, while on 12 December her letter is packed with news of appointments both medical and social.
42 *Corr.3*, p. 77, cited in Cate, p. 142. While she's nursing six-week-old Solange she tells Casimir that Maurice is 'faithful accompanies, goes out with me, sleeps with me. He's my chaperone and my husband.' *Corr.1* #205, GS to Casimir Dudevant 1 [November 1828].
43 Britain seems to have led in the use of animal intestines and membranes as condoms as early as the seventeenth century, but condoms of a variety of materials including fine leather are, though expensive, in use among the middle and upper classes in nineteenth-century France.
44 As Solange will have no surviving descendants, this is a mystery even DNA can't solve.

45 *Corr.1* #182, GS to Hippolyte de Chatiron [10 March 1828], explication p. 440.
46 Something even a rough-and-ready cavalryman, himself no sexual innocent, will doubtless understand.
47 Besides, she writes about him to Zoé in decidedly carnal terms.
48 *Corr.1* #180, GS to Zoé Leroy 2 February [1828].
49 *Corr.1* #180, note 1, p. 437.
50 *Corr.1* #181, GS to Aurélien de Sèze [early February 1828], explication p. 439.
51 *Corr.1* #189, GS to Aurélien de Sèze [10 May 1828], explication p. 450.
52 *Corr.1* #383, GS to Émile Regnault [15 May 1831].
53 *Corr.1* #328, GS to Jules Boucoiran Wednesday [1 or 3 December 1830].
54 https://www.spincemaille.be/go/p771.htm (retrieved 25/6/24).
55 #328.
56 *Corr.1* #344, GS to Charles Duvernet 19 January [1831].
57 'Si de Georges Sand ce portrait / Laisse l'esprit un peu perplex / C'est que le genie est abstrait / En comme on sait n'as pas de sexe.' This is not an era in which a distinction between sex and gender has been formalised in the language https://classes.bnf.fr/essentiels/grand/ess_2339.htm (retrieved 13/11/2024).
58 *Corr.2* #935, GS to Adolphe Guéroult [6 May 1835].

CHAPTER FIVE: BECOMING A WRITER

1 English and French calculations; the fifth floor if you're American. Then called rue de la Seine. She will live at 19 quai de Malquais.
2 *Corr.1* #366, GS to Jules Boucoiran [7 March 1831].
3 *Corr.1* #364, GS to Jules Boucoiran [4 March 1831]. There's also no mention in this letter of Hippolyte's criticism, which provokes her to write again just three days later.
4 At least, it's thought to be about her aunt. *Corr.1* #318, GS to Jules Boucoiran [13 September 1830].
5 Jack, pp. 166–7 claims this is the origin of the lovers' garret retreat in Sand's 1839 novella *Marianna*, and also of the views described in her 1840 novel of student life, *Horace*. But she will have enjoyed these views from several of her Parisian addresses, and the description of the apartment in fact matches the one she gives her son Maurice of the apartment on quai Saint-Michel, where she and Jules arrive in July 1831.
6 *HMV3*, pp. 41–2.

7   He will live until a couple of months short of his ninetieth birthday.
8   *Corr.1* #344, GS to Charles Duvernet 19 January [1831].
9   *Corr.1* #344, GS to Charles Duvernet 19 January [1831].
10 *Corr.1* #344, GS to Charles Duvernet 19 January [1831].
11 In *HMV2*, Ch. 27 she will claim de Latouche takes her on at this first meeting, but at the time she reports only his moderating reaction to 'Aimée'.
12 *Corr.1* #366, GS to Jules Boucoiran [7 March 1831].
13 *Corr.1* #364, GS to Jules Boucoiran [4 March 1831].
14 *Corr.1* #366, GS to Jules Boucoiran [7 March 1831].
15 It's advertised in *Le Figaro* on 17 December.
16 *Corr.1* #387, GS to Mme Gondoüin Saint-Agnan 30 May [1831].
17 *Corr.1* #382, GS to Émile Regnault 10 May [1831].
18 *Corr.1* #386, GS to Émile Regnault [25 May 1831].
19 https://www.gettyimages.co.uk/detail/news-photo/henri-de-latouche-with-george-sand-a-female-student-in-news-photo/159827137. The image is likely to be from 1832 at the earliest, because a news etching will not have been made until she was well known.
20 https://www.museums.cam.ac.uk/lookingatcollections/img/uploads/projects/au-cafe/Latouche-Fragoletta.pdf (retrieved 22/7/24). Balzac defends de Latouche in an article in *Mercure du XIXieme siècle*, reproduced in *Oeuvres Complètes*, Vol. 20. Édouard Maynial will point out that a '*fragoletta*' is a 'little strawberry'; that it's also a name with distant family ties to Casanova, by whom Balzac (and, presumably, de Latouche) is also markedly influenced. Édouard Maynial, 'Balzac et Casanova', *Revue d'Histoire littéraire de la France*, No. 4 (1938), pp. 472–85 https://www.jstor.org/stable/40520507 (retrieved 6/7/24).
21 In this too the future George Sand will follow in his footsteps.
22 *Corr.1*, GS to Émile Regnault [25 May 1831].
23 A sixth floor has since been added.
24 GS, *Horace* (1841–2), Ch. 3 https://www.gutenberg.org/cache/epub/13671/pg13671.txt (retrieved 22/6/24).
25 *Corr.1* #403, GS to Maurice [16 July 1831].
26 *Corr.1* #382, GS to Émile Regnault 10 May [1831].
27 *Corr.1* #397, GS to Émile Regnault [28 June 1831].
28 B. Renault, Lecounte et Pougin, Corbet Ainé, Pigoreau and Levavasseur.

29 Gérard de Nerval, 'Premier Château: 1, La rue du doyenne', *Petits châteaux de Bohême* (*Little Castles of Bohemia*, 1853) https://www.site-magister.com/chateaux.htm (retrieved 24/7/24).

30 De Latouche, helpful as ever, has run an advert for the novel in *Le Figaro*, and then a review – if not an entirely glowing one – which complains of the novel's vulgarities.

31 Heinrich Heine, trans. Charles Godfrey Leland, '19 April 1832' in *French Affairs: Letters from Paris* (London: William Heinemann, 1893), pp. 175, 183–4 https://books.google.co.uk/books?id=8L8LAAAAIAAJ&pg=PR13&source=gbs_selected_pages&cad=1#v=onepage&q&f=false and https://www.laphamsquarterly.org/roundtable/riot-dead (retrieved 24/7/24).

32 The epidemic will last for 169 days. Feargus O'Sullivan, 'Pandemic lessons from the era of *Les Misérables*', Bloomberg UK, 27 April 2021 https://www.bloomberg.com/news/features/2021-04-27/how-paris-transformed-after-cholera (retrieved 24/7/24).

33 *Corr.2* #470, GS to Maurice Dudevant [7 April 1832].

34 https://www.bridgemanimages.com/en/g-dagli-orti/portrait-of-jules-sandeau-aubusson-1811-paris-1883-french-writer-pencil-drawing-from-1831-by-george/nomedium/asset/766866 (retrieved 25/7/24).

35 #470.

36 *Corr.2* #469, GS to Émile Regnault [29 March 1832] (reference to 'poor Jules' in the same letter).

37 George Sand, *Indiana* (Paris: Delmar, 1948), pp. 11, 13.

38 *Corr.1* #46, GS to Marie-Émilie de Wismes 30 January [1823].

39 Sixteen years from now, in 1848, the tiny territory will change its name back to Réunion.

40 *Indiana*, p. 260.

41 'Mme Shelly [*sic*]', trans. Jules Saladin, *Frankenstein: ou le Prométhée moderne* (Paris: Corréard, August 1821). Shelley's creature acquires an entire intellectual formation while squatting in the barn of political radicals who live in rural exile.

42 Geoff Dyer, *But Beautiful* (London: Abacus, 1998), p. 184. George Steiner, *Real Presences* (Chicago: University of Chicago Press, 1989), p. 17.

43 In the atmosphere of *Villette*; from *Lélia* in *Shirley*, Vol. 3, Ch. 4; from *Mauprat* on *Wuthering Heights*; and on *Jane Eyre*, in Rochester's great appeal to Jane, which echoes Sylvia's to Sand's eponymous *Jacques* almost to the point of plagiarism, and from *The Miller of Angibault*, in which the sister of the protagonist goes mad when crossed in love, goes up on the roof and sets

herself and the building on fire https://www.thebrontes.net/reading/s#:~:-text=%5BCB%5D%20read%20George%20Sand%2C,development%20of%20Charlotte%20Bront%C3%AB's%20genius%20%E2%80%A6 (retrieved 2/11/24).

44 'Indiana' in Sir Paul Harvey and J. E. Heseltine (eds), *The Oxford Companion to French Literature* (Oxford: Clarendon Press, 1959), p. 358.

45 Janette McLeman-Carnie, 'Sir Walter Scott and the French press: Paris 1826', *International Review of Scottish Studies*, Vol. 25 (June 2007) https://www.researchgate.net/publication/299499148_Sir_Walter_Scott_and_the_French_Press_Paris_1826 (retrieved 26/7/24).

46 *Corr.2* #513, GS to Layre DeCerfz [3,6 and 7 July 1832].

47 #513. Aurore claims she's most proud of the anecdote about a woman 'renowned for her spirit and beauty' who, reading the novel, writes her lover a letter of reproof and signs it 'Indiana'. He signs his loving response 'Ralph'. In something of the same spirit, Aurore's letter also records the visitor who tells her, 'I am the hero [of *Indiana*]. It's my story, Madame, it's my whole heart.'

48 #513.

49 Charles Fourier, *Théorie de l'unité universelle; Du libre arbitre* (Paris: Librairie Sociétaire, 1841–2), Ch. 3, p. 177 and note 12, p. 187. Honoré de Balzac, *L'Interdiction*, p. 105 https://beq.ebooksgratuits.com/balzac/Balzac_44_Linterdiction.pdf (retrieved 12/12/24).

50 Edmond and Jules de Goncourt, *Journal*, Vol. 3 (Paris: G. Charpentier, 1888), p. 21.

51 Honoré de Balzac to Ewelina Hańska 2 March 1838, Katharine Prescott Wormeley (trans.), *Letters to Madame Hanska* 1833–1846 (Boston: Hardy, Pratt, 1969–70), p. 482 https://www.gutenberg.org/files/54466/54466-h/54466-h.htm#Page_469 (retrieved 2/12/24).

52 Lise Sabourin, 'George Sand, *Elle et lui*', *Studi Francesi*, No. 161 (LIV, II), 2010, p. 390 https://journals.openedition.org/studifrancesi/6695 (retrieved 9/10/24). Also the source for the Balzac and Hetzel quotes.

CHAPTER SIX: THE YEARS OF REBELLION

1 Carl Czerny published exercises for both instruments.

2 *Corr.2* #889, GS to Charles Meure [9 February 1835]. By then she will be writing about a subsequent love, Alfred de Musset.

3 *Corr.2*, 'Note sur les domiciles Parisiens de George Sand pendant la période 1832–1835', pp. 939–40.

4   He mentions taking three weeks to respond to her request (now lost), made in mid-August, because of 'cartophobia', that horror of letter-writing familiar to anyone with a full inbox. *Corr.2* #532, GS to Émile Regnault [20 September 1832], note 1, p. 160.

5   #532.

6   Today this is the École des Beaux-Arts. This garden is larger and closer to the river than its famous *cour de mûrier*.

7   The first surviving letter signed 'George' is dated 15 April 1833. *Corr.2* #617, GS to François Buloz [15 April 1833].

8   Percy Bysshe Shelley, *Queen Mab: A Philosophical Poem, With Notes* (London: P. B. Shelley, 1813).

9   A coincidence: both Hugo and Sand were out of earshot in public gardens when the Uprising started, and didn't realise what was going on until almost too late. He was in the Tuileries, she with Solange in the Jardin de Luxembourg.

10 *Corr.2* #496, GS to Laure Decerfz [13 June 1832].

11 *Corr.2* #508, GS contract with Ernest Dupuy [26 July 1832].

12 The text actually reads 'the first [. . .] on 7th July next', which is clearly an error, since the second, third and fourth follow respectively on '20th December, the third [. . .] on 20th March next year, and the fourth and last [. . .] on the 20th June following'. Was the contract signed late, after the first bill had been handed over, or is 7th an error for 27th – that is, the following day?

13 Offered, in this case, by Musset aîné, Sollier and Company. *Corr.2* #524, GS to Émile Regnault [31 August 1832].

14 *Corr.2* #527, GS to Amédée Pichot [13 September 1832].

15 The sum is confirmed in a letter of the following January when she defends her decision to move to the *Revue des deux mondes* on financial grounds. *Corr.2* #574, GS to Amédée Pichot [19 January 1833].

16 *Corr.2* #524, GS to Émile Regnault [31 August 1832]. The debt is due on 20 September, the novel in instalments from 1 October. Perhaps she hoped to have a first instalment to Dupuy early so as to release her advance.

17 *Corr.2* #523, GS to Émile Regnault [29 August 1832]. But for Aurore-George herself this plea for reassurance may throw up a new set of questions. When she writes about her little daughter missing him, she takes a rare tonal misstep. Motherhood is unlikely to be the thing a young man finds most exciting about his friend's sexy, brilliant lover.

18 *Corr.2* #544, GS to Émile Regnault [18 November 1832].

19 Although this seems to be a matter of her timetable slipping: in August she tells Sainte-Beuve that she's shortly off to 'Berry'. *Corr.2* #693, GS to Sainte-Beuve 25 August [1833]. She takes a week's holiday out of Paris in Fontainbleau in August 1833.

20 Marijke Jonker, 'Gustave Planche, or the Romantic side of Classicism', *Nineteenth-century Art Worldwide*, Vol. 1, No. 2 (autumn 2002) 19thc-artworldwide.org/autumn02/gustave-planche-or-the-romantic-side-of-classicism#:~:text=Gustave%20Planche%20(1808–1857),the%20art%20of%20his%20time. (retrieved 26/8/24).

21 *Corr.2* #555, Gustave Planche to GHD [23 December 1832].

22 Two hundred and fifty francs for a piece of sixteen pages, 350 for one of thirty-two pages – multiples driven by the exigencies of paper-folding.

23 Gustave Planche to GS 14 January 1833, cited in *Corr.2* #561, GS to Charles Gosselin [2 January 1833], note 1, pp. 217–18. The contract with *La Revue des deux mondes* is made by 'Madame Dudevant (Georges Sand)'. *Corr.2* #549 [11 December 1832].

24 Georges Lubin in his biographical note on Planche in *Corr.2*, p. 931.

25 *Corr.2* #574, GS to Amédée Pichot 19 January 1833.

26 George Sand, *Lélia* (Paris: Éditions Gallimard/Folio Classique, 2003), pp. 60, 55.

27 George Lubin will meticulously notate where their paths will already have crossed. *Corr.2* #693, GS to Sainte-Beuve 25 August [1833], note 1, pp. 406–7, where the quotation is also cited.

28 Charles Monselet, *La Lorgnette littéraire: Dictionnaire des grands et des petits auteurs de mon temps* (Paris: Poulet-Malassis et de Broise, 1857) https://gallica.bnf.fr/ark:/12148/bpt6k5834096w.texteImage (retrieved 29/8/24).

29 *Corr.2* #695, GS to Sosthènes de La Rochfoucauld [30 August 1833] (bad-mouthing); *Corr.2* #692, GS to Sosthènes de La Rochfoucauld [second half of August 1833] (sends letter).

30 #693.

31 #693, note 2, p. 407.

32 At any rate, according to Monselet.

33 'Complainte historique et véritable sur le fameux duel qui a eu lieu entre plusieurs hommes de plume très inconnus dans Paris, à l'occasion d'un livre dont il a été beaucoup parlé de différentes manières, ainsi qu'il est relaté dans la présente complainte (sur l'air de la *Complainte du maréchal de Saxe*)', Alfred de Musset, *Poésies Posthumes* (Paris: G. Charpentier, 1888).

34 *Corr.2* #616, GS to Laure Decerfz 1 April [1833].
35 *Corr.2* #672, GS to Sainte-Beuve 24 July 1833.
36 Within days George is already reassuring Marie Dorval that her gossip must have been 'edited' by Dumas. *Corr.2* #649, GS to Marie Dorval Saturday [22 June 1833].
37 By Victor Ducange and Dinaux, 19 June 1827 https://esat.sun.ac.za/index.php/Trente_Ans,_ou_La_Vie_d%27un_Joueur (retrieved 30/8/24).
38 https://gallica.bnf.fr/ark:/12148/btv1b8454268z/f1.item.zoom (retrieved 2/9/24).
39 Alfred de Vigny notes on a letter he has been asked to forward from Sand, 'I have forbidden Marie to respond to this Sapho [sic] who bores her.' *Corr.2* #671, GS to Marie Dorval [18 and 24 July 1833].
40 In early-nineteenth-century Europe women (and men) routinely write to same-sex friends in terms of passionate affection, and share beds with them when visiting or travelling. In societies where marriage is the only sexually intimate relationship permitted, 'best friend'-ships carry an emotional weight it can be hard to understand in the twenty-first-century global North. Marie and George live in the Parisian demi-monde, where promiscuity is not unusual, but French society otherwise precludes experimentation or even serial monogamy.
41 *Corr.2* #649, GS to Marie Dorval Saturday [22 June 1833].
42 https://www.viabooks.fr/article/alfred-de-musset-ou-le-romantisme-exalte-25921 (retrieved 3/9/24). https://www.klosi.com/klosi_news_literature/9420.html (retrieved 3/9/24).
43 https://collections.louvre.fr/en/ark:/53355/cl010090014 (retrieved 3/9/24).
44 Alfred's brother Paul is six years older; his sister Charlotte is nine years younger and will live on into the twentieth century. Alfred's father, over forty when he was born, was a civil servant who wrote alongside his day job: distinguished enough, but not wealthy https://gw.geneanet.org/garric?lang=en&p=alfred&n=de+musset (retrieved 5/9/24).
45 Probably on 24 July 1833. Alfred de Musset and George Sand, ed. Martine Reid, 'Ô *mon George, ma belle maîtresse . . .': Lettres* (Paris: Éditions Gallimard, 2010), pp. 14–15. *Corr.2* #649, p. 368, note 2. Félix Albert Barthelemy Decori (ed.), *Correspondance de George Sand et de Alfred Musset* (Brussels: E. Deman, 1904), pp. 8–10.
46 #672.
47 Reid, pp. 16–17.
48 The Hôtel Britannique, 5–13 August.

49 *Corr.2* #727, GS contract with François Buloz [9 December 1833].

50 In fact George will return home by the mountain route.

51 *Dell influenza delle passioni sul colorito della facia* (Venice: Tipografia Fracasso,1831; revised edition 1838) https://www.vanzella.it/vanzella/scheda.asp?ID=5820 (retrieved 6/9/24).

52 *Corr.2* #801, GS to Sosthènes de La Rochfoucauld [3 or 18 July 1834].

53 *Corr.2* #800, GS to Casimir Dudevant 8 July [1834].

54 Maurice's portrait hangs at Nohant https://artsandculture.google.com/entity/maurice-sand/m04jdqcj?hl=en (retrieved 11/12/24) and in the 1837 engraving by Luigi Calamatta https://www.alamy.com/maurice-sand-reproduction-luigi-calamatta-51801-1869-maurice-sand-reproduction-reproduction-dun-dessin-de-maurice-sand-enfant-conserv-au-muse-de-la-vie-romantique-reproduction-photographique-1837-paris-muse-de-la-vie-romantique-image349584551.html?imageid=E1096CE4-3EAB-4BD0-9480-46DFB755A9F2&p=1261966&pn=1&searchId=be062f018f244f928ced829a45b819f4&searchtype=0 Calamatta's 1845 portrait painting of Maurice, also at Nohant, shows the same striking resemblance https://en.m.wikipedia.org/wiki/File:Maurice_Dudevant-Sand_%281823-1889%29.jpg (retrieved 11/12/24).

55 Probably on 23 August 1834. Reid, p. 109.

56 Where it will be unearthed in 1951 by his last surviving granddaughter. It will first appear, in French translation, in 1897 in Paul Mariéton, *Une histoire d'amour* (Paris: G. Havard fils, 1897).

57 In the twenty-first century this first 1834 portrait will hang at the Musée National Eugène-Delacroix.

58 *Corr.2* #896, GS to Alfred de Musset [22 or 23 February 1835].

59 End of February or start of March 1835. Reid, p. 143.

60 *Corr.2* #900, GS to François Buloz [6 March 1835].

61 *Corr.2* #898, GS to Jules Boucoiran [6 March 1835].

62 *Corr.2* #903, GS to Jules Boucoiran [9 March 1835], *Corr.2* #918, GS to François Buloz [1 April 1835].

63 Though they often stay together, at both Nohant and George's Paris address.

64 Edouard Maynial, 'Le Procès en séperation de George Sand', *Mercure de France*, 1 December 1906, p. 335.

65 *Corr.2* #996, GS to Michel de Bourges [around 22 October 1835], note 2, p. 75. At first glance these terms seem surprising, given Aurore Dudevant's multiple infidelities, public reputation, and the custom of prioritising a

husband's rights of possession. In April, for example, Casimir's lawyer had cited her intimacy with Michel de Bourges among the many items of his 'Griefs against Aurore Dudevant'.

66 'Two documents archived at Chantilly' as Lov., W 948, fol. 40–42. Appendice, *Corr.2*, pp. 847–51.

67 #996.

CHAPTER SEVEN: DUET

1 Even though his parents had married by the time he was born.
2 James Huneker, review of Francis Gribble, *George Sand and Her Lovers*, *The North American Review*, Vol. 187, No. 627 (February 1908), pp. 277–80 https://www.jstor.org/stable/25106084 (retrieved 11/3/24).
3 It was technically illegal for women to wear men's clothes in public in Paris from 7 November 1800 until 4 February 2013 [*sic*] https://daily.jstor.org/rosa-bonheurs-permission-to-wear-pants/ (retrieved 11/5/24).
4 *Corr.3* #1313, note 2.
5 I've translated *Histoire* as 'History' here because, unlike Sand's *Histoire de ma vie*, it aims to be an objective account of public affairs.
6 *Revue des deux mondes*, 15 November 1836. This was a month before the December Berlioz concert, in other words not reporting a particular concert but evoking a cultural world through its most fashionable 'hit' of the season.
7 Bronisław Eduard Sydow (ed.), with Suzanne and Denise Chainaye, *Correspondance de Frédéric Chopin* (3 vols, Paris: Éditions Richard Masse, 1953–60), Vol. 2, p. 208.
8 *Corr.3* #1304, GS to Henri Heine [13 December 1836]. Heine has just moved his life partner 'Mathilde', a Paris shop assistant, in to live with him, so probably feels free to let such follies go over his head.
9 In March 1843 she will perform a Chopin Ballade 'in a really masterly fashion and with great talent' according to 'the Warsaw press'. Alan Walker, *Fryderyk Chopin: A Life and Times* (London: Faber, 2018), p. 285.
10 Then called the Academy.
11 Fryderyk Chopin Institute has the lithograph, inscribed 'pinxit et lith Marie'. The watercolour is at the National Museum of Warsaw www.mnw.art (retrieved 21/10/24).
12 Walker, p. 284. Tad Szulc, *Chopin in Paris: The Life and Times of the Romantic Composer* (New York: Da Capo Press, 2000), pp. 120–24.

13 In 1840 she will, after all, marry someone her own age from their mutual circle. Józef Skarbek was born 13 March 1819, she on 7 January 1819. Their marriage will be annulled after two years, but both will remarry.

14 The protagonist of *Simon* is the son of a village attorney; that of *Poème de Myrza*, the eponymous poet, is an early Christian prophetess. *Mattéa* is the story of a fourteen-year-old girl surrounded by male attention in medieval Venice, and in 'Le Dieu inconnu', a short story, Léa, a woman who has been abandoned, finds peace despite religious persecution when she converts to Christianity.

15 It's like the psychoanalytic idea of cathexis, in which whatever's imbued with deep emotional meaning has a kind of vibrating aliveness about it.

16 Nigel Harkness 'Pour une écriture journalistique féminine? Problèmes d'énonciation et de réception dans les Lettres à Marcie' in Marie-Ève Thérenty (ed.), *George Sand journaliste* (Saint-Étienne: Presses Universitaires de Saint-Étienne, 2011) https://doi.org/10.4000/books.puse.1068. Fourier, who will die this October, proposes the ideal community as a 'phalanx', a kind of semi-agricultural garden city.

17 *Corr.4* #1512, GS to Lamennais [end of May 1837]. His tenure at *Le Monde* will also be brief: by May George is congratulating him on escaping its 'brigands' cave'. But then, a degree of conservative ambivalence about the series he's commissioned is to be expected. For all his eventual influence as a proponent of the separation of Church and State, and in favour of enlarged suffrage, in 1837 Lamennais is still in the middle of his own journey away from the Catholic Church into which he was ordained.

18 Gustave de Gévaudan is the youth she denies seducing.

19 Of Michel de Bourges. *Corr.3* #1213, GS to Marie d'Agoult [12 July 1836].

20 Oliver Hilmes, *Franz Liszt: Musician, Celebrity, Superstar* (New Haven: Yale University Press, 2016), pp. 78, 85.

21 In May he plans to see an old friend in Germany, in June he is at thermal baths and in July he travels to London with piano virtuoso Camilel Pleyel.

22 At 7 rue Grange Batelière from the 18th to the 25th. *Corr. 4* #1719, GS to Théodore de Seynes [19 April 1838].

23 *Corr.4* #1728, GS to Fryderyk Chopin (FC) [end of April 1838].

24 *Corr.4* #1722, GS to Marie Dorval [?22 April 1838], note 1, p. 391. Dorval has sent tickets for a box for her latest performance to George and Charlotte Marliani.

25 *Corr.4* #1748, GS to 'Albert' Grzymała [late May 1838].

26 The date pencilled on it is 23 May 1838, but it seems much more likely that it belongs to May 1837, as years from now Maurice, in cataloguing, will

speculate. In which case it is about Michel de Bourges. *Corr.4* #1740, GS to Charlotte Marliani [23 May 1828?].

27 A variant on her maiden name. She styles herself *Mme* Dupin – almost as if replacing her mother. *Corr.4* #1755, GS to Albert Grzymała [4 June 1838], note 1 p. 445.

28 E. L. Voynich (trans.), *Chopin's Letters* (New York: A. A. Knopf, 1931), p. 446.

29 Voynich, p. 447, and Bronisław Eduard Sydow (ed.), with Suzanne and Denise Chainaye, *Lettres de Chopin et de George Sand* (Palma, Mallorca: Edicions la Cartoixa, no date given), #15, p. 37.

30 He stayed with George in February; this from a letter to Ewelina Hańske. Balzac, *Letters to Madame Hanska*, 2 March 1838, pp. 484–5. Balzac says he arrived on Shrove Saturday, which that year fell on 25 February.

31 *Corr.4* #1579, GS to Dr Marcel Gaubert [20 August 1837]: 'You helped my poor old mother in her final hour.' Dr Marcel Pierre Gaubert edited the four-volume *Cours de pathologie et de therapeutique generals* (Paris: Baillière, 1833–35) from notes of François J. V. Broussais's lectures at the University of Paris, but Broussais's earlier work was *Histoire des phlegmasies ou inflammations chronique* (Paris: Gabon, 1826) https://www.jnorman.com/pages/books/6006/francois-j-v-broussais/histoire-des-phlegmasies-ou-inflammations-chroniques (retrieved 6/11/24). The church was just four blocks away.

32 *Corr.4* #1578, GS to [Félicien Mallefille?] [c.21 August 1837].

33 S. Barles, 'Urban metabolism and river systems: An historical perspective – Paris and the Seine, 1790–1970', *Hydrology and Earth System Sciences*, Vol. 11 (2007), pp. 1757–69 https://hess.copernicus.org/articles/11/1757/2007/hess-11-1757-2007.pdf (retrieved 6/11/24).

34 *Corr.4* #1748, GS to Albert Grzymala [end of May 1838].

35 And these are from the *expurgated* edition of his letters (which omit the 'dirty dream' sentence)! Ethel Lillian Voynich, *Chopin's Letters* (New York: Alfred A. Knopf, 1931), pp. 48, 71, 93.

36 Franz Liszt, *Chopin* (Paris: Buchet-Chastel, 1977), p. 232.

37 Roger Pierrot (ed.), *Honoré de Balzac: Lettres à Mme Hanska* (Paris: Éditions du Delta, 1967), Vol. 1, pp. 584–9.

38 *Corr.4* #1808, GS to Charlotte Marliani [1 November 1838].

39 Full specifications of the vessel: Walker, note 4, p. 373.

40 *Corr.4* #1810, GS to Christine Buloz Monday, 12 [and Wednesday, 14 November 1838].

41 *Corr.4* #1815, GS to Hippolyte Chatiron, 3 December [1838].

42 Carles Manera, 'Cambio agrario y desarrollo industrial no fabril en la isla de Mallorca, 1830–1930', *Revista de Historia Económica / Journal of Iberian and Latin American Economic History*, Vol. 17(2) (1999), pp. 371–410 (retrieved 25/10/24). Gabriel Jover, Ivan Murray, Onofre Fullana and Ricard Soto, 'Feudal colonization to agrarian capitalism in Mallorca: Peasant endurance under the rise and fall of large estates (1229– 1900)', University of Barcelona https://diposit.ub.edu/dspace/bitstream/2445/123369/1/675802.pdf (retrieved 25/10/24).

43 'almost nothing' *Corr.4* #1811, GS to Loius-Édouard Gauttier d'Arc [13 and 14 November 1838], '50 f par mois' *Corr.4* #1812, GS to Charlotte Marliani 14 November [1838]. Both these letters also make clear she has also already reserved three cells at the Charterhouse.

44 *Corr.4* #1812.

45 Sydow et al., *Correspondance*, Vol. 2, pp. 265–6.

46 The huge sum is '5–600 ff', *Corr.4* #1819, GS to Charlotte Marliani [28 December 1838]. Her intervention #1814b, GS to Dr François Cauvière [letter lost: mid-November 1838].

47 It abbreviates either *sin on vent*, 'where the wind blows', or *casa on vent*, 'windy house'. *Corr.4* #1815.

48 *Corr.4* #1810, GS to Christine Buloz 12 and 14 [November 1838].

49 *Corr.4* #1815.

50 GS footnote to FC to Wojciech Grzymała 3 December 1838 #127, Sydow (ed.) https://archive.org/stream/selectedcorrespo002644mbp/selectedcorre-spo002644mbp_djvu.txt (retrieved 28/10/24).

51 *Corr.4* #1822, GS to Alexis Duteil [20 January 1839].

52 Endearments from *Corr.5* #2090, GS to Chopin, Maurice and Solange [13 August 1840]. Chopin's anti-Semitism and financial complaints, Sydow et al., *Correspondance*, Vol. 2, pp. 333, 339, 341.

53 *Corr.4* #1823, GS to Hippolyte Chatiron 22 [January 1839].

54 *Corr.4* #1817, GS to Charlotte Marliani 14 December 1838.

55 *Corr.4* #1819, GS to Charlotte Marliani [28 December 1838].

56 https://www.metoffice.gov.uk/weather/travel/holiday-weather/europe/spain/majorca (retrieved 29 October 2024).

57 Sydow et al., *Correspondance*, #22.

58 Sydow et al., *Correspondance*, note 46.

59 Arthur Hedley (trans. and ed.), *Selected Correspondence of Fryderyk Chopin* (London: William Heineman, 1962), FC to Julian Fontana 28 December 1838, #130 pp. 165–7.

60 FC to Julian Fontana 3 December 1838, Hedley, #128 p. 164.
61 *Corr.4* #1810, GS to Christine Buloz 12 and 14 [November 1838].
62 FC to Wojciech Grzymała 3 December 1838, Hedley, #127, pp. 163–4.
63 He graduated in 1829, dies in 1849.
64 Twenty years after he had published the first set, in 1722, Bach did it all again, which is why they are known as 'The Forty-Eight'.
65 As pointed out by https://books.openedition.org/puc/9822?lang=en (retrieved 19/3/24).
66 *HMV6*, pp. 148–9 https://www.gutenberg.org/files/42765/42765-h/42765-h.htm (retrieved 5/11/24).
67 The title of Goethe's 1809 novel *Die Wahlverwandtschaften*. *Un hiver à Majorque*, originally *Un hiver au midi de l'Europe*, appears in instalments in 1841 and in book form in 1842.
68 It is quarantine law (Edict of 6 October 1751). *Corr.4* #1828, GS to Charlotte Marliani [15 February 1839].
69 #1828.
70 *Corr.4* #1887, GS to Charlotte Marliani [*c*.20 June 1839].
71 *Corr.5* #2332, GS to Pauline Viardot [17 October 1841].
72 *Corr.5* #2210, GS to Michelle Héraeau [16? April 1841] and #2208, GS to Marie de Rozières [15 April 1841].
73 *Corr.4* #1906, GS to Charlotte Marliani [24 July 1839].
74 *Corr.7* #3641, GS to Grzymała [May 1847], pp. 699–702.
75 *Corr.6* #2742, GS to Ferdinand François [12 or 13 November 1843].
76 *HMV6*, p. 171.
77 *HMV6*, p. 156.
78 Pierrot, Vol. 1, p. 527, 15 March 1841.
79 *Corr.6* #2699, GS to Eugène Delacroix [13 August 1843].
80 29 April–17 May.
81 https://en.wikipedia.org/wiki/List_of_administrators_of_the_Com%C3%A9die-Fran%C3%A7aise (retrieved 2/11/24).
82 GS calls Pauline Viardot 'my dear Consuelo' for example in Corr 5 #2508, GS to Pauline Viardot 29 August 1842.
83 *HMV6*, p. 154. It won't have helped that she has made a generous marriage settlement for Augustine, who is herself now engaged to Théodore Rousseau. Augustine, Maurice's third cousin, is descended from one of George's maternal great-grandfathers. She has been brought up by her unwed mother and then with a stepfather, a violent tailor called Joseph Brault. Cate, pp. 537–8.

84 https://gallica.bnf.fr/ark:/12148/bpt6k9657431r/f35.item (retrieved 4/11/24). https://premierssocialismes.edel.univ-poitiers.fr/collection/larevuesociale (retrieved 4/11/24).

85 Michel Dion, *La France profonde: entretiens sur la politique en Lorraine et en Mayenne* (Paris: Messidor Editions Sociales, 1988).

86 https://gallica.bnf.fr/ark:/12148/bpt6k1189449/f10.item.r=George+Sand.langFR (retrieved 5/11/24).

87 In March and April in *Bulletin de la République* (some of which are anonymous), in May in *La Vrai République*. *La Cause du Peuple* lasts for three issues only.

88 It scarcely amounts to either art or portraiture. Brow furrowed above an impressively unfeminine prow of a nose, and hair arranged in a style reminiscent of an imperial wreath, the figure is not merely imperious but actually resembles a Roman emperor. Louvre collection (MAP, AP). Claude Malécot, *George Sand / Félix Nadar* (Paris: Monum, Éditions du patrimonie, 2004), p. 150.

89 Though not before having another little girl, whom they also call Jeanne, in May 1849 https://www.geni.com/people/Jeanne-Gabrielle-Cl%C3%A9singer/6000000010210011656 (retrieved 10/11/24).

90 *Corr.8* #3699, GS to Emmanuel Arago 18–26 July [18]47.

91 *HMV6*, p. 171.

92 *Corr.8* #3702, GS to FC [28 July 1847].

93 Paid for by a collection raised by Delacroix.

94 There's also an unsigned picture, attributed to Charpentier, in which she wears a long ornamental chain, in the collection of Mrs B. Ferra of Valldemossa at Cliché Ruelan in Palma.

95 It's held in the Henry Guttmann Collection of the Hulton picture archive – but is a century too early to have been taken by him.

96 Elizabeth Barrett Browning seems to have adopted barley curls when she changed lady's maid in the early 1840s.

97 George Lubin, *Corr.4*, note on illustrations, p. 986.

CHAPTER EIGHT: DEAR MASTER

1 Henry de Montherlant, *Don Juan, pièce en trois actes* (Paris: Gallimard, 1958), Act 2, Scene 4, l.1048.

2 Matthew Arnold, Obituary for George Sand, cited in George Saintsbury, *Matthew Arnold* (Edinburgh and London: William Blackwood, 1902), Ch. 4

https://www.mirrorservice.org/sites/ftp.ibiblio.org/pub/docs/books/gutenberg/1/6/2/8/16284/16284-h/16284-h.htm (retrieved 6/11/24), and The Poetry Foundation website *Matthew Arnold*: https://www.poetryfoundation.org/poets/matthew-arnold (retrieved 6/11/24).

3   Alexis de Tocqueville, *Souvenirs* (Paris: Calmann-Levy, 1839) pp. 210–11.
4   *Corr.8* #3900, GS to the editors of *La Réforme* and *La Vraie République* [8 April 1848], note 1, p. 391.
5   *Corr.4* #1865, GS to Charlotte Marliani 20 May [1839].
6   Steegmuller and Bray, the first 'Chère maître': #12, GF to GS 5 July [1866]; the first 'Ton vieux troubadour': #204, GF to GS [10 December 1869]; 'Bon comme du bon pain', #204, GF to GS Friday 10 p.m. [10 December 1869].
7   Pierre Milza, *Napoléon III* (Paris: Tempus, 2006), p. 592.
8   Hippolyte dies on 23 December 1848.
9   Hippolyte's daughter is Marie Léontine Chatrion, b. 7 August 1823, m. 27 February 1843 to Théophile Simonnet; her sons are Réné Hippolyte (b. 1844), Edme Pierre (b. 1848) and Albert, who will be born in 1851, a year before she is widowed https://gw.geneanet.org/asantini1?lang=en&n=simonnet&p=-marie (retrieved 10/11/24).
10 *HMV3*, pp. 23, 152.
11 *HMV3*, p. 153.
12 Though onset at twelve will be average for girls living in the global North by the second decade of the twenty-first century.
13 *Corr.5* #2101, GS to Gustave Papet 28 August [1840]. She also asks Gaubert, 'My daughter has undergone a small crisis which is highly natural, but a little too precocious, I believe, although she is well.' *Corr.5* #2100, GS to Dr Paul Gaubert [28 August 1840].
14 *Corr.5* #2223, GS to Ferdinand Bascans [2 and 3 May 1841].
15 *Lettres retrouvées*, p. 21, GS to Emmanuel Arago 18 July 1847.
16 *Corr.9*, note pp. 303–5.
17 Solange names her: 'Jeanne for her father and godfather, Gabrielle for [her mother] and [Solange's mother-in-law] and Béatrice' because it's a name liked by her godmother Mme Sophie Bascans, the tutor with whom Solange boarded. Solange Sand to Sophie Bascans 14 May 1849, quoted in Marie-Louise Pailleron, 'Une petite-fille de George Sand', *La Revue des deux mondes*, October 1950, p. 665 https://www.revuedesdeuxmondes.fr/article-revue/une-petite-fille-de-george-sand/ (retrieved 10/1124). Pailleron (1870–1951) is the granddaughter of François Buloz.

18 Milza, p. 592.
19 https://commons.wikimedia.org/wiki/File:Jeanne_Gabrielle_Cl%C3%A9singer_(1849-1855)_(A).jpg (retrieved 10/11/24).
20 https://www.lanouvellerepublique.fr/indre/le-chateau-de-montgivray-et-sa-legende ; https://montgivray.fr/la-commune/histoire/ (retrieved 12/11/24).
21 https://www.geni.com/people/Solange-Dudevant/6000000010210149724 (retrieved 12/11/24).
22 The edition's an important milestone. For Hetzel, it's a step towards the luxuriously illustrated editions of Jules Verne that will make his reputation; for Maurice, a chance for his work to be seen alongside that of a senior colleague whom Théophile Gautier has called 'without fear of contradiction, the king of illustration'. *La Presse*, 16 June 1845 https://gallica.bnf.fr/ark:/12148/bpt6k429972q/f2.item (retrieved 7/11/24).
23 'Lubins or Lupins' https://worldenoughblog.wordpress.com/2019/06/30/maurice-sand-the-werewolves/ (retrieved 7/11/24).
24 https://www.biodiversitylibrary.org/bibliography/125547 (retrieved 7/11/24) and https://gallica.bnf.fr/ark:/12148/bpt6k5758382f/f4.item (retrieved 7/11/24).
25 *Corr.15* #8618m GS to Alfred Arago 15 March 1860 https://www.geni.com/people/Alfred-Arago/6000000043232476851 (retrieved 7/11/24).
26 *Corr.16* #9059, GS to Pauline Viardot 11 May 1861; #9186, GS to Maurice Sand [1 September 1861].
27 Little realising that despite his cousin's friendship the emperor has already, in a letter dated 9 June 1851, refused funds for a statue honouring her explicitly because of her 'political attitude' https://www.maison-george-sand.fr/en/discover/allegory-of-literature-in-the-guise-of-george-sand (retrieved 19/1/25). 'N Bonap' recorded by Manceau in George Sand's Agenda on 22 December 1852. Anne Chevereau (ed.), *Agenda* (5 vols, Paris: J. Touzot, 1990–3), Vol. 1, p. 7. This is not their first meeting, which was on 15 February. Kelley and Hudson (eds), *The Brownings' Correspondence* #3005, Elizabeth Barrett Browning to John Kenyon 15–16 February 1852.
28 Mary proves her worth by refusing to sleep with her employer: a virtuous choice which relegates her to homeless penury and loss of social respectability. The future couple meet by the mere of the novel's title, its symbolic water that shifty element which can be both dangerous and beautiful, necessary and changeable; and Germain's child Pierre is a sort of chaperone-sponsor at both their meetings there.
29 Her husband is called Landry and she's secretly adored by his brother Sylvinet. Could there be a heavier hand with the nominal determinism: *sylva*, the Latin for woods, and *lands*, the French for moorland?

30 Cited in Scheyder, p. 23.
31 Ernst Haeckel, *Generelle Morphologie der Organismen* (Berlin: Georg Reimer, 1866), Vol. 2, p. 286: 'Unter *Oecologie* verstehen wir die gesammte Wissenschaft von den Beziehungen des Organismus zur umgebenden Aussenwelt, wohin wir im weiteren Sinne alle "Existenz-Bedingungen" rechnen können.' ('By *ecology* we understand the entire science of the relationship of the organism to the surrounding external world, which in a broader sense can include all "conditions of existence".')
32 'Maurice Sand' in Union Internationale de la Marionnette, *World Encyclopedia of Puppetry Arts* https://wepa.unima.org/en/maurice-sand/ (retrieved 19/10/24).
33 *HMV3*, p. 89.
34 Maurice and Lina name their first daughter for her grandmother – *and* for her dead cousin Nini.
35 Sand leaves most of her property, including Nohant and an estate of 143 acres at Chicoterie, entirely to Maurice. Solange receives only an estate at Porte of roughly the same size as Chicoterie. George knows what she's doing: since French law moderates inequity in inheritance, she even leaves a pay-off for Solange. After his widow Lina dies in 1901 their daughters divide the estate, with Gabrielle taking Nohant; but she dies in 1909 and Aurore inherits from her, moves back in and remains in situ as part of the donation agreement until her own death in 1961 at the age of ninety-five https://fr.wikipedia.org/wiki/Domaine_de_George_Sand (retrieved 11/11/24).
36 Edith Wharton, *A Backward Glance: An Autobiography* (London: Dent Everyman, 1993), p. 203. Henry James, letter to Mrs Alfred Sutro, 28 July 1914, in Percy Lubbock (ed.), *The Letters of Henry James*, Vol. 2, Project Gutenberg https://www.gutenberg.org/files/38035/38035-h/38035-h.htm (retrieved 5/4/24).
37 'He was hideous. I could see the tarnishing eyes in the darkness. Oh, the soul had died too.' 'Sur la mort de Chopin', an unpublished MS dated 1852, Bibliothèque Nationale Res.Vmc. ms.23. Marie Dorval dies on 20 May 1849.
38 *Corr.9* #4398, GS to Pierre-Jules Hetzel [10 January 1850].
39 *Corr.6* #3032, GS to Louis Blanc [late November 1844] *et seq.*
40 https://gallica.bnf.fr/html/und/presse-et-revues/histoire-de-ma-vie?mode=desktop (retrieved 17/11/24).
41 See, for example, the anonymous and opinionated French Wikipedia page, which references Simone Bernard-Griffiths et José-Luis Diaz, 'Lire *Histoire de ma vie de George Sand*', Presses Universitaires Blaise Pascal, Clermont-Ferrand, *Cahiers romantiques*, No. 11 (2006), p. 385; Monique Bosco, 'George Sand ou la nouvelle Aurore', *Études françaises*, Vol. 24, No.1

(printemps 1988), pp. 85–93; Corinne Saminadayar-Perrin, 'La littérature au corps. Histoire de ma vie de George Sand', Fabula / Les colloques, Écrivains en performances https://fr.wikipedia.org/wiki/Histoire_de_ma_vie_ (George_Sand) (retrieved 13/6/24).

42 *Corr.8* #3779, GS to Charlotte Marliana 22 December [18]47.
43 *Corr.9* #448, GS to Hetzel [end of April 1850].
44 The rest of the set show a rather plain woman whose great dark eyes are the only clue to her character. In repose, she is frankly jowly. A year later, when Nadar photographs her again, she is a dumpy little woman wearing mourning silk for Manceau. Though by 1874, turbaned and once more in folksy frills, her famous oval face reappears.
45 Diary entry for 11 June 1864, cited https://fr.wikipedia.org/wiki/Alexandre_ Manceau (retrieved 12/11/24).
46 Malécot, pp. 90–91.
47 Like George herself, this protagonist is the product of a liaison between an aristocrat and a performing artist and, as in her *Lucrezia Floriana*, chooses the authenticity and depth of art over a world of society manners.
48 Two years old at the time.
49 The latter is set between three chateaux of George's beloved Vallée Noire in the seventeenth century, the former in the eighteenth in a fictional Loire valley chateau.
50 George calls the butterfly Flavia de Malcolm: is this *Arctia flavia*, the Alpine Yellow tiger moth?
51 *Valvèdre* again explores what traditional gender roles do to a couple. *La famille de Germandre* is a family saga set in the Bourbonnais countryside (today Allier) which adjoins Berry.
52 In *Laura*, crystals have complete interior landscapes into which one can be transported, *La Confession d'une jeune fille* is about a lost child, and *Monsieur Sylvestre* a philosophical novel about a hermit. *La Coupe* is about a magic landscape within a glacier.
53 GS's weekly feuilleton 29 September 1857; opening night of Victor Séjour's *André Gérard* 30 April 1857, recorded in the *Agenda*.
54 Indeed it's here that she arranged to meet Nadar in 1865. In the 1850s she transferred her loyalty to Chez Pinson in the rue de l'Ancienne-Comédie. Malécot, p. 93.
55 Goncourts, Vol. 3, 12 February 1866 https://www.gutenberg.org/cache/ epub/17123/pg17123.txt (retrieved 18/11/24).
56 Steegmuller and Bray, #279, GS to GF 23 July [1871].

57 Steegmuller and Bray, #314, GF to GS 16 [April 1872].
58 Only in 1874, as George's health begins to show her age, will Turgenev instead buy the Viardots a house just west of Paris, in the village of Bougival.
59 A relationship with the friend's sister who became the mother of Guy de Maupassant remains unproven rumour. Jacques-Louis Douchin, *La Vie érotique de Flaubert* (Paris: Éditions Jean-Jacques Pauvert-Carrère, 1984).
60 Steegmuller and Bray, #318, GS to GF 18 May [1872].
61 Brochure, 'George Sand's Garden', Maison de George Sand, 2014.
62 The firm would be renamed Calmann-Lévy only after his death in May.
63 Steegmuller and Bray, #289, GS to GF 25 October [1871].
64 *Corr.24* Annex 4, eyewitness account of Henry Harisse, pp. 655–72, 659.
65 *Corr.24* Annex 4, p. 662.
66 Steegmuller and Bray, #289.
67 *HMV3*, p. 164.
68 Steegmuller and Bray, p. 400.
69 Bibliothèque nationale de France, 'Félix Nadar: George Sand 1864' https://classes.bnf.fr/les-nadar/sand.htm (retrieved 19/12/2024).
70 Elizabeth Hardwick, 'Writing a Novel', in Saskia Hamilton (ed.), *The Dolphin Letters 1970–1979: Elizabeth Hardwick, Robert Lowell and Their Circle* (New York: Farrar Straus Giroux, 2019 and London: Faber, 2020), p. 465.
71 Gustave Flaubert to Louise Colet 16 November 1852, cited in Steegmuller and Bray, p. 3. Charles Baudelaire, *Mon cour mis à nu* (Biblioteca virtual universal), p. 7 https://web.seducoahuila.gob.mx/biblioweb/upload/MON%20COEUR%20MIS%20A%20UN.pdf (retrieved 3/11/24). Friedrich Nietzsche, *Götzen-Dämmerung*, title of 'Wanderings of an Untimely Man 1' https://www.gutenberg.org/cache/epub/7203/pg7203-images.html (retrieved 3/11/24). Cate, p. xvii.

Index

Numbers in **bold** refer to pages with illustrations

Á Kempis, Thomas, 100–1
Apollonie (schoolfriend of GS), 90, 93, 96
Arago, Alfred, 291
Arago, Emmanuel, 270, 286, 291, 305
Aragon, Étienne, 264
Arnold, Matthew, 278–9, 325
L'Artiste, 174
Augustus II, king of Poland and Elector of Saxony (great-great-grandfather of GS), 46, 47, 50

Bach, J. S., 41, 255–6
Balzac, Honoré de: career, 278; death, 299; descriptions of George, 178, 240, 244–5, 261, 297; friendship with George, 193, 213, 244–5, 275, 331; marriage, 299; on de Latouche's work, 164; on Tortoni's café, 107; portrait, 275; publisher, 191; receiving George's work, 174; view of George's work, 179, 325; works, 3, 161, 178, 193–4, 278
Barra, M. (step-grandfather of GS), 17–18
Barrett Browning, Elizabeth: childhood, 119; hair style, 274; health, 258; meeting George, 119–20; quoted, 77, 119–20; reputation, 3; visiting Nohant, 292; works, 194
Bascans, Sophie Lagut, 259
Baudelaire, Charles, 326
Bazouin, Aimée, 127–8
Bazouin, Jane, 87, 127–8
Berlioz, Hector, 174, 231
Berry, Charles Ferdinand, Duc de, 82–3, 107
Bisson brothers, Louis-Auguste and Auguste, 240, 275, 302–3
Bizard, Jean-Baptiste, 112
Blanc, Jean Joseph Louis, 299
Bonjour, Jean-Baptiste, 111–12, 221
Boucoiran, Jules, 143–4, 153–5, 159–60, 199, 217
Brault, Augustine, 265
Brenner, Sophia Elisabet, 47
Brontë, Charlotte, 172–3, 273
Brontë, Emily, 3, 172–3, 273
Browning, Pen, 290
Browning, Robert, 292
Bulletin de la République, 268
Buloz, Christine, 246
Buloz, François: career, 263, 278; commissions portrait of George, 215; contract for *Jacques*, 207; correspondence with George, 218;

Buloz, François: – *cont'd*
  editor of *La Revue des deux mondes*, 191; end of George's contract, 263; financial arrangements with George, 216–17, 251; George's contract, 191, 193, 263; negotiations for George's early novel, 191, 192; publication of *Lettres d'un voyageur*, 219; publication of George's novels, 251; reconciliation with George, 306; refusal to publish *Horace*, 263, 264
Byron, Lord, 194, 205, 229–30

Calamatta, Joséphine, 75–6
Calamatta, Luigi, 75–6, 261, 297
Calmann-Lévy publishers, 289, 296, 318
Caroline (Angélique-Caroline, illegitimate daughter of Sophie-Victoire, half-sister of GS): birth, 18; childhood, 26, 31, 58–9, 61; grandson, 318; name, 18; relationship with mother, 26, 32, 58–9, 61, 83; relationship with sister Aurore, 58–9, 61, 83, 137, 223
Carrel, Armand, 155, 156
La Cause du peuple (weekly), 268
Cauvière, Dr François, 258
Cazamajou, Oscar (son of Caroline), 318
Le Charivari (satirical magazine), 211
Charles X, King, 142
Charpentier, Auguste, 75, 273–6
Chateaubriand, François-René de, 101–2, 205
Chatiron, Catherine, 22, 285
Chatiron, Émilie (de Villeneuve), 121–2, 141–2, 284, 289
Chatiron, Hippolyte (illegitimate son of Maurice Dupin, half-brother of GS): affair with Pepita, 141–2; birth, 22; childhood, 22–3, 49–51, 54–6, 85, 154, 285; daughter, 117, 141, 284; death, 283–4, 289; drinking, 223, 283–4, 284–5; education, 22, 55, 85, 198; family life, 223; finances, 106, 284; friends at La Châtre, 133; grandsons, 284, 318; homes, 22, 145, 152, 284, 289; illegitimacy, 22, 55, 285; marriage, 121–2, 141–2, 284, 289; military career, 85, 89, 98; relationship with father, 285; relationship with grandmother, 49, 58, 107; relationship with half-sister Aurore, 49–50, 56, 89–91, 98, 122, 124–5, 137, 139–40, 152, 153–5, 166, 252, 284–5; relationship with Solange, 284
Chatiron, Marie-Léontine, 117, 141, 284
Chopin, Fryderyk: appearance, 204, 244; career, 233–4, 255, 261, 268–9, 278; chamber concerts, 232, 269; death, 261, 275, 298; engagement to Maria Wodzińska, 232–3, 237, 240, 241; finances, 251–2; financial support from George, 251, 261, 268, 270; first meetings with George, 230–2, 243; health, 233, 241, 250, 254, 257–8, 260, 269, 302, 305; homes, 231, 239, 243, 249, 261–2; last meeting with George, 270–1; life at Nohant, 41, 76, 260–1, 262, 299; Mallorca stay, 246–57; Mediterranean trip, 245–6; pianos, 249, 250, 252; portraits, 225, 227, 239–40, 275, 276; relationship with George, 3, 36, 182, 237–45, 251–4, 260–1, 268–9, 270–1, 275–6, 298,

Chopin, Fryderyk: – cont'd
326; relationship with Solange, 259, 270, 271; sexuality, 242–3, 280; tomb, 271; works, 234, 251, 255–6, 262
Clésinger, Auguste (Jean-Baptiste, son-in-law of GS), 269–70, 271, 287, 288, 320
Clésinger, Jeanne-Gabrielle (granddaughter of GS), 270, 298
Clésinger, Nini (Jeanne-Gabrielle, granddaughter of GS), 287–8, 297, 298
Colet, Louise, 179, 313, 326
Cooper, Fenimore, 191
Courrier de Paris, 309

d'Agoult, Marie, Comtesse, 230–1, 235–6, 278
d'Angers, David, 204
Dames Augustines Anglaises convent: Aurore's confessor, 80, 102, 126; Aurore's grandmother at, 48, 67–9; Aurore's mother at, 69; Aurore's play-writing, 81, 83–4; Aurore's retreat at, 126–7, 154; Aurore's visits, 136, 160; education of Aurore, 67, 70–3, 79–82; foundation, 67–8; school regime, 79–80; site, 67–8; theatrical productions, 81, 83–4, 324–5
Daumier, Honoré, 211
Dauphine of France, Marie-Josèphe, 36, 47–8, 49
de Beaumont, Abbé (uncle of GS), 57–8
de Bourges, Michel: career, 218, 219–20, 222, 277; relationship with George, 218, 219–20, 222, 235
de Grandsagne, Jules, 137, 138, 139
de Grandsagne, Stéphane, 104, 135, 137, 138, 139

de Latouche, Henri: Aurore's appointment with, 157–8; commissioning ghostwritten novel, 166; employment of Aurore as columnist, 158–9, 159–60; *Figaro* editorship, 157–8, 159–60, 164, 196; Paris home, 183, 190; relationship with Aurore, 162, 163–4, 174, 183–4, 190, 242; retirement, 164, 183; sexuality, 163–4, 242; works, 164
de Musset, Alfred: account of duel, 198; appearance, 203–4; career, 204, 277–8; death, 179, 299; drinking, 179, 204, 222, 299; family background, 204, 206; health, 179, 208, 214, 317; Italian trip, 207–8; poetry, 204; portraits of George, **176**, 177–8, 206, 273; portrayal in *Elle et lui*, 178–9, 304; portrayal in *Lettres d'un voyageur*, 210; relationship with George, 177, 178–9, 198, 203–9, 214–17, 226, 246, 281; reputation, 203; Venice stay, 208–9, 214, 215, 246, 317; violence, 216–17, 222; works, 198, 204, 206
de Musset, Paul, 179
de Saxe, Maréchal Maurice de (great-grandfather of GS), 46, 47, 198
de Saxe, Marie-Aurore (grandmother of GS), *see* Dupin de Francueil
de Sèze, Aurélien: appearance, 129; career, 128–9; engagement, 128–9; family background, 129; relationship with Aurore, 129–32, 135, 136–7, 141–2, 143, 214, 244
de Vigny, Alfred, 191, 193, 201
de Wismes, Marie-Émilie, correspondence, 87–92, 98, 121, 122, 124, 125, 132
Decerfz, Laure, 174, 175, 187, 199, 200

Delaborde, Antoine (grandfather of GS), 17, 18
Delaborde, Marie-Lucie (aunt Lucie, later Mme Goüdain Saint-Agnan), 14–15, 16, 18, 26, 69, 155
Delaborde, Sophie-Victoire (mother of GS), *see* Dupin de Franceuil
Delacroix, Eugène: career, 278; double portrait of Chopin and George, 225, 227, 239–40, 276; friendship with George, 76, 215, 261, 262–3, 325; Maurice's publications, 290; Maurice's studies, 76, 259, 289, 291, 302; portrait of George, 215, **224**, 225–7, 239, 274; sexuality, 242; social life, 232; works, 215, 278
Delatouche, Charles, 299, 300
Delavau, François-Charles, 133
Deschartres, Jean-François: appearance and character, 23–4; death and burial of Aurore's grandmother, 105; death and burial of Maurice, 51–2, 105–6; dismissal by Casimir, 113–14; role at Nohant, 23–4, 55, 84–5, 113–14, 135; seeing ghost, 54
Dickens, Charles 194, 267
Didier, Charles, 219
Dion, Michel, 267
Dorval, Marie: appearance, 201; career, 200–1, 263; death, 298; gossip, 200, 202; grandchildren, 299; marriage, 202; message to Chopin, 237; relationship with George, 177, 200–3, 205, 263, 298; sexuality, 201–2
Duban, Félix, 184
Dudevant, Aurore (Dupin de Franceuil), *see* Sand, George
Dudevant, Aurore (Jeanne Claudine Aurore, granddaughter of GS), **38**, 40, 46, 297–8, 312, 319
Dudevant, Casimir (husband of GS): abduction of daughter Solange, 237; affair with Pepita, 141; appearance and character, 106, 148, 244; 'Articles' of married life, 132–3, 136–7; attempt to abduct son Maurice, 237; birth of daughter Solange, 138–9, 287; birth of son Maurice, 116; divorce, 219–22; drinking, 212, 214, 219, 220, 221–2, 284; family background, 108, 114; father's death, 115, 133; father's house at Guillery, 129–30, 131; finances, 115, 127, 130, 133, 142, 152–3, 165–6, 191, 238, 252, 284; health, 212; holiday in Cauterets, 127–8, 129; home in Ormesson, 126; home in Paris, 126; illegitimacy, 108, 114–15; life at Nohant, 114, 127, 133, 185, 211, 222; management of Nohant, 113–14, 131; marriage, 108–9, 130–3, 220–1; marriage contract, 115; meeting Aurore, 107–8; relationship with Aurore, 107, 117–18, 124–5, 127, 130–3, 215; stepmother, 130; 'treaty' with Aurore, 215; violence, 127, 219, 220, 221–2, 269, 284; will, 144
Dudevant, Gabrielle (Jeanne Lucile Gabrielle, granddaughter of GS), **38**, 40, 297–8, 312
Dudevant, Jean-François, Baron, 107, 108, 115, 133
Dudevant, Lina (Marcellina Calamatta, daughter-in-law of GS): appearance, 297; children, 297, 304; family background, 76,

Dudevant, Lina: – *cont'd*
  296–7; George's death, 317–18; marriage, 76–7, 296–7, 304–5, 307; photographed at Nohant, **38**, 40
Dudevant, Marc-François (grandson of GS), 297, 304, 305
Dudevant, Maurice (son of GS): appearance, **74**, 75–6, 213; art studies, 259; birth, 40, 116, 137; career, 76, 283, 289–92, 296; childhood, 116, 120, 121, 126, 136, 144–5, 153–4, 165; children, 76, 297, 304; death, 290, 296; depression, 212–13; drawings, 249; education, 76, 143, 144, 183, 198–9, 212, 214, 237, 252, 259; friendship with Prince Napoléon-Jérôme, 291; health, 212, 238; homes, 126, 136, 144–5, 183, 213, 214, 262, 267, 296, 304; illustrations, 289–90; love life, 265; Mallorca stay, 247, 249; marriage, 76–7, 296–7, 304–5, 307; mayor of Nohant, 268; Mediterranean trip, 245; mother's death, 318; name, 171, 289; Nohant studio, 290; photographed at Nohant, **38**, 40; portrait, **74**, 75–6; published works, 290–1, 296; puppetry, 296, 298, 308; relationship with father, 136, 222, 237; relationship with mother, 153, 154, 162, 165, 212–13, 216, 281, 289–91, 304–5, 306, 318
Dudevant, Solange (*later* Clésinger, Clésinger-Sand, daughter of GS): abduction by father, 237, 287; birth, 40, 141; childhood, 153, 162–3, 165–6, 168–70, 192, 206–7, 221, 285–6, 288; children, 8, 270, 271, 287–8, 297, 298; conception, 138–9, 140, 285; death, 289; dress, 247; education, 199, 214, 252, 259, 286; engagement, 269; homes, 262, 289; Mallorca stay, 247; Mediterranean trip, 245; marriage, 269–70, 287; mother's death, 317–18; name, 138, 287, 289; Paris in time of cholera, 168–9, 288–9; Paris Uprising, 187; paternity question, 138–9, 140, 153; published works, 289; relationship with Chopin, 259, 270, 271, 298; relationship with mother, 153, 162–3, 169–70, 206–7, 265, 269–70, 285–9, 292, 316; relationship with uncle Hippolyte, 284; published works, 289
Dumas, Alexandre, 191, 200, 318
Dupin de Franceuil, Auguste (brother of GS), 30–1, 43–4, 50–1, 54, 121, 137
Dupin de Francueil, Aurore (Amantine-Lucile-Aurore), *see* Sand, George
Dupin de Francueil, Hippolyte (half-brother of GS), *see* Chatiron
Dupin de Francueil, Louis-Claude (grandfather of GS), 48, 102–3
Dupin de Francueil, Marie-Aurore (de Saxe, grandmother of GS): appearance, 44, 57; birth, 47; birth of son Maurice, 48; childhood, 36, 47–8; death, 75, 105; education, 48, 67; education of granddaughter, 58, 60–1, 67, 80–2, 83, 84; family background, 7, 46–8, 49, 58, 83; grave, 105; guardianship of granddaughter, 58–61, 81–3; health, 81–2, 92–3; heir, 55; imprisonment in convent, 67, 68–9; last illness, 75, 92–3, 95–7, 99, 100, 105, 316; life at Nohant,

Dupin de Francueil, Marie-Aurore (de Saxe, grandmother of GS): – *cont'd* 7, 36–7, 40, 85, 295; marriages, 48; motherhood, 120; name, 7, 48; Nohant estate management, 23, 36–7, 295; Nohant estate purchase, 36, 69; Paris apartment, 59, 82, 83, 113, 152; relationship with granddaughter Aurore, 44–5, 46, 49, 55, 56–8, 60–1, 66–7, 69–70, 75, 85–6, 92–3, 316; relationship with grandson Hippolyte, 22, 49, 58; relationship with son, 120; response to son's relationship with Victoire, 21–2, 66; son and family return from Spain, 43–4; will, 106

Dupin de Francueil, Maurice (father of GS): appearance, 19–20, 21; birth of daughter Aurore, 7, 25, 32, 46; birth of son Auguste, 30; birth of son Hippolyte, 22; career, 14, 17, 19, 20, 25–6, 48, 283; childhood, 55, 63, 66, 67; coffin, 105–6; death, 51–5, 56, 64, 106; death and burial of son Auguste, 31, 50–1, 54, 106; education, 23; family background, 17, 46–8; finances, 20; health, 63, 64; horse, 53; Madrid campaign, 26, 28–30; marriage, 15, 16–17, 25–6, 284; name, 48; relationship with daughter Aurore, 25, 50, 80; relationship with son Hippolyte, 285; relationship with Victoire (Sophie-Victoire), 16, 17, 18–22, 25–6; return from Madrid, 31, 44, 49

Dupin de Francueil, Sophie-Victoire (Victoire Delaborde, mother of GS): appearance, 62; birth of daughter Aurore, 14–15, 25, 35; birth of illegitimate daughter Caroline, 18; birth of son Auguste, 30; childhood, 18; children, 31, 34; chorus girl, 18, 56, 69, 155; daughter Aurore's marriage contract, 115; daughter Aurore's wedding, 109; death, 240–1, 284; death of husband Maurice, 51–4; death of son Auguste, 31, 50–1; *demi-mondaine*, 17–21, 48, 85; description of, 33; 'fallen woman', 66; family background, 7, 17–18; finances, 58, 61, 62; health, 62, 240, 284; imprisonment in convent, 69; marriage, 7, 16, 25, 46, 284; meeting Maurice, 19–20; motherhood, 32–3, 52, 56, 61–2, 83, 213, 288; name, 17; relationship with daughter Aurore, 52, 56, 57–8, 61–3, 83, 85, 96–8, 106, 109, 118, 124, 135, 153, 240, 284; relationship with daughter Caroline, 26, 32, 58–9, 61, 83; relationship with husband Maurice, 20–5, 52–3; response to mother-in-law's will, 106; Spanish wartime journey, 26–33, 44–5; visits to Nohant, 44, 61–2, 83, 98, 154, 213

Dupuy, Ernest, 187–9, 193, 196, 197

Duruy, Victor, 282–3

Duteil, Alexis, 252

Duvernet, Charles, 143, 145, 157, 158, 159, 299

L'Eclaireur: Journal des départements d'Indre, du Cher et de la Creuse, 267

Eliot, George, 5–6

L'Europe littéraire, 196, 197

Fanchette (foundling), 264, 293

Favre, Henri, 317

Feuillide, Jean-Gabriel Cappot de, 196–7, 198, 279

Le Figaro, 5, 157–61, 164, 174, 181, 183, 196, 264, 292
Flaubert, Gustave: appearance, 312; correspondence with George, 66, 104, 281, 309, 311, 313, 316, 319–20; death, 317; friendship with George, 42, 66, 281, 309–14, 316–17; George's funeral, 318–19; home life, 42, 311–12, 314, 317; view of George's work, 4; works, 4, 42, 220, 309
Fontana, Julian, 243, 249, 251, 253–4
Fontanier, Mme, 26–7
Fourier, Charles, 178, 235,
Franco-Prussian War, 283, 314

Gautier, Théophile, 166, 167
Gavarni, Paul, 147–8, 163, 310
Gerson, Jean, 101, 102
Godoy, Manuel de, 28–9
Goethe, Johann Wolfgang von, 41, 173, 194, 220, 257, 279
Goncourt, Edmond and Jules de, 178, 310
Gosselin, Charles, 191, 192, 194
Goya, Francisco, 27, 29–30
Grzymała, Wojciech: Chopin's letters, 239, 243, 255; George's letters, 238, 241–2, 243, 250–1, 260; relationship with Chopin, 238, 239, 243–4
Guéroult, Adolphe, 149

Haeckel, Ernst, 296
Hańska, Ewelina, 178, 244, 299
Haussmann, Georges-Eugène, 16, 59, 282, 308
Heine, Heinrich, 168, 191, 232
Héreau, Michelle, 259
Hetzel, Pierre-Jules, 179, 265–6, 282, 289, 299

Hiller, Ferdinand, 232, 243
Hippolyte (illegitimate son of Maurice Dupin de Franceuil, half-brother of GS), *see* Chatiron
Hugo, Victor: exile, 282; George's funeral, 318; Planche's view of his work, 193; social life, 238; view of George's work, 174, 318; works, 3–4, 161, 187, 194

Ingres, Jean-Auguste-Dominique, 76
Isabey, Jean-Baptiste, 112

James, Henry, 107, 195, 298
James, William, 195
Janin, Jules, 174
Journal des débats, 174
Journal de Loiret, 268

Kératry, Comte de, 156–7
Königsmarck, Maria Aurora von (great-grandmother of GS), 4, 46, 47

La Rochefoucauld, Sosthènes, 196–7, 212, 223
Lamennais, Félicité Robert, 235
Lauth, Frédéric, 298
Lavalley, Gaston, 179
Leibniz, Gottfried Wilhelm, 103
Leroux, Pierre, 230, 264
Leroy, Zoé, 128, 129, 131–2, 135–6, 141
Leroyer de Chantepie, Marie-Sophie, 321
Liszt, Franz: concerts, 231, 232; description of George, 244; friendship with George, 218, 236, 313; at Nohant, 41, 235–6; relationship with Marie d'Agoult, 231, 235–6, 246, 278; trip to Geneva and Chamonix, 246; view of George's work, 325; works, 256

Littré, Émile, 155
Lorentz, Alcide-Joseph, 148–9, 166–7
Louis XVIII, King, 82, 129, 197
Louis-Philippe, King, 267
Lubin, Georges, 86, 276, 329
Lumière, Antoine, 324

Macpherson, James, 192
Mallefille, Félicién, 229, 237, 241
Mallorca, winter stay in, 246–57
Mame-Delaunay (publisher), 191
Manceau, Alexandre Damien: appearance, 303; career, 290, 302; cottage at Gargilesse, 303–4, 305; death, 302, 305, 307, 311; diary, 309; health, 302–3, 304–5, 307, 325; at Nohant, 304; relationship with George, 218, 290, 302–6, 303, 307; property at Palaiseau, 305, 307
Marie Antoinette, Queen, 10, 17, 294
Marie-Josèphe, Dauphine, 36, 47–8, 49
Marliani, Charlotte: Chopin recital, 237; friendship with George, 237–8, 258, 286; George's letters, 238, 246, 252, 257–8, 300–1; home, 237, 261, 270, 280
Matuszyński, Jan, 243
Mérimée, Prosper, 199–200, 202, 205
Merle, Jean-Toussaint, 202
Meyerbeer, Giacomo, 174, 231, 232
Michel Lévy Frères, 289, 315
Le Monde, 234–5
Montgivray, chateau, 284, 289
La Moue (periodical), 162
Murat, Général Joachim, 20, 29

Nadar, Félix, 303, 305, 310, 323–5, 327
Napoléon I, Emperor, 11, 16, 46
Napoléon III (Louis-Napoléon Bonaparte), 193, 233, 268, 281–3, 292, 324

Napoléon-Jérôme Bonaparte, Prince, 291, 318
Le National, 155, 197–8
Néraud, Jules, 133, 138
Nerval, Gérard de, 166–7, 173
Nietzsche, Friedrich, 326
Nodier, Charles, 204
Nohant: arrival from Spanish battlefields, 44–6, 49; attic studio for Maurice, 290; Aurore's divorce settlement, 151, 221, 222–3; Aurore's inheritance, 55, 106; Aurore's management, 97, 112; Aurore/George's life between Nohant and Paris, 144, 145, 151, 152, 154, 161, 162, 165, 168, 183, 188, 190, 210, 211, 215, 217; burial of baby Auguste, 51, 54; Casimir's life at, 114, 127, 133, 185, 211; centre of excellence, 41–2; chatelaine Marie-Aurore, 57; Chopin at, 41, 76, 260–1, 262, 299; descriptions, 9, 37, 294–5; distance from Paris, 137, 211, 278; estate management, 23–4, 113–14, 131; garden, **38**, 40, 294–5, 314–15; George as Bonne Dame Nohant, 40, 295, 298; George's funeral, 318–19; George's position as chatelaine, 247–8, 292; graveyard, 50, 54, 105–6, 288, 319; guests, 235, 237, 292, 312; history, 11, 36; income from estate, 152; inherited by granddaughters of GS, 297–8; literary and musical life, 223, 235–6; Maison de George Sand, 9, 331; manor house, 9, 13, 23, **38**, 294; marionette theatre, 41, 296, 298, 308; photograph, **38**, 39–40; portrayal of, 306; purchase, 36, 69; role as salon and retreat, 278;

Nohant: – *cont'd*
  social life, 125, 133, 235; stables, 22, 294, 320; summers at, 258, 262; surroundings, 9; theatres, 41, 308; today, 8–9; wartime military billet, 92
The North American Review, 230

Paganini, Niccolò, 160, 181
Pagello, Pietro, 208–9, 213–16, 226, 246
Paluzzi, Roméo, 298
Papet, Gustave, 190, 258, 317
Paris: boulevard des Capucines, 323–4; cholera epidemic (1832), 168–9, 288–9; Comédie-Française, 263, 278, 320; Commune, 314; Hôtel de Florence, 116, 137–8; literary life, 6, 41, 145, 156, 168, 211; Odéon theatre, 324; quai Malaquais, 183–5; quai Saint-Michel, 164–5, 167, 174–5, 183, 187; Restaurant Magny, 310–11, 316; rue de Chaillot, 259; rue de Condé, 267; rue de Faubourg-Saint-Honoré, 126; rue des Feuillantines, 305; rue Gay-Lussac, 306; rue des Grands-Augustins, 155; rue de la Grange Batelière, 25, 60; rue Laffitte, 230–1, 238, 243; rue Meslée, 15–16, 25; rue Neuve des Mathurins, 59, 82, 83, 113, 115–16, 138; rue Pigalle, 261, 297; rue de Seine, 145, 152; rue Tronchet, 261; Salon des Refusés, 282; Second Republic, 264, 267; square d'Orléans, 261–2; Théâtre de la Gaité, 308; Théâtre du Gymnase, 308; Théâtre de la Porte-Saint-Martin, 308; Three Glorious Days (July 1830), 142–3, 186; Tortoni's café, 107; Uprising (5 and 6 June 1832), 186–7

Paultre, Émile, 190
Pelletan, Eugène, 264
Pepita (nursemaid), 141–2, 153
La Phalange (periodical), 235
Pichot, Amédée, 189, 193
Planche, Gustave, 191, 192–3, 198, 201
Poerio, Alessandro, 203
Pouradier-Duteil, Alexis, 133
Prémord, Abbé, 80, 102, 126
La Presse, 299, 309
Proust, Marcel, 8, 13, 107, 293–4, 301
Pushkin, Alexander, 173
Pyat, Félix, 157, 174

La Réforme, 299
Regnault, Émile: career, 163, 189; friendship with Aurore, 169, 170, 190; friendship with Jules, 163, 169, 189; letters from Aurore, 163, 164, 165, 184, 190
Renan, Ernest, 318
Renault, B. (publisher), 166, 167
Renduel, Ernest, 191
Revue des deux mondes, 191, 193, 197, 198, 210, 211, 216, 225, 263, 306
Revue de Paris, 145, 158–9, 188–9, 193, 199, 309
La Revue indépendante, 264, 265
La Revue sociale, 264, 265
Rinteau, Marie-Genevieve (great-grandmother of GS), 47–8
Roëttiers du Plessis, Angèle (Ange-Justine) and Jacques, 107–8, 109, 114–115, 126, 127
Rogier, Camille, 166–7
Roret, Jean-Pierre (publisher), 170
Roubaud, Benjamin, 193
Rousseau, Jean-Jacques, 41, 102–3, 120, 172, 213, 300–1
Rousseau, Théodore, 166, 167

Saint-Simon, Henri de (and Saint-Simonists), 149, 186
Sainte-Beuve, Charles-Augustin: career, 174, 191; description of George, 325; friendship with George, 197, 216, 310; George's letters, 197–8, 199–200, 205
Salmon, Achille, 152
Sand, George (Aurore Dupin de Franceuil, Aurore Dudevant): family background, 7, 17–18, 46–9, 58, 66–7, 83, 198; birth, 2, 7, 14–15, 33–5, 321; childhood, 7–8, 12–13, 43–4, 49–50, 53–6, 60–3; Spanish wartime journey, 26–33, 44, 246, 289; brother's death, 31–2, 50–1, 121, 137; father's death, 51–5, 56, 64, 106, 137, 154, 284; guardianship, 58–61, 106; education, 58, 67, 70–3, 79–84, 118–19, 123, 192, 259; arranged marriage prospects, 82, 84, 92, 93–4, 98; nursing dying grandmother, 75, 92–3, 95–6, 100, 105, 115, 305, 316; grandmother's death, 105–6; marriage to Casimir Dudevant, 6, 106–9, 122–5, 127; birth of son Maurice, 116; birth of daughter Solange, 138–9; education of children, 76, 143, 144, 154, 183, 198–9, 212, 214, 237, 252, 258–9; life between Nohant and Paris, 144, 145, 151, 152, 154, 161, 162, 165, 168, 183, 188, 190, 210, 211, 215, 217; 'Romantic Rebellion', 36, 151, 182; literary career, 3–5, 41–2, 145, 151, 158–61; columnist on *Le Figaro*, 158, 159–60; first novel published, 170–4; responses to her work, 174, 177, 186, 196–8, 200, 235, 307; Italian tour, 207–8, 212–13; Venice visit, 208–10, 211, 212, 214–15, 246; divorce from Casimir Dudevant, 151, 219–22, 295; mother's death, 240–1; Mediterranean trip, 245–6, 257–8; in Mallorca, 246–57; return to Nohant, 258–9; death, 317–18; funeral, 318–19; obituary, 278–9; memorial statue, 320

APPEARANCE: boyishness (garçonhood), 5, 55, **98**, **110**, 245, 280; bust, 269; clothes, 5, 75, 98, 112, 134, 147, 148–9, 160–1, 226, 230, 303, 321, 327; complexion and colouring, 178, 240, 274, 310; eyes, 240, 273, 303, 327; hair, 60–1, 75, 110, 112, 148, 177, 215, 225, 226, 240, 273–4, 303; height, 5; waist, 147, 177, 274, 327; photographs, **38**, 39–40, 147, 273, 274–5, 297, 303, **322**, 323–5, 327; portraits, 40, **110**, 111–12, **146**, **176**, 177, 179, 221, **224**, 225–7, 239–40, **272**, 273–4, 276, 297; sex, 148–9, 243; statue, 320

FINANCES: allowance from Casimir, 115, 144, 152–3, 165–6, 191; difficulties and debts, 188–9, 216–17; divorce settlement, 151, 221; earnings from journalism, 158, 189, 191; grandmother's will, 106, 115, 152; legal action against Casimir, 238; marriage contract, 115, 152–3; married life, 127; negotiation of advances, 192, 193, 207, 216–17; payments for Sandeau's military exemption, 188, 189, 190, 203; publication of her work, 170, 188–9, 191, 207, 216–17, 251–2; rents, 152; sale of property, 252; supporting Chopin,

FINANCES: – *cont'd*
251–2, 261, 268, 270; writing partnership with Sandeau, 158–9, 166, 170
HEALTH: absence seizures, 63–4; bowel cancer, 317; bowel problems, 147; death, 317–18; digestion problems, 147; fever, 159; flu, 325; gall-bladder disease, 147, 307, 317; gastroenteritis and dysentery, 208; migraines, 62; persistent cough and a racing heart, 127; scabies, 27, 31, 44, 50; state of, 212; teeth pulled, 325; typhoid fever, 147, 307, 317
HOMES: chatelaine of Nohant (Bonne Dame Nohant), 40, 247–8, 294–5, 298; childhood in Nohant, 8–9, 12–13, 44–5, 49–50, 60, 62, 66, 85, 117; childhood in Paris, 25, 46, 59–60; holiday in Cauterets, 127–9; life in Nohant, 13, 41–2, 76, 84–5, 87, 94, 97–9, 114–15, 121, 125, 127, 133, 152, 162–3, 190, 247–8, 292, 294–5, 314–15; life in Paris, 106, 113, 126, 145, 151–2, 155, 164–5, 167, 174–5, 183–5, 230–1, 238, 243, 261–2, 305, 306; life with Alexandre Manceau at Gargilesse, 303–4, 305; life with Alexandre Manceau at Palaiseau, 304–6, 307, 308; Ormesson rental, 126
INTERESTS AND VIEWS: ecology and environment, 41, 65, 262, 296; handwriting, 306; idealism, 65–6, 73, 84, 100, 104, 124, 132, 195–6, 234, 277, 278–9, 320–1; political activity, 149, 156, 257, 263, 264, 267–8, 277, 281–2, 292, 295, 315, 325; principles, 319–221; reading, 100–4; religious position, 71, 80–2, 99–102; riding, 5, 89–90, 93, 95, 100, 102, 112, 119, 133, 134; smoking, 3, 205, 261
NAMES: Aurore, 2, 7, 13, 46, 170, 185, 205, 239, 321; byline Blaise Bonnin, 265, 268; G. Sand, 170, 174–5, 187, 188, 326; George Sand, 147, 170, 185, 192, 205, 321; Georges Sand, 147, 170, 174–5, 185, 186, 187, 191, 192–3, 205; J. Sand, 6, 170; Jules Sandeau nom de plume (with Sandeau), 162, 184; Mme Dudevant, 174, 175, 188; 'Mme Dupin', 238–9; nicknames, 71, 235, 281
RELATIONSHIPS: admirers, 104, 138; arranged marriage prospects, 82, 84, 92, 93–4; connections with Bonaparte family, 291–2; custody of children, 151, 221; divorce from Casimir Dudevant, 219–22, 229; friendship with Balzac, 193, 213, 244–5, 275, 331; friendship with Charlotte Marliani, 237–8, 252, 257–8, 261, 280, 286, 300; friendship with Delacroix, 76, 215, 261, 262–3, 325; friendship with Flaubert, 281, 309–14, 316–17; friendship with Liszt, 236; friendship with Pauline Viardot, 265, 312; friendship with Ursule, 55–6; friendship with Zoé Leroy, 128, 129, 131–2, 135–6, 141; friendships in La Châtre, 133–4, 157, 159, 167; guardianship, 58–61, 106; literary agent, 179, 265–6, 282, 299; marriage to Casimir Dudevant, 108–9, 117–18, 127–8, 130–3, 141–2, 220–1; motherhood, 116–17, 153–5, 162–3, 165, 168–70, 183, 187, 198–9, 206–7, 212, 214, 222–3, 259, 269, 285–9,

RELATIONSHIPS: – *cont'd*
292, 316; mothering her partners, 188, 216, 230, 252, 254–5, 260; publishers, 166, 167, 170, 179, 193, 265–6, 187–8, 191, 197, 211, 216–17, 246, 263, 289, 306, 315; reputation as 'female Don Juan', 3, 155; sexuality, 141, 163–4, 177, 201–4, 280; with Alessandro Poerio, 203; with Alexandre Manceau, 218, 290, 302–6, 307, 311, 325; with Alfred de Musset, 177, 178–9, 198, 203–10, 213, 214–17, 223, 226, 246, 281; with Aurélien de Sèze, 128–9, 131–2, 135, 136–7, 141–2, 143, 214, 244; with Charles Didier, 219; with Chopin, 3, 36, 182, 237–45, 251–4, 260–3, 268–9, 270–1, 275–6, 277, 292, 298, 326; with daughter Solange, 153, 162–3, 169–70, 206–7, 259, 265, 269–70, 292, 316; with father, 25, 50, 80; with Félicién Mallefille, 229, 237, 241; with granddaughters, 40, 76, 287–8, 298, 312; with grandmother, 49, 55, 56–8, 60–1, 66–7, 69–70, 71, 80, 85–6; with half-brother Hippolyte, 49–50, 89–91, 98, 122, 124–5, 137, 139–40, 153–5, 284; with half-sister Caroline, 58–9, 61, 83, 137, 223; with Hermann Müller-Strübing, 299, 302; with Hetzel, 179, 265–6, 282, 289, 299; with Jean Joseph Louis Blanc, 299; with Jules Boucoiran, 199, 217; with Jules Sandeau, 6, 143, 155, 163, 164–5, 169–70, 182–4, 187–90, 199, 207, 244; with Marie Dorval, 200–3, 205, 237, 263, 298–9; with Michel de Bourges, 218, 219–20, 222, 235; with mother, 52, 56–8, 60–3, 66–7, 70, 80, 83, 96–8, 106, 109, 118, 124, 135, 154, 223, 240, 284; with Pierre-François Touzé ('Bocage'), 229, 237; with Pietro Pagello, 208–9, 213–16, 226, 246; with Prosper Mérimée, 199–200, 202, 205; with son Maurice, 153, 154, 162, 165, 212–13, 216, 281, 289–92, 304–5, 306, 318; with Stéphane de Grandsagne, 104, 135, 137, 138, 139; with Victor Borie, 299; writing partnership with Jules Sandeau, 6, 145, 158–9, 162, 166, 170, 174; younger men as lovers, 6, 122, 216, 230, 280, 244, 293, 299, 302

REPUTATION: creation of, 6; literary, 2–3, 174–5, 177, 182, 196–8, 277–9; mannish identifications, 279–81; personal, 3, 141, 155, 199–200, 211, 229, 325–6

WORKS: *Adriani*, 306; 'Aimée', 157–8, 161; *Albine Fiori*, 318; *Antonia*, 307; autobiography (*Histoire de ma vie*), 9, 13–14, 18, 26–7, 32, 33, 35, 45, 51–2, 59, 61–4, 68–9, 72, 86–7, 94–5, 98, 103–4, 157, 260, 285, 299–301, 320, 329–30; *Les Beaux Messieurs de Bois-Doré*, 306; *Cadio*, 315; *Le Château des desertes*, 306; *Claudie*, 307; *Le Commissionnaire* (with Jules Sandeau), 166; *La Comtesse de Rudolstadt*, 264–5; *La Confession d'une jeune fille*, 307; *Constance Verrier*, 307; *Consuelo*, 256, 264–5; *Contes d'une grand-mère*, 312; *Cosima, ou La haine dans l'amour*, 263; *La Coupe*, 307; ecological essays, 64–6; *Les Dames vertes*, 306; *La Daniella*, 306; *La*

WORKS: – cont'd
Dernière Aldini, 234, 251; 'Le Dieu inconnu', 234; early writings, 142; Elle et lui, 178–9, 206, 304; Evenor et Leucippe, 306; La Famille de Germandre, 307; 'La Fille d'Albano' (with Jules Sandeau), 162, 164; La Filleule, 287; Flamarande, 315; Flavie, 307; Francia, 315; François le Champi, vii, 4, 266, 292, 293; Gabriel, 251; Garnier, 207; L'Histoire de France écrite sous la dictée de Blaise Bonnin, 268; Histoire du véritable gribouille, 306; historical fiction, 306–7; Un hiver à Majorque, 86, 257; L'Homme de neige, 306–7; Horace, 165, 263, 264; Impressions et souvenirs, 315; Indiana, 3, 126, 170–2, 173–5, 182, 186–8, 192, 234, 253, 330; Isadora, 266; Jacques, 207, 211, 212; Jean de la Roche, 307; Jeanne, 266, 267; Journal d'un voyageur pendant la guerre, 315; Laura, 307; Légendes rustiques, 289–90; Lélia, 3–4, 177, 186, 190, 193–7, 200, 205–6, 211, 257, 288, 319; Léone Léoni, 211; letters, 86–92, 218–19, 313, 329; Lettres à Marcie, 234–5; Lettres au peuple, 267–8; Lettres d'un voyageur, 86, 206, 210, 219, 231, 234, 330; Lucrezia Floriani, 292, 306; Mlle Merquem, 315; Les Maîtres mosaïstes, 234, 297, 306; La Mare au diable, 1, 4, 36, 266, 292, 293; Le Mariage de Victorine, 308; Marianne Chevreuse, 315; Le Marquis de Villemer, 307, 320, 324; 'La Marquise', 188–9; Mattéa, 234; Mauprat, 234; 'Melchior', 188; Métella, 207; Le Meunier d'Angibault, 266; Molière, 308, 324; Monsieur Sylvestre, 307; Mont-Revêche, 287; Narcisse, 307; Nouvelles lettres d'un voyageur, 315; 'L'ocre', 251; Oeuvres Completes, 234, 289; Oeuvres illustrées de George Sand, 289; Paroles de Blaise Bonnin aux bons citoyens, 268; Pauline, 251; Le Péché de M. Antoine, 266; La Petite Fadette, 266, 292, 293; Pierre qui roule, 315; plays, 263, 306, 308–9, 324; plays written at convent school, 81, 83–4, 324–5; Poème de Myrza, 234; 'La Prima Donna' (as Jules Sandeau), 159; Promenades autour d'un village, 315; La Reine Mab, 185; Le Roi attend, 324; Rose et Blanche (with Jules Sandeau), 162, 164, 166, 167, 170, 191, 192; Le Secrétaire intime, 211; Les Sept cordes de la lyre, 251, 263; Simon, 234; Spiridion, 246, 251, 257, 263; Tamaris, 307; Teverino, 266, 293; Le Théâtre de Nohant, 308; 'To a Poet', 210; La Tour de Percemont, 315; 'Trenmor', 192, 193, 195; L'Usoque, 251; Valentine, 174, 182, 185–6, 187–8, 190–1, 192; Valvèdre, 307; La Ville noire, 307; writing speed, 207, 304, 311; writing style, 219

Sandeau, Jules: appearance, 143, **146**, 244; career, 143, 278; co-authorship, 6, 145, 158–9, 162, 166, 170, 174; education, 143–4; home, 155, 164–5, 174, 184, 190; military service buy-out, 188, 189, 190, 203; relationship with Aurore, 6, 143, 145, 155, 163, 169–70, 182, 184, 187–90, 199, 207, 244; works, 278

Scott, Sir Walter, 173–4
Shelley, Mary, 3, 172, 189–90, 213, 230
Shelley, Percy Bysshe, 185, 189–90, 226, 230
Shelley, Percy Florence, 290
Signol, Alphonse, 166
Simmonet, René (grandson of Hippolyte), 318
Solnit, Rebecca, 42
Spain, wartime trip, 26–31, 52, 58, 246
Spiring, 'Mother' Mary Alicia: appearance, 72; relationship with Aurore, 72–3, 80, 81, 127, 141, 154; role at Dames Augustines Anglaises convent, 71–3
Stendhal, 107, 207–8, 210

Talleyrand-Périgord, Charles-Maurice de, 214, 215
Le Temps, 64, 315
Thiot-Varnennes, Louis Antoine, 220
Touzé, Pierre-François ('Bocage'), 229, 237
Turgenev, Ivan, 312, 319

Ursule (childhood friend of GS), 55–6

Venice, visit, 208–11, 212, 214–15, 246
Verdot, Placide, 39–41, 297
Véron, Désirée, 145, 159
Viardot, Louis, 264, 265
Viardot, Pauline, 265, 291, 312
Villeneuve, Émilie, *see* Chatiron
Villeneuve, René Vallet, Comte de, 94, 104, 106
Viollet-le-Duc, Eugène, 282, 301
La Voix des femmes, 279
Voltaire, 41, 47, 81
La Vraie République, 268

Wharton, Edith, 298
Wodzińska, Maria, 232–3, 237, 240, 241
Woyciechowski, Tytus, 242

About the Author

Fiona Sampson MBE FRSL is a leading British poet, a writer and Romanticist. Professor Emerita of Poetry, University of Roehampton and Senior Research Fellow at Harris Manchester College, University of Oxford, she has received numerous national and international literary awards and been published in thirty-eight languages.

Becoming George completes a trilogy of acclaimed biographies. *In Search of Mary Shelley* was an *Observer*, *Independent*, *Financial Times* and a *Times* Book of the Year. *Two-Way Mirror* was *Washington Post* Book of the Year, *New York Times* bestseller, finalist for the Plutarch Prize & US PEN's Jacqueline Bograd Weld international award for biography.